PATTERNS OF AMERICAN LEGAL THOUGHT

By

G. EDWARD WHITE

THE BOBBS-MERRILL COMPANY, INC.
PUBLISHERS
INDIANAPOLIS • NEW YORK • CHARLOTTESVILLE, VIRGINIA

For John F. Davis
in memory of Valre T. Davis

ACKNOWLEDGMENTS

This book is unusual in that it did not originate with the author, but with others who persuaded me to group some of my essays and to issue them as a unit. I assume, as the persuaders have argued, that a number of readers may not have had access to the essays before; and I hope that those persons may find something of value in them.

I am indebted, as I have been on several previous occasions, to my friends and colleagues William H. Harbaugh, Charles W. McCurdy, and J. Harvie Wilkinson, III. I am also grateful for the interest in the book of Charles Huxsaw and Ward Sims of Michie/Bobbs-Merrill, and for the editorial help of Frances Warren and Richard Thiele.

My family, Susan Davis White, Alexandra V. White, and Elisabeth McC. D. White, provides the emotional base from which my work emanates. That I admire and respect John F. Davis and shall miss Valre T. Davis is vouchsafed in the dedication. George L. White and Frances McC. White are a continuing source of pride for me.

Charlottesville
August, 1978

FOREWORD

"There is absolutely no point in setting up a separate category of legal writing (or law teaching) to be known as 'legal history,'" Yale Law School's Professor Grant Gilmore wrote (p. 146) in his recent, interesting and lively *The Ages of American Law* (1977). Too late, Professor Gilmore, Legal History exists. Gilmore's own *Ages* attests to its presence, and the compiler of *Patterns in American Legal Thought,* Professor G. Edward White of the University of Virginia Law School, agrees.

Legal historians' sophisticated, vigorous, and useful inquiries into the history of American law, including legal thought and concepts, currently exhibit a broad-swinging relevance and sparkle that, ten or fifteen years ago, hardly seemed likely to develop. Indeed, it seems clear that, to paraphrase a recent ex-President of the United States, soon no one will be able justifiably to "kick American Legal History around" any more. To be "kicked around", in the sense of not being considered a respectable area for research and teaching was the fate and condition of American Legal History for a very long time.

Two decades ago, Daniel J. Boorstin, now the Librarian of Congress, characterized American Legal History as a "dark continent." He speculated gloomily that it would remain dim for at least half a century. In 1962 New York University Law Professor John Reid noted unhappily that editors of the nation's major legal periodicals refused to allot review space to what soon became recognized as one of the decade's — indeed, the century's — most important Legal History analyses, James Willard Hurst's *Law and Social Process in United States History* (1960). Reid complained further that when the American Society for Legal History, the only professional association of law-focused historians and history-centered lawyers, wished to honor preeminent legal scholar Roscoe Pound, it could not find a volume of essays in legal History worthy to present to him. White in 1973 echoed this dour refrain noting that "an outstanding characteristic of American legal history in the twentieth century has been the relative absence of scholarship."

Nevertheless, the condition and practice of Legal History and Legal Studies have drastically improved. The three factors primarily responsible — the tenacity of legal historians, the outpouring of their research in quality publications, and the fruition of their calls for curricular reform — are the themes of this Foreword.

The first theme is a tribute to White and other scholars of History and Law who kept the Legal History faith. Even though the scholarly quality of legal history was largely unrecognized, these stubborn, dedicated practitioners continued in their almost defunct speciality. The problems they encountered were legion. With the exception of the decisions and personalities of the United States Supreme Court, other historians studiously ignored the law and its institutions. Simultaneously, the presentist bias of legal training seemed to belittle the importance of history to lawyers.

A further impediment was the division between law and history that had grown up on campuses nationwide. This chasm separated even the small number of law school faculty interested in history from History Department colleagues concerned with the law; general university libraries (and library budgets) from law libraries, to the detriment of both; courses in Constitutional History from political science courses in high court decisional Constitutional Law. Legal History rarely found welcome in any academic departments — History, Law or Political Science — where logic would place it; legal historians were rarely welcomed if they strayed outside their department of formal affiliation.

Happily, reports of Legal History's final or total demise proved to be exaggerated, and the separations are diminishing. In large part resuscitation occurred and is occurring because legal historians, including some premature mourners, worked diligently in terms of research, writing and innovative inter-disciplinary law-history curricula development. Had these busy lawyers and historians merely complained about the need for Legal History research and curriculum innovation, odds are that their peers would have continued indifferent to Legal History or, at best, maintained their view of it as an immature or senile sub-discipline, worthy only of dilettantes' attention. Instead, their achievements transformed complaints into programs and concerns into scholarly adventures.

The second theme is, then, the praiseworthy body of major books, essays, and articles in Legal History, broadly defined, that in the last decade and a half have enriched the field. This outpouring of talent, research skills and persistence, and blessedly often, high literary quality, would score well on any qualitative scale.

As examples of the volume and the quality, in 1971, *Perspectives in American History,* the annual compendium publication of Harvard's Charles Warren Center for Studies in American History, dedicated that issue to the theme "Law in American History." Two years later, Bernard Schwartz' *Law in America: A History* and Lawrence M. Friedman's *A History of American Law* came into print. Both books attended to the law as a profession, to legal education, and to public policy effects on the law as well as the law's impacts on society. In short, as White notes in his review of Friedman's book that forms the first essay in *Patterns,* American Legal History was moving toward healthy maturity.

Interest in the history of the American legal profession and of legal thought proved to be durable; the scholarship, impressive. The bicentennial year was graced by Maxwell Bloomfield's *American Lawyers in a Changing Society, 1776-1876* and Jerold S. Auerbach's *Unequal Justice: Lawyers and Social Change in Modern America.* As noted earlier, Grant Gilmore's *Ages of American Law* appeared in 1977, and journals were sensitive to the merits, and failings, of this concise, effective and iconoclastic consideration of its complex subject. James Willard Hurst's 1960 book could not find law review space; Hurst's 1977 *Law and Social Order in the United States* faced no such bland rejection. And Morton Keller's *Affairs of State: Public Life in Late Nineteenth Century America* takes public law history to frontiers of social and institutional analysis that a de Tocqueville, Bryce, or Beard would have recognized and applauded.

These able, literate, and informative considerations received impressive reinforcement in White's 1976 book, *The American Judicial Tradition: Profiles of Leading American Judges.* In harmony with present broad ideas of what constitutes Legal History, White's *American Judicial Tradition* attends to "the judicial function and property rights" in the chapter on Kent, Story, and Shaw; to state judges as well as national; to judges' concepts of freedom in addition to their decisions and opinions in civil liberties cases.

White has exhibited similar concerns in his periodical scholarship from 1971 to 1977. His "Evolution of Reasoned Elaboration" and "From Sociological Jurisprudence to Realism", both appearing in *Patterns,* are effective arguments in favor of the need to know the historical contexts of significant judicial decisions and opinions. The peril in ignoring context — history — is that the several approaches toward the appellate judicial function, including the twentieth century's "Realism" and "Reasoned Elaboration," are unlikely to be understandable save as slogans, without gauges supplied by Legal History.

White's essays on Oliver W. Holmes, Jr. and Louis Brandeis, in *Patterns,* speak again to this essential point. In addition to the biographical insights he offers on the men, White illuminates also the judicial, legislative and administrative interventions designed to cope with modern enterpreneurships. How we allot decisional power between courts and administrative agencies is a delicate and highly significant question. Of comparable significance is one of White's subjects in the area of civil rights and liberties. White (with J. H. Wilkinson) in "Constitutional Protection for Personal Lifestyles," also in *Patterns,* attends, as few commentators have, to intimate discordances-become-constitutional issues, such as hair and/or dress codes, homosexual relationships, and other "unconventional" lifestyles touched by state laws, but imperfectly accommodated by constitutional law.

Legal History scholars have also analyzed technical aspects of substantive law. In this arena the impressive *oeuvre* of Lawrence

M. Friedman requires special note. Friedman's 1965 *Contract Law in America: A Social and Economic Case Study* was succeeded by his *History of American Law* and by a pride of scholarly periodical articles (in both law and history journals), on legal culture and social development and on the history of law reform, tenement house legislation, testamentary instruments and industrial accidents. White's "Intellectual Origins of Torts in America," reprinted in *Patterns,* Bruce Ackerman's *Private Property and the Constitution* (1977), and William B. Scott's *In Pursuit of Happiness: American Conceptions of Property from the Seventeenth to the Twentieth Century* (1977) are other examples of this increasingly engaging arena of Legal History. Furthermore Morton Horwitz's *The Transformation of American Law, 1780-1860* (1977) received this year's Bancroft Prize, a preeminent mark of professional historians' esteem. What a contrast to 1960! Legal History may not yet have come fully of age. But it has clearly come a very long way.

The third theme in which White's *Patterns of American Legal Thought* is likely to play a prominent role — is curricular innovation and the supply of derivative teaching materials. Increasingly across the academic nation, historians are enriching undergraduate Constitutional History courses with Legal History content, History Departments are offering separate Legal History courses, and full-fleshed interdisciplinary Legal Studies efforts are coming into being. The Legal Studies programs are not designed as pre-law curricula. The philosophical, pedagogical justification of the non-prelaw stress in Legal Studies curricula is that, in Legal History, a viable humanistic-social science discipline exists that is not merely a pre-professional skill accumulation. In short, the scholarly literature of Legal Studies, including Legal History, is more than merely adequate or respectable on its own terms.

On the graduate level, in addition to orthodox MA/PhD offerings in Legal History, several impressive interdisciplinary joint programs have developed recently involving a Humanities and/or Social Science discipline and Law. These joint programs lead commonly to JD degrees, and a Humanities or Social Science advanced degree (MA or PhD) in Anthropology, Economics,

History, Management, Philosophy, Political Science, or Sociology. There are great rewards to be won from such joint graduate programs. Done well, they can enrich the law student and widen greatly the horizons of the non-lawyer participant. The weights, wear, and strains involved in the conception and administration of these joint programs are not light or minor. But the benefits to persons, institutions, and scholarship are worth the costs.

One of the most difficult tasks in creating a viable under-graduate or graduate interdisciplinary Legal Studies program has proved to be the absence of appropriate classroom teaching materials. Until recently there were virtually no courses in Legal History or Legal Studies. Law publishers paid no attention to non-Law parts of campuses. Unsurprisingly, non-Law publishers did not invest funds for preparation of texts or compendia, in the absence of a buying public represented by Legal History-Legal Studies courses.

This hesitation is lessening. The American Bar Association has created a Commission on Undergraduate Education in Law and the Humanities. The primary initial goal of this most promising office is to encourage development of appropriate curricular materials. What is important, and exciting, is that Legal History and Legal Studies courses should, in a reasonably quick pace, enjoy unprecedentedly rich teaching materials; these courses are already enjoying substantial enrollments.

Scholars and publishers are also demonstrating an interest in producing new books suitable for class use. Wythe Holt's 1976 compendium, *Essays in Nineteenth-Century Legal History* (Greenwood) led the way. It is a useful assembly of articles of diverse authorship, drawn from both Law and History journals. These essays attended to historical dimensions of four major arenas of Legal History: schools of Legal History thought, substantive and procedural law, constitutional issues, and the legal profession. An interesting and iconoclastic introductory essay by Professor Holt, "Now and Then: The Uncertain State of Nineteenth-Century American Legal History," offers ideas and insights on the people, institutions, and prospects involved in the included research and writing.

Another, larger compendium of articles of diverse authorship, assembled by Lawrence M. Friedman and Harry N. Scheiber, *American Law and the Constitutional Order: Historical Essays* came into print in 1978. Unlike the Holt compendium, it covers all of American history, not only the nineteenth century. The Friedman-Scheiber volume's author roster is a Who's Who among eminent practitioners in Law and History; the articles are proved founts of ideas and correctives.

It may be, however, that both the Holt and the Friedman-Scheiber compendia will prove to be too ambitious in the number of themes embraced, too costly for students, and, by reason of multiple contributors, too uneven in literary style, pace, and emphases, for continuing use as classroom textbooks. By contrast, White's *Patterns of American Legal Thought* is a compilation in which all the constituent articles are by one author, the compiler. After an introductory thematic section, White's three themes on major schools of Legal History scholarship, aspects of judicial and jurisprudential history, including administrative agencies, and constitutional law history, are examined in ten article reprints.

Patterns offers to the swiftly-growing Legal History and Legal Studies audiences these splendid articles plus connective analytical headnotes by White. The articles were conceived and composed during the years that White conducted the research for, and wrote, *The American Judicial Tradition;* years when he also participated vigorously in developing the University of Virginia's eminent interdisciplinary Law and History programs. White has therefore brought to *Patterns* the insights that original research sometimes provides, the experience that classroom utilization of original research too infrequently allows, and, blessedly, the humility and good humor that permit him to applaud Gilmore's view (p. 11 in *Ages*): "In Heaven there will be no law, and the lion will lie down with the lamb ... In Hell there will be nothing but law, and due process will be meticulously observed."

To return to the comment with which this Foreword began— "There is absolutely no point in setting up a separate category of

legal writing (or law teaching) to be known as 'legal history' " —
I repeat my conviction. Gilmore is not only too late, but incorrect.
Legal History exists because some historians are incurably
law-minded and some lawyers and judges are history-minded. The
fact that all legal materials were created in the past, as Gilmore
noted, has not, with rare exceptions, imbued jurisprudents with the
historian's sense of disciplinary limitations. White's *Patterns of
American Legal Thought* adds a necessary dimension, the
recreation of thought about significant legal subjects.

Harold M. Hyman

May 1, 1978   *William P. Hobby Professor of History*
Rice University
Houston, Texas

TABLE OF CONTENTS

INTRODUCTION

The essays reprinted in this volume represent nearly a decade's work in legal history, jurisprudence, and constitutional law, and I appreciate the opportunity to gather them together under one roof. It is one thing to have portions of one's scholarship assembled, however, and another thing to explain its unities and continuities. It is pleasant to imagine that one's work has an overarching purpose, and with the advantage of hindsight I have been able to identify what seem to me to be some controlling themes. But I confess that to some extent my decisions to explore one or another area of scholarship have not been fully conscious. I have written about subjects and topics that seemed important to me at the time; in retrospect, several still do, although I would not now agree with everything I have said.

Three themes in the history of American legal thought are touched upon in this book. One is the importance of the community of legal scholars in shaping the course of substantive law. I have found that throughout most of American legal history the tacit convictions of groups of scholars have exercised a powerful influence on the direction of scholarly research, and the directions taken by legal scholarship have in turn influenced the doctrinal content of American law. My thinking about the nature and significance of scholarly writing has altered somewhat over the years spanned by this volume, but my conviction remains that legal scholarship is a fertile, though underemphasized, source of insights about the history of law in America.

A second theme of the essays is the significance of the judiciary in American jurisprudence. Edwin Patterson, nearly forty years ago, argued that in "the American view" judges are perceived of as "the center of the juristic universe," * and I am inclined to agree. To say that judges have occupied a prominent place in the history of American legal thought is not to minimize the contributions of other entities, such as groups of scholars or legislatures or

---

* Edwin W. Patterson, *Cardozo's Philosophy of Law,* 88 U. PA. L. REV. 71, 87 (1939).

administrative agencies. It is rather to suggest that Americans have regularly regarded judges as significant oracles, shapers or makers of law, and have cloaked them with the special sort of heroism or villany we reserve for officials who are thought to be capable of affecting all our lives.

Finally, these essays stress the importance for American legal thought of a Constitution with a large accompanying body of interpreted case law. From a comparative perspective, the American Constitution gives our jurisprudence a distinctive character. No other nation has had a history of competing and complementary spheres of law similar to that of the United States. Since the origins of the Constitution one sphere of law, constitutional law, has been designated as "supreme," but its boundaries have never been fixed. Other nonconstitutional spheres of law, such as "common" (judge-made) law, legislative law, executive and administrative law, and even the unofficial "laws" of private groups have coexisted with constitutional law, and the capacity of any of these nonconstitutional spheres to become constitutionalized has varied dramatically with time. The presence of a Constitution as a nebulous but "fundamental" source of law has thus significantly affected the course of American legal thought.

The structure of this volume reflects its thematic emphasis. The first chapter of essays presents a brief overview of each of the themes subsequently discussed. Chapters Two, Three, and Four then explore, in more detail, various patterns of American legal thought. Chapter Two focuses on scholarly writing; Chapter Three on the judiciary; and Chapter Four on constitutional law.

The patterns and themes discussed in this volume should not be regarded as defining the major features of American legal thought. Willard Hurst, the most influential legal historian of his generation, called in 1960 for research on "legislative, executive, and administrative processes"; and on "law's operational significance for the institution of the market." * While Hurst and

---

* Willard Hurst, *The Law in United States History,* 104 PROC. AMER. PHIL. SOC. 518, 523 (1960).

others ** have shown that ideas about the formulation of policy and the distribution of power and economic resources have affected American legal thought, this volume does not stress such themes. Its emphasis is in part a product of my own scholarly interests. I also seek, however, to suggest that American legal thought has been derived from some sources that cannot easily be linked to the legislative session or the economic marketplace. Understanding the history of American legal thought requires, in my view, appreciating its social, intellectual, economic, and political dimensions; and if those of us writing in legal history and jurisprudence are temperamentally or philosophically inclined to emphasize different dimensions, so much the better.

** *See especially* LAWRENCE M. FRIEDMAN, A HISTORY OF AMERICAN LAW (1973); MORTON J. HORWITZ, THE TRANSFORMATION OF AMERICAN LAW, 1780-1860 (1977).

CHAPTER 1. SOME CENTRAL THEMES OF AMERICAN LAW

This chapter of essays presents, in microcosm, the basic themes of the volume. The book review of Lawrence Friedman's *A History of American Law* emphasizes the extent to which legal scholars, like those in other professions and disciplines, conduct their research from starting perspectives which amount to tacit value judgments. These perspectives, when shared by groups of scholars, create "schools" of thought. The value orientations of such schools serve as filters through which data is assessed and analyzed, creating, in less sophisticated presentations than that of Friedman, self-conforming research prophesies. Legal thought in America has been affected, at least since the late nineteenth century, by the presence of shared research perspectives among scholars. Current scholarship in legal history and other areas is only beginning to explore the sociological and philosophical dimensions of schools of thought.

The *Path of American Jurisprudence* gives a more detailed account of the remaining themes emphasized in this study, arguing that a conception of judges as lawmaking officials and a dialectical relationship between "constitutional" and "nonconstitutional" law have served to define the cast of jurisprudence in America.

The Appellate Opinion as Historical Source Material, the remaining essay in this chapter, presents a methodology for exploring legal materials as elements of social and intellectual history. Although I would write the essay somewhat differently today, I am including it because it offers some potential researchers a model against which their own techniques can be juxtaposed.

1

BOOK REVIEW OF LAWRENCE M. FRIEDMAN, A
HISTORY OF AMERICAN LAW

Virginia Law Review, Vol. 59, No. 6 (1973)

It is too much to say that American legal history has come of age with the publication of Lawrence Friedman's *A History of American Law,* the first attempt "to do anything remotely like a general history" [1] of law and legal institutions in America. But the appearance of Friedman's work indicates that a sufficient amount of monographic literature in American legal history exists to allow some form of synthetic treatment. That in itself is an accomplishment, for American legal history has been one of the most unfortunate step-children of the academic profession, disdained by historians and lawyers alike, struggling to establish itself in curricula and to disengage itself from antiquarianism, largely bereft of distinctive or distinguished scholarship.

That Friedman has been the first to attempt a general treatment of American legal history is not without personal significance. He has been a pioneering and innovative contributor to the monographic literature of the field; [2] he has emphasized the historical antecedents of substantive areas of American law; [3] he has attempted to modernize the discipline of legal history by introducing to it the analytical techniques of the social sciences; [4]

---

1. L. FRIEDMAN, A HISTORY OF AMERICAN LAW 9 (1973). [Hereinafter cited as FRIEDMAN.]

2. *E.g.,* Friedman, *Law, Order, and History,* 16 S.D.L. REV. 242 (1971); Friedman, *On Legal Development,* 24 RUTGERS L. REV. 11 (1969); Friedman, *Legal Culture and Social Development,* 4 LAW & SOC'Y REV. 29 (1969); Friedman, *Law Reform in Historical Perspective,* 13 ST. LOUIS U.L.J. 351 (1969); Friedman, *Legal Rules and the Process of Social Change,* 19 STAN. L. REV. 786 (1967); Friedman, *Tenement House Legislation in Wisconsin,* 9 AM. J. LEGAL HIST. 41 (1965); Friedman, *Patterns of Testation in the 19th Century,* 8 AM. J. LEGAL HIST. 34 (1964); Friedman & Ladinsky, *Social Change and the Law of Industrial Accidents,* 67 COLUM. L. REV. 50 (1967).

3. L. FRIEDMAN, CONTRACT LAW IN AMERICA (1965); L. FRIEDMAN, GOVERNMENT AND SLUM HOUSING: A CENTURY OF FRUSTRATION (1968).

4. L. FRIEDMAN, LAW AND THE BEHAVIORAL SCIENCES (1969).

and he is a charter member of the school of thought currently dominant among American legal historians. His *History* illustrates his functions in each of these capacities. Accordingly, it provides a starting point for an analysis of the present state of American legal history.

* * *

An outstanding characteristic of American legal history in the twentieth century has been the relative absence of scholarship. While American legal philosophy and jurisprudence were passing through at least four academic phases since 1900, complete with intellectual controversies and polemics,[5] and while other sub-branches of American history, such as economic history or social history, were exhibiting distinctive patterns of growth and change, American legal history before 1950 produced only isolated studies: treatments of historical periods [6] or particular institutions [7] reflecting the idiosyncratic interests of the scholars involved.

The sporadic nature of intellectual contributions to the discipline can be partially explained by its peculiar methodological problems. Analyzing legal source material requires the technical skills imparted by a legal education: the majority of historians are deterred from doing research in legal materials by their inability to read the relevant sources. Taking the time to acquire the necessary skills, for an historian, is in many instances far more costly than simply choosing a less formidable area of specialization. Other deterrents exist for American lawyers interested in legal history. The methodological techniques of the legal profession, perhaps because of their proven success in analyzing cases and statutes, tend to become the central focus of legal education: substance, on balance, is subordinated to methodology. But history

---

5. *See* White, *From Sociological Jurisprudence to Realism*, 58 VA. L. REV. 999 (1972); White, *The Evolution of Reasoned Elaboration*, 59 VA. L. REV. 279 (1973).

6. *E.g.*, R. POUND, THE FORMATIVE ERA OF AMERICAN LAW (1938).

7. *E.g.*, C. WARREN, THE SUPREME COURT IN UNITED STATES HISTORY (1972).

is not so easily reduced to concrete problems of analysis: descriptions of the flow of change and syntheses of large masses of data are important in rendering it intelligible, and the standard techniques of legal analysis are less helpful in those tasks. Further, modern American legal education, with its emphasis on the contrary uses to which data can be put and the ambivalent nature of reality, may serve as a philosophical deterrent to historical scholarship, which until recently has been seen by its practitioners as an objective search for truth.[8]

These deterrents contributed to the depressed state of scholarly activity in American legal history during the first half of the twentieth century. The one major exception was study of the Supreme Court of the United States. In contrast to the reluctance with which nonlawyers approached most areas of legal research, historians and political scientists enthusiastically analyzed the Supreme Court. However, the result was an unfortunate amalgam of diverse and sometimes opposing perspectives. Political scientists found an interest in the Court as an institution of American government, historians as a repository of socially significant issues. None of the concerns of one group particularly excited the other; indeed, basic assumptions about the proper way to study the Court remained unresolved. As a consequence the Court's work was over-evaluated but seldom illuminated.

Beginning in the 1950's a group of scholars, primarily lawyers some of whom were trained in the social sciences, began a reorientation of the focus of American legal history. Led by Willard Hurst, the most prolific legal historian of his generation, and using the University of Wisconsin as its common intellectual base, the group advocated a twofold shift in the primary concern of American legal historians: from national themes to predominantly local issues and from public (constitutional and administrative) to private (business and commercial) law. Hurst himself began a massive empirical study of the legal history of the lumber industry

---

8. *See* White, *The Appellate Opinion as Historical Source Material,* 1 J. INTERDISCIPLINARY HISTORY 491 (1971).

in Wisconsin, and on the basis of his exploratory research wrote essays [9] suggesting that fruitful connections could be drawn between the growth of private law in America and changing patterns of economic development.

Following Hurst, a "Wisconsin School" of legal historians embarked on a series of monographic studies involving the relationship of private law to economic development. As their focus came to coincide with one previously identified by economic and business historians, a measure of interdisciplinary cooperation began to emerge. At the same time the social sciences developed distinctive methodologies which gave more attention to analysis of empirical data; the Wisconsin School enthusiastically seized upon these methodologies. The result was both an outpouring of monographs and the advancement of a new set of generalizations about the development of law and legal institutions in America. The first was the observation that law in America had functioned not as a divine body of rules but as a "rational tool" [10] which interest groups used to secure particular goals. Private law was the creation of private parties and groups with distinct aims in mind; its purpose was to ensure certainty and predictability for these groups.

Following from this generalization was a second: since economic or commercial interest groups were relatively easy to identify, and since the ordinary function of law was to accomodate the needs of those groups, the central focus of scholarship in legal history should be on economic issues and their relationship to the normal workings of legal institutions. Issues in "high politics," as Hurst called them,[11] were to be eschewed for the more mundane affairs of the free enterprise system and its legal appendages. Legal

9. J. W. HURST, THE GROWTH OF AMERICAN LAW: THE LAW MAKERS (1950); J. W. HURST, LAW AND THE CONDITIONS OF FREEDOM IN THE NINETEENTH CENTURY UNITED STATES (1956); J. W. HURST, LAW AND SOCIAL PROCESS IN UNITED STATES HISTORY (1960).

10. FRIEDMAN, *supra* note 1 at 25.

11. HURST, LAW AND SOCIAL PROCESS IN UNITED STATES HISTORY, *supra* note 9, at 18.

history came to be identified in economic terms; its phases were correlated to the waves of entrepreneurial innovation and consolidation that marked the nineteenth and early twentieth centuries in America.

Implicit in the economic and commercial orientation of the Wisconsin School was a deemphasis of the ideological themes of American legal history except insofar as they touched upon those particular areas. Although the school was responsive to the empirical innovations in social science methodology of the 1950's and sixties, it ignored the formation of an increasingly sophisticated vocabulary for addressing nonempirical data, such as the concepts of national myths, ideals, and symbols developed by the American Studies movement to analyze ideological developments. The result was a juxtaposition in the Wisconsin School of painstaking empirical research with unrefined and simplistic generalizations about historical trends.[12]

* * *

Friedman is a product of the Wisconsin School and shares its assumptions. He cites the "work, personality, and spirit" of Hurst as a "major influence;"[13] he credits "the atmosphere of ferment"[14] at Wisconsin as generating his interest in legal history and the relation of law to the social sciences; he admits to having "surrendered [him]self wholeheartedly to some of the central insights of social science";[15] he emphasizes in his *History* "the separate histories of the law of the fifty states" and "the more mundane workings of the system"[16] rather than constitutional law and the Supreme Court. He sees law as "an instrument" used by "the people in power" to "push or pull toward some definite

---

12. *See, e.g.,* Hurst's chart of "shifts in time among principal and secondary preoccupations of public policy" from 1620 to 1900 in LAW AND THE CONDITIONS OF FREEDOM, *supra* note 9, at 40.

13. FRIEDMAN, *supra* note 1, at 11.

14. *Id.*

15. *Id.* at 10.

16. *Id.* at 11.

goal." [17] In short, he offers not so much a general history of American law as a history which attempts to "redress the balance" [18] by focusing on the particular levels of the American legal system that have received attention from the Wisconsin School. His work is ultimately an argument for the proposition that American legal history can derive its identity as a discipline from the concerns and assumptions of the Wisconsin scholars: that it can center its focus on the reaction of private law to economic trends.

Friedman has deliberately deemphasized constitutional law and jurisprudence in his *History.* There is relatively little on the history of the Bill of Rights; the Alien and Sedition Acts receive only a cursory mention; Leonard Levy's recent study of the origins of the Fifth Amendment [19] is not cited; the relationship between religion and law in colonial America is not emphasized; the Zenger trial and free speech problems in the eighteenth century are not discussed. Nor do the major constitutional issues of the early nineteenth century receive much attention. Some of Marshall's decisions articulating the power of the national government in a federal system are alluded to, but others, such as *McCulloch v. Maryland,*[20] are not; the Taney Court's modification of Marshall's theories in such cases as *Cooley v. Board of Wardens*[21] is not mentioned. The early nineteenth-century constitutional cases that Friedman treats are those which have an impact on economic themes: *Dartmouth College*[22] and its effect on the status of corporations; *Charles River Bridge*[23] and its implications for state-supported economic expansion. With certain exceptions, such as a minor treatment of civil rights in the context of the Reconstruction Amendments,[24] the pattern after the Civil War is the same. The "main themes in the law" are the uses of land,

---

17. *Id.* at 25.
18. *Id.* at 10.
19. L. LEVY, THE ORIGINS OF THE FIFTH AMENDMENT (1968).
20. 17 U.S. (4 Wheat.) 316 (1819).
21. 53 U.S. (12 How.) 299 (1851).
22. Trustees of Dartmouth College v. Woodward, 17 U.S. (4 Wheat.) 518 (1819).
23. Proprietors of the Charles River Bridge v. Proprietors of the Warren Bridge, 36 U.S. (11 Pet.) 420 (1837).
24. FRIEDMAN, *supra* note 1, at 298-301.

the regulations of business, the emergent role of labor unions, changes in the law of corporations, and the interaction between social welfare legislation and the economic theory of laissez-faire.

Developments in jurisprudence receive a similar deemphasis. Friedman devotes some attention to the great treatise writers of the early nineteenth century, Kent, Story, Simon Greenleaf and Theophilus Parsons, and to their post-Civil War counterparts, Thomas Cooley, Christopher Tiedeman, and John Forrest Dillon, and brings the history of juristic scholarship into the twentieth century. He has a brief treatment of legal realism and its impact on twentieth-century legal education. But he ignores such developments as the influence of an "instrumentalist" conception of law on judicial decision-making in the early nineteenth century [25] and its manifestation in the opinions of such judges as Lemuel Shaw. Nor does he treat the rise of "mechanical jurisprudence," an artificial method of inductive reasoning common to the late nineteenth century by which judges reasoned syllogistically downward from initial premises to results. Similarly omitted is the counter-movement of sociological jurisprudence, conceived by Roscoe Pound and others in the early twentieth century as a protest against the mechanical school; and the decline of realism in the years immediately preceding World War II, with the consequent rise of a new school of jurisprudence that emphasized the obligation of judges to give detailed and coherent reasons for the results they reached.[26]

In the face of his stated attempts to provide a "social history of American law" in which law is seen "not as a kingdom unto itself ... but as a mirror of society," [27] Friedman's failure to include these areas of American legal history is significant. Insofar as ideological change is an important facet of a civilization's development, this omission is a serious one. We have no help from

---

25. *Cf.* Horwitz, *The Emergence of an Instrumental Conception of American Law, 1780-1820,* in D. FLEMING AND B. BAILYN, 5 PERSPECTIVES IN AMERICAN HISTORY 287 (1971).

26. *See* White, *supra* note 5.

27. FRIEDMAN, *supra* note 1, at 10.

Friedman in attempting to analyze such historical phenomena as the relationship between the social assumptions of the Enlightenment and the framing of the Constitution; the parallels between the early nineteenth century reform literature concept of an organic community and the emergence of a community welfare standard by which judges tested the validity of legislation; the connections between social Darwinism, a prevalent ideology of the late nineteenth century, and the doctrine of substantive due process, developed by judges after the Civil War; or the validity of the theory advanced by Alexander Bickel [28] that Warren Court activism was stimulated by early twentieth century assumptions about the inevitability of progress.

But all of this is not to say that there is not a good deal of interesting information and rewarding analysis in Friedman's *History*. He gives us an excellent guide to the development of substantive law in the states. We can determine the status of civil procedure in early nineteenth century North Carolina,[29] the division of the crime of murder into degrees in early nineteenth century Missouri [30] and the contrasting treatments of the insanity defense after the Civil War in Iowa and New Hampshire.[31] We can explore the status of married women as property holders in Mississippi in the 1830's; [32] the legal techniques employed by Illinois and Nebraska to regulate railroads during the late nineteenth century; [33] Michigan's treatment of mortgages at the turn of the last century; [34] the growth of the doctrine of charitable immunities in Massachusetts and Maryland; [35] or the gradual efforts to achieve uniformity in state laws governing sales and

---

28. *See generally* A. BICKEL, THE SUPREME COURT AND THE IDEA OF PROGRESS (1970).
29. FRIEDMAN, *supra* note 1, at 131.
30. *Id.* at 249.
31. *Id.* at 515.
32. *Id.* at 185-86.
33. *Id.* at 305-06.
34. *Id.* at 374.
35. *Id.* at 416.

negotiable instruments.[36] These pieces of information do more than satisfy an antiquarian curiosity. They provide us the antecedent reference points to which the law, in its process of change, is continually recurring, and thereby help to explain its anomalies and irregularities. They lend persuasive weight to Friedman's thesis that law is inevitably "molded by economy and society." [37] Each of these local laws is a microcosm of social attitudes of a distinct time and place. The conception of women in antebellum Mississippi affects their very limited autonomy as property holders; agrarian hostility to the symbols of an advancing urban and industrial civilization helps generate the Granger legislation regulating railroads. In these examples we can see law in an instrumentalist capacity, as Friedman would like us to see it.

Friedman's work is also a full demonstration of the pervasive relationship in America between law and economic development. He documents, in a chapter on law and the economy from 1776 to 1847, the active role of government in promoting entrepreneurial ventures and the supervisory powers it enacted as a condition of its promoter role. Although this revisionist approach to a period in American economic history once inaccurately characterized as dominated by theories of laissez-faire is not new,[38] Friedman's is the first attempt to popularize it on a wide scale.

Other chapters pursue the same theme. One ties shifts in the legal doctrines governing the use of property and commercial transactions to the expanded meaning of property rights and the outgrowth of commerce in the early nineteenth century. Another deals with the modification of land use concepts in the face of the increasingly industrial character of post-Civil War America. Another traces the growth of regulation of business enterprise in the later nineteenth century, during which American government changed its stance toward business enterprise from sponsor to

---

36. *Id.* at 468-73.

37. *Id.* at 10.

38. It appeared in the 1940's in such works as Oscar and Mary Handlin's *Commonwealth* (1947) and Louis Hartz's *Economic Policy and Democratic Thought: Pennsylvania, 1776-1860* (1948).

sometimes reluctant regulator and trustee. Another deals with the rise of the corporate form of business enterprise and the consequent growth of the law governing corporations. Even some of the major social issues of the nineteenth and twentieth centuries are seen to have an economic tinge: Friedman treats the legal problem of slavery primarily as a form of property holding; he views the philosophy of administrative regulation, an ideological innovation of the twentieth century, as a response to the emergence of giant business organizations.

In addition to his concern with state and local law and the adjustment of the legal system to economic change, Friedman is interested in the educational patterns, literary habits, and styles of practice of the legal profession. Hence we are shown the changes in legal education from the apprenticeship system of the eighteenth and early nineteenth centuries to the rise of law schools with Joseph Story's appointment to Harvard as a full-time professor in the 1830s to the eventual emergence of the law school as a necessary step in the process of being called to the bar. We are also given some indication of the curricular revolutions of American law schools. Friedman traces the lecture system, dominant in the early nineteenth century and not necessarily confined to legal subjects; the use of nonannotated casebooks and the Socratic method of classroom teaching under Langdell at Harvard in the 1870s; the reactions against the case method and the attempts to reintegrate law with other disciplines that have variously appeared, with mixed success, since the 1930s.

Friedman has also demonstrated the close relationship between the state of legal education and the production of technical literature. In general, the more autonomous the methodology of analyzing legal materials taught in the law schools, the less necessity for the appearance of treatises as academic tools. Thus the early nineteenth century, with its relatively short supply of lawbooks and rudimentary state of legal education, saw the appearance of the first great wave of treatises. With the advent of the case method after the Civil War, treatises and textbooks largely disappeared from the law schools, to reappear as practical guides to the practice of law. With the innovations of the twentieth century, the treatises came to take on a more academic character and even to represent jurisprudential points of view. Samuel Williston's *Contracts* was "fully armored against the intrusion of any ethical, economic, or social notions whatsoever;"[39] Arthur Corbin's *Contracts* attempted to describe the relation of legal doctrines to their social context.

Finally, Friedman gives us brief overviews of American legal history in the colonial period and in the twentieth century. His main themes in both chapters are the interplay between the diversity of economic and social conditions that has characterized life in America and the continual attempts to make our legal system uniform. This framework serves Friedman for discussions of twentieth century legal reform movements as well as for descriptions of the organization of colonial courts. It is a highly workable one. As numerous commentators on American civilization have pointed out, our history has been in large measure an effort to develop a unifying set of distinctively American social values out of an extraordinary diverse, multifaceted and polarized cultural experience. The major cultural crises of our civilization, from the Revolutionary War through the Civil War to the Vietnamese War, have been times when a surface consensus of values has disintegrated under pressure from competing groups who interpret its meaning in radically different ways. Against those episodes can be juxtaposed other periods, the 1830s, the post-Civil War generation, the 1950s, when American civilization seems to have achieved a certain surface unity, as manifested in the collective enshrinement of a national model of success: the self-made man, the captain of industry, or the organization man. In discussing legal institutions in the framework of a dialectic between homogeneity and cultural pluralism Friedman has found a rich and powerful theme.

* * *

---

39. FRIEDMAN, *supra* note 1, at 593.

Throughout his discussion run Friedman's persistent organizing assumptions: the permanency of social change and the resultant "growth" of law; the "rational" use of the legal system to achieve particularistic economic ends; and the instrumentalist nature of historical change, in which nothing happens by accident, and "nothing is autonomous," but everything is "molded" [40] purposively by mankind in the rational pursuit of its goals. These assumptions require as much evaluation as Friedman's substantive emphases, for the two are inevitably linked.

On becoming fascinated with the remarkable *usefulness* of economic theory — its skill at assembling, synthesizing, and manipulating data, its reduction of obtuse phenomena to simple, workable concepts and systems, the kinetic energy of its methodology, in which one is constantly busy with the graph or the equation — one may be tempted to ignore the fact that it rests on unproven starting assumptions about behavior and that those assumptions, once accepted, clear away many nasty complexities for the sake of a manageable working model. The difficulty is that the very clearing away may ultimately hinder understanding instead of improve it; that too easy a transition from the model to the "real world" may be made. In that transition an admirably clear but perhaps overly simplistic and even wrongheaded description of social behavior may result. For example, the very act of assuming that individuals *make* history — that they develop institutions in their own image and use them for their own purposes, create events rather than react to them, "mould" rather than undergo "accidents" — may oversimplify at the outset.

To be sure, individuals aspire after power and status, elites are created, elites use their influence to achieve various parochial goals, and social change is affected by the pressures that elites generate. But that is not in any sense a complete description of the process of history. As in the lives of individuals, so in the life of a culture a series of random, disoriented, and inexplicable events occur. Persons react — not always "rationally" unless that term has lost its meaning — and their reactions make a difference, even

---

40. *Id.* at 10.

though they cannot be said to have been thought out in advance. At any point in time there are a series of limitations on the capacity of a nation's citizens to perceive and think, a set of cultural blinders that prevent certain options from being entertained or even considered. And even within the cognizable framework resulting from the shared values of a nation at a moment in time, there are options which, with hindsight, seem culturally determined rather than truly chosen. One need only examine the process of decisionmaking in foreign affairs from 1950 to 1970 to see the extent to which all the decisionmakers, whatever their individual shades of disagreement, were prisoners of the mythologies of the cold war.

So perhaps the most fundamental difficulty with Friedman's view of American legal history is that he takes "nothing as historical accident." [41] If by that he means that law and legal institutions in America must necessarily reflect the goals and values of their contemporary social context, one can hardly quarrel. But to say that social institutions are "mirror[s] of society" [42] is a truism. If, however, he intends to inject a thoroughly purposive quality into the relation of social groups and the legal system, as if the latter is entirely created or used by the former so that it is the equivalent of "an instrument," [43] one is given pause. However attractive the notion of the law as an on-going, functioning, purposive process [44] used reasonably by rational men in the pursuit of their common goals, it is surely more than that, and its history in America has embodied more than the pushing or pulling of "people in power . . . toward some definite goal." [45] Our legal institutions, over time, have been to an important extent repositories of the helplessness and prejudices of mankind and the disorderliness and absurdities of our experience.

---

41. *Id.*
42. *Id.*
43. *Id.* at 25.
44. *Cf.* H. HART & A. SACKS, THE LEGAL PROCESS iii (tent., ed., 1958).
45. FRIEDMAN, *supra* note 1, at 25.

But these are mainly matters of philosophy rather than historiography. At one level Friedman's *History* has succeeded admirably. It has demonstrated the coming maturity of the discipline of American legal history by building a synthesis — itself an argument for a particular point of view — from the growing monographic literature in the field. The important contributions of the Wisconsin School and its predecessors, the Handlins,[46] Hartz,[47] Levy,[48] Friedman and Ladinsky,[49] Goodrich,[50] Hurst,[51] Kimball,[52] Scheiber,[53] serve as foundations for Friedman's generalizations. Once isolated voices in the historical wilderness, those contributions are now seen as part of an overall framework, and private law and economic development have become central source materials of American legal history. There are successes in Friedman's *History*: his work is an excellent reference for the state of common law doctrine in a given locality at a particular time. He has provided abundant leads for the student who wants further detail on the topics Friedman has described. And, perhaps most importantly, he has helped demonstrate the predominantly conflict-free nature of the legal system in America. That system is intended to resolve conflict; at its heart, the countless ordinary private transactions managed daily by practitioners and their clients, it effectuates this resolution without undue stress or strain. "Great" constitutional law cases give the system an appearance of turmoil and conflict that is partially illusory; in ordinary and mundane ways, it adapts and adjusts to changing conditions with

---

46. O.and M. Handlin, *supra* note 37.

47. L. Hartz, *supra* note 37.

48. L. LEVY, THE LAW OF THE COMMONWEALTH AND CHIEF JUSTICE SHAW (1957).

49. Friedman and Ladinsky, *Social Change and the Law of Industrial Accidents,* *supra* note 2.

50. C. GOODRICH, GOVERNMENT PROMOTION OF AMERICAN CANALS AND RAILROADS, (1960).

51. J. W. HURST, LAW AND ECONOMIC GROWTH: THE LEGAL HISTORY OF THE LUMBER INDUSTRY IN WISCONSIN 1836-1915 (1964) and sources cited *supra,* note 9. supra, note 9.

52. S. KIMBALL, INSURANCE AND PUBLIC POLICY (1960).

53. H. SCHEIBER, OHIO CANAL ERA (1969).

relative ease, and an emphasis on private law transactions helps to illustrate its flexibility and resilience.

But Friedman's work cannot be called a full treatment of the history of American law, only a redressing of a previous overemphasis on national and public law themes. American legal history has been an interplay of the ordinary workings of private actions with issues of high politics. In addition to patterns of economic and attendant legal change, it has contained issues of profound ideological significance, such as the tension between egalitarian and humanitarian ideals and the system of slavery, the pressure placed upon historic notions of fairness and justice by sociopathic criminals, the limits of the power of a government to invade the privacy of its citizens in the name of the national interest, the rights of legislative majorities to impose their collective social views on unwilling minorities.

Each of these issues raises questions of constitutional interpretation. Each involves the area where law, politics, and ideology interact to define the social values of a nation. None receives treatment in Friedman's work, yet they are surely part of American legal history. Friedman might respond by pointing out that these issues have received treatment in other places and that no one-volume history can be all-inclusive. But even granting this rejoinder, American legal history simultaneously occurs on a series of levels, from the level of the daily work of the average practitioner, to the level of the steady, changing flow of substantive doctrine from the law offices, treatises, and courts, to the level of the large constitutional issues at the Supreme Court. Thus there is a sense in which Friedman's *History* is like a cathedral without a dome: its foundations are intact and a structure has been built on them, but nothing caps it.

Perhaps only when we have as rigorous a treatment of the ideological dimensions of American law as we have had of its "more mundane workings" [54] can such an intellectual edifice be constructed. Before such an effort is possible, there may be

---

54. FRIEDMAN, *supra* note 1, at 11.

necessary as extensive a monographic investigation of particular problems in the relationship of ideas to law in America as the Wisconsin School has undertaken for economic subjects. This undertaking may be neither as attractive nor as successful. But in any case, Friedman's *History* should not be regarded as a stopping place, except for the conferral of some deserved praise.

THE PATH OF AMERICAN JURISPRUDENCE

Univ. of Pennsylvania Law Review, Vol. 124, No. 5 (1976)

This Article seeks to identify some indigenous characteristics of American jurisprudence, to offer an explanation for their presence, and to explore some of their ramifications over time. The principal thesis of the Article is that the social and intellectual climate in which the English common law functioned in America was markedly unlike that in England, and that this climate, which included the experiences of the American Revolution, stimulated attitudes toward law and legal institutions that were unique rather than derivative. These attitudes have remained part of the educational experience of American lawyers since the eighteenth century, notwithstanding the dramatic changes in American society in the last two hundred years.

Three unique features of American jurisprudence emerge: the belief that "common" or "nonconstitutional" law,[1] however defined, must continually reflect currently held social attitudes; the tradition of a written constitution as the ultimate source of legal principles; and the delegation of lawmaking power to a "constitutionalizing" agent of government. The function of that agent (primarily but not exclusively the judiciary and most often the Supreme Court, representing the federal judiciary) is to integrate constitutitional principles with changing social attitudes and values as manifested in nonconstitutional "laws." Part One of the Article discusses the origins of each of these features; Part Two assesses some of their implications for the development of constitutional law and legal scholarship in America. Although much of the material discussed here may be familiar, the Article seeks to offer some fresh perspectives.

---

1. The term "common law" as used herein refers, first, to nonstatutory English law received in the American colonies prior to the Revolution; second, to nonstatutory law propagated by American judges and juries prior to the passage of the Constitution; third, to nonstatutory, nonconstitutional law propagated by judges from the passage of the Constitution to the end of the second decade of the

I. THE ORIGINS OF AMERICAN JURISPRUDENCE

A. *Common Law and Social Attitudes in Prerevolutionary America*

The patterns of English settlement in colonial America were diverse. Some colonies began as self-conscious missions, others episodes in adventure and enterprise.[2] In every colony, however, differences from England became apparent immediately. Severity of climate and terrain, an abundance of open land, sparsity of population, remoteness from centers of commerce, learning, and culture, and the absence of established settlements with formal status distinctions and social habits meant that England could not be duplicated in America. Although colonial towns often attempted to transplant English customs and practices,[3] modifications were inevitable. From this experience came a tacit assumption of colonial life: English institutions were to be perpetuated in America only if they could be made to harmonize with the new environment.

Examples were the offices of lawyer and judge. By the seventeenth century the English bench and bar had become professionalized, with structured patterns of education and achievement.[4] America did not have enough lawyers, clients, or source materials to replicate such an approach. By the revolutionary generation professionalization of the colonial bars had only begun. (High-level judgeships remained available to

---

nineteenth century. The term "common law" is used only metaphorically in referring to developments after 1820 that reveal an entrenched role for the judiciary. The term "nonconstitutional law" includes statutory, administrative, and judicial lawmaking outside the ambit of the Constitution.

2. Compare the Puritans' seventeenth century settlement of Massachusetts with the Duke of York's "conquest" of New York in the same century.

3. One example is described in S. POWELL, PURITAN VILLAGE (1963).

4. *See* D. BOORSTIN, THE AMERICANS: THE COLONIAL EXPERIENCE 195-97 (1958); Plucknett, *The Place of the Legal Profession in the History of English Law,* 48 L.Q. REV. 328, 332-36, 338-39 (1932). The professionalization of the English bar was reflected in the specialization of English lawyers. "Barristers" comprised the top echelon of the English bar and pleaded in the High Courts. "Attorneys" initiated court action for a client but were not permitted to plead in the High Courts. "Solicitors" could neither plead in the High Courts nor initiate lawsuits, but dealt with a client's routine legal problems. D. BOORSTIN, *supra,* at 195-96.

nonlawyers throughout the eighteenth century.)[5] As county courts, which combined legislative, executive, and judicial functions, became centers of trade and social intercourse in the colonies, the office of justice of the peace came to resemble that of an ombudsman, having varied informal powers of a quasilegal nature. Untrained judges like John Dudley of New Hampshire, who "never was able to write five consecutive sentences in correct English," [6] came to equate "law" with roughspun equities. Dudley is reported to have instructed a jury "to do justice between the parties, not by any quirks of the law out of Coke or Blackstone — books that I never read and never will — but by common sense as between man and man." [7] Thomas Hutchinson, who served as Chief Justice of the Massachusetts Superior Court despite his lack of legal training, confessed that "[t]he most I could pretend to was when I heard the Law laid on both sides to judge which was right." [8]

Even those colonial lawyers and judges who sought to keep current with English practice found a difficult time of it. Few published reports of decisions existed in the colonies; law libraries containing English reports were few and incomplete; English precedents were irregularly followed and given uneven weight.[9] English emphasis on the technicalities of pleading in the seventeenth century compounded the difficulty of adhering to English law. In arcane English practice the most minor error in a writ rendered it defective and invalidated the claim; such practice required thorough mastery of the writ system. While some colonial lawyers undoubtedly became experts in the intricacies of the writ

---

5. *See* D. BOORSTIN, *supra* note 4, at 195-202. Many states still have nonlawyer judges in courts not of record. The Supreme Court is currently considering the constitutionality of Kentucky's practice of having nonlawyer judges preside over criminal trials. North v. Russell, 516 S.W.2d 103 (Ky.), *vacated,* 419 U.S. 1085 (1974), *prob. juris. noted,* 422 U.S. 1040 (1975).

6. C. BELL, THE BENCH AND BAR of NEW HAMPSHIRE 40 (1894).

7. *Quoted in* D. BOORSTIN, *supra* note 4, at 201.

8. *Quoted in* 1 LEGAL PAPERS OF JOHN ADAMS xli (L. Wroth & H. Zobel eds. 1965).

9. *See* D. BOORSTIN, *supra* note 4, at 199; G. WOOD, THE CREATION OF THE AMERICAN REPUBLIC 1776-1787, at 296-97 (1969).

system,[10] others distinguished between formal English "law" and "reason," "equity," or "justice." [11] Alexander Hamilton noted that it was the practice in eighteenth century New York to "attend to" reported English decisions, but to reject them "where the injustices of them could be pointed out." [12]

The most detailed study of prerevolutionary law in America presently available, William Nelson's analysis of Massachusetts, finds a strong correlation between consensual social attitudes and common law practices. Massachusetts, Nelson argues, was for much of its colonial history unified in the belief that a stable, hierarchical, "christian" social order deserved perpetuation.[13] Law was consciously employed in numerous ways in Massachusetts to perpetuate such an order. Technicalities of pleading were preserved if they corresponded to meaningful technicalities of life: one could be thrown out of court, for example, if one called a yeoman a "laborer" or a gentleman a "yeoman." [14] But technicalities would not be tolerated if they offended a communal sense of justice. "[I]f one is under obligation from the ties of natural justice to pay another money and neglects to do it," Judge Edmund Trowbridge announced in 1772, "the law gives the sufferer an action on the case. . . ." "[M]ere justice & equity" were "sufficient foundation" to bring an action.[15] Overly voracious economic individualism, Nelson maintains, was perceived as undermining social stability; consequently Massachusetts courts sought to compensate victims of shrewd or unscrupulous business practices. Contract law in prerevolutionary Massachusetts,

---

10. *See, e.g.,* J. SMITH & P. CROWL, COURT RECORDS OF PRINCE GEORGES COUNTY, MARYLAND 1696-1699 (1964).

11. G. WOOD, *supra* note 9, at 298-99.

12. *Quoted in* 1 THE LAW PRACTICE OF ALEXANDER HAMILTON 51 (J. Goebel ed. 1964). *See* D. BOORSTIN, *supra* note 4, at 200-01; G. WOOD, *supra* note 9, at 297-99.

13. *See generally* W. NELSON, AMERICANIZATION OF THE COMMON LAW (1975).

14. *Id.* at 75-76.

15. Palfrey v. Palfrey, in W. CUSHING, NOTES OF CASES DECIDED IN THE SUPERIOR AND SUPREME JUDICIAL COURTS OF MASSACHUSETTS 1772-1789, at 1, 92, 98-99, *quoted in* W. NELSON, *supra* note 13, at 55.

according to Nelson, "probably furthered ethical unity and stability in the allocation of wealth and status at the expense of economic efficiency."[16]

While it helped perpetuate social and economic stability, the common law in Massachusetts was also used to promote morality and religiosity, primarily through public prosecution of "immoral" sexual offenses. Fornication that resulted in the birth of illegitimate children was punished regardless of whether the offenders subsequently married; in nearly all cases the party prosecuted was the woman.[17] Drunkenness, blasphemy, "spreading falsehoods," and being a "common scold" were also indictable criminal offenses.[18] Punishment for these crimes — normally a fine coupled with a whipping or some similar reprimand[19] — was designed to hold the offender up to public censure. Imprisonment was rare and "criminals" were drawn from all strata of society.[20] The primary purpose of the criminal law appears to have been the enforcement of community standards of morality. Civil suits for defamation, fraud, malicious prosecution, and the recovery of unpaid debts served a similar function. Creditors were awarded extensive remedies, in Nelson's view, not because of their political power but because their cause was regarded as just, and the evil of which they complained — failure to discharge a financial obligation — was considered especially pernicious.[21]

A final suggestive finding of Nelson's is Massachusetts' efforts to limit the lawmaking power of judges. The numerous informal powers of judges and the infrequent availability of legal sources fostered judicial discretion. Massachusetts sought to limit that discretion either by emphasizing adherence to precedent or by

---

16. W. NELSON, *supra* note 13, at 62.
17. *Id.* at 37-38.
18. *Id.* at 38-39.
19. *Id.* at 15.
20. *Id.* at 40.
21. *Id.* at 44-45.

using juries as lawmakers as well as factfinders.[22] The second device was probably more effective than the first because judges often misread, ignored, or were not aware of English decisions. Except for certain rules of evidence, juries had almost unlimited discretion to ignore judicial instructions and "find the law" themselves.[23] Their decisions could be based on local custom even if it departed from common law rules. Jury decisions did not bind other juries, allowing room for individual equities to enter into a case. Judges often gave instructions to juries seriatim, inviting a choice among conflicting views of a controversy. Motions seeking appeal from jury verdicts were rarely granted.[24]

In sum, Nelson maintains that Massachusetts colonists "freely received the common law of England as the basis of their jurisprudence but simultaneously reserved the unfettered right to reject whatever parts of that law were inconsistent with their own views of justice and morality or with their own needs and circumstances." [25] If Nelson's analysis is sound, "law" in colonial Massachusetts seems to have been not only indistinguishable from dominant social attitudes but localistic and possibly even "democratic." The common law appears to have been less a tool of elites than a reflection of widely held views, albeit views that served to perpetuate a stable and stratified social order. An older English view of law as a realm of mysteries interpreted by a trained elite and handed down to a complaisant populace[26] seems to have been altered, at least in Massachusetts, by the realities of colonial life.

Systematic studies of whether other colonies conformed to the pattern of Massachusetts in their use of law and legal institutions are lacking. Although important ideological differences and settlement patterns distinguished the colonies, features similar to those Nelson identifies as having influenced the development of

---

22. *Id.* at 20.
23. *Id.* at 3, 28.
24. *Id.* at 27.
25. *Id.* at 30.
26. *See generally* J. GOUGH, FUNDAMENTAL LAW IN ENGLISH CONSTITUTIONAL HISTORY (1955).

common law in Massachusetts were present in each. Every colony suffered a shortage of trained lawyers and judges; no colony possessed an abundance of English source materials; each was isolated from Europe and made up of communities linked to each other only by rudimentary transportation; in none was colonial government (as opposed to local government) an omnipresent force.[27] In all the colonies judges performed legislative and administrative functions, in all those for which evidence is available they decided cases by appeal to equitable considerations as well as to English doctrines, and in all they reserved the right to disregard common law rules when they were unsuited to the American environment. Hence it it not unlikely that an association of common law with currently dominant social attitudes and values took place throughout the colonies, although the substantive content of common law doctrines, and of social attitudes as well, varied from colony to colony.[28] The critical unanswered question about colonial common law is whose values it perpetuated. That question can be answered only by further studies of individual colonies. Whatever the answer to that question, a conventional notion of common law as a formal entity which can be understood apart from its social and intellectual context will likely have to be abandoned.

B. *The Impact of Natural Rights Thought and a Written Constitution*

Environmental differences between England and America became apparent immediately to settlers in the New World, leading to the frank modification of English common law doctrines, as in the application of common law dower rights to uncultivated American lands.[29] It was ideology, however, more than geography, that ultimately produced the rift between England and its American colonies. The American Revolution was in part the product of natural rights theory. In the 1760's England suddenly

---

27. *See generally* D. BOORSTIN, *supra* note 4; R. HOFSTADTER, AMERICA AT 1750: A SOCIAL PORTRAIT (1971).
28. *See* W. NELSON, *supra* note 13, at 3.
29. *Id.* at 9.

sought to modify colonial practices that it had long tolerated. In response to attempted modifications, the colonists defined their practices as grounded in inalienable rights, denied the authority of Parliament to usurp such rights, and eventually went to war to secure the ancient rights and liberties of Englishmen.[30] The colonists drew mainly on three sources in asserting their rights: the legacy of British constitutional history, the charters of individual colonies, and the philosophical insights of Enlightenment theoreticians.[31] Once they achieved independence, colonial leaders set out to create a governmental structure consistent with natural rights thought.

One of the intriguing questions about the American Revolution is why radical versions of natural rights thought found such widespread acceptance in America, so that a society with comparatively little economic discontent or social unrest became a seedbed of subversion and treason in the name of liberty. The importance of early eighteenth century English radicalism in shaping the perspective of American revolutionaries has been documented; [32] how did views marginal in England come to be dominant in America? One possibility is the different institutional structure of government in the colonies. By the mid-eighteenth century Americans were accustomed to a much greater freedom from governmental interference than their counterparts in

---

30. *See generally* B. BAILYN, THE IDEOLOGICAL ORIGINS OF THE AMERICAN REVOLUTION (1967); E. MORGAN, THE BIRTH OF THE REPUBLIC (1956).

31. *See generally* B. BAILYN, *supra* note 30.

32. *Id.* at 34-54. A group of English writers and politicians waged a relentless, scathing attack on the powers and prerogatives of the King's ministers. The English radicals feared the growth of executive power at the expense of Parliament and accused the King's ministers of manipulating members of Parliament by bribery, extravagant favors and pensions, preferment, and the bestowal of lucrative offices upon them. The radicals believed that the ministry, through its lackeys in Parliament, levied taxes upon the people to support its drive for power and enhance its ability to manipulate and control Parliament, thereby drawing all power unto itself. They charged that the ministry maintained a standing army ostensibly to protect the public but in fact to strengthen the ministry's domination. *Id.* Although these ardent oppositionists achieved little popular support in their own time in England, their writings were enormously influential among the American colonists. *Id.* at 51.

England. For the colonists Parliament, the Privy Council, and the Crown were remote bodies; colonial governors were often mere functionaries; colonial assemblies reflected the parochial interests of their constituencies. The notion of autonomy from governmental control was part of the reality of the American experience; in this context talk of inalienable rights against the state was not so revolutionary.[33]

Other contributing factors may have been the identification of America with newness, exploration, and freedom from the European past; the generally secular character of American settlements by the Revolution, which made Enlightenment ideas about the primacy of man palatable; the fact that American growth occurred after the Glorious Revolution's reduction of the power of the monarchy and articulation of ideas that were to become the foundations of natural rights theory in America.[34] Whatever the explanation, the idea of natural rights gained a foothold in America and became a self-fulfilling prophecy as Great Britain sought to tighten her administration of the colonies in the 1760's and 1770's. In all government lay the seeds of tyranny, as the Stamp Act, the Sugar Act, and the Boston Port Act demonstrated. The people could not expect full protection of their liberties from government officials; officeholding bred corruption and the coveting of power.[35] The only way to protect the inalienable rights of the people was to record those rights in writing. The term "constitution," which

---

33. E. Morgan, *supra* note 30, at 8-12.

34. *See, e.g.,* J. LOCKE, *The Second Treatise of Civil Government,* in TWO TREATISES OF GOVERNMENT 121-247 (T. Cook ed. 1947). *See generally* C. BECKER, THE DECLARATION OF INDEPENDENCE (1922).

35. The influence of English radicalism was especially felt in this regard. *See* note 32 *supra.* The colonists had read the claims of English radicals that the King's ministers were grasping for power and corrupting the legislature, all to the detriment of English liberties and the English constitution. Suddenly in the 1760's England began to impose controls on the colonists, including taxes, and decided to maintain a standing army in North America. Many Americans viewed these controls with great alarm, especially in light of their reading of the English radicals. The colonists feared that such measures were part of a conspiracy to deprive them of their liberties. B. BAILYN, *supra* note 30.

26

had traditionally referred to the corpus or general framework of British laws and institutions, took on a new meaning. In eighteenth century American political thought "constitution" came to refer to a body of fundamental principles, extracted from human experience, which, in written form, set the limits of governmental power. Older charters of rights and liberties for individual colonies, originally conceived as general references rather than guarantees of fundamental political rights, were reinterpreted as efforts to codify first principles of government. The permanent preservation of rights in a written constitution came to be regarded as a necessary bulwark against tyranny; the unwritten British constitution would not suffice.[36]

The idea of a written constitution imparted a new dimension to law in America. Law was, in addition to a manifestation of current social attitudes, a body of universal principles. The very universality of those principles gave them permanence; hence law could not change completely with time and circumstance, but could change only in conformity with the mandates of the Constitution. A Pennsylvanian declared in 1776 that "[m]en entrusted with the formation of civil constitutions should remember that they are *painting for eternity*: that the smallest defect or redundancy in the system they frame may prove the destruction of millions." [37] Among the difficulties posed by a constitution was its effect on the common law heritage of Americans. Would a constitution supplant the common law, or would it be superimposed upon the common law? Who was to determine the application of universal principles to concrete situations? How were areas of American life not governed by specific constitutional provisions to be treated?

Despite the momentousness of these questions, the revolutionary generation in America gave them little attention. The authors of the Declaration of Independence and the framers of the Constitution were concerned primarily with declaring certain

---

36. *Id.* 175-89; G. Wood, *supra* note 9, at 259-68.

37. Anonymous, The Genuine Principles of the Ancient Saxon or English Constitution 34 (1776) (emphasis in original), *quoted in* B. Bailyn, *supra* note 30, at 184.

principles of natural rights to be "self-evident" and with effectuating their theory of popular sovereignty. They were apparently satisfied with letting the common law continue to develop independent of constitutional control and with codifying a tripartite system of governmental powers without deciding which of the three branches of government would have final authority to interpret what had been codified.[38]

C. *The Emergence of the Judiciary in the Early Nineteenth Century*

Colonial judges were among the officials whose peremptory treatment of liberties natural rights theorists feared. Little in the colonial experience suggested that the judiciary would emerge eventually as the chief institutional protector of civil liberties and the primary interpreter of the Constitution. The status of judges in prerevolutionary Massachusetts was probably representative: judges were generally prominent men without legal training whose power to differ from community sentiment was sharply curtailed by the community.[39] The possibility of judicial discretion,[40] although recognized, was not applauded.[41] The courts, a commentator noted five years after the Declaration of

---

38. *See* Levy, *Judicial Review, History, and Democracy: An Introduction,* in JUDICIAL REVIEW AND THE SUPREME COURT 1-8 L. Levy ed. 1967) [hereinafter cited as JUDICIAL REVIEW]; Thayer, *The Origin and Scope of the American Doctrine of Constitutional Law,* in *id.* 43-63. Some framers and supporters of the new Constitution, most notably Alexander Hamilton, urged that the courts have the authority to interpret the Constitution, noting that state courts already exercised the power of judicial review over state legislation. THE FEDERALIST Nos. 78, 80, 81 (B. Wright ed. 1961) (A. Hamilton); Levy explains Hamilton's support for judicial review in *The Federalist* as a political tactic in the struggle for ratification rather than as an expression of the framers' intent. JUDICIAL REVIEW, *supra,* at 6.

39. W. NELSON, *supra* note 13, at 32-33.

40. "Judicial discretion" in this context refers to the freedom of judges to decide cases in accordance with their own predilections rather than as indicated by precedent, statute, or the values of the community. *See generally* Dworkin, *The Model of Rules,* 35 U. CHI. L. REV. 14 (1967); Raz, *Legal Principles and the Limits of Law,* 81 YALE L.J. 823, 842-54 (1972).

41. G. WOOD, *supra* note 9, at 298.

Independence, "must take the law as it is, and by all due and proper means execute it, without any pretense to judge if it's right or wrong." [42] Allowing judges to set aside a law, James Madison wrote in 1788, "makes the Judiciary Department paramount in fact to the Legislature, which was never intended and can never be proper." [43]

Yet in the late eighteenth and early nineteenth centuries the judiciary emerged as a creative lawmaking force. One factor explaining this development was the ambiguous status of legislative bodies in a republic. Americans seemed to regard state legislatures as autonomous but manifested uneasiness about limitless powers in Congress. A major purpose of a written constitution was to place permanent checks on governmental power; if Congress alone could determine the meaning of the Constitution, that purpose might be defeated. As for the Executive, no right-thinking American patriot was prepared to invest unlimited discretionary power in an office that bore trappings of monarchy. From its origins American constitutionalism differed from the British model in rejecting the notion of absolute sovereignty in any branch of government. Government actions were to conform to the principles of the Constitution, which were not identified with any group save the people at large.[44]

In the context of American constitutionalism a theory of judicial interpretation first began to develop. Attempts to make "law" synonymous with written codes invariably run into problems of coverage: The language of constitutions or statutes cannot anticipate every contingency. In novel contexts some interpretation of language is required. In the framers' debates in the Constitutional Convention, and in the earliest years under the

---

42. Trenton Gazette, Apr. 18, 1781, *quoted in* G. WOOD *supra* note 9, at 302.

43. James Madison's Observations on Thomas Jefferson's Draft of a Constitution for Virginia, Oct., 1788, in 6 THE PAPERS OF THOMAS JEFFERSON 315 (J. Boyd ed. 1952) (footnote omitted).

44. But *see* C. BEARD, AN ECONOMIC INTERPRETATION OF THE CONSTITUTION OF THE UNITED STATES (1913).

Constitution, the possibility that Congress would act as chief interpreter was given serious consideration. The argument for congressional interpretation rested on the assumption that law is the will of the sovereign and the judiciary is bound to follow it; because Congress represents the sovereign people, it should declare their will. This argument ultimately foundered on the belief that law was bounded by the natural rights principles embodied in the Constitution, which even the will of the legislature could not contravene. Yet appeals to the Constitution were meaningless unless someone interpreted the document; if the legislature could not, who could? John Marshall seized upon this dilemma to develop the concept of independent judicial review in *Marbury v. Madison.*[45]

Marshall's argument in *Marbury* intertwined three propositions: First, the Constitution is the supreme source of law in America, to which the legislature is subordinate; second, ultimate construction of the Constitution by a legislature runs counter to the first proposition, because it would make constitutional principles synonymous with the legislative will; third, the proper interpreter of the Constitution in situations in which it clashes with legislative acts is the judiciary, because the judiciary is empowered only to declare the law, not to make it. Hence the true meaning of the Constitution is ascertainable only through judicial interpretation.[46] Once Americans had decided to have a constitution with a tripartite governmental structure, Marshall's argument implied, they had necessarily decided to have an independent judiciary, because the Constitution was supreme and yet its coverage was not preordained, and judges could be counted on to be disinterested expositors of constitutional principles.

Marshall's position was not unassailable. Adherence to a declaratory theory of the judicial function did not eliminate the problem of judicial discretion.[47] A group of thinkers as convinced

---

45. 5 U.S. (1 Cranch) 137 (1803).

46. *Id.* at 176-79. Hamilton expounded these principles in *The Federalist.* Note 38 *supra.*

47. *See generally* sources cited note 40 *supra.*

of man's susceptibility to corruption and tyranny as the revolutionary generation was not likely to be sanguine about judical disinterestedness.[48] Interpretive powers in the judiciary secured a foothold in America not only because of Marshall's ingenuity but because of changes in the social and economic climate of the nation. In the years following the framing of the Constitution social and economic developments helped break down the patterns of stability, order, interdependence, and hierarchical social organization that had marked colonial settlements. The expansion and transformation of the economy (especially in its transportation sector), the decline of organized religion, the growth and diffusion of population, the development of a more heterogeneous ethnic base, the lure of vacant land, and the emergence of literature deemphasizing social obligations and emphasizing individual freedoms and accomplishments combined to disrupt the communal homogeneity and solidarity of prerevolutionary America.[49] As the American environment changed, law became more of a vehicle for facilitating individual action and accomplishment.[50]

For reasons that have not yet been explained fully[51] the judiciary, at both the federal and state levels and with respect to both constitutional and common law issues, came in the early nineteenth century to assume a posture of promoting social welfare by fostering individual entrepreneurial activity. In the process judges expanded their interpretive powers. By the close of

---

48. For a useful survey of the variety of attitudes on judicial review at the time of the framing of the Constitution, see JUDICIAL REVIEW, *supra* note 38.

49. The following sources discuss specific aspects of early nineteenth century American culture: G. TAYLOR, THE TRANSPORTATION REVOLUTION (1951); T. SMITH, REVIVALISM AND SOCIAL REFORM (1957); R. WADE, THE URBAN FRONTIER (1959); H. SMITH, VIRGIN LAND (1950); A. KAUL, THE AMERICAN VISION (1963).

50. *See generally* J. HURST, THE GROWTH OF AMERICAN LAW (1950); W. NELSON, *supra* note 13.

51. *But see* Horwitz, *The Emergency of an Instrumental Conception of American Law,* 1780-1820, in LAW IN AMERICAN HISTORY (5 PERSPECTIVES IN AMERICAN HISTORY) 287 (D. Fleming & B. Bailyn eds. 1971) [hereinafter cited as LAW IN AMERICAN HISTORY].

Chief Justice Marshall's tenure in 1835 the Supreme Court had emerged as a consistent, if not constant, supporter of the right to unrestricted use and enjoyment of one's property;[52] it also had emerged as a formidable lawmaking force. Meanwhile local community control of judicial decisionmaking diminished; judges began to reserve the law-declaring function for themselves in the areas of riparian rights, admiralty, and damages,[53] among others, and to articulate their decisions in terms of principles of wider applicability.[54] That Americans tolerated this aggrandizement of judicial power suggests that judicial decisions were furthering values that had come into prominence, such as freedom and predictability in the conduct of individual affairs, and that other values, such a community solidarity, which had served as checks on judicial discretion in colonial America, had declined in significance. The breadth of the judiciary's new constituency remains a matter of historical debate.[55] It is clear, however, that in an atmosphere of increasing deemphasis of community solidarity and a growing emphasis on individual initiative judges solidified their position as the primary interpreters of the Constitution and the leading architects of changing common law doctrines. With the emergence of the judiciary in this dual capacity an indigenous American jurisprudence was born.

---

52. The Court's protection of private property rights was achieved primarily by an expansion of the scope of the Constitution's contract clause. *See e.g.,* Fletcher v. Peck, 10 U.S. (6 Cranch) 87 (1810); New Jersey v. Wilson, 11 U.S. (7 Cranch) 164 (1812); Sturges v. Crowninshield, 17 U.S. 70, 7 Wheat. 122 (1819); Trustees of Dartmouth College v. Woodward, 17 U.S. 250, 7 Wheat. 518 (1819). For a discussion of the Marshall Court's protection of private property rights through the contract clause, see B. WRIGHT, THE CONTRACT CLAUSE OF THE CONSTITUTION 3-53 (1938). A sophisticated treatment of Marshall's theory of property rights is found in R. FAULKNER, THE JURISPRUDENCE OF JOHN MARSHALL (1968).

53. These areas are discussed briefly in Horwitz, *supra* note 51, at 289, 322-24.

54. W. NELSON, *supra* note 13, at 117-64; Horwitz, *The Transformation in the Conception of Property in American Law* 1780-1860, 40 U. CHI. L. REV. 248 (1973).

55. *See* W. NELSON, *supra* note 13, at 165-74. The pervasiveness of entrepreneurial values in the population at large in the early nineteenth century, *see* I. WYLLIE, THE SELF-MADE MAN IN AMERICA (1954), suggests that the judiciary may have been responding to widely held attitudes. It is possible, however, that the

D. *The Creation of an American Jurisprudence*

By the second decade of the nineteenth century the distinctive features of American jurisprudence were established. The colonial experience had produced an impression of common law more as a repository of social attitudes than as a mysterious body of rules. Notwithstanding a view of judging that assumed that "law" was sufficiently finite to be "discovered," Americans had not equated law with a set of rules that compelled obedience whether reasonable and just or not. The "brooding omnipresence" of law in America was essentially the omnipresence of natural rights, the "higher law" to which one could appeal. The American colonists continually had revised or abandoned English common law doctrines if they were inequitable or inefficient; the colonists had come to believe that law was meaningless apart from its social context.

If the years prior to the Revolution had nurtured a distinctively American attitude toward law, the revolutionary generation refined this attitude by giving law another dimension. By introducing a supreme, permanent source of law, the framers of the Constitution checked any jurisprudential inclination to conform law entirely to dominant social attitudes. Certain legal principles, the Constitution suggested, were to be virtually immune from change. Future events and ideas might alter the meaning of law only up to a point; certain rights, powers, privileges, and limitations were unalterable. Superimposed upon a fluid and diverse body of common law in America was a more rigid body of constitutional law.

But even the Constitution was not free from change. The generality of its language and the incompleteness of its coverage, in short, the need for its interpretation, meant that contemporary social attitudes could affect its meaning. With the origins of an American jurisprudence came a complex relationship between

---

enhanced role of the judiciary is attributable to the judges' responsiveness to the needs of an economic elite. *See* L. FRIEDMAN, A HISTORY OF AMERICAN LAW 99-100 (1973).

common law,[56] constitutional law, and changing social perceptions. The Constitution set limits on the permissible range of federal and state activity. For example, states could not interfere with previous contracts between private parties [57] and the federal government could not try persons twice for the same offense.[58] At the same time, the Constitution apparently left a vast amount of activity free of its coverage, allowing a considerable body of nonconstitutional law to develop.

The above developments created a continuing possibility of tension between newly created nonconstitutional doctrines, reflecting changing social attitudes, and constitutional principles. In areas apparently untouched by constitutional law a network of common law relationships emerged; but when a common law or legislative concept or doctrine, or a private practice, took on sufficient social significance, it became a matter of "constitutional" concern. Competitive transportation franchises, neither prohibited nor permitted by the language of the Constitution, were eventually attacked as inconsistent with the contract clause, and the Supreme Court was forced to settle the matter in favor of competition.[59] The institution of slavery borrowed a number of common law property doctrines to organize its relationships; eventually those doctrines were judged to reflect constitutional rights violated by states unsympathetic to slavery or, alternatively, judged to offend the civil rights of blacks. Thus the property rights of slaveholders [60] and the citizenship status of freed slaves [61] became questions of constitutional law. The domain

---

56. *See* note 1 *supra.*

57. U.S. CONST. art I, § 10.

58. U.S. CONST. amend. V.

59. In Charles River Bridge v. Warren Bridge Co., 36 U.S. 341, 11 Pet. 420 (1837), the Massachusetts legislature had given plaintiffs a franchise to build a toll bridge over the Charles River. Forty-three years later, the legislature granted a franchise to another corporation to build a bridge (without tolls) over the same river. The first corporation suffered a loss of revenue, but the Court rejected its claim that the granting of the second franchise violated the contract clause.

60. *E.g.*, Strader v. Graham, 51 U.S. (10 How.) 82 (1851).

61. *E.g.*, Dred Scott v. Sandford, 60 U.S. (19 How.) 393 (1857). *See also* text accompanying notes 118-20 *infra.*

of common law, which mostly had developed independently of constitutional law, nevertheless became a recurrent source of constitutional issues; conversely, the resolution of constitutional issues regularly had common law implications.

The principal institution for resolution of the tension between the common law and the Constitution came to be the judiciary. Doctrines or legal entities that had ancient common law origins, such as eminent domain or the corporation, became revitalized in nineteenth century America and eventually were given constitutional sanction by judges.[62] In addition, the nineteenth century judiciary became the chief creator of constitutional limitations on private conduct. The same judges who pioneered in harmonizing innovative common law doctrines with the Constitution — Joseph Story, Roger Taney, Lemuel Shaw — also stressed the implications flowing from the Constitution's recognition of slavery as a legitimate institution.[63]

The indigenous character of American jurisprudence is fully discernible by the middle of the nineteenth century. A uniquely broad definition of "common law," a reverence for natural rights principles as embodied in the Constitution, and a high tolerance for judicial lawmaking in nonconstitutional and constitutional contexts are evident. Major themes of American legal history can be viewed as outgrowths of these central features of American jurisprudence.

Three such themes will be traced in the following section of this Article. The first is the presence of transient constitutional "doctrines," analogous to the doctrinal creations of common law courts. The notion that the Constitution, supposedly a source of

---

62. On James Kent's contributions to the development of eminent domain, see generally J. HORTON, JAMES KENT: A STUDY IN CONSERVATISM (1939); on Joseph Story's role in the emergence of the corporation, see G. DUNNE, JUSTICE JOSEPH STORY AND THE RISE OF THE SUPREME COURT (1970).

63. A thorough account of Story's and Shaw's ambivalence toward the slavery issue is R. COVER, JUSTICE ACCUSED (1975). For Taney's involvement with the issue, see C. SWISHER, ROGER B. TANEY (1935); C. SWISHER, THE TANEY PERIOD 1836-1864 (1974) [hereinafter cited as THE TANEY PERIOD].

permanent principles, can be glossed by judges, and the evidence that such glosses rise and fall in prominence, testify to the close interplay in American jurisprudence of changing social mores, common law adjudication, and constitutional interpretation.

A second theme is the competitive interaction of constitutional and nonconstitutional law, particularly in the late nineteenth and twentieth centuries when statutory and administrative lawmaking proliferated, causing a redefinition of "common law" adjudication. Judges have continued to play a creative role as lawmakers despite the plethora of statutory and administrative "laws" that have emerged since the Civil War. The role of the judiciary as a constitutionalizing agent, charged with the simultaneous duties of conforming changing social attitudes and practices to constitutional principles and of accommodating the Constitution's coverage to emerging values, has been maintained. But the much larger body of nonconstitutional law in modern America and the increased presence of alternative lawmaking institutions has changed the process of constitutionalization for the judiciary and complicated the relationship between constitutional and nonconstitutional law.

A third theme is the relationship between broad changes in juristic perspectives and changing conceptions of legal scholarship, with special reference to lawyer historians' successive definitions of "legal history." Analysis of the interplay of constitutional and nonconstitutional law in American history reveals the presence, in different time periods, of dominant juristic attitudes which express distinctive perspectives on law and legal institutions. At some times in American history such perspectives insist on a wide ambit for constitutional principles, so that nonconstitutional law is perceived as pregnant with potential constitutional issues and the judiciary is invited to apply constitutional principles to a wide variety of ordinary legal relationships. In other periods the dominant perspective reserves the Constitution for a limited number of issues, and active experimentation in nonconstitutional areas is encouraged. In some periods influential jurists perceive a rigid analytical separation between constitutional and nonconstitutional law; in others constitutional and non-constitutional lawmaking are thought of as discrete parts of an intergrated legal process. The same perspectives that produce one or another of the above emphases affect the subjects and methodologies of legal scholarship.

The "path" of American jurisprudence, as traced in this Article, consists of selected thematic corollaries to the proposition that unique attitudes about law and the judiciary emerged in nineteenth century America. In addition to the themes upon which the Article focuses, one broader characteristic can be noted. Since the "creation" of an American jurisprudence, American lawyers and legal scholars have not thought about law in the same manner as have their English counterparts with a similar common law heritage. The close association of "law" with current social attitudes and the decisions of an activist, "lawmaking" judiciary has not only immersed American judges in contemporary social issues, but has made a rigid separation of law from politics appear artificial to Americans. The identification of common law with currently dominant social attitudes and of constitutional law with natural rights has interfused "law" and "justice" for Americans. A definition of law as merely a body of rules appears unrealistic in the American context. However much American jurists have been interested in portraying law as a "science" with governing universal axioms and concepts,[64] the effort has never entirely succeeded. From the nineteenth century to the present, "policy," "morals," and "law" have been interwined in American jurisprudence, despite juristic attempts to separate them.

II. SOME THEMES OF AMERICAN JURISPRUDENCE

A. *The Rise and Fall of Constitutional Doctrines*

One of the characteristics of a jurisprudence that creates a permanent source of law in a constitution but requires that the source be continually interpreted in light of changing social perceptions is the appearance of fluctuating trends in constitutional interpretation. A manifestation of such trends is the changing status of various constitutional "doctrines," or judicially created glosses on broad language in the Constitution. Constitutional doctrines represent judicial efforts to conform constitutional law to dominant modes of thought, thereby reinforcing public confidence in the judiciary as a constitutionalizing agent. Three variables affect the current status of constitutional doctrines: the stature of particular social values at various times in American history, the textual support (or lack thereof) for a particular value as a constitutional "right," and the current state of public confidence in the judiciary as a lawmaking force. Two constitutional doctrines, "liberty of contract" and "privacy," serve as illustrations.

1. Liberty of Contract

Prior to the Civil War constitutional protection of entrepreneurial activity from governmental interference was secured primarily through the contract clause of the Constitution.[65] Enterpreneurs were not entirely free from governmental regulation despite that clause. Most economic ventures required state subsidization, and in chartering franchises states reserved the power to amend a charter's terms, thereby avoiding a contract clause challenge. State/private economic partnerships and state regulation of the economy were common, if controversial, notions.[66] After 1860, however, the purchasing power of private individuals increased markedly, entrepreneurs undertook ventures without public capital, state governments reduced their regulatory operations, and theories of economic individualism rose in popularity. By the last decades of the

---

64. There have been times when this interest has been considerable. *See* note 178 *infra*. *See generally* White, *From Sociological Jurisprudence to Realism: Jurisprudence and Social Change in Early Twentieth Century America*, 58 VA. L. REV. 999 (1972).

65. *See* B. WRIGHT, *supra* note 52, at 27-88.

66. *See generally* O. HANDLIN & M. HANDLIN, COMMONWEALTH (1969); 2 A. HOWARD, COMMENTARIES ON THE CONSTITUTION OF VIRGINIA 1126-30 (1974); J. HURST, LAW AND THE CONDITIONS OF FREEDOM IN THE NINETEENTH-CENTURY UNITED STATES (1956).

nineteenth century massive enterprises had appeared which were accustomed to doing business free from any governmental regulation.

Social, intellectual, and economic trends increasingly favored unregulated private activity. The fourteenth amendment's due process clause apparently codified "liberty" as a paramount value, and the clause was interpreted to protect corporations.[67] In this atmosphere treatise writers interpreted "liberty" in the due process clause to encompass freedom to "contract" — to buy and sell one's services on the terms for which one bargained.[68] By the late nineteenth century a climate favorable to incorporation of antiregulationist economic theories into the Constitution had developed. First the state [69] and then the federal [70] judiciary announced as a principle of constitutional law that no state could pass legislation that interfered with the right of an individual to contract freely.

Liberty of contract undoubtedly served the interests of enterprises that were in strong bargaining positions and wanted to maintain a predictable and modest level of compensation for their employees. The doctrine did not assure that their expenditures for wages would remain constant, considering that the market for employee services fluctuated, but it allowed them to hire employees at the "going rate" regardless of its inequities. In the late nineteenth century, however, as industrial enterprise matured and the population of the United States grew and

---

67. Santa Clara County v. Southern Pac. R.R., 118 U.S. 394 (1886). On economic life in the late nineteenth century, see E. KIRKLAND, INDUSTRY COMES OF AGE (1961).

68. On the juristic origins of liberty of contract, see C. JACOBS, LAW WRITERS AND THE COURTS (1954).

69. *E.g.,* Godcharles & Co. v. Wigeman, 113 Pa. 431, 6 A. 354 (1886); State v. Goodwill, 33 W. Va. 179, 10 S.E. 285 (1889); Ritchie v. People, 155 Ill. 98, 40 N.E. 454 (1895).

70. Missouri Pac. Ry. v. Nebraska, 164 U.S. 403 (1896), was the first case in which the Supreme Court invalidated a state statute through use of the due process clause in an economic context. Allgeyer v. Louisiana, 165 U.S. 578 (1897), was the first case in which the Court explicitly recognized a fourteenth amendment "liberty" to contract. *Id.* at 589.

diversified, unregulated industrialism produced an underclass of subsistence workers whose existence because a matter of public concern. Disease, violence, and poverty were discernible adjuncts to industrial growth. Gaps between the income levels and life styles of the "captains of industry" and industrial workers offended egalitarian traditions. Efforts to alleviate the casualities of industrialism were undertaken, initially by private agencies and eventually by the states in the form of wage and hour legislation.[71] That legislation encountered the liberty of contract principle.

In passing upon the validity of state wage and hour legislation the judiciary confronted another example of dissonance between contemporary social trends and constitutional principles. Adherence to the liberty of contract doctrine would invalidate nearly any piece of social welfare legislation designed to confer benefits on persons who could not obtain those benefits in a free market; to invoke liberty of contract meant to oppose increasingly popular humanitarian views. On the other hand, validation of social welfare statutes emasculated the principle of economic liberty. For a time the Supreme Court clung to freedom of contract.[72] After severe academic criticism, however,[73] the Court decided that liberty of contract was only a doctrine, not a principle of fundamental law, and that having been "interpreted" into being, the doctrine could be interpreted into obscurity.[74]

In the process, however, the Supreme Court was forced temporarily to qualify its power as a constitutionalizing agent. The attack on liberty of contract stressed that the notion was a fiction,

---

71. Late nineteenth and early twentieth century perceptions of the costs of mature industrialism are described in R. BREMNER, FROM THE DEPTHS (1956); S. FINE, LAISSEZ FAIRE AND THE GENERAL-WELFARE STATE (1956).

72. *E.g.,* Adair v. United States, 208 U.S. 161 (1908); Adkins v. Children's Hosp., 261 U.S. 525 (1923), *overruled,* West Coast Hotel Co. v. Parrish, 300 U.S. 379 (1937).

73. *E.g.,* Pound, *Liberty of Contract,* 18 YALE L.J. 454 (1909).

74. West Coast Hotel Co. v. Parrish, 300 U.S. 379 (1937). In that case Chief Justice Hughes, for the majority, said that "[t]he Constitution does not speak of freedom of contract. . . . Liberty under the Constitution is . . . subject to the restraints of due process, and . . . regulation which is reasonable in relation to its subject and is adopted in the interests of the community . . . ." *Id.* at 391.

because true equality of bargaining power did not exist between the employers and employees of industrial America; that it was based on an economic philosophy unsupportable in twentieth century America; that in invoking liberty of contract judges were approving that philosophy; and that judges should not read their social and economic views into the Constitution.[75] Further judicial adherence to an outmoded idea would have revived the spectre of judicial tyranny. Implicit in the recognition of the judiciary as a constitutionalizing agent had been the assumption that judge-made glosses on the Constitution would reflect contemporary social attitudes, not the personal views of judges. Hence coincidentally with the attack on the liberty of contract doctrine came calls for a reduced judicial role in constitutional interpretation, in which the courts would assume a permissive stance toward legislative innovations.[76] This stance assumed implicitly that the Constitution could accommodate legislative solutions to social problems if they were devised on a rational basis. In seeking to curtail the judiciary's power to scrutinize legislative solutions, critics wanted to oust judges from their position as the primary link between social change and constitutional principles.[77]

2. Privacy

Liberty of contract passed into oblivion after 1937, leaving the circumscribed constitutionalizing role for courts its unpopularity

---

75. *See* Lochner v. New York, 198 U.S. 45, 74 (1905) (Holmes, J., dissenting).

76. This was part of the message of Justice Holmes' dissent in *Lochner:*

This case is decided upon an economic theory which a large part of the country does not entertain. If it were a question whether I agreed with that theory, I should desire to study it further and long before making up my mind. But I do not conceive that to be my duty, because I strongly believe that my agreement or disagreement has nothing to do with the right of a majority to embody their opinions in law. . . . The Fourteenth Amendment does not enact Mr. Herbert Spencer's Social Statics. *Id.* at 75.

77. In 1912 Theodore Roosevelt called for "the exercise of the referendum by the people themselves in a certain class of decisions of constitutional questions in which the courts decide against the power of the people to do elementary justice." 19 THE WORKS OF THEODORE ROOSEVELT 258 (H. Hagedorn ed. 1925).

had helped foster. The manner in which the constitutional doctrine of privacy was announced and the doctrine's delayed arrival were functions of the persistence of a narrowly defined constitutionalizing role for the judiciary. The Supreme Court refused to give substantive content to the fourteenth amendment's due process clause throughout the 1940's, 1950's, and 1960's,[78] a refusal applauded by the commentators.[79] The Court said in *Ferguson v. Skrupa*,[80] "We have returned to the original constitutional proposition that courts do not substitute their social and economic beliefs for the judgment of legislative bodies . . . ."[81] In the meantime, however, legislative solutions to social problems had proved to have some costs of their own. Legislatures could infringe individual rights as well as protect them; being a ward of the government could result in loss of one's freedom.[82]

One consequence of active government was increased governmental involvement in people's lives. Distribution of the benefits conferred by social welfare legislation, for example, required an administrative apparatus that supposedly needed a plethora of information about the program's beneficiaries.[83] In

---

78. *See, e.g.,* Olsen v. Nebraska, 313 U.S. 236 (1941); Lincoln Fed. Labor Union v. Northwestern Iron & Metal Co., 335 U.S. 525 (1949); Day-Brite Lighting, Inc. v. Missouri, 342 U.S. 421 (1952).

79. *See, e.g.,* McCloskey, *Economic Due Process and the Supreme Court: An Exhumation and Reburial,* 1962 SUP. CT. REV. 34.

80. 372 U.S. 726 (1963).

81. *Id.* at 730.

82. In the 1940's and '50's the Court was reluctant to upset restrictive legislation of any kind, except in the first amendment area. *See, e.g.,* Board of Educ. v. Barnette, 319 U.S. 624 (1943); Thomas v. Collins, 323 U.S. 516 (1945). Cases like Skinner v. Oklahoma, 316 U.S. 535 (1942), invalidating an Oklahoma sterilization statute on equal protection grounds, were rare. But by the 1960's the Court had come to use the equal protection clause in a "substantive" manner, striking down legislative classifications that amounted to "invidious discrimination" against beneficiaries of government largesse. *See, e.g.,* Shapiro v. Thompson, 394 U.S. 618 (1969).

83. In some government programs, such as social security, participation (symbolized by a social security number) gave interested parties access to general

numerous other respects twentieth century American civilization reduced one's opportunities for privacy. Sophisticated electronic devices made eavesdropping and wiretapping relatively easy tasks. The telephone, the camera, and the advent of mass media sharply reduced distances between oneself and one's neighbors. Urban living became an exercise in insulating oneself from crowds. The private lives of public figures and the extraordinary experiences of otherwise unknown persons became matters for commercial exploitation.

Despite the growing consciousness of the value of privacy in the twentieth century, "privacy" was slow to become a constitutionally protected "right." The delayed constitutionalization of privacy was in part a function of the early twentieth century contraction of the judiciary's constitutionalizing function. Academic and judicial criticism of "substantive" judging caused the Supreme Court to assume a posture of deference toward legislative regulation of economic affairs ıfter the 1930's; this tolerance was extended tacitly to regulation of noneconomic matters. If the federal government and the states could regulate hours and wages, why could they not regulate social activity? From the 1930's to the 1960's the answer was that they could, within reasonable limits,[84] with the sole exception of speech, which many justices felt the first amendment singled out for special protection.[85]

In this context the Connecticut birth control cases,[86] which tested the constitutionality of a statute prohibiting the use of contraceptive devices by married persons, came before the Supreme Court. The Connecticut law, which conceivably justified searches of private homes to ensure that birth control was not being practiced, appeared not to infringe any constitutional rights

---

information about the participant; in others, such as welfare, administrators were far more zealous in their quest for information, to the point of searching the homes of recipients to ensure that their qualifications for largesse were bona fide. *See* Parrish v. Civil Serv. Comm'n, 66 Cal. 2d 260, 425 P.2d 223, 57 Cal. Rptr. 623 (1967); Reich, *Midnight Welfare Searches and the Social Security Act,* 72 YALE L.J. 1347 (1963).

84. United States v. Carolene Prods. Co., 304 U.S. 144 (1938).

85. *See* note 82 *supra.*

86. Poe v. Ullman, 367 U.S. 497 (1961); Griswold v. Connecticut, 381 U.S. 479 (1965).

PATTERNS OF AMERICAN LEGAL THOUGHT

then recognized by the Court. No right of privacy is mentioned in the Constitution, and the law seemed not to violate any constitutionally protected "liberties," because "liberty" in the fourteenth amendment had been stripped of most its substantive content. Yet the birth control cases were clearly substantive due process cases, although, of course, not explicitly so. As in the liberty of contract decisions before 1937, the Court was urged to give substantive meaning to "liberty" in the fourteenth amendment. The essential difference was that this time the meaning would not be an economic one.

Recognizing the substantive due process implications of the birth control cases, the Court in *Griswold v. Connecticut*[87] took pains to dissociate itself from that position. "Overtones of some arguments," Justice Douglas wrote for the majority, "suggest that *Lochner v. New York,*" a liberty of contract opinion, "should be our guide. But we decline that invitation. . . . We do not sit as a super-legislature to determine the wisdom, need, and propriety of laws that touch economic problems, business affairs, or social conditions. [The Connecticut law], however, operates directly on an intimate relation of husband and wife . . . ."[88] That relationship was found worthy of constitutional protection because the very idea that police could search the sacred precincts of marital bedrooms for telltale signs of the use of contraceptives is "repulsive."[89] The Court wanted to afford protection to "zones of privacy";[90] but the constitutional basis of a "right" of privacy was never specified definitively. Justice Douglas could only identify "penumbras, formed by emanations" from specific guarantees in the Bill of Rights.[91]

The advent of the right of privacy demonstrates that when a contemporary value becomes sufficiently prominent it will receive

---

87. 381 U.S. 479 (1965).
88. 381 U.S. at 481-82 (citations omitted).
89. *Id.* at 485-86.
90. *Id.* at 484.
91. *Id.*

constitutional recognition, but the form in which it is recognized will be determined not only by the Constitution's text but by current conceptions of the constitutionalizing function. The *Griswold* opinion was both ingenious and absurd: ingenious because Justice Douglas' reading of Bill of Rights provisions demonstrated that if privacy was not a right enumerated in the Constitution, it was arguably one of its core values; absurd because of the tortuous interpretation the Court endured to avoid the highly unpopular doctrine of substantive due process.[92] Seven years after

---

92. The Court not only felt constrained in *Griswold* to deny that its holding resurrected the discredited due process analysis of an earlier time, *see* text accompanying notes 88-91 *supra,* it suggested, both in *Griswold* and in Roe v. Wade, 410 U.S. 113 (1973), that the right of privacy had long been protected implicitly by the Court. The Court seemed to suggest that its holdings in *Griswold* and *Roe* did not so much announce a "new" right of privacy as they added further dimensions to an implicitly recognized right. Thus in *Griswold* Justice Douglas cited, *inter alia,* NAACP v. Alabama, 357 U.S. 449 (1958); NAACP v. Button, 371 U.S. 415 (1963); and Schware v. Board of Bar Examiners, 353 U.S. 232 (1957), to argue that the Court had safeguarded privacy before in its protection of freedom of association. 381 U.S. at 483-84. He also pointed to the Court's decisions under the fourth and fifth amendments as examples of the Court's past recognition of the right to privacy. *Id.* at 484-85.

Justice Blackmun, in an effort to root the *Roe* decision firmly in the Court's prior cases, said:

The Constitution does not explicitly mention any right of privacy. In a line of decisions, however, going back perhaps as far as *Union Pacific R. Co. v. Botsford,* 141 U.S. 250, 251 (1891), the Court recognized that a right of personal privacy, or a guarantee of certain areas or zones of privacy, does exist under the Constitution. In varying contexts, the Court or individual Justices have, indeed, found at least the roots of that right in the First Amendment, *Stanley v. Georgia,* 394 U.S. 557, 564 (1969); in the Fourth and Fifth Amendments, *Terry v. Ohio,* 392 U.S. 1, 8-9 (1968), *Katz v. United States,* 389 U.S. 347, 350 (1967), *Boyd v. United States,* 116 U.S. 616 (1886), ... in the penumbras of the Bill of Rights, *Griswold v. Connecticut,* 381 U.S., at 484-485; in the Ninth Amendment, *id.,* at 486 (Goldberg, J., concurring); or in the concept of liberty guaranteed by the first section of the Fourteenth Amendment, see *Meyer v. Nebraska,* 262 U.S. 390, 399 (1923).... [These decisions] make it clear that the right [to privacy] has some extension to activities relating to marriage, *Loving v. Virginia,* 388 U.S. 1, 12 (1967); procreation, *Skinner v. Oklahoma* 316 U.S. 535, 541-542 (1942); contraception, *Eisenstadt v. Baird,* 405 U.S., at 453-454; ... family relationships, *Prince v. Massachusetts,* 321 U.S. 158,

Griswold The Court was still not prepared to make the right of privacy a "liberty," although it was prepared to free it from the marital relationship in the contraception context and include in it "the right of the *individual,* married or single, to be free from unwarranted governmental intrusion into matters so fundamentally affecting a person as the decision whether to bear or beget a child." [93]

A year later, however, the Court was more willing than before, though not without hestiation,[94] to place the right of privacy in the fourteenth amendment's substantive guarantee of liberty. The Court found in *Roe v. Wade* [95] that the right of privacy was "broad enough to encompass a woman's decision whether or not to terminate her pregnancy" in certain circumstances, "whether [that right] be founded in the Fourteenth Amendment's concept of personal liberty and restrictions upon state action, *as we feel it is,* or, as the District Court determined, in the Ninth Amendment's reservation of rights to the people ...." [96] Justice Stewart, who dissented in *Griswold* but concurred in *Roe,* bluntly summarized the trend:

> [I]t was clear to me then, and it is equally clear to me now, that the *Griswold* decision can be rationally understood only as a holding that the Connecticut statute substantively invaded the "liberty" that is protected by the Due Process Clause of the Fourteenth Amendment.

---

166 (1944); and child rearing and education, *Pierce v. Society of Sisters,* 268 U.S. 510, 535 (1925) ....

410 U.S. at 152-53.

The lengthy citation to prior holdings under the first, fourth, and fifth amendments demonstrates how loath the Court was to appear to be substituting its own social judgment for that of state legislatures under the rubric of substantive due process.

93. Eisenstadt v. Baird, 405 U.S. 438, 453 (1972).

94. *See* note 92 *supra.*

95. 410 U.S. 113 (1973).

96. *Id.* at 153 (emphasis supplied).

> As so understood, *Griswold* stands as one in a long line of . . . cases decided under the doctrine of substantive due process . . . .[97]

Privacy might never have become a constitutional right independent of the right to liberty were it not for the Court's understanding of the early twentieth century loss of confidence in the judiciary as the institution primarily charged with translating changed social perceptions into constitutional law. The perception that the conditions of twentieth century life threatened privacy values still would have been the catalyst for constitutional protection of those values, but the right of privacy might well have been subsumed earlier, unhesitantly, and explicitly, in the broader guarantee of "liberty." Liberty of contract emerged because the text of the Constitution provided an explicit recognition of the right to "liberty" and ingenious jurists and judges were able to include "contract" in that liberty; it disappeared because freedom of contract eventually was preceived to be a false liberty, given the conditions of American life. Privacy emerged in its present form (or lack thereof) because the constitutional text *does not* explicity protect it, because its protection was widely perceived to be vital, and because the unpopularity of the judicial constitutionalization of liberty of contract precluded the arguably more straightforward approach of interpreting "liberty" to include "privacy."

Privacy is as much a "doctrine" as liberty of contract; it protects currently significant values, here the autonomy of one's person and one's interest in being secluded. It may come to resemble liberty of contract in terms of its acceptance by judges as inalienable and sacred. It may also fall into disrepute. Numerous other constitutional doctrines, from the judicial "rule of reason" articulated in the late nineteenth century rate cases [98] to "overbreadth" in the first amendment area today,[99] while perhaps

---

97. *Id.* at 167-68 (Stewart, J., concurring) (footnote omitted).

98. *See, e.g.,* Chicago, M. & St. P. Ry. v. Minnesota, 134 U.S. 418 (1890); Smyth v. Ames, 169 U.S. 466 (1898).

99. *See, e.g.,* Shelton v. Tucker, 364 U.S. 479 (1960); United States v. Robel, 389 U.S. 258 (1967); Zwickler v. Koota, 389 U.S. 241 (1967); Coates v. Cincinnati, 402 U.S. 611 (1971).

not as pervasive in their impact, are amenable to similar analysis.

B. *The Changing Interplay of Constitutional and Nonconstitutional Law*

One might wonder why the Supreme Court attempted to constitutionalize privacy at all, given its omission from the text of the Constitution and given twentieth century skepticism about "substantive" judging. Some judges, including Justice Frankfurter, themselves espoused a limited view of the judiciary's constitutionalizing powers and opposed the Court's involvement in privacy cases.[100] The Court's decision to reach the privacy issue in *Griswold,* after declining to pass on the constitutionality of the Connecticut statute three years earlier in *Poe v. Ullman,*[101] evidenced its renewed confidence in the ability of constitutional law to solve social problems. This confidence paralleled the expansion of constitutional law in the 1950's and '60's into areas that had long been regarded as nonconstitutional territory.[102] The developments of the 1950's and '60's illustrate that just as nonconstitutional and constitutional law have interacted throughout American history, they have also competed, their preceived jurisdictions expanding and contracting. Although the judiciary has attempted, as part of its constitutionalizing function, to identify the jurisdictional boundaries of nonconstitutional and constitutional law, it has not dictated those boundaries. The boundaries have been dictated implicitly by prevailing conceptions of the judiciary's proper role as a constitutionalizing agent. Those conceptions have been influenced not only by the presence of a written Constitution, the changing social and economic context of American history, and the

---

Overbreadth may already have "peaked" in its primacy as a doctrine: *see* Broadrick v. Oklahoma, 413 U.S. 601 (1973).

100. In announcing the judgment of the Court in Poe v. Ullman, 367 U.S. 497 (1961), Justice Frankfurter seized upon the relative absence of prosecutions under the Connecticut birth control statute as a means to avoid reaching the merits of the case. *Id.* at 507-09.

101. *Id.*

102. *See* notes 146-49 *infra* & accompanying text.

current public stature of the courts, but also by the complexities of a federal system of government.

Each of the above variables came into play in the "great cases" decided by the Marshall Court. *Gibbons v. Ogden* [103] is an example. That case was decided late in Marshall's tenure; the pattern of "final" interpretation of the Constitution by the Supreme Court had already been established. *Marbury v. Madison,* [104] *Fletcher v. Peck,* [105] *Trustees of Dartmouth College v. Woodward,* [106] *McCulloch v. Maryland,* [107] and *Cohens v. Virginia,* [108] taken together, evidenced the Court's involvement in and resolution of highly charged social issues and implicitly communicated a national judiciary's concern with ostensibly local questions. *Gibbons* was in the same vein. It was first an exercise in judicial interpretation of the constitutional principle of interstate commerce; second, an inquiry into the monopoly status of state-supported steamboat companies; third, a test of the Court's ability to function in a "common law" capacity, in this instance by assessing and responding to emerging entrepreneurial values; and fourth, an inquiry into the prospective scope of the federal judiciary's supervision, through its mandate to interpret the Constitution, of state economic regulation.

Potentially competing in *Gibbons* were two roles for the judiciary in America: that of common law synthesizer and that of constitutional interpreter. The common law in America had become highly localized by the time of the Constitution: Parochial points of view had created diverse common law rules and doctrines. The growing influence of the judiciary in the states in the late eighteenth and early nineteenth centuries was in part a product of its ability to modify existing common law doctrines to reflect changing parochial attitudes. *Gibbons* raised the question whether

---

103. 22 U.S. (9 Wheat.) 1, 212-21 (1824).
104. 5 U.S. (1 Cranch) 137 (1803).
105. 10 U.S. (6 Cranch) 87 (1810).
106. 17 U.S. (4 Wheat.) 518 (1819).
107. 17 U.S. (4 Wheat.) 316 (1819).
108. 19 U.S. (6 Wheat.) 264 (1821).

a federal judiciary, in the person of the Supreme Court, could perform its role as interpreter of constitutional principles in a manner consistent with the now entrenched role of common law judges. *Gibbons,* then, presented a delicate problem of constitutionalization: Could the Court maintain the integrity of constitutional principles without offending the emergent American version of common law adjudication? Could it secure a result acceptable to the many factions of the populace while preserving its power to scrutinize local laws in the name of the Constitution?

The great success of Marshall's opinion in *Gibbons,* described as "one of the most powerful efforts of the human mind that has ever been displayed from the bench of any court" [109] and the "one and only . . . 'popular' " [110] decision of Marshall's career, was its ability to integrate "common" and "constitutional" lawmaking. Marshall refined ancient English doctrines about the use of navigable waters to conform to the interstate character of American rivers; he lent support to the value of economic competition as opposed to protectionist values; he provided a powerful stimulus for the expansion of trade and commerce into the interior of the American continent. These positions were consistent with influential American common law adjudication. Marshall expanded the meaning of the Constitution's commerce clause, embracing navigation in its coverage, at the same time as he expanded the potential range of federal regulatory power (although that power would lie dormant for many years hence), and thereby increased the potential power of the federal judiciary to decide commercial questions affecting local interests. *Gibbons* was vintage American common law adjudication and activist constitutional interpretation in the same case. It achieved a harmony between the component parts of the early nineteenth century system of American jurisprudence.

But jurisprudential integration of the *Gibbons* variety was the rare exception throughout the nineteenth century. First, the

---

109. New York Evening Post, Mar. 5, 1824, *quoted in* C. WARREN, HISTORY OF THE AMERICAN BAR 395 (1911).

110. A. BEVERIDGE, 4 THE LIFE OF JOHN MARSHALL 445 (4 vols. 1919).

"common law" function of the judiciary became complicated by the increased presence of state statutes promoting new policies. Second, the function of the judiciary in constitutional interpretation became complicated by the collapse of "natural law" as an extra-constitutional source to which judges could appeal. Third, social issues appeared, most notably slavery, that had ominous implications for prospective harmony between the federal government and the states. Fourth, population growth and territorial expansion in the nineteenth century interacted with the legacy of local consciousness from colonial times to produce a thoroughgoing regionalization of nineteenth century American society. All these factors combined to create a potential for competition between constitutional and nonconstitutional law. In the *Dred Scott* case [111] that competition placed the Supreme Court in an insoluble dilemma.

In the uncertain atmosphere of rapid economic change in early nineteenth century America, state legislatures and prospective entrepreneurs sought ways of promoting growth without undermining economic security. Various versions of state-private economic partnerships developed, with varying degrees of state regulation of entrepreneurial activity.[112] In general, the thrust of this development was a greater proliferation of state statutes and a subtle alteration of the "common law" function of the judiciary. Leading common law judges, such as Lemuel Shaw of Massachusetts, sensed their vulnerability as "lawmakers" in the face of legislative activity, yet were reluctant to surrender their lawmaking powers altogether.[113] Their responses, which varied in degree and in content from state to state, can be described generally as professed deference to legislative authority and retention of a "supplementary" interpretive role to aid state legislatures in implementing their desired policies. The judges'

---

111. Dred Scott v. Sandford, 60 U.S. (19 How.) 393 (1857); *see* text accompanying notes 118-20 *infra*.

112. *See* sources cited note 66 *supra*.

113. A comprehensive treatment of Chief Justice Shaw's decisions is found in L. LEVY, THE LAW OF THE COMMONWEALTH AND CHIEF JUSTICE SHAW (1957).

approach has been described as "instrumentalist": [114] It sought to fuse statutory and common law in the pursuit of desired social policies.

The "common law" component of American jurisprudence was thus significantly altered by the middle of the nineteenth century, with serious implications for the continued primacy of judicial lawmaking in nonconstitutional areas. Indeed, some who feared judicial power sought to restrict severely the freedom of common law judges to make law by implementing a general codification of American laws which everyone could understand and which would require little judicial interpretation.[115] At the same time juristic thought evinced an increasing skepticism about the independent viability of natural law. Appeals beyond the Constitution to "general principles which are common to our free institutions," [116] such as Justice William Johnson had made in *Fletcher v. Peck,* came into disfavor.[117] The consequence of this last development was a recognition of the Constitution as the exclusive source of natural rights principles, and a tacit reluctance to permit judicial use of "higher law" sources other than the Constitution's text. This exerted strong pressure on the Constitution to incorporate prevailing notions of reason and justice, and attendant pressures on the judiciary to effectuate that incorporation. Complicating matters even more was the demise of consensual values which accompanied the collapse of natural law as an independent entity during the nineteenth century regionalization of American life.[118]

The *Dred Scott* case came to a Supreme Court caught up in these swirling pressures. Under Chief Justice Taney the Court had shown signs of developing an "instrumentalist" posture, promoting regionalism and industrial expansion by deferring to the judgment of state legislatures, despite the legacy of broad federal

---

114. Horwitz, *supra* note 51.

115. *See* R. COVER, *supra* note 63, at 140-44; P. MILLER, THE LIFE OF THE MIND IN AMERICA 49-109, 239-65 (1966).

116. Fletcher v. Peck, 10 U.S. (6 Cranch) 87, 143 (Johnson, J., concurring).

117. For an account of the disappearance of "natural law" as an entity independent of the Constitution, see R. COVER, *supra* note 63, at 33-193.

118. *See* text accompanying note 49 *supra*.

primacy bequeathed it by former Chief Justice Marshall.[119] Constitutional adjudication by the Taney Court became an exercise in political compromise between clashing regional interests. Could the Court maintain its position of primacy in the area of slavery by endorsing certain states' solutions to the slavery problem, thereby constitutionalizing the common law property doctrines as they had been applied to slaves? Or should the Court, as the final interpreter of the supreme source of natural rights in America, confront squarely the conflict between slavery doctrines and natural rights principles, resolving that conflict one way or the other as a matter of constitutional law?

The juristic dilemma of *Dred Scott* was thus a dilemma brought about by conflict between two types of law and two judicial roles. In seeking to address this dilemma the Court received little guidance from an appeal to consensual values or to fundamental principles. No national consensus existed on how to "solve" the problem of slavery; the Constitutional text was explicitly ambiguous about the place of the institution in a republic based on natural rights principles, especially equality; and appeals to natural law itself were no longer permissible. Hence the Taney Court could only guess whether a full-blown constitutionalization of the legal doctrines governing slavery, which *Dred Scott* accomplished by freeing those doctrines from regional contexts and permitting their extension into new territories, would resolve the slavery question conclusively. The Court, of course, guessed wrong. The constitutional principle of natural rights and the common law doctrines governing slavery were in in irreconcilable conflict and could not be integrated.

The "wrong guess" in *Dred Scott* lowered the stature of the Court drastically and threatened the continued primacy of judges as lawmakers. But in the forty-odd years after 1870 the judiciary was able to reassert and even expand its lawmaking power, again

---

119. *See, e.g.,* Cooley v. Board of Wardens, 53 U.S. (12 How.) 299 (1852); License Cases, 46 U.S. (5 How.) 504 (1847); City of New York v. Miln, 36 U.S. (11 Pet.) 102 (1837); Charles River Bridge v. Warren Bridge Co., 36 U.S. 341, 11 Pet. 420 (1837); THE TANEY PERIOD, *supra* note 63, at 360-65, 370-77.

by successfully integrating constitutional and nonconstitutional law. Several factors contributed to this judicial renaissance. First, the federal judiciary's interpretive powers were potentially expanded by the adoption of the Reconstruction Amendments,[120] which placed constitutional limitations on the states through an impressively broad and general textual apparatus highlighted by such terms as "liberty," "due process," and "equal protection." Second, institutional competitors of the judiciary suffered a decline in public esteem. The public viewed Congress and the state legislatures as partisan and corrupt, the executive branch as inconsequential.[121] Third, a new conception of the relationship between the individual and the government emerged, emphasizing the ability of Americans, especially those in the business community, to master their own destinies and to organize their own affairs. Governmental control of the economy became unfashionable: The state-private partnerships of the antebellum period survived the Civil War but declined thereafter; hostility developed toward state statutes regulating industrial enterprise, and, in general, regulation by the states declined even in areas in which regulation could have been constitutional.[122] Finally, the excitement generated by rapid industrialization, coupled with the dissipation of sectional animosities, superficially united Americans behind an ethic of material progress, which became a new "first principle" cognizable by constitutional law.[123] The interaction of these factors made possible a series of judicial accommodations of constitutional provisions to new nonconstitutional developments.

One can identify several such accommodations: liberty of contract, based upon the stringent rules of the common law of contracts; the expansion of the term "persons" in the due process

---

120. U.S. CONST. amends. XIII, XIV, XV.

121. *See generally* L. WHITE, THE REPUBLICAN ERA 1869-1901 (1958).

122. *See* J. HURST, *supra* note 66; E. KIRKLAND, DREAM AND THOUGHT IN THE BUSINESS COMMUNITY, 1860-1900 (1956); A. PAUL, CONSERVATIVE CRISIS AND THE RULE OF LAW (1960).

123. *See* P. BUCK, THE ROAD TO REUNION 1865-1900 (1937); R. GABRIEL, THE COURSE OF AMERICAN DEMOCRATIC THOUGHT 281-99 (2d ed. 1956).

clause of the fourteenth amendment to protect the corporate form of enterprise,[124] itself a "common law" creation; a construction of the fourteenth amendment's equal protection clause to permit "equal" racially segregated facilities.[125] Unlike the *Gibbons* Court, the late nineteenth century Court did not innovate in the area of constitutional interpretation but simply incorporated nonconstitutional innovations by reference. Liberty of contract was a creation of jurists and state courts; the inclusion of corporations within the meaning of "persons" was conceived by railroad lawyers seeking to prevent legislative encroachment on their clients' holdings;[126] the doctrine of "separate but equal" was developed by white legislators in the South.[127] Only occasionally was the Court required to innovate on its own, as in the *Knight* case,[128] in which the Court sought to accommodate the Sherman Act[129] to the Constitution for the purpose of protecting yet another nonconstitutional innovation, the conglomerate enterprise or "trust." In *Knight* the Court had to come up with a novel reading of the commerce power to exclude manufacturing enterprises.

By and large, then, the Court's stance was that of toleration of nonconstitutional innovations rather than activism as such. But toleration became a form of judicial activism. The expanded Constitution served, in the late nineteenth and early twentieth centuries, both as a bulwark against legislative encroachments on private enterprise and as a blueprint for continued legislative

---

124. Santa Clara County v. Southern Pac. R.R., 118 U.S. 394, 396 (1886); *see also* text accompanying note 67 *supra.*

125. *E.g.,* Plessy v. Ferguson, 163 U.S. 537 (1896).

126. *See* B. TWISS, LAWYERS AND THE CONSTITUTION 60-61, 94 (1942).

127. The Court's deference to legislatures in the segregation cases should not be considered abdication of its constitutionalizing function. The deference was professed rather than actual: In *Plessy,* for example, the Court announced a doctrine that effectuated what it perceived to be the prevailing social attitude. Actual deference to legislative judgment, exemplified by the "rationality" standard later applied to legislative judgments, *see* text accompanying notes 137 & 138 *infra,* represents the Court's decision to refrain from conceptualizing social attitudes it views as currently prevailing.

128. United States v. E.C. Knight Co., 156 U.S. 1 (1895).

129. 15 U.S.C. §§ 1-7 (1970).

efforts to achieve racial segregation. The judiciary as a constitutionalizing agent functioned as a "negative power, the power of resistance," [130] against attempts by government or private groups to curtail activities based on values and attitudes the Court perceived as dominant.

As late as World War I important state courts, such as the Court of Appeals of New York, persisted in this variety of resistance,[131] and a majority of Supreme Court justices consistently thought of the Constitution as a source of protection for particularistic values through the 1920's.[132] By 1940, however, a much more limited jurisdictional definition of "constitutional law" had become accepted, nonconstitutional law innovations had proliferated in changed forms, and both the "common law" and "constitutional" powers of the judiciary had been curtailed sharply. Again, a mix of social and intellectual factors contributed to this sudden change. Economic crisis prompted a dramatic expansion of the regulatory powers of the federal government, particularly through administrative agencies. That crisis was one facet of a growing awareness of the costs of mature industrialism, including discrepancies in income, status, and health which mocked America's alleged commitment to egalitarianism. The judiciary's open resistance to experimental state and federal legislation that tried to alleviate some of these costs rebounded to its political disadvantage. Most importantly, the posture of resistance initiated by the late nineteenth century judiciary became characterized, as it continued into the twentieth century, as a selective, partisan reading of the Constitution, a substitution of the will of the judge for the will of the law.

That charge revived an old and painful theme. Despite the close identification of common law adjudication with the promotion of

---

130. Letter from Justice Stephen Field to the Chief Justice and the Associate Justices of the Supreme Court of the United States, Oct. 12, 1897, in 168 U.S. 713, 717.

131. *See, e.g.,* Ives v. South Buffalo Ry. Co., 201 N.Y. 271, 94 N.E. 431 (1911), invalidating a New York workmen's compensation statute.

132. 1 W. SWINDLER, COURT AND CONSTITUTION IN THE TWENTIETH CENTURY 223-303 (2 vols. 1969).

dominant social attitudes in colonial and revolutionary America, despite the thoroughgoing activism of Chief Justice Marshall and the policymaking posture of mid-nineteenth century judges, and despite the particularistic glosses on the Constitution written by judges at the close of the nineteenth century, judges were not prepared to acknowledge themselves as lawmakers. Nor, in the main, were they so perceived. When Justice David Brewer announced in 1893 that "the courts make no laws," "establish no policy," "never enter into the domain of public action," and "do not govern," [133] his intended meaning was not ironic. His attitude was rather a posture thought necessary to maintain the independence of a judiciary that was by and large not democratically selected. To suggest openly that judges "made law" was to raise the spectre of unchecked judicial bias and to revive the eighteenth century fears of judicial tyranny.

Yet in the 1920's and '30's the effect of individual bias in judicial decisionmaking was fully addressed. In a time of rapidly changing perceptions about governmental regulation of economic and social affairs, it seemed that many justices of the Supreme Court and judges on lower court subscribed to nineteenth century social theories and equated them with "law." Their attitudes, once exposed, cast serious doubt on the premises of impartiality and humility from which the American judiciary supposedly started.[134] The long-term result of this crisis of legitimacy for the judiciary was the triumph of a "realistic" understanding of judicial lawmaking and the advent of jurisprudential theories oriented toward curbing judicial power.[135]

An important side effect of this altered view of judging was a redefinition of the interaction between nonconstitutional and

---

133. PROCEEDINGS OF THE NEW YORK BAR ASSOCIATION 46 (1893).

134. For a discussion of the embattled status of courts in the 1930's, see R. JACKSON, THE STRUGGLE FOR JUDICIAL SUPREMACY (1941).

135. The relationship of realism to the Court-packing cases of the 1930's is discussed in White, *The Evolution of Reasoned Elaboration: Jurisprudential Criticism and Social Change*, 59 VA. L. REV. 279, 281-82 (1973). *See generally* R. JACKSON, *supra* note 134, at 124-96.

constitutional law in America. The association in the public mind of certain constitutional doctrines with the social predilections of judges paved the way for a contracted view of the Constitution's jurisdiction and a corresponding expansion of lawmaking by public institutions (legislatures and especially administrative agencies) and private groups.[136] No one case represented the trend, but a general pattern emerged. Private groups, legislatures, and agencies regulated the activities of Americans through multifaceted rules, contracts, union-management negotiations, and statutes. The ambits of traditional common law judging and constitutional adjudication were redefined to insure greater judicial deference to the "reasonable" decisions of private and especially public lawmakers.[137] Only in egregious cases, such as the appropriation of property without just compensation [138] or the failure to provide aggrieved parties with minimal procedural safeguards,[139] did the judiciary scrutinize the acts of other lawmaking institutions. Application of the due process clause was limited to procedural matters; the equal protection clause was understood to invalidate only "arbitrary" (as opposed to "reasonable") classifications.[140] Self-conscious judges assumed postures consistent with the trends. Felix Frankfurter stressed the self-imposed limitations of his office; [141] Learned Hand wondered whether the role of the judiciary in constitutional adjudication was anything more than communicating the "moral adjurations" of the Bill of Rights.[142]

By the 1950's the above pattern had spawned a novel set of insights into law in America, which emphasized the process by which legal institutions interact rather than the content of law

---

136. "Lawmaking" by private groups means the ordering of social and economic relationships by nongovernmental institutions.

137. *See, e.g.,* Nebbia v. New York, 291 U.S. 502, 525 (1934).

138. *See, e.g.,* United States v. Causby, 328 U.S. 256 (1946).

139. *Cf.* Bowles v. Willingham, 321 U.S. 503 (1944).

140. *See, e.g.,* Railway Express Agency, Inc. v. New York, 336 U.S. 106 (1949).

141. *See* F. FRANKFURTER, OF LAW AND MEN 16-30, 53-56 (1956).

142. *See* L. HAND, THE BILL OF RIGHTS 1-30, 56-77 (1958).

itself.[143] If postwar American lawmakers — "private orderers," agencies, legislatures, and courts — understood their respective functions and operated within their limits of competence, the "legal process" would produce efficient and just laws.[144]

At first this conception of law and legal institutions appeared to depart from the traditions of American jurisprudence in minimizing the roles of the Constitution and the judiciary. The primary lawmaking agents appeared to be private groups and the new public lawmakers. The judiciary seemed destined to revert to a passive stance, losing most of its "common law" powers to legislatures and administrative agencies and constitutionalizing areas only when "neutral principles" of constitutional law justified the intrusion.[145] In a different context these hypothetical roles for judges and the Constitution might have been realized. Events of

---

143. For a recent discussion of substantive values embodied in law, see L. FULLER, THE MORALITY OF LAW (1964).

144. The terms "private ordering" and "legal process" were created and introduced into the law school curriculum by H. HART & A. SACKS, THE LEGAL PROCESS (tenth. ed. 1958).

145. Cf. Wechsler, Toward Neutral Principles of Constitutional Law, 73 HARV. L. REV. 1, 14-20 (1959).

> Let me repeat what I have thus far tried to say. The courts have both the title and the duty when a case is properly before them to review the actions of the other branches in the light of constitutional provisions, even though the action involves value choices, as invariably action does. In doing so, however, they are bound to function otherwise than as a naked power organ; they participate as courts of law. This calls for facing how determinations of this kind can be asserted to have any legal quality. The answer, I suggest, inheres primarily in that they are — or are obliged to be — entirely principled. A principled decision, in the sense I have in mind, is one that rests on reasons with respect to all the issues in the case, reasons that in their generality and their neutrality transcend any immediate result that is involved. When no sufficient reasons of this kind can be assigned for overturning value choices of the other branches of the Government or of a state, those choices must, of course, survive. Otherwise, as Holmes said in his first opinion for the Court, "a constitution, instead of embodying only relatively fundamental rules of right, as generally understood by all English-speaking communities, would become the partisan of a particular set of ethical or economical opinions . . . ."

Id. 19 (footnote omitted).

the 1950's and '60's, however, propelled the federal judiciary into a far more active lawmaking stance, resulting in a marked expansion of the ambit of constitutional law and a renewed judicial interest in ensuring that nonconstitutional innovations of the twentieth century conformed to newly perceived constitutional mandates.

The early twentieth century reorientation of juristic emphasis had minimized the substantive content of individual rights and the power of the judiciary to preserve rights against the state. Amid enhanced governmental planning, pressures for national solidarity, and the unprecedented economic crisis of the 1930's and '40's, a deemphasis of individual autonomy seemed appropriate. After the Second World War, however, revelation of the atrocities of Nazi "planning" fostered an environment conducive to more searching scrutiny of discrimination and inequality in American life. But the process of governance in America continued apace, the nonconstitutional lawmakers of the 1930's maintaining their presence and viability. Their laws represented a complex adjustment of conflicting interests by administrators and legislatures, or negotiated compromises among interested groups. They did not define their task, however, as the vindication of individual rights and liberties; when pressure for that vindication came, especially in the area of civil rights, they appeared hesitant or unwilling to respond. A void was created for the swift affirmation of principles of liberty and equality, given a new meaning by the Second World War and exemplified by a heightened sense of the constitutional rights of individuals. Into that void stepped the Warren Court.

The boundaries between constitutional and nonconstitutional law were blurred once again as the Warren Court found that state or federal legislation segregating public schools,[146] apportioning voter representation,[147] fashioning rules of criminal procedure,[148]

---

146. Brown v. Board of Educ., 347 U.S. 483 (1954).

147. Baker v. Carr, 369 U.S. 186 (1962).

148. *E.g.,* Gideon v. Wainwright, 372 U.S. 335 (1963); Miranda v. Arizona, 384 U.S. 436 (1966).

compelling prayers in public schools,[149] or suppressing "subversive" speech [150] violated constitutional principles. Over a period of about fifteen years, beginning in the mid-1950's, the Warren Court continually expanded the meaning of constitutional rights and held other lawmaking institutions accountable to the dictates of the Constitution. As lower courts followed the trend, the judiciary revived one of its major roles. The constitutionalization process took on a new but not unprecedented form. Unlike the "passively activist" courts of the late nineteenth century,[151] the mid-twentieth century judiciary constitutionalized nonconstitutional law by requiring existing governmental institutions to confer procedural safeguards on persons affected by their decisions or to use "fair" or "equal" standards in their decisionmaking.[152] The late nineteenth century judiciary, in contrast, had sought to prevent government from regulating the affairs of private persons. Whereas in the late nineteenth century the judiciary permitted nonconstitutional doctrines to infiltrate into the corpus of constitutional law, in the mid-twentieth century the judiciary imposed constitutional principles upon the already expanded domain of nonconstitutional law in modern America. The courts constitutionalized current values and attitudes before they had been identified or adopted by other institutions.[153]

C. The Juristic Perspectives of American Legal Scholarship: Changing Conceptions of Legal History in America.

Although the shifting interplay of constitutional and nonconstitutional law and the rise and fall of constitutional doctrines are dominant themes in the history of American jurisprudence, they are made even more discernible by the phenomenon of periodization in American history. Interactions between events and ideas have produced basic shifts in cultural

---

149. Engel v. Vitale, 370 U.S. 421 (1962).

150. *E.g.,* Yates v. United States, 354 U.S. 298 (1957).

151. *See generally* text accompanying notes 121-30 *supra.*

152. *See, e.g.,* Levy v. Louisiana, 391 U.S. 68 (1968); Miranda v. Arizona, 384 U.S. 436 (1966); Griffin v. Illinois, 351 U.S. 12 (1956).

153. *See also* text accompanying notes 103-13 *supra.*

values and attitudes which lend themselves, with the perspective of hindsight, to rough characterizations and demarcations. Historical periodization is a present-oriented phenomenon: The value orientation of a past "era" or "generation" is implicitly compared or contrasted with the present value orientation of the historian. The history of blacks in America became revitalized with the advent of the civil rights movement in the 1960's; the same is true of the history of women in the 1970's. Not only do the heroes and villains of history change with time; [154] so do the subjects of historical inquiry and the methodologies by which those subjects are approached. Historical writing by legal scholars is no exception. However faithfully lawyer historians try to reproduce the past, their sense of historical progression and demarcation and their modes of observation and analysis are products of the present.

The purpose of this section is to suggest that the "juristic mix" of various periods in American history — the complex interaction of ideas and events that produces a discernible social and intellectual perspective — affects conceptions of legal history just as it affects conceptions of the Constitution, nonconstitutional law, and judging. Moreover, the "legal history" written by lawyers at various times complements other juristic positions advanced at the times. The scholarly contributions of influential lawyer historians from four periods in American history will be used as illustrations.

The most influential legal historians of the late eighteenth and early nineteenth centuries, when American jurisprudence took on its distinctive character, were James Kent and Joseph Story.[155] As noted, between 1790 and 1840 common law and constitutional law proliferated but did not often compete: Constitutionalization could sometimes be effectuated without strain, and judges functioned creatively both as constitutional interpreters and as common law

---

154. For example, changing public attitudes toward Thomas Jefferson are discussed in M. PETERSON, THE JEFFERSON IMAGE IN THE AMERICAN MIND (1960).

155. *E.g.,* J. KENT, COMMENTARIES ON AMERICAN LAW (1826-1830); J. STORY, COMMENTARIES ON EQUITY JURISPRUDENCE (1836); J. STORY, COMMENTARIES ON THE CONSTITUTION OF THE UNITED STATES (1838).

adjudicators.[156] Few serious conflicts between parochial common law rules and constitutional principles developed; when they did, as in the case of slavery, provisional resolutions took place. Law and legal institutions were expanding; American jurisprudence was in a phase of growth. In this atmosphere the scholarship of Kent and Story, themselves judges as well as scholars, supplied an authoritative corpus of "law" — rules, principles, axioms, and doctrines, of "common," "constitutional," and "natural" origin — that could guide the affairs of a new nation. Story's and Kent's methodological approach to their subject matter was synthetic. They combed diverse sources and extracted seemingly authoritative rules and doctrines, analogous to the "great principles" on which Marshall rested his decisions. Their scholarship was comprehensive, encompassing all existing fields of nonconstitutional and constitutional law; their methodology was designed to filter the contributions of the ancients through the special perspective of the new American republic. Legal history for them was part of the grand design of American jurisprudence. They reinforced the wisdom of the past by restating it, discarding whatever they perceived as inapposite or inimical to the American experience.[157]

The grand integrative syntheses of ancient and contemporary materials that characterized Kent's and Story's legal history complemented the simultaneous, and generally noncompetitive, expansion of common and constitutional law in the early nineteenth century. Both developments were linked to an interest among American jurists in creating an indigenous jurisprudence. Just as the common law was becoming "Americanized" and the principles of a written Constitution were interpreted as contributing to the uniqueness of the American republic, so the great treatises of Kent and Story produced a nationalistic version of legal history, in which

---

156. *See* text accompanying notes 103-13 *supra.*

157. *See generally* G. DUNNE, *supra* note 62; L. FRIEDMAN, *supra* note 55, at 288-92 (Kent); J. HORTON, *supra* note 62; J. MCCLELLAN, JOSEPH STORY AND THE AMERICAN CONSTITUTION 61-193 (1971).

selected insights of ancient jurists were shown to be applicable to the American experience.

The next major American legal historian of the nineteenth century was Oliver Wendell Holmes, Jr.[158] Holmes' *The Common Law*, published in 1881, was in one sense a protest against certain intellectual assumptions of some of his contemporaries,[159] but was in another sense representative of late nineteenth century juristic perspectives. Holmes believed that the dominant legal theories of his time were to be derived from nonconstitutional sources. The "principle" that "loss from accident must lie where it falls," [160] for example, emerged from the experience of the marketplace. By emphasizing common law subjects and by attempting to develop a theory through which majoritarian impulses could operate, Holmes' analysis was analogous to the approach of late nineteenth century judges who sought (perhaps unconsciously) to expand the Constitution to encompass widely accepted nonconstitutional doctrines.

Holmes' approach to legal history in *The Common Law* was representative of his age in a more fundamental sense. Whereas Kent's and Story's methodology had been intended to amass a useful storehouse of relevant information from the past, Holmes' method in *The Common Law* was intended, as he later stated, to free his generation from the past.[161] The function of history in *The Common Law* was to show the futility of erecting legal rules based on logic: Rules never survived their utility in a particular context. Because rules could not be immutable, contemporary Americans

---

158. Important theoreticians, including Thomas M. Cooley, Sidney George Fisher, Francis Lieber, Joel Parker, John Norton Pomeroy, and Robert Rantoul, surfaced among legal scholars between 1840 and 1870, but their scholarship was not historically oriented. P. PALUDAN, A COVENANT WITH DEATH (1975), analyzes the work of Cooley, Fisher, Lieber, Parker, and Pomeroy.

159. "The life of the law has not been logic: it has been experience." O.W. HOLMES, THE COMMON LAW 1 (1881).

160. *Id.* 94.

161. O.W. HOLMES, *Law in Science and Science in Law*, in COLLECTED LEGAL PAPERS 210, 225 (1920).

were free to derive their own, based on "the felt necessities" [162] of the times.

Story and Kent used legal history as a vehicle for a grand synthesis; Holmes used data from the past as raw material for a theory. Story and Kent had been selective in their methodology, but not in their subject matter. They presented their audience of neophyte jurists with a wealth of information that revealed, almost coincidentally, the primacy of certain "principles" such as the inviolability of property rights.

Holmes presented his readers with what he considered an appropriately deterministic explanation of the law's growth over time.[163] Holmes argued that law responds to unconscious and changing majoritarian impulses, so that it can never be static. To understand the course of legal history one only has to recognize and accept the primacy of majority will. Then one could be satisfied, in a democracy, with the knowledge that "the crowd" was "getting all it wanted" and reserve the pleasure of critizing the crowd for the folly of its judgments.[164]

Holmes' interest in history as a source of a theory was congenial to the thinking of late nineteenth century jurists. The late nineteenth century was an age of conceptualism, in which judges and scholars sought clear and practicable governing rules or

---

162. O.W. HOLMES, *supra* note 160, at 1.

163. *See* G. GILMORE, THE DEATH OF CONTRACT 14-31 (1974) for a discussion of Holmes' analysis of common law principles:

> It seems perfectly clear that Holmes was, quite consciously, proposing revolutionary doctrine and was not in the least interested in stating or restating the common law as it was. He was, at the time he wrote the lectures which make up *The Common Law,* as learned in the history of the law — including the law of contracts — as any lawyer in the English-speaking world. Yet his analysis of the true meaning of "consideration" comes forth almost naked of citation of authority or precedent. He starts with an off-hand reference to what is commonly "said" and commonly "thought." However, what is clear to Holmes "has not always been sufficiently borne in mind" by others. Whereupon, we are off to the races at a dizzying clip.

Id. 20-21 (footnotes omitted).

164. *See, e.g.,* 1 HOLMES-LASKI LETTERS 207 (Howe ed. 1953).

doctrines in both constitutional and nonconstitutional law. But the relativism of Holmes' end product was less acceptable to his peers. (*The Common Law* made its greatest impact in the twentieth century, when its relativism came to be viewed as philosophically sound and its deference to majoritarian lawmaking seemed to make good sense.) [165] Holmes' theory was too unpredictable and passive for late nineteenth century jurists. They sought the affirmative development of workable doctrines and rules. They prized certainty in the law. They wanted law to be a science with governing axioms and concepts. They were eager to perform the exercises in syllogistic logic that Holmes decried. Ultimately, they believed that truth was an ascertainable entity, whereas Holmes found "truth" in the "majority vote of that nation that could lick all others." [166]

For all the originality of Holmes' perspective in *The Common Law,* and for all of its affinity to the leading edge of late nineteenth century jurisprudence, his approach was too unconventional to be influential in its own time. Holmes refused to reduce his relativistic theories to rigid concepts from which judges could deduce results. Roscoe Pound, who never achieved the insight or vision of Holmes, was for a time more influential. It was Pound rather than Holmes who provided the principal bridge between nineteenth century juristic conceptualism and the empirically oriented "realist" thinking of the early twentieth century.

Pound made his initial impact on the legal profession as a critic of conceptualism, which he called "mechanical jurisprudence." [167] Conceptualist thinking was a product of the same late nineteenth century juristic mix that generated the expansion of constitutional law to incorporate emerging nonconstitutional doctrines.[168] The distinguishing features of conceptualism were controlling

---

165. *See generally* White, *The Rise and Fall of Justice Holmes,* 39 U. CHI. L. REV. 51, 56-65 (1971).

166. O.W. HOLMES, *Natural Law,* in COLLECTED LEGAL PAPERS 310 (1920).

167. Pound, *Mechanical Jurisprudence,* 8 COLUM. L. REV. 605 (1908).

168. *See* text accompanying notes 121-30 *supra.*

assertions — whether axioms, maxims, glosses, or doctrines —
which were announced to be true and then used as the basis for
syllogistic reasoning to an end result. The doctrine of liberty of
contract was one such assertion; it yielded the result, in one case,
that a statute regulating the permissible number of working hours
in the baking industry was unconstitutional.[169] The distinction
drawn between "manufacture" and "commerce" in the *Knight* case
was another.[170] Pound attacked conceptualist opinions as oblivious
to changing social conditions and imprisoned in their own ritualistic
logic, which he felt rested primarily on a priori postulates.[171] But
while calling for a "sociological jurisprudence" by which courts
would broaden their inquiries and increase their social
awareness,[172] Pound continued to employ a conceptualist
methodology in his historical scholarship.

Foremost among his use of conceptualist devices was his use of
classification. Pound attempted to undermine the primacy of
mechanical jurisprudence by showing that it was only one of
several "schools" in the history of juristic thought. Nineteenth
century American jurisprudence, he argued, had included a
"creative" school, a "historical" school, and an "analytical" school;
mechanical jurisprudence was simply the analytical school in its
latter stages of decay.[173] Pound did not define the characteristics
of each of the "schools" clearly, but he made his point clearly
enough: Because ideas moved in and out of vogue over time, no
one idea could claim universality. The purpose of mechanical
jurisprudence had been to create and to utilize "universals," [174] but
that purpose was futile.

Or so Pound seemed to be saying in his reformist writings of the
early twentieth century. As sociological jurisprudence became

---

169. Lochner v. New York, 198 U.S. 45 (1905).

170. United States v. E.C. Knight Co., 156 U.S. 1 (1895). The distinction allowed
a corporation controlling over 90% of the nation's sugar production to avoid the
strictures of the Sherman Act.

171. Pound, *supra* note 73, at 457.

172. Pound, *The Need of a Sociological Jurisprudence,* 19 GREEN BAG 607 (1907).

173. Pound summarized his earlier views on the history of juristic thought in R.
POUND, THE FORMATIVE ERA OF AMERICAN LAW 93-118 (1938). *See also* Pound,
supra note 172, at 608-10.

174. R. POUND, *supra* note 173, at 110.

more orthodox in legal scholarship, however, and as Pound himself became part of the established academic order as Dean of Harvard Law School, the affinity of his thinking with conceptualism became apparent. Pound conceived of history not merely as a series of changing "felt necessities," but as a progression of refined truths. There was a "taught legal tradition" [175] that remained constant in the face of change; stability and predictability in adjudication were values to be prized; natural law, in different embodiments, was a continuous thread of American jurisprudence.[176] Pound eventually suggested that the "legal order" could be "partioned" into compartments: In some, such as property and commercial transactions, the late nineteenth century desire for certainty should predominate; in others, such as administrative and constitutional law, "the flexibility required for the individual life" [177] should be accommodated. The initial classification determined the subsequent treatment, just as the initial maxim had set forth the process of syllogistic reasoning in late nineteenth century judicial decisions.

Hence Pound stood firmly in the mode of nineteenth century conceptualist thinking; his link to subsequent juristic developments in the twentieth century came chiefly from his recognition that the context of law was broader than "scientific" conceptualism admitted,[178] and consequently that a variety of institutions could perform lawmaking functions simultaneously. In his characterization of history as a source of permanent truths and in his conviction that a conceptualist methodology could extract these truths, however, Pound was far closer to the mechanical jurists

---

175. *Id.* 82.

176. *Id.* 110-16.

177. *Id.* 118.

178. *Cf.* C. LANGDELL, SELECTION OF CASES ON THE LAW OF CONTRACTS viii (2d ed. 1879) (Preface to the First Edition): "Law, considered as a science, consist of certain principles or doctrines. . . . [T]he number of fundamental legal doctrines is much less than is commonly supposed . . . ." In 1886 Langdell asserted that "all the available materials" of the science of law were "contained in printed books." RECORD OF THE COMMEMORATION, NOVERBER FIFTH TO EIGHTH, 1886, ON THE TWO HUNDRED AND FIFTIETH ANNIVERSARY OF THE FOUNDING OF HARVARD COLLEGE (1887), *quoted in* A. SUTHERLAND, THE LAW AT HARVARD 175 (1967).

than to Holmes or to the "skeptical realists" [179] he quarreled with in the 1930's.

After the Second World War still another perspective on legal history emerged. An important facet of this perspective, embodied in the scholarship of James Willard Hurst,[180] was a deemphasis of "great cases" and constitutional law as subjects for historical inquiry. Hurst used Pound's "partition" [181] of the legal order to emphasize the significance of lawmaking by private groups and virtually to eliminate constitutional law from his field of inquiry as a legal historian.[182] Hurst's conception of legal history was, like previous conceptions, a product of the juristic mix of his time.

Hurst, like many other postwar legal scholars, became fascinated with the complex network of nonconstitutional lawmaking institutions — courts, legislatures, agencies, and private groups — whose development he witnessed in mid-twentieth century America. These scholars sought to develop a juristic posture consistent with their acceptance of modern theories of the lawmaking capacity of judges, their support of trends toward curbing the constitutionalizing function of the judiciary, and their recognition of the continued vitality of private enterprise in a regulated economy. The concept of law as a process served as their rallying point. It made possible both a partition of the legal order into institutional compartments and the retention of a vision of an integrated system; it focused upon carefully defined institutional roles consistent with institutions' respective lawmaking capabilities; it identified actions by private groups that

---

179. R. POUND, *supra* note 173, at 28.

180. J. HURST, THE GROWTH OF AMERICAN LAW (1950); J. HURST, LAW AND THE CONDITIONS OF FREEDOM IN THE NINETEENTH-CENTURY UNITED STATES (1956); J. HURST, LAW AND SOCIAL PROCESS IN UNITED STATES HISTORY (1960) [hereinafter cited as LAW AND SOCIAL PROCESS]; J. HURST, LAW AND ECONOMIC GROWTH (1964); Hurst, *Legal Elements in United States History,* in LAW IN AMERICAN HISTORY, *supra* note 51, at 3.

181. Pound, *The Theory of Judicial Decision,* 36 HARV. L. REV. 940, 956-58 (1923).

182. "[M]easured by continuity and impact upon distribution of functions basic to social life, much law has been constitutive which does not fit the conventional historical preoccupation with formal constitutional law." Hurst, *supra* note 180, at 7-8.

could fairly be called exercises in making law. For these scholars, lawmaking was rational in the sense that the legal process was "purposive" [183] and interrelated. The perceived rationality of the system depended upon rational action by each of its component parts. Judicial decisions had to be "reasoned" and "principled"; statutory interpretation focused on the "purpose" of statutes; agencies had to justify their "expertise." An understanding of the institutional division of the lawmaking function was a prerequisite to rational decisionmaking.

Hurst's approach reoriented scholarship in American legal history. It deemphasized "issue[s] of high politics," [184] invited empirical studies of the economic implications of lawmakers' decisions, stressed the important lawmaking role of private groups, and, in short, equated legal history with social histories of "private lawmakers" and their interaction with common law courts and legislatures. In the place of Poundian abstractions came a series of monographic studies of nonconstitutional topics. By the 1970's this perspective had become sufficiently entrenched that a general history of American law "deliberately kept to a minimum the story of constitutional law" and displayed the "influence [of Willard Hurst] . . . on every page." [185]

Conceptions of American legal history, in their successive emphases, reflected the changing juristic patterns marking the path of American jurisprudence. Parallels between Kent's and Story's approach and early nineteenth century perspectives on common law adjudication and constitutional interpretation have been noted.[186] The attractiveness to the late nineteenth century judiciary of nonconstitutional innovations as potential constitutional principles paralleled Holmes' interest in deriving general theories of law from the common law and nonlegal practices. Pound's conceptualism reflected an early twentieth century interest in confining constitutional and nonconstitutional

---

183. H. HART & A. SACKS, *supra* note 144, at iii.
184. LAW AND SOCIAL PROCESS, *supra* note 180, at 17.
185. L. FRIEDMAN, *supra* note 55, at 11.
186. Text accompanying notes 156 & 157 *supra*.

law to their proper ambits. Hurst's rediscovery of the importance of lawmaking by private groups and legislatures mirrored mid-twentieth century efforts to define the powers of the judiciary narrowly and to recognize the multifaceted character of lawmaking in modern America. The most recent juristic mix, exemplified by an expanded jurisdiction for constitutional law and a greater tolerance for judicial scrutiny of nonconstitutional lawmaking in the name of constitutional principles, has not yet produced a parallel conception of legal history.

The recent tendency of American legal historians to equate legal history with the study of "private" law assumes a separation between "legal" and "constitutional" history that is untenable, given the character of American jurisprudence. American legal history has been what each generation has chosen to make it, and recent efforts have redressed an earlier overemphasis, particularly among nonlawyer historians, on political and constitutional developments. But the path of jurisprudence in America reveals a continuous interaction among constitutional law, nonconstitutional law, and "private ordering," based on currently dominant ideas and values and on social and economic relationships. It also reveals an indispensable role for the judiciary as forger of links among those entities. Portraits of "legal history" that ignore the multiple sources of law in America and minimize the role of the judiciary are incomplete.

III. CONCLUSION: SOME PRELIMINARY REFLECTIONS ON THE "JURISTIC MIXES" OF AMERICAN JURISPRUDENCE

This Article has argued that certain developments that came to fruition in the early nineteenth century have given American jurisprudence its distinctive character. They include the identification of "common" (subsequently nonconstitutional) law with currently dominant social attitudes and values, the designation of a written Constitution as the supreme source of American law, and the creation of a special role for the judiciary as a constitutionalizing agent. The Article has suggested that

71

important constitutional law decisions and influential legal scholarship in the course of American history can be reassessed from a point of view that stresses the unique features of jurisprudence in America.

If the point of view adopted in this Article stimulates further inquiry one of its premises must be submitted to more rigorous investigation. The premise is that at various times in American history ideas and events have interacted to produce a "juristic mix" out of which has emerged a dominant, distinctively new perspective on law and legal institutions.

It is not at all clear how a "juristic mix" congeals to produce a dominant intellectual perspective. This Article has attempted to identify salient features of the American intellectual and social landscape that seemed likely to have been important elements in the creation of novel modes of juristic thought. The process of combination remains elusive, however. In particular, the problem of determining the respective weight of events on ideas and ideas on events requires much greater attention. It seems far too simple to assert that certain "significant" events change the thinking of persons exposed to them. Are the events significant because of their intrinsic extraordinariness or because they are perceived as significant? If the latter, so perceived by contemporaries or historians? If contemporaries, what accounts for such a perception?

Although one can identify "conceptualist" or "realist" or "process" perspectives, and maintain that such perspectives played an important part in determining the respective ambits of constitutional and nonconstitutional law or in affecting the stature of judges as creative lawmakers, one cannot easily determine precisely how or why those perspectives surfaced when they did. Much more serious attention must be given to the impact of ideas on law and legal institutions, especially to the notion that dominant ideas serve as unarticulated values, forces that skew perceptions of events and institutions.

American jurisprudence, then, is much more than what appears in this preliminary survey of its origins and development. It is also the aggregate of a series of shifting dominant juristic perspectives. When the origins and impact of those perspectives are examined more rigorously we may be closer to understanding jurisprudential developments more fully. This Article outlines a path, but the rest of the wilderness remains.

THE APPELLATE OPINION AS HISTORICAL SOURCE MATERIAL

The Journal of Interdisciplinary History, Vol. 1, No. 3 (1971)

American legal history has recently piqued the curiosity of historians and legal scholars seeking to make connections between their respective disciplines. Underlying this interest is the assumption that the working materials of the legal profession — cases, statutes, treatises, and the like — reflect to some degree the changing patterns of American civilization and may fruitfully be viewed as indices of the general tone of American culture at various points in time. This assumption may seem hardly worth lingering over, especially to historians accustomed to noting the ways in which institutions and ideas in America have taken on distinctive forms during particular time periods. Yet the inclusion of appellate court decisions in the general category of materials considered "representative" of the style and substance of intellectual contributions at a given point in American history raises a number of troublesome problems in interdisciplinary communication. I am concerned here with identifying some of those problems and with proposing one methodological approach designed to alleviate them. Specifically, my focus is on the factors that distinguish appellate opinions from the general mass of recorded social phenomena available to the historian, the relationship between these factors and the development in the legal profession of a particular set of techniques for analyzing material, and some of the implications of this development for the potential scholar in legal history.

By focusing upon some of the problems in a historical treatment of appellate court decisions, I am, of course, eschewing the "rather ordinary matter" of legal history, which Hurst has found so stimulating, for what he calls "issues of high politics."[1] This is not to suggest that appellate decision-making should necessarily be the central concern of legal historians. My emphasis upon appellate

---

[1]. JAMES WILLARD HURST, LAW AND SOCIAL PROCESS IN UNITED STATES HISTORY (Ann Arbor, 1960), 18.

decisions stems primarily from the fact that they have traditionally been the core materials of legal education in America — the practice field, as it were, on which a set of professional analytical techniques have been tried out. An understanding of the factors distinguishing the appellate opinion from other published sources of its time can therefore lead to an understanding of the distinctive ways in which the legal profession orders its source material and ultimately to some sense of the differing biases of the disciplines of law and history.

When a historian attempts to analyze past opinions of the Supreme Court or federal or state appellate courts, his first problem is normally to learn how to read the opinion, a process which requires not only mastering jargonistic terms such as respondent, demur, hold, or remand, but understanding, at least in a rudimentary sense, the manner in which social situations are transposed into legal cases. Consider, for example, the case of an intellectual historian examining a variety of documents with a view toward understanding the positions on matters of public policy taken by influential and articulate men of the period. Should he attempt to include the opinions of appellate judges among his sources, he will be confronted with the following complicating factors: First, judges, in their professional role, only decide *cases* — their statements are made in the framework of a dispute between two parties that has been couched in certain legal terms and which they are asked to resolve in those terms; second, each case, in the American judicial system, is considered to be a discrete set of facts, the resolution of which has conclusive significance only for that fact-situation or one identical to it; third, the judge's role is defined as that of an informed and impartial arbiter of disputes whose decision is allegedly based on the legal "merits" of a case rather than on any personal inclinations of his own.

Each of these factors has a restrictive effect on judicial language. The first confines it to words and phrases of legal significance; for example, was the defendant negligent (in a case involving an auto accident), did he lack the requisite intent (in a murder case), or was there consideration for a promise (in a case involving the making of a contract). The second factor creates a division, familiar to lawyers, between language used to decide the precise legal point at issue or to justify that decision, and language of a more general nature (dicta) whose import is far less clear. The third stimulates among the judiciary a process of self-conscious depersonalization of their function, which may ultimately result in abdication of the arbiter role, as when Justice Felix Frankfurter resolved not to participate in a case testing the power of the District of Columbia Transit Authority to forbid the playing of radios in buses in Washington, D.C., on the grounds that his feelings were too "strongly engaged as the victim of the practice in controversy." [2] As a consequence of these formal constraints, the tone and substance of an appellate decision at a particular time may more closely resemble those of another decision from a much earlier period than those of a contemporary non-legal document; in addition, the decision may conceal rather than reveal the social attitudes of an individual judge.

Thus the historian approaching appellate decisions may find that his understanding of the ebb and flow of political ideologies in American history is not an entirely useful guide to case analysis, because legal issues and judicial decisions are difficult to characterize in ideological terms. It is often difficult to assess, for example, whether or not a particular decision upholding the rights of an employee against his employer is a "liberal" one, even if it occurs at a time when "liberals" generally sided with employees in labor-management conflicts. Indeed, a historian's sense of the ideological currents of a particular time period may encourage him to impose a characterization on legal materials that they will not bear.

The process of appellate decision-making also has its effect upon the scholarship of individuals with legal training. The techniques employed in appellate courts, where counsel present opposing arguments on the legal issues in question and judges in their decisions pay considerable attention to the previous findings of

---

2. Public Utilities Comm. v. Pollack, 343 U.S. 451 (1952).

other courts on similar or analogous issues, often find their way into less specialized efforts by legal scholars.

Pound, for example, has characterized the development of legal history in America as a process whereby social, political, and economic conditions of time and place create a "pressure of new demands" upon the "taught legal tradition" which results in "new reasoned applications of the technique in which . . . judges had been trained." Social phenomena, in Pound's view, are analogous to pieces of evidence presented in a brief or an oral argument: They are "fitted into the traditional [legal] system in their interpretation and application." [3] Pound emphasizes the existence of a distinctive self-perpetuating set of responses to experience — a taught legal tradition — which can exist apart from, and at the same time order, its social context.

Pound's description of legal history suggests a second manifestation of the influence of the appellate court model upon legal scholarship: the prevalence of what might be called an advocate's worldview. Such a view sees society as being shaped by what two legal scholars have called "the compulsive force of human desires" and "the compulsive logic of the facts of interdependence." In this view "every human being wants what he wants as intensely as he wants it," but "every human being . . . has to reckon with the fact that other people want what they want in the same way also." [4] Society is therefore a complex of potentially hostile but interdependent interests, the welfare of which depends on mutual accommodation. In this complex, the role of one who has mastered the techniques of advocacy — who has learned how to frame, argue, and resolve the conflicts of opposing interests — is enormously important for the promotion of social welfare. The apparatus of the legal profession thus becomes a force for social stability and tranquility: In a world where desires are compulsive and interdependence is inescapable, those who possess the techniques necessary to resolve disputes and issue mutually

---

3. ROSCOE POUND, THE FORMATIVE ERA OF AMERICAN LAW (Boston, 1938), 82, 83, 86.

4. Henry M. Hart and Albert Sacks, *"The Legal Process"* (unpub. ms., 1958), 114.

satisfactory authoritative directions are bulwarks against societal self-destruction.

In terms of legal history, this view has manifested itself in a juxtaposition of the continuity of a legal tradition and the diversity of its social context: Pound is again illustrative. Writing of the nineteenth century, he found that "the course of judicial decision has been characteristically steady and uniform ... through five generations of rapid political, economic, and social change, bringing about a communis opinio over the country as a whole on the overwhelming majority of legal questions, despite the most divergent ... political, economic, social, and even racial conditions." "The outstanding phenomenon" of American legal history was, for Pound, "the extent to which a taught tradition ... has stood out against all manner of economically or politically powerful interests." [5]

In the language of contemporary American historians, the above characterization emphasizes consensus within the legal profession and conflict among the rest of society. But this distinction is an artificial one: the fact that the legal profession is, to some extent, able to translate social pressures into terms (cases, briefs, opinions) which it can manipulate and resolve does not mean that it is isolated from those pressures which do not come within its boundaries; nor can those disputes settled through the processes of law necessarily be said to symbolize the alleviation of more general social grievances. If the Supreme Court declared that nonreligious conscientious objectors could resist fighting in the war in Vietnam on moral grounds, the general anxiety created in America by that war would by no means be relieved.

A further effect of the appellate model upon legal scholarship, and consequently upon the writing of legal history by lawyers, can be seen in the techniques employed by the legal profession in dealing with authoritative legal statements (such as rules, precedents, and statutes) made in the past. The American legal system presumes such statements to represent, at the moment of their enactment, valid guidelines for the future as well as the

---

5. POUND, THE FORMATIVE ERA, 82, 83.

present, but it allows that presumption to be overcome in the form of challenges to the validity of the statements; in this fashion the system remains responsive to social change. A major portion of the work of judges and advocates involves testing the applicability of past legal pronouncements to present situations and consequently reassessing the validity and relevance of the social assumptions and policies of a prior time. Presentmindedness, then, is built into legal training; indeed, that training tends to encourage skepticism toward directives enacted at too remote a time period (more recent precedents, other things being equal, are preferred in a litigation), and to provide ammunition, in the form of the techniques of advocacy, for attacking the precepts of the past. Hence the American legal historian with legal training faces a dilemma because the very techniques that aid him in analyzing legal materials, by reason of their presentist bias, tend to de-emphasize the historical dimensions of those materials.

In addition to affecting the language and methodology of its actors, the process of appellate decision-making in America makes use of the element of time in distinctive ways. In the first place, as Henry Hart and John McNaughton have pointed out, appellate decisions have a double time dimension: "at the moment of their making, they speak from the present to the future ... at the moment of their application, they speak out of the past to the present." [6] Appellate judges are conscious that their decisions are retesting the validity of past precedents and laying down guidelines for future conduct — guidelines that will themselves be retested. This affects the character of appellate decisions as social documents. The opinions of appellate judges, in addition to being more self-constrained and depersonalized than letters, diaries, novels, treatises, newspapers, magazines, and other standard materials of social and intellectual historians, are more difficult to locate in time, because one of the functions of the opinion is to preserve, through generalized and indeterminate language, a sense of continuity between past, present, and future. The

---

6. Henry M. Hart and John McNaughton, *"Evidence and Inference in the Law,"* DAEDALUS, LXXXVII (1958), 42, 43.

historian looking for "period" language or social attitudes in an appellate opinion has to reckon with this tendency.

A second time-related problem is that of cultural lag. The presence in appellate opinions of elements intended to convey a sence of continuity, plus the time delays imposed by backlogs in trial and appellate court dockets, can play havoc with attempts to match legal materials with historical trends. Take, for example, a trend considered significant by historians: the emergence of heavy industry in the Northeast after the Civil War. This phenomenon is generally felt to have had a substantial effect on the course of American civilization after 1865: One can find ample evidence of the impact of industrial life and its models of success, such as the "captain of industry," on the social theories of late nineteenth-century Americans.[7] One might also expect rapid industrialization to be reflected in an extensive modification of prior legal doctrines in the latter portion of the nineteenth century, as the courts took cognizance of the inapplicability of legal principles formulated in a pre-industrial age. Such modification did indeed take place, but in a haphazard and uneven fashion: In certain areas, such as nuisance, many courts merely reaffirmed notions of land use that had been formulated prior to the advent of industrialization.[8]

The historian, on observing an apparent reluctance on the part of late-nineteenth-century courts to take immediate cognizance of social change, may be tempted to characterize the judiciary of the period as "conservative."[9] But such a characterization tends to

7. *See generally* EDWARD KIRKLAND, DREAM AND THOUGHT IN THE BUSINESS COMMUNITY (Ithaca, 1956); IRVIN WYLLIE, THE SELF-MADE-MAN IN AMERICA (New Brunswick, 1954). Whether the Civil War advanced or retarded industrialization is a question on which there is little agreement. See Thomas C. Cochran, "*Did the Civil War Retard Industrialization?*" MISSISSIPPI VALLEY HISTORICAL REVIEW, XLVIII (1961), 197-210; Stephen Salisbury, "*The Effect of the Civil War on American Industrial Development,*" in Stanley N. Katz and Stanley I. Kutler (eds.), NEW PERSPECTIVES ON THE AMERICAN PAST (Boston, 1969), I, 416-424.

8. For an illustrative reaffirmation of preindustrial concepts of nuisance, *see* Lossee v. Buchanan, 51 N.Y. 476 (1873).

9. For example, ROBERT G. MCCLOSKEY, AMERICAN CONSERVATISM IN THE AGE OF ENTERPRISE (Chicago, 1951) and THE AMERICAN SUPREME COURT (Chicago, 1960).

ignore the function of time in the legal process. When economic and technological innovations result in different ways of using space, as they did in the latter portion of the nineteenth century, these new uses may or may not pose legal problems that need to be settled in the courts, for they may or may not have been anticipated by some prior legal directive. For example, municipal ordinances regulating horsedrawn traffic on city streets may be adequate for automobiles if their terminology is sufficiently broad to include both types of transportation under a general category such as "vehicles"; they may, however, prove inadequate if they make judgments about traffic regulation based on the assumption that all vehicular traffic is horsedrawn. The continued use in the courts, then, of rules and principles formulated in an earlier period in time is a natural product of a system that innovates, for the most part, through glosses on generalities rather than through abrupt departures from prior rules, and is not necessarily an indication of conservatism among the judiciary.[10]

Moreover, challenges to existing doctrines fostered by changing social conditions are delayed by the process of litigation. Assume that an influx of heavy industry has radically altered the residential pattern of a city: Factories have clustered near waterfront locations and have through a combination of noise, traffic, and smoke made living conditions in their vicinity less than desirable. One could imagine this situation stimulating a re-evaluation of doctrines concerned with land use, property rights, nuisance, and so on; but such re-evaluations would take place within the framework of litigation, and might hence be considered years after the social conflict that spawned them had been generated.

I have referred above to some of the ways in which the appellate model, with its emphasis upon the techniques of advocacy, has influenced the cast of scholarship in the legal profession. A more general manifestation of this influence may be seen in the differing

---

10. For a different view, which sees lag as "present-minded pragmatism rather than long-term rational planning," see Lawrence M. Friedman and Jack Ladinsky, "Law and Social Change in the Progressive Era," in KATZ AND KUTLER, NEW PERSPECTIVES, II, 195-200.

use by legal scholars and historians of value judgments in an empirical presentation. A perusal of law reviews and historical journals shows that articles in the former generally take the form of argumentative propositions on an aspect of public policy, with the author's empirical findings used in support of this argument, whereas articles in the latter are rarely argumentative in the same sense. Historians seem to be searching for some kind of objective reality in the past, piling information on top of previous information in an attempt to get closer to truth. Their arguments are directed at previous generalizations made by their predecessors on the basis of too limited or faulty evidence; their "revision" of these generalizations is presented as part of a continuing professional search for what "really" happened. This stance is in contrast, by and large, to that of legal scholars, who are interested not so much in what happened or is happening as in what should have happened or should happen.

This difference stems in part from the kinds of subjects to which the two disciplines address themselves. In large measure legal scholarship deals with unresolved contemporary problems for which more than one solution exists; the task is to assess the problem and discern the optimum solution. In this setting there is much to be said in support of an argumentative presentation. Historians, however, confront problems that, for better or worse, have been "solved"; the question for them is often why, given the complex of factors in operation at the time that the solution was reached, it should have taken the particular form that it did. An appropriate answer to this last question, it is generally assumed, requires scholarly detachment: If a historian is too outraged by a particular result (such as the imposition of martial law in Southern states in the Reconstruction period), he may in an assessment of that policy emphasize certain factors influencing its formulation (sadism and vindictiveness in the personalities of influential Congressmen) at the expense of others (the reluctance of Southern states to enfranchise freed Negroes).[11] A shorthand way of

---

11. *See* Bernard A. Weisberger, *"The Dark and Bloody Ground of Reconstruction Historiography,"* JOURNAL OF SOUTHERN HISTORY, XXV (1959), 427-447.

representing this phenomenon is to characterize the scholarly ideal of the historian as objectivity; by contrast, that of the legal scholar might be persuasiveness.

At the extremes, the disciplinary ideals appear very far apart: If one assumes that law is "a science not only of what is but what ought to be"[12] and that the legal system in America is an open-ended vehicle for policy debate, the formulation of a coherent set of social values appears to be a prerequisite for effective functioning within that system, and objectivity, in the sense of value-free detachment, an inappropriate stance. That is, if commentators on past legal decisions were precluded from persuading their audience that those decisions were "wrong" in the sense of being inapplicable or irrelevant to present conditions, the system would lose its receptiveness to change. Yet, insofar as that persuasion reflects present-minded evaluations of past phenomena, it moves away from the historical ideal of objectivity.

The divergence of the disciplinary ideals is not so marked in American legal history. First, the process employed in American courts of testing past decisions against present circumstances insures that at some point most precedents will become "invalid" in the sense of having no authoritative applicability. At this point one could argue that the present-mindedness essential to a persuasive critique of the decision is no longer necessary: The decision has become a historical curiosity. Second, it may be fair to say that the degree to which scholars remain "curious" about a past decision once it has lost its authority depends on present circumstances; that is, the decision of a historian to study a particular topic or time period and his reaction to it are heavily influenced by the fashions of his own time. In this sense "objectivity" on the part of the historian is unrealizable and even unnecessary.

Nevertheless, the different modes of presentation and idealized objectives of legal scholars and historians can force the legal historian to walk an analytical tightrope. The orthodox method of scholarly criticism of appellate opinions by lawyers consists of a

---

12. Hart and McNaughton, *"Evidence and Inference."* 42.

rigorous dissection of the internal logic of the opinion in order to expose (and perhaps question) its tacit assumptions. In this task, the critic is admittedly interested in determining whether the starting premises of the judge are valid; should he find them invalid, his role resembles that of a lobbyist. But the legal historian, if he takes this tack, has a rather different function, that of showing that there is a historical explanation for the premises on which the opinion rests: for example, prevailing beliefs concerning the sanctity of private property against encroachments by the State. Ideally, the fact that such beliefs may presently be in disrepute plays no part in the analysis, but it is a difficult task to employ the analytical methods of an argumentative mode of discourse to arrive at a "detached" result.

Thus far I have been concerned with raising some of the problems that historians might encounter in utilizing appellate opinions as source materials. The question such an approach may raise is whether in the face of these difficulties historians should continue their well-established custom of paying scant or cursory attention to appellate cases, or whether some method of analysis intended to anticipate the problems can be formulated. In the remainder of this essay I shall sketch the form one such method might take.

The method seeks to emphasize both the distinctive professional characteristics of the judicial process and the extent to which judicial decision-making mirrors broader social and ideological trends in American culture. It rests on four assumptions about the judiciary in America: First, judges, because of their authoritative role, are subjected to certain constraints which are internalized in the form of approved techniques of judicial decision-making, such as following precedent, testing general doctrines in terms of particular fact-situations, and publishing formal, reasoned justifications of their results; second, they are subjected to a variety of extraprofessional pressures stemming from the fact that they hold elective or high appointive office; third, individual judges interpret their function by weighing their social and political inclinations against the constraints of their role, with the result that as many potential theories of judicial performance exist as there are individual judges; fourth, since the operational vehicle for formulating theories of performance is the opinion, and since opinions are published documents open to criticism by a judge's peers and by readers both within and without the legal profession, the wide range of potential interpretations of judicial performance becomes narrowed to certain interpretations that are fashionable at different points in time.

It is therefore possible to identify in American appellate decisions the presence of certain ratiocinative styles during various time periods. By ratiocinative style I mean the manner in which a judge rationalizes the end result of his opinion — the way in which he manipulates the various sources of authority and persuasion (precedent, "public policy," etc.) at his disposal. At some points in time judges place greater reliance on precedent or the authority of their office; at others they are more concerned with changing social conditions that question a precedent's import, or are more apt to downgrade their authority to pass on questions in the face of a judgment by another institutional body, such as a legislature or an administrative agency.

The presence of shifting ratiocinative styles in American appellate opinions is particularly suggestive in light of the fact that at least since the early nineteenth century the core elements of the appellate decision-making process have remained constant: that is, appellate courts have continually followed the principles of searching for applicable precedents (which has also been termed deciding "like cases alike"), depersonalizing the judicial function, and elaborating the reasons for their results. Despite this institutional constancy, there have been marked shifts in the manner of opinion-writing: A notable example is the replacement in the early twentieth century of what Pound termed "mechanical jurisprudence" — in which "the judicial function was taken to be one of discovery of the definitely appointed precept ... by an absolute method admitting of no scope for anything but logical identification of the actual precept ... and mechanical application thereof" — with a style that de-emphasized syllogistic logic and judicial omniscience and emphasized attention to "prevalent moral and political theories and intuitions of public policy."[13]

If the process of appellate opinion-writing is thought of as subsuming a number of elements — the professional and extraprofessional constraints upon the judge, his temperamental inclinations, his consciousness of acceptable modes of presentation at given times — an analysis of that process would appear to raise a number of historical questions. To what extent can comparisons be made between the ratiocinative styles of appellate opinions in particular time periods and modes of discourse in other disciplines at the same time? To what extent can the weight given to precedents and the use of syllogistic logic be said to represent certain assumptions about the locus of institutional power in America at given times? If such assumptions can be identified, are they shared by political or social movements extant at the time? How, in short, do prevailing cultural attitudes at given points in the history of American civilization penetrate the self-contained and self-perpetuating appellate court system?

What I propose is a correlation of prevailing cultural attitudes and appellate ratiocinative styles at various times in American history. It is difficult, however, to evaluate "prevailing cultural attitudes" without having previously formulated some index of them; hence a more precise correlation might be between the decisions of appellate courts and political or ideological movements, such as "Jacksonian Democracy," or "progressivism," which had widespread appeal during a particular time span. The first step in such a correlation would be to characterize the social assumptions and modes of thought and expression that distinguished the "Jacksonians" or "progressives"; the next would be to inquire whether these assumptions and modes could be found in appellate opinions at roughly similar points in time, taking into account the factor of time lag in the courts. The inquiry would necessitate an analysis of the internal structure of the opinions and would hence given some attention to the distinctive characteristics

---

13. Roscoe Pound, *"Mechanical Jurisprudence,"* COLUMBIA LAW REVIEW, VIII (1908), 605; THE FORMATIVE ERA, III.

of the appellate opinion as a primary source for historical research. The ultimate concern, however, would be to locate the opinion in a historical context.

The following analysis of Judge Benjamin Cardozo's celebrated opinion in *MacPherson v. Buick,*[14] a case decided by the Court of Appeals of New York in 1916, is intended to serve as an example of how some of the above suggestions might be put into practice. The *MacPherson* case was considered during the ascendancy of the Progressive Movement; Cardozo had, in fact, run for a state judgeship on the Progressive ticket. Generally speaking, Progressive social thought was concerned with exposing the inadequacies of established social philosophies and in positing new ends, purposes, and ideals for society; but it envisioned the retention, in purified form, of existing institutional structures.[15] With respect to the judiciary, for example, Progessives railed against the obstructiveness and arbitrariness of a number of late-nineteenth-century decisions, and demanded that judges in the future be more responsive to changing economic and social conditions, but advocated the continued existence of the judicial branch as an independent locus of power, provided that it kept its house in order.[16] The climate of Progressivism was beneficial for those members of the judicial profession who advocated reform from within — that is, those who exhibited a sense of the inadequacy of prior decisions and sought to expand the functions of the judiciary, while at the same time retaining a firm commitment to the integrity, independence, and authority of their office.

The *MacPherson* case presented a familiar, though ticklish, problem for common law judges, and one to which Progressive

---

14. 217 N.Y. 382 (1916).

15. *See generally* RICHARD HOFSTADTER, THE AGE OF REFORM(New York, 1960); DAVID M. NOBLE, THE PARADOX OF PROGRESSIVE THOUGHT, (Minneapolis, 1959).

16. *See* WOODROW WILSON, THE NEW FREEDOM (New York, 1913); HERBERT CROLY, THE PROMISE OF AMERICAN LIFE (New York, 1909) and PROGRESSIVE DEMOCRACY (New York, 1913); CHARLES MCCARTHY, THE NEW IDEA (Madison, 1912); ROBERT LAFOLLETTE, LAFOLLETTE'S AUTOBIOGRAPHY (New York, 1919); WALTER LIPPMANN, DRIFT AND MASTERY (New York, 1914).

critics of the judiciary were particularly sensitive. The Court of Appeals of New York was asked to reexamine a longstanding precedent in light of its questionable applicability to a new fact situation. In *Winterbottom v. Wright*, an 1842 decision, the Court of the Exchequer in England had held that a supplier of mail coaches, under contract to the Postmaster General, was not liable to third parties not in "privity" of contract with it for injuries resulting from defects in the coaches caused by the supplier's negligence. In *MacPherson* a roughly analogous situation existed: The Buick Motor Company had supplied automobiles to dealers for their eventual sale to the public; one Donald C. MacPherson had purchased an automobile from a dealer; a wheel of the automobile collapsed, injuring MacPherson, who sought compensation from the Company. The question for the Court of Appeals was whether the doctrine of *Winterbottom v. Wright* should control the *MacPherson* situation, in which case the Company's liability for any defective wheels that it had negligently failed to discover on inspection would be limited to persons in privity of contract with it, in this instance the dealer.[17]

The complicating factors in the *MacPherson* situation involved the state of the early-twentieth-centry American automobile industry, in its infancy but perceived as having enormous growth potential. On the one hand, automobiles in America in 1916 were like carriages in England in 1842 in that the assemblers of their component parts anticipated use of the finished product by the general public, not merely those to whom they supplied that product; on the other, automobiles were not like carriages in that they had the potential to travel at much greater speeds and hence conceivably submit their occupants to greater risks. Moreover, the position of early-twentieth-century American automobile manufacturers vis-à-vis the national economy as a whole was rather different from that of mid-nineteenth-century English carriage manufacturers: In 1842 carriages were the major mode

---

17. 217 N.Y. 382, 384 (1916); Warren Seavey, *"Mr. Justice Cardozo and the Law of Torts,"* HARVARD LAW REVIEW, LII (1939), 372, 376, 377.

of transportation in England and had been so for decades; in 1916 the place of the automobile with respect to the American transportation system was ambiguous and the future role of automobiles in the American economy highly speculative. Finally, the question of which interests should bear the risks of potentially dangerous economic activities was a more complicated one for American courts in 1916 than for English courts in 1842, by reason of the increased costs and dangers attendant upon the emergence of an advanced industrial society, and by reason of a growing public awareness of, and reaction against, the protected position industrial manufacturers had enjoyed in the latter part of the nineteenth century. In this vein, the doctrine of the nonliability of manufacturers to those outside privity with them had been subjected to mounting criticism by legal scholars, and had met with certain exceptions in the courts as the twentieth century dawned.[18]

The *MacPherson* case thus presented the Court of Appeals with an opportunity to demonstrate the common law's responsiveness to changing social conditions, but apparently at its own expense: to find for the plaintiff it seemed necessary to overrule or demonstrate the inapplicability of *Winterbottom v. Wright.* The triumph of Cardozo's opinion in *MacPherson* is that he solved this problem by avoiding it: He altered legal doctrine, disposed of *Winterbottom,* and apparently linked the New York court with the forces of social change in a manner that emphasized the continuity and stability of the appellate decision-making process.

Cardozo began his analysis of the question presented by the *MacPherson* case, which he stated to be "whether the defendant owed a duty of care to any one but the immediate purchaser," with a statement of what he considered to be the governing legal principle. "The foundations of this branch of the law, at least in this state," he noted, "were laid in *Thomas v. Winchester.*" Beneath the didacticism of this statement lay a degree of artfulness: *Thomas v. Winchester* had excepted those who falsely labeled

---

18. Seavey, *"Mr. Justice Cardozo,"* 372, 377-378.

poisons from the protection of the *Winterbottom* rule while reaffirming the general validity of that rule; in that sense Cardozo's choice of the phrase "this branch of the law" in the context of *MacPherson* was misleading. Cardozo was quick to sharpen his focus, however, speaking of "the principle of the distinction" of *Thomas v. Winchester,* and noting that "there has never in this state been doubt or disavowal of the principle" although "there may at times have been uncertainty or even error" in its application. The result of this opening series of statements was to replace *Winterbottom v. Wright* with an alternative authority at the very outset of the opinion. Through a deliberately ambiguous use of the term "principle," Cardozo placed an exception to an arguably governing precedent at the center of the stage rather than the precedent itself, thus suggesting that the exception might cover the facts of *MacPherson*: "the principle of the distinction is for present purposes the important thing." [19]

In the next portion of the opinion Cardozo refined his mode of analysis. After having asserted the relevance of the *Thomas* exception to *MacPherson,* he then sought to demonstrate that relevance by making the exception work for him. He cited a series of cases which allegedly illustrated that in New York there had "never . . . been doubt or disvowal of the [*Thomas*] principle." The first two of these cases, *Loop v. Litchfield* and *Losee v. Clute,* found no liability in the absence of privity, following the *Winterbottom* rule and not the *Thomas* exception; Cardozo, however, stated that the cases exemplified "a narrow construction of the [*Thomas*] rule." The second pair of cases, *Devlin v. Smith* and *Statler v. Ray Manufacturing Co.,* demonstrated, in Cardozo's terms, "a more liberal spirit." Both followed the *Thomas* exception, the first applying it to an improperly constructed scaffold and the second to a defective coffee urn: The manufacturer was held liable to parties not in privity of contract with him. In his analysis of the *Devlin* and *Statler* cases, Cardozo turned a flaw in their reasoning

---

19. 217 N.Y. 382, 385 (1916).

to his advantage. The *Thomas* principle, he noted, originally pertained only to substances, such as poison bottles, that were by their nature dangerous to human life; scaffolds and coffee urns were not such substances. Although the court in *Statler*, for example, had stated that a coffee urn "was of such a character inherently that . . . it was liable to become a source of great danger to many people, . . . no one thinks of [an urn] as an implement whose normal function is destruction." Nor was a scaffold "inherently a dangerous instrument"; it became destructive "only if imperfectly constructed." One explanation for this anomaly, Cardozo concluded, was that the *Devlin* and *Statler* courts "may have extended" the *Thomas* rule; "if so, this court is committed to the extension." [20]

By this point in the opinion, the *Thomas* holding had become transformed from a special exception to *Winterbottom* to Cardozo's working principle, and the transformation had been made to seem as if it had been effectuated by past courts rather than Cardozo himself. A possible explanation of the *Devlin* and *Statler* results is that the courts in each case felt that to deny liability to the plaintiff on the grounds that he was not in privity with the defendant would be particularly unfair and unjust, since the absence of contractual relations appeared to be a heinously irrelevant reason for refusing a third party compensation for injuries he very probably could neither have anticipated nor avoided, particularly when the defendant-manufacturer had reason to know of the potentially dangerous character of the article in question and of its likely use by third parties. The *Thomas* precedent, in this vein, was a helpful if not entirely analogous means of achieving a result essentially dictated by considerations of equity. Yet Cardozo's focus was largely on the *Thomas* precedent as precedent: his purpose was to demonstrate that "Thomas v. Winchester became quickly a landmark of the law . . . there has never in this state been doubt or disavowal of [its] principle." In so doing he was attempting to instill his original

---

20. *Ibid.,* 382, 385-387.

assertion that "the foundations of this branch of the law . . . were laid in *Thomas v. Winchester*" with an authority of its own, thereby showing that it was not an assertion but a fair reading of the relevant cases. By the close of this portion of the *MacPherson* opinion, Cardozo had suggested that those cases demonstrated a "trend of judicial thought" toward extending the *Thomas* rule to a series of *Winterbottom*-type situations: a builder of a defective building, a manufacturer of an elevator, a "contractor who furnished a defective rope with knowledge of the purpose for which the rope was to be used." [21] Although Cardozo took no position on the merits of these last examples, they served to reinforce his own inference that *Thomas,* not *Winterbottom,* governed *MacPherson.*

At this point in the opinion Cardozo, who could have proceeded directly to judgment for the plaintiff on the basis of the *Thomas* principle as it had emerged from precedents, took an additional preliminary step. Citing Lord Esher's opinion in *Heaven v. Pender,* Cardozo introduced the general "conception of a duty, irrespective of contract, imposed upon the manufacturer by the law itself." Lord Esher's opinion had stated that when a manufacturer supplied articles for use by another "under such circumstances that every one of ordinary sense would . . . recognize at once that unless he used ordinary care and skill with regard to the condition of the thing supplied . . . a duty arises to use ordinary care and skill as to the condition or manner of supplying such thing." Violation of such a duty gave rise to an action for negligence, and the right to bring that action, according to Cardozo's interpretation of Lord Esher's decision, was "not to be confined to the immediate buyer," but extended "to the persons or class of persons for whose use the thing is supplied." Cardozo conceded that Lord Esher's opinion "may not be an accurate exposition of the law of England," that it "may need some qualification even in our own state," and that it "may involve errors of inclusion and of exclusion." Nevertheless, he judged its "tests and standards, at least in their underlying principles," to be "the tests and standards of our law." [22]

---

21. *Ibid.,* 387.
22. *Ibid.,* 388-389.

Cardozo was thus prepared for his holding in *MacPherson:* "the principle of *Thomas v. Winchester* is not limited to poisons . . . and things of like nature . . . which in their normal operation are implements of destruction. If the nature of a thing is such that it is reasonably certain to place life and limb in peril when negligently made, it is then a thing of danger . . . . If to the element of danger there is added knowledge that the thing will be used by persons other than the purchaser, and used without new tests, then, irrespective of contract, the manufacturer of this thing of danger is under a duty to make it carefully." In "such circumstance," Cardozo stated, "the presence of a known danger, attendant upon a known use, makes vigilance a duty." The decision, in his judgment, had "put aside the notion that the duty to safeguard life and limb grows out of contract and nothing else;" it had "put the source of the obligation where it ought to be — in the law." [23]

Having combined in his holding his interpretation of the *Thomas* line of cases with Lord Esher's formulation of a duty irrespective of contract, Cardozo briefly reflected on the implications of that combination for the *MacPherson* case. "From this survey of the decisions," he stated, "there thus emerges a definition of the duty of a manufacturer which enables us to measure this defendant's liability. Beyond all question the nature of an automobile gives warning of probable danger if its construction is defective. . . . The defendant knew the danger. It knew also that the car would be used by persons other than the buyer. . . . The maker of this car supplied it for the use of purchasers from the dealer just as plainly as the contractor in *Devlin v. Smith* supplied the scaffold for use by the servants of the owner. Yet the defendant would have us say that he was the one person whom it was under the legal duty to protect. . . . The law does not lead us," Cardozo continued, "to so inconsequent a conclusion. Precedents drawn from the days of travel by stage coach do not fit the conditions of travel today. The principle that the danger must be imminent does not change, but

---

23. *Ibid.,* 389-390.

the things subject to the principle do change. They are whatever the needs of life in a developing civilization require them to be." [24]

The *MacPherson* opinion, then, demonstrates not only Cardozo's skill in manipulating precedents in order to make an exception swallow up a rule but also an understanding of the *sub rosa* policy considerations implicit in those precedents. Cardozo announced that "a definition of the duty of a manufacturer" emerged from "a survey of the decisions"; in actuality, that definition arose from Lord Esher's dictum and Cardozo's unexpressed belief that the decisions were groping toward positions like that expressed in the dictum. Cardozo never expressly stated that the *Devlin* or *Statler* cases, for example, extended *Thomas* because of a sense of the injustice of the privity standard in certain situations, but he nevertheless gave clear evidence that an extension had taken place and that his court was committed to that extension.[25] Similarly, he noted that the tests and standards of liability formulated in *Heaven v. Pender* were "the tests and standards of our law . . . at least in their underlying principle," suggesting that those "principles" had been exemplified by the *Thomas* line of cases. By the time that Cardozo applied his definition of the duty of the manufacturer to the *MacPherson* situation, the reader had the impression that that definition had long existed in New York state, even though it had not previously been articulated. Yet, in light of the fact that *Thomas,* while making an exception for falsely labeled poison bottles, reaffirmed the *Winterbottom* rule, in light of the special facts of *Devlin* and *Statler,* and in light of the reaffirmation of the *Winterbottom* rule by the Court of Appeals eight years prior to *MacPherson,*[26] there seems to be little evidence supporting this impression.

In the final analysis, *MacPherson* appears to represent a perception on Cardozo's part that "the needs of life in a developing

---

24. *Ibid.,* 390-391.

25. *See* 217 N.Y. 382, 393, discussion of "the underlying principle" of Devlin v. Smith.

26. Torgeson v. Schultz, 192 N.Y. 156 (1908).

civilization" required a new allocation of risks in the relationship between automobile manufacturers, automobile dealers, and the public, and an extraordinary infusion of that perception into the materials of his opinion, so that it appeared to emerge out of the past rather than out of the consciousness of the judge. "Precedents drawn from the days of travel by stage coach do not fit the conditions of travel today," Cardozo noted in disposing of *Winterbottom,* but at the same time he had used precedents from those days to lend authority to his interpretation of the *MacPherson* situation. In his realization that "the things subject to principle . . . change," he brought within the judicial consciousness a sense of social flux and complexity that posed a counterweight to arbitrariness. *MacPherson* was one of those cases, later celebrated by Cardozo, in which the judge's task was to reconcile a past precedent with his perception of present needs;[27] Cardozo performed that task by arriving at modern solutions through traditional means. His interpretation of his function was hence in harmony with that of the leading edge of social thought of his time.

The primary goal of the method just illustrated is to preserve some sense of the autonomy of appellate opinions while investigating them for historical purposes. The method employs analytical techniques and makes assumptions that are perhaps most familiar to the intellectual historian; for these reasons it may prove inapplicable to that area of legal history which does not deal with appellate opinions. Even in its narrow context, it cannot claim to have "solved" any of the problems of interdisciplinary communication raised earlier; language, methodology, the function of time, and value judgments are basic difficulties associated with primary source research in history. Where the method may make some contribution is in its effort to reduce the material contained in appellate opinions to terms historians can understand and utilize without altogether losing sight of the distinctiveness of that material.

---

27. *Ibid.,* 390-391; BENJAMIN CARDOZO, THE NATURE OF THE JUDICIAL PROCESS (New Haven, 1921), 142-166.

CHAPTER 2. SCHOLARLY THOUGHT

The essays included in this chapter, taken together, reveal the changing focus of my recent research on the contributions of American legal scholars. *The Intellectual Origins of Torts in America* reflects my current interest in extending the techniques of social and intellectual history to analyses of private law subjects. That essay also reflects my enhanced sense of the importance of what I call "disciplinary matrixes" (conditions producing shared research perspectives among groups of scholars) in shaping American legal thought.

When compared with the two preceding essays in this section, *The Intellectual Origins of Torts in America* presents me with an analytical difficulty. I assume, in both *From Sociological Jurisprudence to Realism* and *The Evolution of Reasoned Elaboration,* that dominant schools of American jurisprudential thought (sociological jurisprudence, Realism, etc.) emerge as responses to social conditions. I then proceed, in those essays, to describe and analyze the social conditions that "generate" such schools. But *The Intellectual Origins of Torts* suggests that I consider the relationship between ideas and events to be more complex than I previously assumed.

The last suggestion should be made explicit. To the extent that the two earlier essays assume that events, or other social phenomena, "cause" jurisprudential schools to emerge, I would not now endorse that view of causation. It seems to me that the relationship between dominant ideas or values and "significant" events in the history of a profession is extraordinarily complex and difficult to characterize. Events cannot categorically be said to cause the emergence of ideas, nor can ideas categorically be said to skew perceptions of events. Much more work and thought needs to be done, in my judgment, before a theory of the interaction of ideas and events in the history of American legal thought can be proposed.

Of course if one shares my earlier assumptions about the relationship between ideas and their social context *From*

Sociological Jurisprudence to Realism and *The Evolution of Reasoned Elaboration* may prove congenial. Moreover, I believe that the essays provide a mini-history of twentieth-century schools of legal thought, and emphasize some of the distinguishing features of jurisprudential attitudes that have too often been lumped together.

FROM SOCIOLOGICAL JURISPRUDENCE TO REALISM: JURISPRUDENCE AND SOCIAL CHANGE IN EARLY TWENTIETH-CENTURY AMERICA

Virginia Law Review, Volume 59, No. 2 (1972)

This Article describes the displacement of one mode of American jurisprudence by another in the first three decades of the twentieth century. During that period Realism succeeded Sociological Jurisprudence as the dominant strain in American legal thought. Although the earlier mode was generative of the latter, the exponents of the two saw them as antagonistic. Conceived and defined by law professors, the two modes of thought were explicated through argument and counterargument. But their mutual opposition was not merely rhetorical; it stemmed from differing views on such fundamental questions as the relation between morality and law and the nature of judicial decision-making.

The backdrop to the struggle between Sociological Jurisprudes and Realists was the passage of American political, social, and intellectual history from a period dominated by the Progressive Movement to one dominated by the spirit of the New Deal. This change was not an essentially evolutionary process, although it has sometimes been so described.[1] Although the New Deal borrowed much of the rhetoric and some of the governmental apparatus of Progressivism, its followers made some strikingly different social assumptions from those of the Progressives. Just as Sociological Jurisprudence was the jurisprudential analog to Progressivism, so Realism was the analog to the New Deal.

In the comparisons between the jurisprudential modes and social movements that follow, Progressivism and the New Deal are primarily considered in terms of their ideas, values, and governing assumptions. This is not to deemphasize their political or economic impact, but rather to facilitate comparison with the mode of jurisprudence in vogue during each of these eras. The political and

---

1. *See, e.g.,* A. Link, American Epoch (1955); A. Schlesinger, The Coming of the New Deal (1959).

economic reforms initiated by Progressivism and the New Deal were primarily the results of what their proponents felt to be new social insights. These insights simultaneously revealed themselves to jurisprudential scholars.

Since both Progressivism and Sociological Jurisprudence on the one hand, and the New Deal and Realism on the other, envisaged themselves as movements protesting the credos of an existing intellectual order, the chronology of this analysis begins in the late nineteenth century, before the first pair of ideologies became dominant. Part One traces the rise of Progressivism as a critique of late nineteenth-century social thought and the concurrent emergence of Sociological Jurisprudence as a protest against the "mechanical jurisprudence" [2] of the last quarter of the nineteenth century. Part Two describes the circumstances surrounding the rise of Realism and the birth of the New Deal. Part Three advances some tentative conclusions about the relationship of jurisprudential movements to social change.

From Mechanical Jurisprudence to Sociological Jurisprudence

The late nineteenth century in America illustrates the difficulty of attempting to describe judicial behavior in catch phrases. The majority of late nineteenth century judges were the strictest of strict constructionists and the most tenacious defenders of property rights. Yet they could not be considered champions of judicial self-restraint and could only partially be called conservatives. Late nineteenth-century jurisprudence attempted, along with other disciplines of the time, to find some solutions to the persistent problem of economic instability.[3] Prior to the Civil War, the presence of state regulation and the immaturity of industrial enterprise meant that the pace of economic change could in some measure be controlled, although prosperity could not be

---

2. The term was coined by Roscoe Pound in *Mechanical Jurisprudence,* 8 COLUM. L. REV. 605 (1908).

3. *See generally* E. KIRKLAND, DREAM AND THOUGHT IN THE BUSINESS COMMUNITY, 1860-1900 (1956).

assured.[4] After 1865 massive developments in interstate transportation, coupled with enormous strides in technology and industrial production, placed severe pressure on the regulatory apparatus.

The federal government responded to the post-Civil War surge of economic expansion by designing policies, such as land grants to railroads, to increase its momentum. Beyond that it took no action; laissez-faire was the general watchword of the times. Laissez-faire, however, did not mean the utter absence of regulation, it merely meant shifting the burden of regulation from artificial entities, such as governments, to "natural" ones, such as the market and its iron laws. Behind the apparent indifference to the course of economic development on the part of late nineteenth-century policymakers lay the convictions that the economy was fated to rise and fall at regular intervals; that the laws of the marketplace were invariably sound; and that man had a discernible and predictable nature.[5]

Obsession with ineluctable rules, principles, and axioms became characteristic of the academic disciplines of the time. By applying a curious combination of spiritualism and Darwinism, economists, natural scientists, and sociologists discovered universal absolutes that governed their fields. Competitive man and the self regulating market were united in a permanent fluctuating alliance. One had only to discover these truths: political, economic, sociological, and biological theories flowed from the discovery.[6]

Jurisprudence was likewise attracted to the universal principle. Judges began their decisions by making verbal distinctions, defining concepts in useful ways. They then pronounced their definitions as axiomatic. From then on it was a rush downward to the result: the axiom was applied to the facts of a case, and certain

---

4. *See generally* S. BRUCHEY, THE ROOTS OF AMERICAN ECONOMIC GROWTH, 1607-1861 (1965).

5. S. FINE, LAISSEZ-FAIRE AND THE GENERAL WELFARE STATE (1956); E. KIRKLAND, BUSINESS IN THE GILDED AGE (1952).

6. *See generally* R. HOFSTADTER, SOCIAL DARWINISM IN AMERICAN THOUGHT, 1860-1915 (1944); I. WYLLIE, THE SELF-MADE MAN IN AMERICA (1954).

things "inevitably" followed. "Manufacture" was not "commerce." One could easily see the distinction between the two activities. An intent to monopolize the manufacture of sugar in the United States did not imply an intent to monopolize commerce, since the processes were discrete. Hence the Sherman Act, which prohibited the monopolization of any part of commerce in the United States, did not apply to a corporation manufacturing over 90% of the sugar in the nation.[7]

Alongside this tendency toward what the elder Justice Harlan once called "subtle and ingenious verbal criticism"[8] the judges of the late nineteenth century placed a compassion for vested property rights. In doing this they were not acting in a "conservative" fashion. For several centuries the theory of property rights had been that they were derived from the state. Although these rights could not be taken away unfairly, their initial conferral was at state suffrance. Under this theory, states in the early nineteenth century gave monopoly franchises to build canals, bridges, and turnpikes, reserving the right to regulate the franchises or even to withdraw them.[9] The late nineteenth-century notion of an absolute right to private property free from any governmental interference was revolutionary. When they protected sugar corporations from government regulation, the courts were not acting in a conservative fashion; they were sanctioning a radical change in the relationship between private individuals and the state.

In another sense, however, the judicial defense of individual property rights was a conservative response. In situations where two classes of persons were in unequal bargaining positions, the courts often found a property right lurking somewhere in the facts, and they tended to use this finding to preclude governmental aid to the disadvantaged class. In 1905 the case of *Lochner v. New York*[10] demonstrated that late nineteenth-century ways of

---

7. United States v. E.C. Knight Co., 156 U.S. 1 (1895).

8. Civil Rights Cases, 109 U.S. 3, 26 (1883).

9. For the practice of this theory in Massachusetts, see O. HANDLIN, COMMONWEALTH (1947).

10. 198 U.S. 45 (1905).

thinking had continued into the twentieth. The Supreme Court declared that a state law regulating the number of hours worked by bakers interfered with the bakers' right to sell their services at whatever terms they wished. Since those terms, in 1905, were largely dictated by the employers, the decision actually protected their right to work their employees as long as they could.

Decisions such as *Lochner* were symbolic manifestations, for some, of the evils of unregulated industrial capitalism. Beginning in the first years of the twentieth century, an increased awareness of the costs of mature industrialism began to penetrate the rhetoric of politicians and social theorists.[11] In their eyes, laissez-faire stimulated poverty, created and rewarded "special interests," nurtured monopolies and trusts, and discriminated against the farmer and the workingman. The absence of economic regulation led to unbridled economic power, which led to the corruption of public officials. Yet the executive branch of the government was indifferent to these conditions, Congress and state legislatures were accomplices in their creation, and judges were blind to their meaning. A greater sense of public responsibility needed to be instilled in these institutions.[12]

The Progressive movement united these critiques and gave them an intellectual foundation. Progressivism began with the assumptions that society was in a constant state of flux and that man had the capacity to progress by directing this inevitable change toward beneficial ends. Consequently it affirmed the worth of evaluating social theories on the basis of contemporary experience. Such testing of the allegedly universal laws that governed intellectual disciplines often demonstrated their fallacy.

---

11. *See generally* R. BREMNER, FROM THE DEPTHS (1956); S. HAYS, THE RESPONSE TO INDUSTRIALISM, 1885-1914 (1957). Contemporary examples are R. HUNTER, POVERTY (1904); W. RAUSCHENBUSH, CHRISTIANITY AND THE SOCIAL CRISIS (1907); J. RYAN, A LIVING WAGE (1906).

12. *See generally* G. MOWRY, THE ERA OF THEODORE ROOSEVELT (1958). Contemporary accounts are collected in THE MUCKRAKERS (A. & L. WEINBERG ed. 1964). *See also* H. CROLY, THE PROMISE OF AMERICAN LIFE (1909); W. LIPPMANN, DRIFT AND MASTERY (1914); L. STEFFENS, THE SHAME OF THE CITIES (1904); L. STEFFENS, THE SHAME OF THE STATES (1911).

The rules of the marketplace produced extreme poverty and outrageous wealth; they did not further progress. It was no longer enough to justify governmental indifference to economic and social inequalities by appeal to Darwinist religiosity which informed the exploited that "God helps those who help themselves." In order to achieve progress government paternalism was needed to promote the common good.

Thus as political reformers the Progressives sought to expand the public sector of government in order to substitute decision-making by an educated and efficient group of impartial administrators for decision-making by partisan representatives of special interest groups. Progressivism believed in the management of government by experts and advocated the expansion of the executive branch, primarily in the form of administrative regulatory agencies, at the expense of Congress and the courts. It also urged regulatory and welfare legislation at both the state and federal levels and demanded judicial tolerance for such legislation. Progressives criticized judges for being unresponsive to social and economic conditions and asked them to take greater notice of the casualties which unregulated industrialism created.[13]

Concomitant with this general Progressive attack on the performance of governing institutions came a specific critique of late nineteenth-century judicial methodology. One of the earliest examples was Justice Holmes' dissent in *Lochner,* where he repudiated the judicial tendency to announce general social propositions as truths and to reason downward from them in the decision of specific cases. This technique, in his opinion, approached arbitrariness. It demonstrated the extent to which judges could use their office to expound, in the form of authoritative pronouncements, their own political, economic, social views. *Lochner* had been decided on an economic theory which a great portion of the country did not entertain. More importantly, the theory had not been empirically tested; it was merely announced as true. This constituted, in cases examining the validity of state

---

13. *E.g.,* H. CROLY, *supra* note 12; C. McCARTHY, THE WISCONSIN IDEA (1912).

regulatory legislation, an impermissible substitution of judicial views for those of the legislature.[14]

Three years after Holmes' *Lochner* dissent, Roscoe Pound hailed it as "the best exposition of . . . sociological jurisprudence" extant in America. For Pound Sociological Jurisprudence was "the movement for the adjustment of principles and doctrines to the human conditions they are to govern rather than to assumed first principles." [15] Pound had been foremost among those who, in the first decade of the twentieth century, exhorted jurists to abandon their method of deducing decisions from predetermined conceptions. In 1905, in the face of "growing popular dissatisfaction with [the] legal system," he called for a philosophy of law founded on a sound knowledge of the elements of social and political science.[16] In 1907 he maintained that the most logical and skillfully reasoned rules might defeat the end of law in their practical administration because they were not adapted to the environment in which they were to be enforced.[17] In 1908 he exposed the "condition of mechanical jurisprudence" [18] allegedly prevalent among early twentieth-century judges, in which conceptions were developed logically at the expense of practical results through an artificial process of legal reasoning.[19] And in 1910 he implored his brethren in the legal profession to "look to economics and sociology and philosophy and cease to assume that jurisprudence is self-sufficient." [20]

In a long article in the 1911 and 1912 issues of the *Harvard Law Review,* Pound announced the emergence of Sociological Jurisprudence as a discrete and definable philosophy of law.[21]

---

14. 198 U.S. at 75.
15. Pound, *Liberty of Contract,* 18 YALE L.J. 454, 464 (1909).
16. Pound, *Do We Need a Philosophy of Law?* 5 COLUM. L. REV. 339, 344, 351 (1905).
17. Pound, *The Need of a Sociological Jurisprudence,* 19 GREEN BAG 607 (1907).
18. Pound, *supra* note 2.
19. Pound, *supra* note 15, at 457.
20. Pound, *Law in Books and Law in Action,* 44 AM. L. REV. 12, 35, 36 (1910).
21. Pound, *The Scope and Purpose of Sociological Jurisprudence,* 24 HARV. L. REV. 591 (1911) and 25 HARV. L. REV. 489 (1912).

Among its common elements, he maintained, were a realization of "the backwardness of law in meeting social ends"; [22] discontent with prevailing modes of juristic thought and juridical method; [23] an insistence upon study of the actual social effects of legal doctrines; [24] and a belief in "the equitable application of law," by which judges eschewed the illusory certainty of legal rules for "reasonable and just solutions of individual causes." [25]

Pound's emphasis on understanding changing social phenomena rather than static universal rules, his belief in social planning through scientific expertise, and his commitment to "equity" and "justice" were congenial to Progressives. His 1911 critique of the New York State Court of Appeals' decision in *Ives v. South Buffalo Ry. Co.*[26] is illustrative. The *Ives* decision had declared unconstitutional a 1910 New York labor law providing for workmen's compensation. The passage of the law was a classic Progressive exercise in policymaking. In 1909 the New York legislature had created a fourteen-member bipartisan commission to determine the liability of employers to their employees for industrial accidents and to inquire into the efficiency, cost, justice, merits, and defects of industrial accident laws in sister states and foreign countries. The commission presented a detailed report to the legislature in 1910, in which, as the court in *Ives* stated, it claimed that the New York system of dealing with industrial accidents was economically, morally, and legally unsound, basing this claim on a voluminous array of statistical tables, extracts from the works of philosophical writers and the industrial laws of many countries.

On the basis of the commission's recommendations, the legislature enacted a workmen's compensation law. When it invalidated that law, the majority in *Ives* stated that "under our form of government ... courts must regard all economic,

---

22. 25 HARV. L. REV. at 510.
23. *Id.*
24. *Id.* at 514.
25. *Id.* at 515.
26. 201 N.Y. 271, 94 N.E. 431 (1911).

philosophical, and moral theories, attractive and desirable though they may be, as subordinate to the primary question whether they can be molded into statutes without infringing upon the letter or spirit of our written Constitutions." [27] Pound described the judicial state of mind that produced the *Ives* decision as akin to that of a law professor who had degree candidates state that the English feudal system was introduced by William the Conqueror in 1086. As a matter of historical fact the statement was inaccurate, but the professor considered it a "question of law," since it had appeared in Blackstone, an "infallible source." "Of course," Pound wrote of the *Ives* ruling, "economic, moral, and philosophical theories of today could have no more bearing on [the court's reading of the text] than historical study of today, in the mind of [that professor], could have upon the legal dogma as to what was legal history." [28]

Pound's theories about the proper direction of jurisprudence found support in the writings of Joseph Bingham, a law professor at Stanford. Bingham, in articles in the *Michigan Law Review* written in 1911 and 1912, advanced two generalizations that closely paralleled Pound's observations.[29] The first was that legal rules and principles were merely mental processes. Bingham felt that judicial enunciation of a rule or principle of law was by no means "a fundamental and essentially authoritative thing"; so to assert was to "confuse the content of knowledge with its form or with the mode of its expression." [30] Bingham decried the tendency of some judges of his day "to search the authorities for general considerations of law which seem to be applicable to their cases, to determine which of these statements was sufficiently supported by authority to stand as 'law,' to interpret these established statements and to decide the case by application of the

---

27. *Id.* at 287.
28. Pound, *supra* note 17, at 611.
29. Bingham, *What Is the Law?* 11 MICH. L. REV. 1, 109 (1912); Bingham, *The Nature of Legal Rights and Duties,* 12 MICH. L. REV. 1 (1913).
30. 11 MICH. L. REV. at 7, 13.

interpretations." [31] This method accounted, in his opinion, for "much of the backwardness of the law." [32]

Bingham's second proposition tied in with his first: "the law" was not a set of rules and principles but "an external field of concrete phenomena" and should hence be studied with the same care that was devoted to other fields of scientific investigation.[33] He suggested that "the working field" of students of the law included "the organization of the institutions and agencies of ... government, their concrete operations and effects, and the causal facts which bring about those operations." [34] Bingham pointed to "a movement which portends changes in our administration of justice" that he felt to be "gaining momentum all over the country." [35] He maintained that the movement could be "directed and controlled towards true and permanent progress" if lawyers and judges would place a greater emphasis on the thorough study of the facts of government, their causes, and their concrete effects.[36] The result of this effort would yield a better comprehension of the functions of the judicial office and a consequent improvement of the administration of justice through "more uniformly enlightened and progressive decisions and careful, scientific legislation." [37]

Criticism of the craftmanship of early twentieth-century judges was the principal bond between Holmes, Pound, and Bingham. Each attempted to expose certain fallacies underlying judicial opinion-writing, e.g., that judges should reason downward from universal principles and that judges need not be concerned with extralegal phenomena in their decisions, and to suggest that effective judicial performance came not from obeisance to such principles but from an awareness of the social context of adjudication. Beyond that the three men began to diverge. Holmes

---

31. *Id.* at 16-17.
32. *Id.* at 18.
33. 12 MICH. L. REV. at 26 n.24.
34. 11 MICH. L. REV. at 9.
35. *Id.* at 119.
36. *Id.* at 119-20.
37. *Id.* at 120-21.

merely complained that it was inappropriate for judges to utilize their office as a means of expounding their economic prejudices; he did not prescribe the ways by which they might become more sophisticated economists. This was consistent with his tendency to make few affirmative proposals in the name of intellectual development or social change. He tended to adopt a passive approach, relying on what he termed "the marketplace" to produce ideas or policies for a given point in time.[38] Pound and Bingham were much more concerned with specific proposals for jurisprudential reform; in that sense their views were closer to the mainstream of Progressive thought.[39] In particular, Pound and Bingham were at one with the Progressives in their faith that social planning could be made a "science" through expert interpretation of empirical phenomena, in their desire to make the authoritative institutions of American government more sensitive to the complexities of twentieth-century life and more efficient in their response to those complexities, and in their perception that human life was governed not by fixed rules or principles but by change.

Despite these areas of agreement, Pound and Bingham diverged on an issue that was of equal importance to Progressives: the rôle of common moral principles. One of the elements of Progressivism was a belief that social change could of itself promote continuity and stability through the reaffirmation of consensual moral values. The Progressives were both absolutists and relativists. Although society was in a process of constant change, certain patterns of behavior, such as honesty, industry, and temperance, should remain constant. Put another way, Progressives believed that although effective social planning recognized the necessity of adjusting principles to changing conditions, it nonetheless proceeded from shared principles and attempted to achieve ideal social ends.[40]

---

38. *Cf.* White, *The Rise and Fall of Justice Holmes,* 39 U. CHI. L. REV. 51, 75 (1971).

39. *See* D. NOBLE, THE PARADOX OF PROGRESSIVE THOUGHT (1958); White, *The Social Values of the Progressives,* 70 SO. ATL. Q. 63 (1971).

40. White, *supra,* note 39.

In the writings thus far considered neither Pound nor Bingham specifically addressed the question of whether legal institutions should consciously attempt to perpetuate certain values or to attain certain ideals. They had neither evaluated the potential of law as a cohering, homogenizing social force nor attempted to describe what Lon Fuller later came to call law's "inner morality." [41] But a comparison of one of Bingham's articles with a long essay Pound wrote in 1923 on judicial decision-making reveals a divergence between the two men that had significant ramifications for the development of American jurisprudence in the late 1920's and 1930's.

Bingham prefaced a discussion on legal rights and duties with the observation that "the term *right* or the term *wrong* is but an asserted label which cannot be appreciated accurately except in the light of the purposes which inspired and the mental processes which produced the application." [42] A certain method might be "right," Bingham argued, in the sense of being effective to produce specific results, but there was "no external measure of the correctness or incorrectness of a particular assertion of moral rectitude or delinquency." [43] In making that assertion Bingham risked the criticism, as he pointed out, "of all who insist on the existence of an external supernatural force which promulgates or establishes . . . an absolute, unassailable moral justice, and also of all who would contend that there actually exist . . . moral unitary rules and principles which may be discovered and demonstrated." The "conflict between such criticism and my philosophy," Bingham maintained, "I cannot hope to reconcile." [44]

The thrust of Bingham's remarks was directed at those who insisted that public standards of morality be regarded as authoritative guides for what he called "the operation of . . .

---

41. Fuller's most comprehensive statement of the "inner morality" of law appears in L. FULLER, THE MORALITY OF LAW (2d ed., 1970).

42. Bingham, *The Nature of Legal Rights and Duties,* 12 MICH. L. REV. 1, 2 (1912).

43. *Id.*

44. *Id.* at 2-3 n.3.

governmental law-determining machinery." [45] He conceded that there existed "a predominant and potent public opinion on the 'morality' of a large proportion of ordinary sorts of conduct" but argued that this predominant opinion was in many important particulars uncertain, varying, and indefinite and might differ from the leading enlightened opinion of the day.[46] Hence a public consensus on moral issues could not be the conclusive arbiter of decisions on legal questions.[47]

If Bingham was suggesting that those in authoritative positions in the "governmental law-determining machinery," such as judges, need not be constrained by traditional legal principles or by prevailing standards of public morality, his position was largely repudiated by Pound in 1923. In a three-part article in that year,[48] Pound set forth a theory of judicial decision-making that diverged from Bingham and represented a partial retreat from his own earlier jurisprudential views.

Two components of that theory are of present interest. The first is Pound's qualification of his previous condemnations of mechanical jurisprudence. He maintained in the second and third parts of his article that the assumptions governing much of late nineteenth-century judicial decision-making were "quite at variance with the facts" but "nevertheless represent[ed] an ideal of judicial decision to which for some purposes, and in some connections, the administration of justice ought to conform." [49] In particular, the mechanical ideal was appropriate to the law of property and to commercial transactions, since one fee simple was like every other and no individuality of judicial product was called for as between one promissory note and another.[50] There were instances, Pound argued, in which the process of judicial decision-making could and should consist of "a selection from

45. *Id.* at 3.
46. *Id.*
47. *Id.*
48. Pound, *The Theory of Judicial Decision,* 36 HARV. L. REV. 641, 802, 940 (1923).
49. *Id.* at 825.
50. *Id.* at 952.

among fixed precepts of determined content" and a "mechanical ascertainment of whether the facts fit the rule." [51] He maintained that jurists could partition the "field of the legal order," setting off the part involving repetition and calling for rule from the part "involving unique situations, calling for standards and for individualized application." [52] The error of the late nineteenth century had not been in formulating a mechanical ideal, which in Pound's view represented "a distinct gain for the legal order," but in seeking to extend this ideal over the whole domain of law. "The social interest in the individual human life," Pound wrote, "presses for better securing, and theories of property and contract are inadequate thereto." [53]

The phrase "the social interest in the individual human life" described the second major component of Pound's 1923 theory of judicial decision-making. It too represented a modification (in this instance an elaboration) of Pound's earlier work. Pound's previous writings had criticized the "exaggerated" importance courts attributed to individual rights [54] and at the same time had decried the tendency of mechanical jurisprudence to ignore the fact that each case allegedly represented a unique set of empirical phenomena. For Pound these two criticisms were in apposition rather than in opposition because he was interested in the individual in his role as a part of a complex and interdependent society. He postulated three stages in the development of enlightened judicial decision-making: first, a perception of social interdependence, which would result in a greater awareness of the societal responsibilities of individual activity; second, a realization that judicial decisions could not be isolated from their social context and a consequent infusion of extralegal phenomena, gathered by use of the social sciences, into the judging process; and finally, "social engineering," where judges "[would] generalize the claims of the parties as individual human claims . . . subsume the claims

---

51. *Id.* at 947.
52. *Id.* at 958.
53. *Id.* at 825.
54. *E.g.,* Pound, *supra* note 16, at 344.

so generalized under generalized claims involved in life in a civilized society in the time and place, and endeavor to frame a precept or state a principle that will secure the most of these social interests that we may with the least sacrifice." [55]

Pound's conception of judicial decision-making as part of the larger process of social engineering received its first detailed formulation in the third part of the 1923 article. The significant aspect of that formulation for present purposes is suggested by the phrase "subsume [individual human claims] under generalized claims involved in life in a civilized society in the time and place. . . ." Pound wanted judges to keep in mind the common values held in priority by a society at a point in time and to perceive individual cases as symbolic representations of "conflicting and overlapping claims . . . involved in civilized social life." [56] As such he wanted to insure that judges take cognizance of the "body of philosophical, political and ethical ideas as to the end of law . . . with reference to which . . . the traditional ideas of application and decision . . . are continually reshaped." [57]

Pound's insistence that judicial decision-making was continually influenced by current moral, political, and social ideas allowed him to suggest that adjudication could function as a force for moral cohesiveness in society. "Current moral ideas," he argued, were "drawn upon continually" in the judging process, but "seldom consciously." [58] Effective judicial decision-making, in Pound's theory of social engineering, proceeded from a consciousness among judges "of the role of ideal pictures of the social and legal order." [59] Since those ideal pictures rested in part on prevailing notions of morality, judges, in ascertaining the origins of the pictures, needed to discern the common moral principles of their time. That examination would help them understand to what extent

---

55. Pound, *supra* note 48, at 955.
56. *Id.* at 954-55.
57. *Id.* at 645.
58. *Id.* at 948.
59. *Id.* at 958.

their decisions were motivated by "personal pictures" and to what extent by "general pictures." [60]

Pound had previously criticized over-personalized judicial approaches to social problems. Hence, in suggesting that judges determine "how far they may act upon ... ideal pictures with self-assurance," [61] he was urging them to legitimatize their decisions by demonstrating how they reflected common moral values rather than merely their own idiosyncracies. And since Pound saw "legal social engineering as a part of the whole process of social control," [62] a judicial announcement of prevailing public attitudes on moral questions served not only to articulate those attitudes but to sanctify them.

Pound's 1923 theory of Sociological Jurisprudence paralleled the social hypotheses of the Progressive movement in two respects. First, in his bifurcation of the legal order into those portions where the values of continuity, stability, and regularity were prized and those where flexibility and individuality were paramount, Pound demonstrated the same desire to preserve continuity in change that marked Progressive thought. Second, through his device of an "ideal element" in adjudication Pound summoned up the vision of a society motivated by a search for common goals, these resting on shared moral principles. Law, being the basis by which society cohered, was for both Pound and the Progressives a repository of moral values.

By 1923 Pound's blueprint for enlightened judicial decision-making appeared to differ from Bingham's formulations, and in some respects from Pound's own earlier views, in its definition of the locus of judicial authority. In Pound's view society at large approved certain techniques for resolving the claims of competing interests in various areas of the law; approval signified a coherence with respect to the promotion of certain values — security in matters involving property and commercial transactions, flexibility elsewhere. To fulfill his social function

---

60. *Id.*
61. *Id.*
62. *Id.*

properly, a judge was bound to make decisions that reflected common values: the closer the relationship between any given decision and these values, the more authoritative that decision.

Since in many instances the values represented in litigation were imperfectly expressed or incoherent, judges had a large measure of freedom to make their own interpretations and resolutions. But in Pound's formulation the judiciary functioned as an active repository of social values: demonstrating a sensitivity to the legal and social subcategory into which a given case fell, utilizing appropriate techniques of legal analysis, seeking empirical information, giving conscious attention to the perceived purposes and goals of contemporary society. The processes, forms, and techniques of judicial decision-making and opinion writing were symbols of social and professional constraints on the judge. And because professional constraints, such as syllogistic reasoning, were themselves socially derived, as evidenced by mechanical jurisprudence, ultimately a judge's authority should emanate from his skill at perceiving and articulating the social interests and values presented by his cases.

In Pound's view, then, there should exist at any given point in the history of a civilization both an unarticulated consensus as to what constituted society's pressing concerns and accepted techniques for judicial decision-making that related to the social concerns of that time or previous times. He concluded that judges should utilize these techniques in such a way as to reveal their awareness of the burning issues of their age. The manner of utilization for Pound was virtually formulaic, consisting primarily of classifying litigations into various categories depending upon the "generalized claims" each exhibited and promoting certainty, flexibility, or some other social value in accordance with the classification. Adjudication under Pound's scheme was systematic, depersonalized, formal, and constrained. Judges were primarily social and professional beings.

115

FROM SOCIOLOGICAL JURISPRUDENCE TO REALISM

At nearly the same moment that Pound announced his synthesis, a variety of legal scholars, lawyers, and judges began writing articles asserting that because judges were primarily individuals, the process of adjudication was impressionistic, idiosyncratic, informal, and intuitive. Within less than ten years after the appearance of Pound's 1923 *Harvard Law Review* article, an alternative theory of judicial decision-making had emerged which severely criticized Pound's basic assumptions and whose underlying set of values represented a divergence from that of the Progressives. Nonetheless the exponents of that theory, who came to call themselves Realists, hailed Pound as one of their mentors and claimed Bingham as one of their number.[63]

A stimulus to the emergence of Realism was the changed face of Progressivism in the 1920's. The movement did not, as historians once thought, disappear in that decade.[64] The federal administrative apparatus Progressivism had erected, including the Federal Trade Commission and the Federal Reserve Board, remained intact; states continued to pass welfare legislation; the most popular political figure of the time, Herbert Hoover, called himself a Progressive and promoted the respected Progressive values of efficiency, honesty, morality, and social engineering.[65] But the sense of optimism and cheerfulness about the eventual destiny of man that had pervaded America prior to World War I had vanished with that experience. Progressivism rested, finally, on the concept of progress, a composite of the inherent perfectibility of man and the permanently dynamic quality of society. The First World War made progress a hollow belief.

Morality too, in its old-fashioned form, seemed vanished with the war. A reexamination of traditional standards of morality had been

---

63. *See* Purcell, *American Jurisprudence between the Wars,* 75 AM. HIST. REV. 424, 425 (1969).

64. *See* Link, *What Happened to the Progressive Movement in the Twenties?,* 64 AM. HIST. REV. 833 (1959); Tindall, *Business Progressivism: Southern Politics in the 1920's,* 62 SO. ATL. Q. 92 (1963).

65. *See generally* R. WILBUR & A. HYDE, THE HOOVER POLICIES (1937).

stimulated by Progressivism itself; as its adherents became more impressed with the notion of social change and the impermanence of ideas and institutions, they came to question the inviolability of their own moral principles.[66] Divorce rates rose sharply in the early twentieth century; traditional definitions of sex roles were challenged.[67] The war, with its images of holocaust and meaningless death and its mood of social instability, accelerated this process. Earnestness, a favorite state of the prewar years, was replaced by cynicism; social responsibility gave way to alienation, virtuousness appeared as hypocrisy.[68]

In keeping with this shift in attitudes was a growing interest in the behavioral sciences, with their emphasis on sexuality and their relativistic view of human nature and morality. In the nineteenth century academic interest had centered on the natural and physical sciences. In the early years of the twentieth century the focus shifted to the so-called "social sciences": statistics, ethnology, economics, sociology. When pre-war Progressives spoke of a "scientific" approach to social problems, they normally analogized to one of the social sciences; Pound's social engineering was a variant on the same theme. But after World War I, the term "science" increasingly included the behavioral sciences, notably psychology and cultural anthropology. The primary impact of the behavioral sciences was their suggestion that the personalities of humans and even nations or cultures could be studied empirically. Once the human psyche had been explained, enthusiasts felt, its impact on the institutions and artifacts of society could be better understood.

In studying social phenomena, behavioral scientists utilized techniques first developed to analyze the personalities of individuals. When they applied their techniques to the social arena,

---

66. *See generally* H. MAY, THE END OF AMERICAN INNOCENCE (1959).

67. W. O'NEILL, DIVORCE IN THE PROGRESSIVE ERA (1967); W. O'NEILL, EVERYONE WAS BRAVE (1969).

68. *See generally* M. COWLEY, EXILE'S RETURN (1934); W. LEUCHTENBERG, THE PERILS OF PROSPERITY, 1914-32 (1958).

they stressed the observation that society was a collection of individual human beings, each in some sense unique, whose interactions were motivated by their personal needs and drives. The best indication of the future direction of the various agencies of the American government, for example, was a "scientific" understanding of the psychic structure of the individuals involved in the daily operations of those agencies and the nature of their interpersonal relationships.[69] The sub-discipline of institutional analysis, a field which increasingly attracted political scientists and economists in the 1920's, focused its attention on the manner in which social institutions functioned. In the numerous daily operations of private and public enterprises, institutional analysts felt, lay the data necessary for a fruitful understanding of modern society.

The thrust of behavioral science research was that human behavior was idiosyncratic and often irrational and that external sanctions on personal actions were actually products of an individual's own psyche. This insight was subversive of collective behavior standards based on external phenomena, such as religious or moral beliefs. All these beliefs were indistinguishable from one's superego, and their permanency was questionable. This appeared to suggest that collective moral values, on which the Progressives had placed such faith, were ephemeral and perhaps even nonexistent.

In the early 1920's legal scholars began to apply the insights of behavioral science to their own profession. Some, notably Underhill Moore and the economist-turned-lawyer Walton Hamilton, were primarily concerned with investigating the entire gamut of legal institutions from a new perspective. Moore announced in 1923 that legal institutions were "complex aggregate[s] of many specific group habits." [70] "Each of the specific group habits," he noted, was in turn "an aggregate of the individual habits of the members of

---

69. *See, e.g.*, J. DEWEY, HUMAN NATURE AND CONDUCT (1922); W. McDOUGALL, PSYCHIATRY (1923).

70. Moore, *Rational Basis of Legal Institutions*, 23 COLUM. L. REV. 609, 613 (1923).

the group." [71] The study of legal institutions should begin "with the motivation of habit formation, stabilization, modification, and obliteration, with the 'drives,' whether instinctive or otherwise, which motivate one to behave habitually, and the impulses which push in another direction." [72] Here Moore felt the insights of psychologists would be useful.[73]

Most legal scholars, however, applied the teachings of behavioral science more strictly. To their eyes psychology opened up a new dimension of insight into the process of judicial decision-making. Judges were human beings, and human beings performed their social roles in accordance with their own needs and drives, then found reasons to justify (the psychologists said "rationalize") their conduct. In 1922 Charles Grove Haines catalogued a variety of personal, political, and economic influences, including psychic traits, social background, and familial ties and values, which affected judges' decisions.[74] Three years later Max Radin pointed out that judges were capable, like other human beings, of manipulating evidence and rationalizing their personal value judgments.[75] In the process of statutory interpretation, he maintained, judges took advantage of the fact that statutes were general statements which could "be extended pretty widely and contracted pretty narrowly." [76] "If you are a little clever," Radin noted, the statute "will catch or let out the situation you are deciding." [77]

As the twenties waned, interest in the psychological aspects of the judicial process intensified. In 1927 Herman Oliphant of Columbia Law School, in his presidential address before the

---

71. *Id.*

72. *Id.*

73. *Id.*

74. Haines, *General Observations on the Effects of Personal, Political, and Economic Influences in the Decisions of Judges*, 17 ILL. L. REV. 96, 116 (1922).

75. Radin, *The Theory of Judicial Decision: Or How Judges Think*, 11 A.B.A.J. 357 (1925).

76. *Id.* at 361.

77. *Id.*

Association of American Law Schools, contended that in resolving cases judges made intuitive choices both with regard to results and to the manner in which they were reached.[78] Oliphant accepted the inevitability of judicial choice, but asked that it be made more conscious and methodical through a "complete and constant self-consciousness as to methods of thought and procedure." [79] A year later Hessel Yntema asserted that the judicial process was "an emotive experience in which principles and logic play a secondary part." [80] He urged commentators to "probe the purposes and prejudices implicit in the judge's reaction to the concrete case." [81] And in 1929 the observations of Yntema and the others received strong support from an unexpected source. Federal District Judge Joseph Hutcheson confessed that his decisions were impressionistic and subjective.[82] Even when precedents, rules, or customs made the decision a clear one, Judge Hutcheson admitted to deciding cases "more or less offhand and by rule of thumb." [83] And "when the case is difficult or involved," he maintained, "I . . . give my imagination play, and brooding over the cause, wait for the feeling, the hunch — that intuitive flash of understanding which makes the jump-spark connection between question and decision." [84] Assuming that "the intuitional faculty" was "essential . . . to great judging," Hutcheson called for increased attention in law schools to "those processes of the mind by which . . . decisions are reached." [85]

The same year Judge Hutcheson's views appeared the stock market crashed and the Great Depression began. Symbolically, the

---

78. Oliphant, *A Return to Stare Decisis* (pts. 1 & 2), 14 A.B.A.J. 71, 159 (1928).
79. *Id.* at 161.
80. Yntema, *The Hornbook Method and the Conflict of Laws,* 37 YALE L.J. 468, 480 (1928).
81. *Id.* at 481.
82. Hutcheson, *The Judgment Intuitive: The Function of the "Hunch" in Judicial Decision,* 14 CORNELL L.Q. 274 (1929).
83. *Id.* at 278.
84. *Id.*
85. *Id.* at 288.

two events marked another repudiation of some stock assumptions about American culture on which Progressivism had been nurtured. Even though Americans had not known a major depression in the century, prosperity was not permanent after all. Nor was the capitalist system, which could seemingly thrive whether regulated or not,[86] omnipotent. Nor was man necessarily capable of mastering his economic environment: in this instance, incompetent use of the system of securities speculation had directly contributed to the crash, and no expert had perceived the extent of that folly. Nor was the future necessarily an improvement upon the past. If the Great War had not taught that lesson, the aftermath of the crash surely did. One by one the truths of early twentieth-century America were exposed as myths. The gap between illusion and reality seemed ever-widening.

The year 1930 marked the full scale emergence of a new theory of American jurisprudence which contained within it an alternative to Pound's view of adjudication. That year witnessed a selective gathering of strands from Sociological Jurisprudence and the behavioral sciences into a loose theoretical patchwork termed "the realist movement," "realist jurisprudence," or, most commonly, Realism. The principal collectors, Karl Llewellyn and Jerome Frank, may be considered the primary exponents of Realism not because their views were most representative of the movement (most of the individuals who considered themselves Realists were disinclined to allow their colleagues' views to represent their own), but because they were the most anxious of their peers to see themselves as members of a jurisprudential "school," to attempt to state its canons, and to criticize other schools. Consequently, of all the Realists, Llewellyn's and Frank's views received the most attention within the legal community; critics of Realism continually assumed that these two men were its leading exponents and often

---

86. Gabriel Kolko has argued in THE TRIUMPH OF CONSERVATISM (1963) and RAILROADS AND REGULATION, 1877-1916 (1965) that the regulation of industry initiated under Progressivism was sponsored by the regulatees and increased their profits.

121

based their attacks on the movement exclusively on a reading of their work.

Llewellyn's celebrated article "A Realistic Jurisprudence — The Next Step," [87] was the first self-conscious statement of Realism. Llewellyn's jurisprudential point of reference was what he labeled, in his distinctive shorthand, a "behavior-content" approach. This method attempted to apply the findings of behavioral scientists to areas first identified by the sociological jurists. Llewellyn urged, for example, that "careful study of the instrumentalism, the pragmatic and socio-psychological decision elements" in adjudication be combined with "careful study of [its] effects on the society concerned." [88]

In particular, Llewellyn combined a sense of the sterility and artificiality of legal rules with a belief in the importance of manipulation and rationalization in governmental decision-making. He formulated a distinction between "real" rules and "paper" rules, the former being convenient shorthand symbols for the practices of the courts, the latter "the accepted doctrine of the time and place — what the books there say 'the law' is." [89] Building on this distinction, Llewellyn advocated an exposure of paper rules for what they were: tacit communications between governmental officials telling each other whether to follow or deviate from published institutional dogma. The communication took place, Llewellyn maintained, in "the handling of official formulae." [90] To understand the extent to which rules purportedly followed by courts were real or paper, one sought "the real practice on the subject, by study of how the cases do in fact eventuate." [91] Llewellyn suggested that "the point of reference for all things legal" be "consciously shifted to the areas of contact, of interaction, between official regulatory behavior and the behavior

---

87. Llewellyn, *A Realistic Jurisprudence — The Next Step*, 30 COLUM. L. REV. 431 (1930).
88. *Id.* at 447 n.12.
89. *Id.* at 447-48.
90. *Id.* at 451.
91. *Id.* at 450.

of those affecting or affected by [it]" and away from "the rules and precepts and principles which have hitherto tended to keep the limelight." He styled this suggestion "a sophisticated reversion to a sophisticated realism." [92]

Llewellyn, with his interest in the interactions of public officials with their constituencies, echoed the institutional analysts; Jerome Frank's version of Realism emphasized judicial psychoanalysis. Frank's *Law and the Modern Mind*[93] appeared, much to Frank's consternation, slightly later in 1930 than Llewellyn's article, but its impact was equally striking. After paralleling Llewellyn in cataloguing the recent exposure of the impermanency, flexibility, artificiality, and uncertainty of legal rules and principles,[94] Frank turned to his main theme: the personality of the judge was the pivotal factor in legal administration and consequently "law may vary with the personality of the judge who happens to pass upon any given case." [95]

For Frank a number of things followed from this proposition. First, the process of judging, according to psychologists, began with tentatively formed conclusions, not with premises from which conclusions were subsequently worked out.[96] "[R]espectable and traditional descriptions of the judicial ... process" had failed to admit this.[97] Second, the idiosyncratic biases of the judge were the most important determinants in explaining judicial decision-making. These biases manifested themselves not only in the manner by which judges rationalized their results but more significantly in the way they interpreted the "facts" of a case. In hearing evidence, Frank argued, the judge's sympathies and antipathies were likely to be active. "His own past may have created plus or minus reactions to women, or blonde women, or men with beards, or Southerners, or Italians, or Englishmen.... Those memories ... may affect the judge's initial hearing of, or

---

92. *Id.* at 449.
93. J. FRANK, LAW AND THE MODERN MIND (1930).
94. J. FRANK, *supra* note 93, at 3-75.
95. *Id.* at 111.
96. *Id.* at 100.
97. *Id.* at 101.

subsequent recollection of, what the witness said, or the weight of credibility which the judge will attach to the witness's testimony." [98] Third, variations in the law brought about by personality differences among judges were concealed by "verbal contrivances ... which conceal judicial disharmony." [99] Foremost among these were legal principles which enabled judges "to give formal justifications — rationalizations — of the conclusions at which they otherwise arrive" and consequently served as devices for concealing rather than disclosing what the law was. [100] Fourth, the continual use of these contrivances apparently persuaded many judges "that the announced rules are the paramount thing in the law" and "that uniformity and certainty are of major importance and are to be procured by uniformity and certainty in the phrasing of rules." [101]

Once these truths were revealed, Frank maintained, a more scientific view of law could emerge. If judges accepted the fact that they were inevitably biased in their interpretation of facts and the law which governed those facts, they might well concentrate on improving the manner in which they obtained evidence and "come to grips with the human nature operative in themselves." [102] Frank proposed three exercises for judges: employing experts to aid them in the fact-finding process; training themselves "in the best available methods of psychology" in order to "become keenly aware of [their] own prejudices, biases, antipathies, and the like"; [103] and abandoning "the phantasy of a perfect, consistent, legal uniformity," for a "clear, sane, progressive ... legal skepticism." [104]

With the publication of Frank's and Llewellyn's contributions, the relationship between Sociological Jurisprudence and Realism became clearer. Pound, Llewellyn, and Frank shared a belief that

---

98. *Id.* at 106.
99. *Id.* at 111.
100. *Id.* at 130.
101. *Id.* at 154.
102. *Id.* at 147.
103. *Id.* at 147.
104. *Id.* at 147. Frank reiterated many of these notions a year later in an article entitled *Are Judges Human?* 80 U. PA. L. REV. 17 (1931).

the process of judicial decision-making could be improved by an abandonment of artificial logical concepts and an increased use of empirical data gleaned from "scientific" studies of contemporary social phenomena. They also tended, on a larger scale, to link expertise, "science," and progress, and to argue that contemporary jurisprudence should recognize the tendency of civilizations to define and aspire after social purposes and ends. They believed in social engineering and argued, as Llewellyn put it, "that the trend of the most fruitful thinking about law has run steadily toward regarding law as an engine." [105] They called for research into the actual operations and practices of governmental institutions to determine how ideas and concepts were modified by their social context.

These common values were overshadowed, however, by the sharp differences between Pound and the principal Realists on two issues: the worth of legal rules and the place of moral values in the law. The differences were first aired in criticisms of Pound by Llewellyn and Frank in 1930. Llewellyn's was the milder. He called Pound "a man partially caught in the traditional precept-thinking of an age that is passing." [106] Pound's "pioneering thoughts," Llewellyn maintained, had not been "integrated," since " 'sociological jurisprudence' remains bare of most that is significant in sociology." [107] Llewellyn also implicitly criticized Pound when he ridiculed discussions of law that made the Progressive assumption that there was "*a* 'society' " and were able to discover "social objectives." "Where is the unity," he asked, "the single coherent group?" [108]

Frank's 1930 attack on Pound was more personalized and intense. Pound's theory of judicial decision-making, Frank argued, was based on an artificial separation of "property cases" from "human conduct" cases. This separation was unreal, first, because property and commercial transactions were often unique; second, because Pound assumed that abstractions were independent

---

105. Llewellyn, *supra* note 87, at 464.
106. *Id.* at 434.
107. *Id.* at 435 n.3.
108. *Id.* at 461.

125

entities, having an objective existence apart from the persons affected, an assumption psychologists had shown to be erroneous; and third, because Pound too sharply differentiated between one department of law which required the application of abstract rules and another department which called for the just and painstaking study of the novel facts of the particular case.[109] "Every case," Frank felt, "presents the question of the extent to which the judge should adhere to settled precedents as against flexible modification of the precedents." [110] In sum, Frank maintained that Pound, who had exposed the evil consequences of the theory of mechanical jurisprudence, nevertheless tried to justify it in an extensive portion of lawmaking.[111] He was "aware of the judicial realities, yet reluctant to relinquish entirely the age-old legal myths." [112]

Pound chose the March, 1931 *Harvard Law Review* testament to Holmes for his counterattack on Realism. The setting was meaningful for Pound: he was among the notables of the legal profession solicited by the *Review* to pay tribute to Holmes on his ninetieth birthday. Chief Justice Charles Evans Hughes, Judge Benjamin Cardozo, Holmes' ancient friend and longtime correspondent Sir Frederick Pollock, and the noted legal historian Theodore F. T. Plucknett made commemorative remarks; sandwiched in between their tributes was Pound's *The Call for a Realist Jurisprudence.*

Added to Pound's protest was the appearance of a sweeping criticism of Frank's *Law and the Modern Mind* by Mortimer Adler in January, 1931.[113] Adler had maintained that Frank and his associates, including Oliphant, Yntema, and Bingham, were "blindly convinced" that science was "strictly empirical and in close contact with reality." [114] In applying to the study of law "the latest claims of this or that group of psychologists, sociologists and anthropologists," Adler wrote, Frank and his fellow Realists had

---

109. J. FRANK, *supra* note 93, at 207-13.
110. *Id.* at 213.
111. *Id.* at 213-16.
112. *Id.* at 215.
113. Adler, *Legal Certainty,* 31 COLUM. L. REV. 91 (1931).
114. *Id.* at 92.

made an "illicit conversion of what are merely theories and questionable empirical findings into hard realities and indisputable facts." [115] Further, Frank exhibited for Adler an "utter failure to understand the character of formal logic," an indictment which had serious consequences.[116] Adler argued that there was certainty and probability in the law — in "the demonstration of rules," if not in the prediction of decisions.[117] This was the insight about the law which Pound, Cardozo, and others had made, if not analyzed; Frank had "made no attempt to understand this insight, [but] everywhere dismissed it." [118] In sum, Frank and the other Realists had demonstrated a "philosophical incompetence and naivete." [119]

Pound echoed Adler's observations in his 1931 critique of the Realists.[120] His major differences with Realism, he stated, involved the place of judicial psychoanalysis as an evaluation tool for the jurist, the function of rules in adjudication, and the part played by ideals and values in the legal process. In elaborating on the first two of these differences he used language similar to that of Adler. The "psychological neo-realism of the moment," he wrote, was not "wholly emancipated from the ... dogmatism with which it reproache[d] older types of juristic thought." [121] Moreover, it was "dogmatic and unreal to be blind to the extent to which the administration of justice attains certainty through rule and form...." [122] In stating his third point of contention with the Realists, by contrast, Pound utilized his own distinctive terminology. "Received ideals," he maintained, "... are actual and everyday phenomena of the legal order. The question at bottom is whether a faithful representation of realities shall paint them in the foreground or instead shall put in the foreground the subjective features in the behavior of particular judges." [123]

---

115. *Id.*
116. *Id.* at 100.
117. *Id.* at 101.
118. *Id.* at 102.
119. *Id.* at 107.
120. Pound, *The Call for a Realist Jurisprudence,* 44 HARV. L. REV. 697 (1931).
121. *Id.* at 706.
122. *Id.* at 707.
123. *Id.* at 699.

To state the question in this fashion was, for Pound, to answer it. "One of the conspicuous actualities of the legal order," he maintained, was the impossibility of divorcing what lawmakers did from what they ought to do or what they felt they ought to do.[124] "Valuings of traditional ideals with respect to the actualities of the social and legal order," Pound felt, were "as much in touch with reality ... as psychological theories of the behavior of particular judges in particular cases." [125] In conclusion, Pound called for the incorporation of "a theory of ... the ends of the legal order" and "a theory of values," [126] into "a program of relativist-realist jurisprudence." [127]

The final clarification of the differences between Pound and his fellow sociological jurists [128] and the Realists came in Llewellyn's June 1931 response to Pound, *Some Realism about Realism.*[129] Llewellyn, with Frank's aid,[130] identified some twenty Realists,[131] catalogued their writings to show that Pound's characterizations of Realism were inaccurate or distortive,[132] and described nine common points of departure that Realists shared.[133] Four of these points are of interest for the light they shed on the relationship between Sociological Jurisprudence and Realism. The Realists shared, Llewellyn maintained, a conception of law in flux and of

---

124. *Id.* at 700.

125. *Id.*

126. *Id.* at 711.

127. *Id.* at 710.

128. Pound's best-known supporter was John Dickinson, who criticized the Realists in two 1931 articles, *Legal Rules: Their Function in the Process of Decision* and *Legal Rules: Their Application and Elaboration,* 79 U. Pa. L. Rev. 833 and 1052, respectively (1931). Llewellyn also included Felix Frankfurter as a sociological jurist rather than a Realist.

129. Llewellyn, *Some Realism about Realism — Responding to Dean Pound,* 44 Harv. L. Rev. 1222 (1931).

130. "Jerome Frank," Llewellyn wrote, "refused me permission to sign his name as joint author to this paper, on the ground that it was my fist which pushed the pen. But his generosity does not alter the fact that the paper could not have been written without his help." *Id.* at 1222, n.∗.

131. *Id.* at 1226-28, n.18.

132. *Id.* at 1226-33.

133. *Id.* at 1235-38.

judicial creation of law; a conception of society in flux, and "in flux typically faster than the law, so that the probability is always given that any portion of law needs reexamination to determine how far it fits the society it purports to serve"; the "*temporary* divorce of Is and Ought for purposes of study," so that the observation of social phenomena was "uncontaminated by the desires of the observer or by what he wishes might be or things ought (ethically) to be"; and a distrust of the theory that "traditional prescriptive rule-formulations are *the* heavily operative factor in producing court decisions." [134]

Llewellyn's language was more qualified in the 1931 article than it had been a year earlier. He backed away, for example, from saying that traditional legal rules had no meaning in the decision of any case.[135] In addition, he placed strong emphasis on the "evaluation of any part of law in terms of the effects," which to him meant studies of the working of legislatures and administrative agencies as well as courts.[136] But, by and large, the debate between Pound and the sociological jurists and Llewellyn and the Realists focused on judicial decision-making, and by 1931 centered on what could then be seen as two issues: the place of morals or ethics in the law and the identification of the factor (traditional legal rules or the rationalizations of the judge) most crucial in the creation of a judicial decision.

If these differences between the sociological jurists and the Realists are placed alongside elements they shared in common, such as beliefs in a continually fluctuating social order and the inextricable relationship between the changing values of that order and legal development, one can see how Realism evolved out of and yet threatened Progressivism. Early twentieth-century Sociological Jurisprudence could just as easily have been termed Progressive Jurisprudence. Its philosophical premises — the inevitability of change, ultimate confidence in the ability of governmental mechanisms to respond to change, a desire to

---

134. *Id.* at 1236-37.
135. *Id.* at 1237.
136. *Id.*

maintain certain traditional values in the face of change, a belief in the violability of common social ends and shared moral values, and a faith that moral and ethical "rights" could be perceived and distinguished from "wrongs" — were those of Progressivism at large. Realism affirmed some of these premises and discarded others, notably the inherent worth of traditional values and the tendency toward moral or ethical absolutism.

In repudiating the assumption of the Progressives that American society was founded on a set of fundamental common values and traditions, the Realists were positing a different relationship between governing authorities and the persons they governed. A major Progressive justification for the re-entrance of elites into public life was the belief that members of those elite groups either shared overriding moral concerns with the public or could, through "the white light of public opinion," be forced to share them. Elites derived their authority from a reciprocal relationship with the public, not merely from their expertise or positions of power.[137] The Realists, notably in their observations on the judiciary but also in their evaluation of the other governing branches, redefined the authority-populace relationship. They dismissed the popular check on authority as a sham and focused on the ways in which persons in authority performed the functions of their office through manipulation or rationalization. They undertook this redefinition not because they wanted to replace government by elites with some alternative form, but because they saw the popular shibboleths employed by judges and other authority figures to justify their decisions as superfluous euphemisms that only concealed the decision-making process. By stripping these artificial coverings from the engines of society, the Realists reasoned, their internal parts would be revealed and perhaps put in better working order. The Realists' scrutinies of public officials were undertaken not in order to make them less responsive to "special interests" but to enable them to understand themselves and the manner in which their offices functioned in order that they could perform more "scientifically."

---

137. *See* White, *supra* note 39, and sources cited therein.

The same assumptions made by the Realists were made by the framers of the New Deal. The New Dealers were also demythologizers. They set out to eradicate the notions that private property was sacred and that self-help was the only way to deal with adversity. They announced that traditional bogeys such as the belief that government distribution of economic benefits was equivalent to socialism were shams: the only thing the nation's citizens had to fear was fear itself. They preferred experimentation and empiricism to theorizing: it was not as important to articulate any philosophy of problem-solving as it was to try to solve problems. Despite their interest in improving the economic position of lower-income families, they were less interested in representative government than the Progressives. They preferred government experimentation conceived and executed by elites, with the primary governing institutions being administrative agencies, whose staffing and activities were not subject to a popular check.[138]

The world of the Realists and the New Dealers was one in which the traditional values had been at least temporarily abandoned in favor of concentration on the "realities" of politics and government — shifting alliances, power trade-offs, the processes of administration, the selling of legislative programs. To the New Dealers and those Realists who called for ongoing investigations of the way governing institutions functioned, this focus was merely a recognition of psychological truth. But to former Progressives, this apparent unconcern for fundamental moral principles was outrageous. Their shock manifested itself in increased criticism of the New Deal.[139] Progressive opponents of the New Deal attacked it in four respects: its unsound fiscal policies, with their emphasis on deficit spending; its delegation of excessive, unchecked power to the Executive branch of

---

138. *See* H. ICKES, THE NEW DEMOCRACY (1934); R. TUGWELL, THE BATTLE FOR DEMOCRACY (1935). *See also* P. CONKIN, THE NEW DEAL (1969).

139. For a general account of Progressive criticism of the New Deal, *see* O. GRAHAM, AN ENCORE FOR REFORM (1967).

government; its disregard for the concept of a collective national consensus based on moral principles in favor of one based on the accommodation of competing interest groups; and its subversion of traditional American individualism brought about by rewarding collective organizations, such as labor unions.[140]

Each of these attacks stemmed from a belief that longstanding patterns of social and political behavior in America were a source of stability and a repository of confidence. There were certain things one could take for granted about American society: that it promoted individual initiative, that it rewarded thrift, that it was based on discernible notions of morality, and that it would not tolerate too much power in its leaders. These had apparently been characteristics of the American nation since its inception. The New Dealers seemed to regard them as simply part of some accumulated national folklore that had little to do with the business of government.[141]

Ultimately, the conflict between the Progressives and the New Dealers, like that between the Sociological Jurisprudes and the Realists, came down to one between a relativistic or absolutist approach to morals. Just as the Realists had denied the existence of any law beyond the individualistic decisions of judges, so the New Dealers denied the existence of a moral role for governing officials except in a transparently symbolic capacity. Later in the 1930's, as the Axis powers came to pose a threat to America that had distinct moral overtones, the position of the Realists became a source of acute embarrassment; and leading Realist spokesmen were forced to say that they had believed in natural law all along.[142] The transformation of the New Dealers from pragmatists to moralistic patriots was less painful, especially since concentrated executive power was useful in wartime and the war effort stimulated the nation's economy.

---

140. *Id.* at 24-43.

141. *Cf.* T. ARNOLD, THE FOLKLORE OF CAPITALISM (1937).

142. *E.g.,* J. FRANK, LAW AND THE MODERN MIND (1949 ed.); Llewellyn, *On Reading and Using the Newer Jurisprudence,* 40 COLUM. L. REV. 581 (1940).

Some Observations on Jurisprudence and Social Change

It has been a thesis of this Article that the interaction of events with ideas produces certain dominant ideologies in American society at points in time. Developments in jurisprudence, like those in politics, art, literature, the sciences, and academic disciplines, reflect the presence of those ideologies. Although the subject matter of jurisprudence differs from that of art or history, its concerns at a point in time are similar. This is not to say that every jurisprudential writer, any more than every artist or historian, shares or even perceives the dominant ideology of his time. Nor is it to say that the presence of that ideology can be adequately explained: one may not adequately understand how "earnest" comes to be an approved state of mind for one generation and "hard-boiled" a state of mind for another,[143] but one can perceive the transformation taking place.

If this theory has any validity, it should hold not only for the Sociological Jurisprudes and the Realists but for other jurisprudential schools. Without the benefit of detailed observation, I believe that at least two other jurisprudential movements of the twentieth century can be analyzed in a similar fashion. The first is the group of essays by legal scholars appearing in the 1950s which suggested that judicial opinions should aspire to state, through elaborately reasoned analysis, the conflicting social values at stake in a case and decide the case in accordance with legal principles of general applicability which themselves represented an accommodation of values.[144] This jurisprudential theory appears to parallel a pluralistic, consensus-oriented view of American society advanced by political scientists and historians at the same time [145] and motivated, perhaps, by the interaction of the

---

143. On the "hard-boiled" mood of the 1930s, see D. WECTER, THE AGE OF THE GREAT DEPRESSION 251 (1948).

144. *E.g.*, Bickel and Wellington, *Legislative Purpose and the Judicial Process: The* Lincoln Mills *Case,* 71 HARV. L. REV. 1 (1957); Hart, *The Time Chart of the Justices,* 73 HARV. L. REV. 84 (1959); Wechsler, *Toward Neutral Principles of Constitutional Law,* 73 HARV. L. REV. 1 (1959).

145. As evidenced in R. DAHL, WHO GOVERNS? (1961); and L. HARTZ, THE LIBERAL TRADITION (1955).

New Deal interest-group model of politics with the pressures for national solidarity brought about by the Cold War.

A second example is the current concern for minority rights in a majoritarian society, especially when those rights can be identified with fundamental Constitutional guaranties. Some examples of this concern are the critiques of consensus history and pluralistic political science advanced by recent scholars; [146] and the discovery that governmental processes designed to accommodate competing interests may deprive unrecognized minorities, such as consumers, from any viable participation in decisions affecting them.[147] A recent article criticizing the jurisprudential bias of the Nixon administration has articulated the concern in this fashion: "The constitutional theory on which our government rests is not a simple majoritarian theory. The Constitution, and particularly the Bill of Rights, is designed to protect individual citizens and groups against certain decisions that a majority of citizens might want to make, even when that majority acts in what it takes to be the general or common interest." [148] It may be that yet another jurisprudential school will evolve which takes its point of departure from statements of this kind. This school might affirm the courts' active participation to resolve the grievances of minorities, even though a majority of the nation's citizens are indifferent or unsympathetic to those grievances. Under such a formulation a traditional role of courts as places where a discontented citizen can have his complaint heard is revived at the expense of a conception of courts as enforcers of consensual beliefs.

If developments in jurisprudence can be seen as components of ideological responses to social change, perhaps the discipline can be liberated from its recurrent fixations with such problems as the nature of law and the superiority of positivism to natural law and vice versa. This analysis would suggest that there are different

---

146. *E.g.,* P. BACHRACH, THE THEORY OF DEMOCRATIC ELITISM (1967); TOWARDS A NEW PAST (B. BERNSTEIN ed. 1968).

147. *See* L. KOHLMEIER, THE REGULATORS (1969).

148. Dworkin, *The Jurisprudence of Richard Nixon,* 17 NEW YORK REVIEW OF BOOKS 27 (1972).

conceptions and philosophies of law that meet changing social needs at various points in time and that it is more fruitful to examine how those conceptions and philosophies have evolved and what contemporary functions they serve than to assess their ultimate soundness.

THE EVOLUTION OF REASONED ELABORATION: JURISPRUDENTIAL CRITICISM AND SOCIAL CHANGE

Virginia Law Review, Volume 59, No. 2 (1973)

The development of American jurisprudential criticism over the past forty years often suggests that critical schools arise in response to, and depend for their vitality on, perceived social needs whose fulfillment is felt by a group of legal scholars to be central to the nation's future. This is not to say that academic criticism of the judiciary is essentially result-oriented and still less that it is oriented to justify particular outcomes in particular pieces of litigation. But the moral sensibility of scholars is necessarily molded by their social experience, and critical intelligence is in the end an arm of moral sensibility.

This Article represents a further exploration of a thesis advanced in an essay which appeared recently in this journal.[1] That essay suggested that jurisprudential contributions, like those of other academic disciplines, reflect the social needs and ideological concerns of various points in time, and analyzed the relationship between Sociological Jurisprudence and Realism against the backdrop of social changes in America in the first three decades of the twentieth century. This Article considers the relationship between jurisprudential criticism and social change from the 1930's to the present.

The Article traces the history of Reasoned Elaboration,[2] a mode of Supreme Court criticism. The view of the Article is that Reasoned Elaboration emerged in the late 1930's and the early 1940's when certain social experiences — particularly the threat of totalitarianism and the circumstances surrounding the Court-packing crisis of 1937 — generated overwhelming academic

---

1. *See* White, *From Sociological Jurisprudence to Realism: Jurisprudence and Social Change in Early Twentieth-Century America.* 58 VA. L. REV. 999 (1972).

2. The phrase was originated by Henry M. Hart and Albert M. Sacks in THE LEGAL PROCESS 161ff (tent. ed. 1958). For a more extended definition see notes 24-26, *infra*, and accompanying text.

hostility to jurisprudential Realism, and that the tenets of Reasoned Elaboration, at first largely methodological and concerned with the manner in which the judges articulated their decisions, inevitably took on substantive content with the explosive loss of social consensus on first principles in the 1960's. The Article concludes by suggesting that Reasoned Elaboration, in its classic form, is ill-suited to the 1970's and by proposing an alternative set of critical guidelines.

FROM REALISM TO REASONED ELABORATION

Realist Jurisprudence, christened and developed by Karl Llewellyn and Jerome Frank in 1930 and 1931 [3] and popularized throughout the 1930's, had three principal components. The first was a relativistic approach to morals and ethics. Some Realists, Llewellyn and Frank among them, were skeptical about the place of moral and ethical "oughts" in the legal process; others, including Walter Wheeler Cook, Underhill Moore, Walter Nelles, Edward Robinson, and Thurman Arnold, eschewed absolute moral values altogether.[4] Changes in laws were often couched in terms of moral ideals, argued Arnold, but these ideals were merely slogans contrived by lawmakers to appeal to the emotions of the public. They were not "principles of truth," but only manifestations of "symbolic thinking and conduct which condition[ed] the behavior of men in groups" [5] and which had no intrinsic substance.

A second component of Realism consisted of what its advocates called an "institutional" approach to decision-making. Drawing on contemporary scholarship in the behavioral sciences, many Realists maintained that the primary locus of lawmaking in America was the daily interaction of government officials (notably

---

3. *See* J. FRANK, LAW AND THE MODERN MIND (1930); Llewellyn, *Some Realism about Realism — Responding to Dean Pound,* 44 HARV. L. REV. 1222 (1931); Llewellyn, *A Realistic Jurisprudence — The Next Step,* 30 COLUM. L. REV. 431 (1930).

4. *See* T. ARNOLD, THE FOLKLORE OF CAPITALISM (1937); E. ROBINSON, LAW AND THE LAWYERS (1935); Cook, *Scientific Method and the Law,* 13 A.B.A.J. 303 (1927); Moore, *Rational Basis of Legal Institutions,* 23 COLUM. L. REV. 609 (1923); Nelles, Book Review, 33 COLUM. L. REV. 763 (1933).

5. T. ARNOLD, THE SYMBOLS OF GOVERNMENT iv (1935).

judges and agency administrators) with the individuals and interests they governed. The idiosyncrasies of judges, the ongoing relationship between regulatory agencies and their regulatees, and the internal operations of governing institutions, these men argued, were far more the stuff of "law" than were abstract legal rules or theories. Consequently they called for empirical studies of the institutions of government in order to determine how the governmental apparatus might be made more responsive to contemporary social needs.[6]

The third notable element of Realism was its repudiation of formalistic, deductive logic in judicial opinions as an artificial construct employed to conceal the subjective preferences of the judge. Legal "rules," "principles," and precedents had no permanent, general applicability; they were merely pseudo-authoritative pegs on which a desired result could be hung. Llewellyn distinguished between the "paper" rules announced in opinions and the "real" rules whose "significance ... appear[ed] only *after* the investigation of the ... behavior" of the actors involved in the decision.[7] Frank read rules out of the judging process altogether: they were means by which judges justified a result they had previously reached on the basis of intuitive "hunches" (a process confirmed for Frank by Judge Joseph Hutcheson, a fellow Realist).[8] The traditional deference of the judicial profession to precedent was for Frank a sham: in his view judges "manipulate[d] the language of former decisions." [9] As a consequence of this manipulative feature of the formal opinion-writing process, the Realists argued, no general principle announced in a case had in reality any broad applicability, for it

6. *See, e.g.,* Frank, *Realism in Jurisprudence,* 7 AM. L. SCHOOL REV. (1934); Hamilton, *The Problem of Anti-Trust Reform,* 32 COLUM. L. REV. 173 (1932); Llewellyn, *A Realistic Jurisprudence — The Next Step, supra* note 3; Moore & Hope, *An Institutional Approach to the Law of Commercial Banking,* 38 YALE L.J. 703 (1929); Yntema, *The Hornbook Method and the Conflict of Laws,* 37 YALE L.J. 468 (1928).

7. Llewellyn, *A Realistic Jurisprudence — The Next Step, supra* note 3, at 444.

8. Hutcheson, *The Judgment Intuitive: The Function of the "Hunch" in Judicial Decision,* 14 CORNELL L.Q. 274 (1929).

9. J. FRANK, *supra* note 3, at 148.

merely justified the impressionistic judgment of one judge. On the same set of facts, another judge might make a different judgment based on a different "principle."

In each of its major facets Realism was a jurisprudence congenial to the America of the early 1930's. In the first years of the Great Depression, Americans found that one of the foundations of their society, the superiority of a loosely regulated capitalist system and its accompanying mythologies (the sanctity of private property, the virtue of self-help) had crumbled, and they had to find some way to rebuild in sounder form. In undertaking this task their environment was one of economic deprivation; their mood, cynicism; their fantasy heroes, hardboiled men of action; their academic tools, the behavioral sciences; their philosophy of government, experimentalist and pragmatic.[10] The demythologizing tendencies of the Realists, their commitment to decision-making by experiment, their preference for empiricism rather than abstraction, even their questioning of moral absolutes, were in harmony with the spirit of the first New Deal. Frank, Felix Cohen, and Arnold were among the Realists who saw a close connection between the goals of their movement and the needs of a depression-ridden society.[11] The relationship between Realism and the political culture of the 1930's was made manifest by President Roosevelt's Court-packing plan of 1937, wherein Realist theories were used by Roosevelt's supporters to expose the biases of justices who voted to strike down New Deal legislation.[12]

But by 1937 certain forces had come to the fore that stimulated the downfall of Realism and the rise of Reasoned Elaboration. These forces may be grouped into two categories, one set

---

10. *See generally* THE AMERICAN WRITER AND THE GREAT DEPRESSION (H. SWADOS ed. 1966); THE GREAT DEPRESSION (D. SHANNON ed. 1960); D. WECTER, THE GREAT DEPRESSION (1949); Purcell, *American Jurisprudence Between the Wars: Legal Realism and the Crisis of Democratic Theory,* 75 AM. HIST. REV. 424 (1969).

11. *See* T. ARNOLD, THE FOLKLORE OF CAPITALISM, THE SYMBOLS OF GOVERNMENT, *supra* notes 4 & 5; Cohen, *The Problem of a Functional Jurisprudence,* 1 MODERN L. REV. 5 (1937); Frank, *supra* note 6.

12. *See, e.g.,* Hart, *An Argument on the President's Side,* HARV. ALUMNI BULL. 767 (1936). *See generally* R. JACKSON, THE STRUGGLE FOR JUDICIAL SUPREMACY (1941).

responding to the presence of totalitarianism and the other cohering around the problem of preserving the professional competence of the Supreme Court. The content of these two central problems changed from the 1930's to the 1940's, but their presence remained constant.

The year 1937 marked the emergence of fullblown attacks on the Realists. By 1945 advocates of Realism had lost their critical momentum and were largely on the defensive. The chief cause of this sudden decline of influence was a perceived relationship between their moral relativism and the rise of amoral totalitarian governments. Frightened by the spectre of Nazi Germany and Fascist Italy, American intellectuals sought a means of distinguishing their culture from that of those regimes. One apparently clear distinction, they found, was the presence in America of pervasive moral ideals, such as liberty and democracy. These ideals were absolutes in that they served to define the nature of American civilization; yet the Realists were asserting the relativistic nature of morals and ethics and championing pragmatism. It was not difficult, pursuing this line of reasoning, to see Realism as an intellectual precursor to totalitarianism. If law, as Llewellyn had maintained, was simply *"[w]hat ... officials do about disputes,"* [13] it could be made synonymous with simple force. This was in fact the credo of the totalitarian regimes: might makes right. By denying any relationships between law and moral principles, Philip Mechem, Edgar Bodenheimer, Roscoe Pound, Lon Fuller, and Rufus Harris argued, Realism was "prepar[ing] the intellectual ground for a tendency toward totalitarianism." [14]

---

13. K. LLEWELLYN, THE BRAMBLE BUSH 12 (1930).

14. E. BODENHEIMER, JURISPRUDENCE 316 (1940); *see* L. FULLER, THE LAW IN QUEST OF ITSELF (1940); R. POUND, CONTEMPORARY JURISTIC THEORY (1940); Harris, *Idealism Emergent in Jurisprudence,* 10 TUL. L. REV. 169 (1936); Mechem, *The Jurisprudence of Despair,* 21 IOWA L. REV. 669 (1936).

In its most extreme form the attack on Realism came close to equating it with treason. Catholic law professors and theologians, of whom the most outspoken was Francis Lucey, maintained that pragmatism, relativism, and behaviorism were subversive doctrines inevitably leading to the ascendancy of an agnostic, absolutist state. "Democracy versus the Absolute State," thundered Lucey as the United States geared to resist the Axis powers, "means Natural Law versus Realism." Lucey, *Natural Law and American Legal Realism: Their Respective Contributions to a Theory of Law in a Democratic Society,* 30 GEO. L.J. 493, 533 (1942).

In the face of this attack, some Realists, including Llewellyn and Frank, sought to modify their early views on the place of moral values in the law. By 1940 Llewellyn was "ready to do open penance" [15] for suggesting that "the heart and core of Jurisprudence" [16] could be determined empirically; it was related to ethical values and purposes.[17] Frank ultimately came to affirm "the fundamental principles of Natural Law" [18] as the basis of modern civilization.

While Realism's potential affinity for totalitarianism was viewed as affirmatively dangerous, another set of concerns was emerging in the legal community to which Realism apparently offered little assistance. The Supreme Court, in invalidating certain New Deal legislative programs, wrote several opinions that gave to the Constitution various interpretations characterized by many commentators as inept or disingenuous.[19] The Court's actions raised the spectre of professional incompetence in its members and in so doing called attention to the small amount of attention given that problem by the Realists. The original thrust of Realism, an attack on prevailing formalistic theories of judicial decision-making, had been negative. Caught up in the excitement of their new insights, the Realists and their followers had not devoted much consideration to the positive guidelines that judges ought to follow in their work. But the Court, with its apparently willful intervention against the New Deal on behalf of private property, had made that question an important one.

---

15. Llewellyn, *On Reading and Using the Newer Jurisprudence,* 40 COLUM. L. REV. 581, 603 (1940).

16. *Id.*

17. *Id.* at 593.

18. J. FRANK, *supra* note 3, at xvii (1939 ed.).

19. *See, e.g.,* Justice Roberts' opinion in United States v. Butler, 297 U.S. 1, 53 (1936). The *Butler* case was handed down January 6, 1936. Between that date and June, 1936, twenty-seven law reviews and bar journals commented on the opinion. The comments varied in length and revealed a panorama of views on the merits of the case and the political and economic implications of the opinion. But not one comment attempted to defend the logic of Mr. Justice Roberts' tenth amendment argument, and most approached the position taken by Charles S. Collier that the argument was "a genuine logical disaster." Collier, *Judicial Bootstraps and the General Welfare Clause,* 4 GEO. WASH. L. REV. 211, 227 (1936).

After the Second World War, the focus of concern with totalitarianism shifted, but a spirit of moral revulsion against antidemocratic regimes remained. The Nurenberg trials dramatized the continued belief of American intellectuals in the moral principles on which their civilization was allegedly based. Having halted the expansion of the inhumane Axis powers and having subjected Nazi leaders to the dictates of "higher law," Americans awoke to the saber-rattling of the Soviet Union, another godless, totalitarian regime. "[T]he foundations of all things are being re-examined," wrote Henry Hart in 1951; it was time to reassert "[t]he moral claims of settled law in a constitutional democracy." [20] "We have begun to ask ourselves," Mark DeWolfe Howe observed in the same year, "whether . . . there are not some standards of decency so fundamental and so permanent they may properly be described as absolute." [21]

The concern over judicial competence had also survived the war. The task of judging had been complicated by the increasingly complex and interdependent character of postwar American society. The major reforms of the New Deal remained intact, leaving a vast regulatory apparatus affecting the lives of thousands of persons; the private sector of the economy appeared poised on the threshold of expansion, and the public sector showed similar signs of growth; previously powerless groups, such as labor unions, had emerged as major social forces. It appeared that effective living in postwar American society was tied to efficient allocation of social and economic resources by managing elites, of which the judiciary was one. Lon Fuller, writing in 1946, called for judicial "formulas and methods that would reconcile conflicting interests and bring a new distribution of power into a pattern of order and justice." [22]

In attempting to modify Realism to respond to these two sets of problems, postwar legal scholars came upon what they regarded as a significant insight. Although the Realists had observed that judges "made" law rather than merely "found" it, they had failed

---

20. Hart, *Holmes' Positivism — An Addendum,* 64 HARV. L. REV. 929, 937 (1951).
21. Howe, *The Positivism of Mr. Justice Holmes,* 64 HARV. L. REV. 529, 545 (1951).
22. Fuller, *Reason and Fiat in Case Law,* 59 HARV. L. REV. 376, 393 (1946).

sufficiently to explore the implications of that observation. In their rush to show that judges were human beings, motivated in their decisions more by their own values than by legal "rules," the Realists had unduly minimized the place of institutional constraints in judicial decision-making. For to speak, as some Realists had, of institutional "personalities" [23] meant not only that the decisions of governing bodies were affected by their personnel; it meant that the decisionmakers were in turn affected by their institutional roles. And this insight, generally true of officeholders, applied most particularly to judges, who were required to make public the justifications for their decisions, thus inviting comment on their performance.

In emphasizing the disingenuous aspects of the use of precedent, rule, and doctrine, the Realists had made too simplistic an appraisal of the function of the rationalization process in judicial opinions. They had failed to grant due respect to the fact that a judge's use of these devices was itself constrained by the expectations of others. A new set of questions about judicial decision-making emerged, revolving around the *reasoning* of opinions. Had the courts adequately articulated reasons for its result? What assumptions lay behind the reasoning process? To what extent did the judge appeal to technical considerations, social policies, philosophical principles, and moral values?

These questions were responsive to the two sets of problems previously discussed. The articulation process was the vehicle through which a judge's professional competence was revealed. A judge who failed to give reasons for his decisions did not meet his obligation to allow the public to evaluate the manner in which he was performing his office. Secondly, articulation of the reasoning process in opinions highlighted the difference between a society, such as America, where law allegedly attempted to conform to public notions of reasonableness and fairness, and totalitarian regimes where law was synonymous with the fiats of officials. To assert, as some Realists had, that "[i]t is not what the judges say

---

23. *See* note 6, *supra* and accompanying text.

which is important but what they do" was to arrive, Henry Hart wrote in 1951, at the "monstrous conclusion that reason and argument, the conscious search for justice, are vain." [24]

THE TENETS OF REASONED ELABORATION

As legal scholars of the 1950's grew increasingly convinced of the importance of judicial rationalization, they came to criticize its contemporary manifestations and to formulate a new set of ideals and standards for judicial decision-making. Reasoned Elaboration, a catch phrase coined by Henry Hart and Albert Sacks in 1958,[25] came to summarize those ideals and standards. The phrase, as applied to the Supreme Court, demanded, first, that judges give reasons for their decisions; second, that the reasons be set forth in a detailed and coherent manner; third, that they exemplify what Hart called "the maturing of collective thought"; [26] and fourth, that the Court adequately demonstrate that its decisions, in the area of constitutional law, were vehicles for the expression of the ultimate social preferences of contemporary society.

Beginning in 1951, the *Harvard Law Review* initiated the practice of inviting legal scholars to write Forewords to its analysis of the Supreme Court's work for the preceding term. These Forewords came to serve as the major forum of Reasoned Elaborationist jurisprudence in the 1950's. Building on the observations and assumptions of their predecessors, the authors of successive Forewords gradually expanded and sharpened the focus of their critique until it came to encompass each of the above demands.

Early Forewords decried the Vinson Court's tendency to dispose of cases without giving any reasons at all. Louis Jaffe, in his Foreword to the 1950 term, argued that the Court had shirked the elementary business of guiding and directing the lower courts and

---

24. Hart, *Holmes' Positivism — An Addendum, supra* note 20, at 933.

25. Hart and Sacks felt that "[t]he gradual spread of the obligation of reasoned decision and elaboration" was "one of the major phenomena of contemporary law." H. Hart & A. Sacks, *supra* note 2, at 170.

26. Hart, *The Supreme Court, 1958 Term — Foreword: The Time Chart of the Justices,* 73 HARV. L. REV. 84, 100 (1959).

the legal profession by denials of certiorari petitions and by the issuance of per curiam opinions even in cases of apparent first importance.[27] Three years after Jaffe's Foreword, Albert Sacks made a similar criticism of the 1953 term. Sacks was apprehensive that the Court's use of per curiam opinions might impede the application of its decisions by lower courts and by the Bar as a whole. He called for criticism that would evoke in the Court a greater awareness of the need to explain its actions.[28]

In an article in the *Harvard Law Review* in 1957, Alexander Bickel and Harry Wellington implored the Court not only to give reasons, but to set forth their reasoning process fully. Bickel and Wellington argued that the Court's opinions had shown an increasing incidence of "the sweeping dogmatic statement, of the formulation of results accompanied by little or no effort to support them in reason, in sum, of opinions that do not opine and of per curiam orders that quite frankly fail to build the bridge between the authorities they cite and the results they decree." [29] A decision that did not attempt to gain reasoned acceptance for the result, asserted the authors, did not make law "in the sense which the term 'law' must have in a democractic society." [30] A necessary prerequisite of opinion-writing, in their view, was rationally articulated grounds of decision.[31]

Henry Hart, in his Foreword to the 1958 term, set forth the third criterion of Reasoned Elaboration, making a marked departure from Realism by assuming that, given adequate time and discussion, the thinking of judges about particular cases, perhaps initially a product of their idiosyncratic presuppositions, could mature into something more synonymous with "reason," a suprapersonal construct.[32] This view freed the judiciary from the

---

27. Jaffe, *Foreword to The Supreme Court, 1950 Term,* 65 HARV. L. REV. 107, 108, 109, 112, 113 (1951).

28. Sacks, *Foreword to The Supreme Court, 1953 Term,* 68 HARV. L. REV. 96, 103 (1954).

29. Bickel & Wellington, *Legislative Purpose and the Judicial Process: The Lincoln Mills Case,* 71 HARV. L. REV. 1, 3 (1957).

30. *Id.* at 5.

31. *Id.* at 6, 35.

32. Hart, *supra* note 26.

Realist prison of inevitable human bias. It assumed that for every judicial problem there was ultimately a "reasonable" solution — reasonable in terms of the value preferences of American society at a particular point in time. This solution could be reached, despite human frailties, if judges would take the time and effort to discuss openly their views of cases, compare them with the views of their colleagues, and articulate as fully as possible the general areas of ultimate concordance.[33]

Hart's formulation drew the ire of Thurman Arnold, who claimed that "there is no such process as [the maturing of collective thought], and there never has been; men of positive views are only hardened in those views by such conferences." [34] But Arnold was bucking the scholarly tide: Erwin Griswold, in commenting on the Hart-Arnold debate, sounded a more representative note. "Judge Arnold's argument wholly fails," [35] Griswold wrote. "[M]any times clearly held views of mine have been radically changed by discussions with associates or colleagues, often people with very different outlooks from mine. . . . To me 'the maturing of collective thought' is a profound reality." [36] Although it was clear that judges did make law, Griswold argued, the process was a "self-effacing" [37] one which required "intellectual detachment and disinterestedness." [38]

This dimension of the reasoning process proved attractive but elusive for scholars as Reasoned Elaboration matured. A case in point was Herbert Wechsler's 1959 Holmes Lectures, where he proposed that constitutional issues be decided in accordance with "neutral principles." [39] Wechsler began by assuming that courts,

---

33. *Id.*

34. Arnold, *Professor Hart's Theology*, 73 HARV. L. REV. 1298, 1312 (1960).

35. Griswold, *The Supreme Court, 1959 Term — Foreword: Of Time and Attitudes — Professor Hart and Judge Arnold*, 74 HARV. L. REV. 81, 85 (1960).

36. *Id.*

37. *Id.* at 94.

38. *Id.*

39. Wechsler, *Toward Neutral Principles of Constitutional Law*, 73 HARV. L. REV. 1 (1959). Some of Wechsler's readers had difficulty understanding the meaning of his "neutral principles." *See* Miller & Howell, *The Myth of Neutrality in Constitutional Adjudication*, 27 U. CHI. L. REV. 661, 671, 694 (1960); Pollak, *Racial*

especially in constitutional law cases, faced issues that involved choice among competing values or needs. Neutrality for Wechsler did not mean that judges should refrain altogether from taking positions on social issues: they were, in fact, fated to condemn or condone the activities of the other branches of government. He did, however, imply that judges were required to support their choices by a "type of reasoned explanation," [40] which involved reaching judgment on analysis and reasons transcending the immediate result. Only decision-making that rested "on grounds of adequate neutrality and generality" [41] was for Wechsler "genuinely principled." [42] The critical point of the decision-making process, for Wechsler, came when a judge sought to relate the case before him to myriad past and future cases presenting potentially similar issues.[43] Generalizing a result in such a manner meant invoking principles of law covering a variety of fact situations. But it meant more than that, because the legal principles themselves represented a society's value choices with regard to the regulation of social conduct. Inevitably, therefore, a judge, in resting his decision on any more than an ad hoc basis, was making a statement about the social values of his age.

In the area of constitutional law, particularly, the close connection between general principles of law and social values could be seen. As a judge reached beyond the facts of the case for a broader rationale on which to decide it, there would come a moment, Wechsler felt, when he should be aware that the case ultimately presented a "conflict in human claims of high dimension" [44] — the conflict in *Brown v. Board of Education*,[45] for example, between equality regardless of color and freedom of association. A "principled" decision, for Wechsler, would be one where this ultimate conflict was perceived, articulated, and

---

Discrimination and Judicial Integrity: A Reply to Professor Wechsler, 108 U. PA. L. REV. 1, 32 (1959); Brown, Book Review, 62 COLUM. L. REV. 386, 387 (1962).

40. Wechsler, *supra* note 39, at 15.
41. *Id.*
42. *Id.*
43. *Id.*
44. *Id.* at 34.
45. 347 U.S. 483 (1954).

resolved in a manner that gave guidance for the subsequent resolution of similar conflicts. Unprincipled decisions, by contrast, were those where this level of the adjudication process was not perceived or not articulated. Neutrality in this context meant that judges should subordinate their personal predelictions to the competing values cases presented.

With the advent of Wechsler's thesis Reasoned Elaboration reached its maturity. Its standards for judicial competence, if followed, met the overriding needs of postwar American jurists, for they presupposed a judiciary involved with the management of a complex contemporary society, mindful of the need to meet high standards of clarity and competence in its rationalization process, and dedicated to the articulation and maintenance of the general moral principles that bound Americans together. In the world of the Reasoned Elaborationists judges neither found law in the old-fashioned sense nor made it in the sense of the Realists; they reasoned toward it and then articulated their reasoning processes.

At its maturity, Reasoned Elaboration appears to have embraced certain policy goals which were to foreshadow its future confrontation with the activist Warren Court in the 1960's. First, it favored institutional conservatism in the judiciary. Since principled decision-making required a full understanding of the competing social values at stake in a case, judicial intervention was premature where those values were dimly perceived or articulated.[46] In the context of the 1950's, institutional conservatism was the equivalent of political conservatism, for in emerging areas of social conflict, such as race relations, the executive and legislative branches of government had largely remained indifferent to change.[47]

Second, the Reasoned Elaborationists, reflecting their academic orientation, emphasized technical and professional expertise in

---

46. Wechsler, for example, concluded that a number of Vinson and Warren Court race relations decisions, including Terry v. Adams, 345 U.S. 461 (1953), Shelly v. Kraemer, 334 U.S. 1 (1948), and, most conspicuously, Brown v. Board of Educ., 347 U.S. 483 (1954), could not be justified on grounds that could be deemed "neutral principles."

47. *See generally* W. MURPHY, CONGRESS AND THE COURT (1962).

opinion-writing. Their model of an enlightened opinion contained qualities associated with professional success among legal scholars: thoroughness, soundness, clarity, and internal consistency. Their interest in craftsmanship reflected their own desire to participate actively in shaping the professional progress of the Court.

Third, and most important, the Reasoned Elaborationists had highly developed and sophisticated views about the proper relationship of the Supreme Court to other governing institutions. They were anxious to preserve the Court's prestige by ensuring that it did not overstep the limits of its function and thereby take itself into areas of decision-making in which it was not equipped to deal, and in which it was sure to clash with other branches of government. The proper way to prevent such quixotic forays was to impress upon the Court's members a sense of the kinds of controversies which were justiciable and which sorts of analytical processes were likely to produce respected opinions. The doctrine of judging by neutral principles spoke to these considerations. It suggested that the Court either make decisions that accorded with broadly held social values or refrain from decision-making.

On the other hand, Reasoned Elaboration was designed to protect American society from the excesses of an unbridled judiciary. By insisting that opinions be justified through a process of articulated reasoning and that the process itself be internally consistent, the movement was attempting to impose an academic check on the judiciary. In the view of the Reasoned Elaborationists, a court's power and influence depended on its reputation for disinterested decision-making. Sustained, impartial academic criticism of the Court's opinions would deter decisions made through excess or by fiat.

In sum, the institutional theories of Reasoned Elaboration attempted to reconcile an elitist judiciary with the egalitarian premises of American society. Since Supreme Court Justices were members of a professional elite, they had an obligation to meet professional standards of competence, as determined by other elite members, notably law professors. Their institutional prestige was partially dependent on their meeting those standards. But since

149

their function was not only academic but political, they had an additional obligation to meet performance expectations derived from their role as policymakers in one of the branches of American government. These expectations rested on the premise that the judiciary was not a representative or democratic institution and should not encroach upon the prerogatives of the popularly elected branches. By staying within the confines of their institutional role and justifying their decisions in terms of standards derived from that role, Justices were being competent professionals and good democrats at the same time.

REASONED ELABORATION AND ACTIVISM: THE DILEMMA OF THE 1960's

The delicate institutional role postulated for the judiciary by Reasoned Elaboration was incompatible with the brand of activism that emerged in the Warren Court. Stimulated by the postwar transformation of racial attitudes, the Warren Court set out on a wholesale reexamination of the discriminatory practices of American institutions. A shifting majority of its members assumed that American citizenship imported transcendental guaranties of fair and equal treatment, and they took it upon themselves to ensure that those guaranties were recognized.

In the process, the meaning of terms such as "due process of law" and "equal protection of the laws" changed. In place of the older judicial technique of undertaking an even-handed weighing, in equal protection cases, of the legitimacy of the state's interest in making a discriminatory classification and the right allegedly invaded by that classification, the Warren Court substituted an approach which elevated certain rights (such as voting) by declaring that they were "too fundamental to be ... burdened or conditioned." [48] It de-emphasized historical and institutional factors that have served to circumscribe them. Other considerations, including precedent and the intent of the framers,

---

48. Harper v. Virginia Bd. of Elections, 383 U.S. 663, 670 (1966).

paled in the face of what Justice Harlan called "current egalitarian notions of how a modern democracy should be organized." [49]

The Warren Court's open espousal of "an ideology of unrestrained egalitarianism" [50] caused great anxiety for devotees of Reasoned Elaboration. At first they admired the Court's vision, but they became increasingly uneasy over the methods of adjudication that accompanied it. The 1960's witnessed a series of attempts by the Reasoned Elaborationists to alleviate this tension. These initially took the form of efforts to square the Warren Court's activities with the Reasoned Elaboration theory of jurisprudence. Later, an increasingly sharp estrangement from the Court began to emerge.

For Alexander Bickel the tension focused upon the notion of principled decision-making. Bickel believed that the Warren Court's enhanced sensitivity to social issues augured the emergence of a variety of legal problems that could not easily be resolved in a principled fashion. He attempted to meet this problem by emphasizing a variety of techniques, such as standing, ripeness, denials of certiorari, and dismissals of appeals, through which the Court could make provisional resolutions of issues without issuing full-blown opinions, pending the formation of some broad social consensus.[51]

To Bickel's dismay, the Warren Court did not use the devices he suggested. On the contrary, he came to feel that the Court, impressed by ideals of furthering progress and doing justice, had too hastily ventured into the areas of school desegregation and reapportionment and had produced a plethora of "unprincipled" opinions.[52] Bickel's concern was shared by Philip Kurland, who as early as 1964 had accused the Court of insisting "that its rulings

---

49. *Id.* at 686 (dissent of Harlan, J.).

50. *Id.*

51. Bickel, *The Supreme Court, 1960 Term — Foreword: The Passive Virtues,* 75 HARV. L. REV. 40 (1961). *See also* McCloskey, *The Supreme Court, 1961 Term — Foreword: The Reapportionment Case,* 76 HARV. L. REV. 54, 66 (1962).

52. A. BICKEL, THE LEAST DANGEROUS BRANCH 70 (1962).

be carried to their dryly logical extremes," [53] and who in 1969 charged that the overriding premises of the Court's opinions in such areas as federalism, reapportionment, and school desegregation were simplistic.[54]

Thus Reasoned Elaborationists moved, through the fifties and sixties, from an original dissatisfaction with the tendency of the Vinson Court toward per curiam opinions to sweeping attacks on the social assumptions of the Warren Court. Their initial straining to accommodate their principles to Warren Court decisions had given way, in the face of what they considered to be unbridled judicial excesses, to disenchantment and alienation. However, not all legal scholars became thus estranged from the Court.

The same egalitarian pressures that had stimulated the Warren Court produced a body of literature supporting the Court's actions [55] and dissenting from the tenets of Reasoned Elaboration.[56] In 1971, Judge Skelly Wright published an open repudiation of the "fundamental axioms" of the Reasoned Elaborationists.[57] Judge Wright argued that the students of the 1960's had become a new generation of lawyers educated in a new tradition. "[F]or them," he maintained, "the [Warren] Court was the one institution in the society that seemed to be speaking most consistently the language of idealism which we all recited in grade school." [58] The members of this new generation, for Judge Wright, "see no point in querulous admonitions that the Court should restrain itself from combatting injustice now in order to preserve

---

53. Kurland, *The Supreme Court, 1963 Term — Foreword: "Equal in Origin and Equal in Title to the Legislative and Executive Branches of the Government,"* 78 HARV. L. REV. 143, 165 (1964).

54. Kurland, *Toward a Political Supreme Court,* 37 U. CHI. L. REV. 19 (1969).

55. *See, e.g.,* A. COX, THE WARREN COURT (1968); Black, *The Unfinished Business of the Warren Court,* 46 WASH. L. REV. 3 (1970).

56. Clark, *A Plea for the Principled Opinion,* 49 VA. L. REV. 660 (1963); Gunther, *The Subtle Vices of the "Passive Virtues" — A Comment on Principle and Expediency in Judicial Review,* 64 COLUM. L. REV. 1 (1964).

57. Wright, *Professor Bickel, The Scholarly Tradition, and the Supreme Court,* 84 HARV. L. REV. 769, 784 (1971).

58. *Id.* at 804.

itself to combat a coup later on." [59] In contrast, the generation that adopted Reasoned Elaboration as its standard was influenced by the Stalin era, which fostered the conventional wisdom of the Cold War, and was a time scarred "by worries of Court packing and judicial obstructionism," [60] an era that bred cynicism, caution, and "protective[ness toward] fragile institutions." [61] These values had paled, Judge Wright maintained, in the face of the inspiration of the 1960's for a modern generation.[62]

Judge Wright believed that Reasoned Elaboration might well be headed for obsolescence. He stopped short, however, of a full-blown discussion of the grounds for this belief. One form such a discussion could take would make use of the analysis already applied to the legal theories of the past four decades: a description of the social forces emerging in the 1970's, suggestions regarding their implications for jurisprudence, and an evaluation of the continued impact of Reasoned Elaboration in light of those implications.

SOCIAL CHANGE, THE DIALECTIC OF CONSTITUTIONAL ADJUDICATION AND REASONED ELABORATION IN THE 1970's

Emerging Social Phenomena

It is possible to identify at least three characteristics of American society in the 1970's that have immediate relevance to discussions of the proper function of the Supreme Court. The first is the emergence of new, fragmented, vocal "minorities" [63] who lack power and status, who perceive discrimination directed at them on a variety of grounds, and who are anxious to air their grievances publicly and impatient to have those grievances resolved. Unlike the minorities whose concerns received national attention in the 1960's, these groups are not primarily racial or

---

59. *Id.*
60. *Id.*
61. *Id.*
62. *Id.*
63. I include women as a "minority" notwithstanding the fact that they compose a majority of the total American population.

ethnic in composition. Racial and ethnic groups continue to articulate their concerns, but many of the techniques that they pioneered are now being adopted by groups who perceive their disadvantaged position to rest on economic considerations (consumers or environmental organizations), sexual attitudes (women or homosexuals), or a combination of moral assumptions and bureaucractic imperatives (prisoners).

None of these "new" minorities has hitherto enjoyed extensive access to the traditional grievance-resolution mechanisms of the political process. But this fact has not deterred any of them from attempting to voice their discontent, and, with the aid of the media and of organizations established to protect the rights of disadvantaged persons, the groups have managed to dramatize their problems on a wide scale without having access to standard political channels. The emergence of these new minorities is one of the striking characteristics of contemporary American society.

A second feature of contemporary life in the United States revolves around the relationship of American citizens to the different branches of their government. There is an acknowledged gap between the goals of officeholders and those of their constituents, as well as a widespread judgment that those same officeholders are furthering their own goals while merely paying lipservice to their constituents' needs. Thus, while regulatory agencies are charged with the duty of regulating the activities of industrial enterprises in the public interest, they actually define "public interest" to be synonymous with the needs of their regulatees. Likewise, members of reviewing boards entrusted with establishing standards for the granting of licenses in the interests of public health determine that the "public health" is furthered by their private financial gain.[64] The critics of operational government, both established officeholders [65] and advocates of the

---

64. *See generally*, L. KOHLMEIER, THE REGULATORS (1969); Reich, *The New Property*, 73 YALE L.J. 733 (1964).

65. *See, e.g.*, Elman, *Administrative Reform of the Federal Trade Commission*, 59 GEO. L.J. 777 (1971); Johnson, *Consumer Rights and the Regulatory Crisis*, 20 CATHOLIC U.L. REV. 424 (1971).

new interest groups,[66] are linked in their perception that terms such as "public interest" and "social welfare" have lost their meaning: the terms are capable of such wide, divergent, and contradictory interpretations that they are useless as standards of performance.

At the same time the judiciary has assumed a contrasting posture. The federal courts, in particular, have established a legacy of competence in dealing with emerging social problems. Beginning with *Brown* in the 1950's, the Supreme Court assumed that one of its functions was to respond to the needs of emergent minorities insofar as those needs could be squared with the values of libertarianism and egalitarianism. Initiated at a time when other branches of government were largely unresponsive to demands of disadvantaged groups, the Warren Court's activism conditioned the public to expect participation by that Court, and courts generally, in emerging areas of social controversy. The Burger Court, for its part, has continued to meet this expectation, and has added to it, by involving itself in the death penalty [67] and Pentagon Papers [68] controversies.

A final and possibly the most significant aspect of American culture in the 1970's is the disintegration of common values or goals. In the place of consensual values around which members of American society can cohere stand sets of polar alternatives — permissiveness and regimentation, militancy and fatalism, cynicism and fantasy.[69]

The interaction of these features of contemporary American society suggests a serious problem. A combination of the continuing emergence of new minorities, the loss of confidence in the notion of public service on which officeholders base their authority, and the residue of expectations engendered by the Warren Court appears to make vital the continued presence of the Supreme Court as a guarantor of the credibility and stature of the

---

66. *See, e.g.,* R. FELLMUTH, THE INTERSTATE COMMERCE OMISSION (1971).
67. *See* Furman v. Georgia, 408 U.S. 238 (1972).
68. *See* New York Times Co. v. United States, 403 U.S. 713 (1971).
69. *See generally* W. O'NEILL, COMING APART (1971).

governmental process. The Court gave dignity to the grievances of racial and ethnic minority groups in the 1960's by grappling with their complaints, thereby giving them recognition and easing their eventual entry to the political arena; it now comes to consider a similar function with respect to the newly emerging minorities of the seventies. But how can the Court perform this function in the face of a disintegration of consensual values? How can it meet the "felt necessities of the times" if Americans cannot agree on what these necessities are? Resolution of this problem necessitates further examination of both the special sensitivity of minority rights and the role played by consensual values. The framers of the Constitution were concerned with the potential tyranny of majorities, which they associated with demagoguery and mob rule. In codifying certain rights they established the moral principle that many minority prerogatives may not be undermined by majorities, even if the majorities perceive such action to be in the general interest.[70] Although they confined that principle to enumerated instances, some of their enumerations (such as "equal protection" and "due process") were strikingly broad. An inevitable question, therefore, is which specific minority rights can be said to fall within the broad enumerations and thereby merit special protection. In answering this question the Court of necessity must look beyond constitutional language to cultural values.

The Dialectic of Adjudication

In interpreting constitutional language, the Court should not merely search for the collective wisdom of the nation. That search would be fruitless at a time marked by the absence of collective values. Rather, the Court must attempt to assist in the creation of that wisdom by calling to mind the existence or non-existence of a relationship between the asserted rights of current minorities and constitutional principles. That is precisely what the Warren Court did in *Brown,* suggesting that the quest on the part of black school children for access to public schools of their choice embodied

---

70. *See* Dworkin, *The Jurisprudence of Richard Nixon,* 17 N.Y. REV. BOOKS 27 (1972).

values of fairness and equality that were endemic to American society. It urged the affirmation of those values in the context of public education, despite the inconveniences and anxieties that such an affirmation caused and despite the preference of many Americans not to give the values a high priority in the educational context.

Once the Supreme Court has attempted to influence the public in this fashion, a majority of the public has several options in response. It may applaud the decision and comply with it; it may protest the decision or its implementation in varying degrees, but stop short of taking affirmative legal action to repeal it; it may take affirmative action through its legislative representatives, thereby inviting the Court to scrutinize the action's constitutionality; or, it may take affirmative action in the form of a constitutional amendment. Only in the last case is that public majority asserting any ultimate authority over the Court. While its actions in the second and third cases may erode the authority of Court's decision, they do not strike at the authority of the Court itself.

The Court's initial decision that asserted minority rights deserve the status of constitutional protection, then, is an *authoritative* one but one that has not yet been *legitimated.* It is authoritative because it rests on the generally acknowledged status of the Court as a viable and respectable governmental institution, but it is not legitimated because the Court's attempt to influence popular opinion has not yet met with a response. The process of influence and response is a *dialectical* one. The Court makes an initial judgment that some minority claims rise to the level of constitutionally protected rights, and others do not. The public responds to that judgment. The Court may take note of the public's response. At some point in time, the initial judgment is legitimated or revised.

The source of legitimacy, in this formulation, is not merely the consensual values of American society at a point in time, nor is it simply majoritarian sentiment. The source is rather the dialectical process itself — the interaction of the Court's authority with the needs of its constituents. The fact that a particular decision of the

Court with regard to minority rights is not responsive to the needs of the majority does not mean that it will not be legitimated, given the special place of minority rights in American culture and given the Court's historic role in defining that place.

Legitimacy comes, then, when the dialectical process reveals that the Court is generally perceived as having made a "right" decision, not necessarily one that is popular in an ephemeral, immediate sense, but one that embodies values — equality and liberty conspicuous among them — that have over time emerged as endemic to American civilization, at least as it is currently perceived. "Rightness," like the dialectical process itself, is ultimately a function of history. If a Court is "wrong" in its definition of the kinds of rights that exist against the state, as was the Court in the early 1930's, its decisions are not legitimated and its authority is threatened. But rightness and wrongness do not depend exclusively on consensual values or on the majority will, canons of judicial deference and neutral principles notwithstanding.

A New Look at Reasoned Elaboration

The jurisprudential ideal for the Supreme Court formulated by the Reasoned Elaborationists is, accordingly, historically unsound and currently inappropriate in two respects. For the reasons suggested above, the Reasoned Elaborationist tenet of "principled decision-making," which requires the Court to postpone resolution of controversies until there is a discernible social census on the issues in question, is based on a conception of the relationship between the Court and the public which may be flawed. But even if reasonable men may differ on that point, "consensus" has taken on a new meaning in contemporary America. The very presence in the courts of issues raised by isolated minorities implies an absence of consensus on those issues. The complainants in these cases are demanding, in fact, that a system of consensual politics has functioned to exclude their positions. If the Supreme Court postpones decision on these issues in order to allow them to ripen for principled resolution it cannot help but amplify the exclusionist character of a system based upon "consensual" values.

In addition, the theory of institutional interrelationships posited by the Reasoned Elaborationists has been called into question by recent trends. Reasoned Elaboration assumed that the limited role it advocated for the Court followed from the fact that the judiciary was an unrepresentative, elitist institution in a democratic society that believed in representative government. The corollary to this axiom was that the popularly elected branches of government were not elitist and were representative. But if that corollary comes to be disclaimed, and the popularly elected branches come to be seen as neither egalitarian nor representative, while the judiciary, in the person of the Court, takes an egalitarian posture, the distinction breaks down and with it fall the strict limitations on judicial behavior that flow from it.

If the Reasoned Elaborationist ideal of judicial performance is at least partially obsolete, what alternative jurisprudential standards shall the Court follow? The emergent social forces previously described and their jurisprudential implications seem congenial with certain guidelines for decision-making. The pressure to resolve minority grievances and the assumed absence of any consensus as to how they should be resolved suggest, for example, that the Court will have to make a number of intuitive judgments.

The discovery of intuition in the judicial process caused great excitement among the Realists, but this element has always been part of judging: it is a necessary technique of a profession charged with the responsibility of making "fair" and "just" decisions on the basis of less than complete information. The dangerous aspect of judicial intuition in the American system of government, of course, is that it can result in the tentative imposition of the subjective biases of a small group of persons on the public at large. But there is a traditional means of protecting the public from judicial fiat: the requirement, underscored by the Reasoned Elaborationists, that judges give reasons for their results, and the consequent disqualification of certain types of reasons as nothing more than illegitimate statements of personal prejudice.[71]

---

71. An opinion, for example, which announced as its reason for decision the fact that the Court was not impressed with the physical appearance of counsel for the

The requirement of reasoning and the distinction between legitimate and illegitimate reasons can harmonize with a dialectical theory of constitutional adjudication. In articulating the basis for his intuitive judgment, a Justice should reach for arguments which make use of reasons that apply to deeply embedded cultural values and thereby transcend his own biases. That process of reaching was associated by Reasoned Elaboration with the concept of neutral principles. But, unlike that solution, under this formulation the Court does not wait until it perceives that a social consensus exists with regard to a particular issue; Justices decide cases intuitively and then search to justify their intuitions by making arguments directed at a wide audience. The effectiveness of their arguments ultimately turns on the extent to which they can demonstrate that a given result furthers values which American society has traditionally considered of high importance, and is in that sense "right" and "just." Over time, the rightness of a result may be called into question; just as the Constitution is capable of changing interpretations, the collective insights of Justices are capable of being repudiated. But the possibility of repudiation should not deter the Court from deciding difficult cases in emerging areas of social controversy.

Social responsiveness, of course, is not the equivalent of support for social change. It is possible under these guidelines for the Court to entertain grievances from minority groups and yet not invariably resolve those grievances in a manner that expands the rights or powers of those groups. Certain recent appointees of the Court, it is said,[72] have shown a tendency to erode protections for disadvantaged members of society and to assert the primacy of legislative fiats at the expense of persons on whose rights those fiats infringe. Assuming this indictment to be fair, one may well deplore this tendency. These proposed guidelines, however, stop short of requiring the Court to resolve controversies involving

---

petitioner would be so patently lacking in legitimacy as to undermine the Court's authority to make decisions. Intuitive judgments require legitimation; legitimacy is tied to the reasoning process in opinions.

72. *See* Bender, *The Techniques of Subtle Erosion*, 245 HARPER'S, May 18, 1972, at 25-30; Dworkin, *supra* note 70, at 35.

disadvantaged groups by consistently accepting the arguments of the disadvantaged. In keeping with its historic function, the Court may ascertain, subject to the response of the public, which minority rights rise to constitutional stature. At some point blanket indifference to minority grievances leads to a loss of legitimacy; but where this point comes is a matter for history to decide.

In addition to the requirement that the Court give reasons for its results, other strictures of Reasoned Elaboration retain current value. Reasoned Elaboration's requirement that judicial decisions should attempt to cohere around more than a perfunctory statement of the result seems timely. If the Court in its contemporary role is expected to decide hard cases in emerging areas of the law, it must make an effort to achieve something like a final disposition of the issues raised by those cases in order to act as an institution that truly resolves grievances. Coherence is particularly difficult to achieve in controversial developing areas, but the alternatives — provisional resolution of the issue through a "passive" device or a raft of individual opinions joined only by their concurrence in the result — do not meet the Court's responsibility genuinely to respond to social change. The tendency of the Burger Court to entertain such "hard" issues as those raised by the Pentagon Papers [73] and dealth penalty [74] cases would seem contemporary-minded, but the use in these cases of short per curiam opinions with majority Justices concurring individually is troublesome, for the public is left with an insufficient understanding of the basis on which the Court as an institution has resolved the issues at stake.

CONCLUSION

In sum, the suggested guidelines borrow in part from both Realism and Reasoned Elaboration but interject an additional standard for Supreme Court performance. The Realists' sense of the intuitive aspects of judging is retained, along with their implicit

---

73. *See* New York Times Co. v. United States, 403 U.S. 713 (1971).
74. *See* Furman v. Georgia, 408 U.S. 238 (1972).

assumption that the Supreme Court, despite institutional constraints, has considerable freedom to intervene in areas of "unripened" social controversy. The insistence of the Reasoned Elaborationists upon institutional conservatism is thereby abandoned. On the other hand, Reasoned Elaboration's demand for an articulation of the reasoning process in opinions seems as relevant to the seventies as it was to the fifties and sixties. The suggestion that Court majorities cohere around more than cryptic justifications for their decisions could be interpreted as another call for matured collective thought. But that concept was introduced in the context of pleas for a limited and restrained role for the Court; these guidelines point to a role that is wide ranging and potentially innovative.

Insofar, however, as neither Realism nor Reasoned Elaboration fully embraced the notion of a dialectical process of constitutional adjudication, the present guidelines depart from these schools. The Realists gave so little consideration to the institutional constraints on judges that the concept of legitimation, as herein used, was not part of their calculus. Although certain Reasoned Elaborationists, notably Bickel, spoke of "colloquies" between the Court and society at large, those colloquies were seen primarily as means by which consensual values and their attendant neutral principles could be discovered and passively reflected by the Court. The present guidelines assume such entities to be undiscoverable, but propose that the Court go on making "hard" decisions notwithstanding, justifying their results by appeal to constitutional principles that have shown an ability to withstand time and change.

In the final analysis no theory of jurisprudence or mode of Supreme Court criticism can survive the passing of the social milieu from which it emerges. As the Burger Court attempts to meet its obligations in the seventies, and as courtwatchers attempt to help define those obligations, recurrent questions about judicial decision-making and opinion-writing, similar to those asked by the Realists and the Reasoned Elaborationists, will be posed again. The context of those questions, however, will have altered, and that alteration, regardless of how dimly it may be perceived, will in the long run make all the difference.

THE INTELLECTUAL ORIGINS OF TORTS IN AMERICA

Yale Law Journal, Vol. 86, No. 4 (1977)

The emergence of Torts as an independent branch of law came strikingly late in American legal history. Although Blackstone and his contemporaries, in their 18th-century efforts to classify law, identified a residual category of noncriminal wrongs not arising out of contract,[1] Torts was not considered a discrete branch of law until the late 19th century. The first American treatise on Torts appeared in 1859,[2] Torts was first taught as a separate law school subject in 1870,[3] the first Torts casebook was published in 1874.[4]

A standard explanation for the emergence of an independent identity for Torts late in the 19th century is the affinity of Tort doctrines, especially negligence, to the problems produced by industrialization.[5] I argue, in what follows, that the process by which Torts emerged as a discrete branch of law was more complex and less dictated by the demands of industrial enterprise than the standard account suggests. Changes associated with industrial enterprise did provide many more cases involving strangers. And those cases did play a part in the emergence of Torts as an independent branch of law. But those cases alone were not

---

1. Blackstone's *Commentaries* had separate chapters on trespass and nuisance and referred to torts as "all actions for trespasses, nuisances, defamatory words, and the like." 3. W. BLACKSTONE, COMMENTARIES *117. The general classification system of Blackstone's *Commentaries* is discussed in note 13 *infra*.

2. I F. HILLIARD, THE LAW OF TORTS iii-iv (Boston 1859). *See* L. FRIEDMAN, A HISTORY OF AMERICAN LAW 409 (1973).

3. *See* THE CENTENNIAL HISTORY OF THE HARVARD LAW SCHOOL 29 (1918).

4. J. AMES, SELECT CASES ON TORTS (1874). *See* Rothenberg, Book Review, 23 U.C.L.A. L. REV. 373, 377 (1975).

5. *See, e.g.,* L. FRIEDMAN, *supra* note 2, at 262, 409; M. HORWITZ, THE TRANSFORMATION OF AMERICAN LAW, 1780-1860, at 85-99 (1977); Gregory, *Trespass to Negligence to Absolute Liability,* 37 VA. L. REV. 359, 368, 377-79, 382 (1951). *See also* Roberts, *Negligence: Blackstone to Shaw to ? An Intellectual Escapade in a Tory Vein,* 50 CORNELL L.Q. 191, 204-05, 213 (1965).

sufficient. Also necessary was a reorientation of thinking about classifications of law itself. The emergence of Torts owed as much to changes in jurisprudential thought as to the spread of industrial machines.

In brief, this article maintains that the interaction of three trends in the late 19th century fostered the development of Torts as a separate legal subject. The first trend was an impulse toward "conceptualization" among American intellectuals, including legal scholars. A manifestation of the advent of "Victorian" culture in America, the impulse sought universal principles in academic fields of study. It stressed "scientific" methodologies and substituted secular theories for religious dogma. The second trend was the collapse of the system of common law writ pleading, whose jurisprudential scaffolding, once functionally effective, became too random and arbitrary to satisfy those interested in achieving regularity and expediency in legal proceedings.[6] A third trend was the gradual change of the standard tort case from one involving persons in closely defined relations with each other to one involving strangers. As judges and academics sought to extract a set of universal principles from this new prototypical tort situation, the notion of a general, but severely limited, theory of civil obligation emerged. That notion, slow to be articulated, influenced the transformation of the older tort of neglect into the modern tort of negligence, with its generalized principles and its fault prerequisite for liability. With the convergence of these trends, Torts came to be conceived as a discrete legal subject in treatises, casebooks, and law school curricula.[7]

---

6. Horwitz argues that the promotion of thses values was significant concern of mid-19th century judges and jurists. *See* M. HORWITZ, *supra* note 5, at 258-66.

7. The late emergence of Torts as a separate branch of law cannot be explained merely by reference to changes in the pattern of American legal education. It is true that the generalized categories of modern American private law — Property, Contracts, Torts, etc. — were not universally employed in the early 19th century. *See* THE CENTENNIAL HISTORY OF THE HARVARD LAW SCHOOL 24, 73-75 (1918); A. REED, TRAINING FOR THE PUBLIC PROFESSION OF THE LAW 139, 146 (1921). Law school courses in what would now be considered subtopics of a general field — Bills and Notes, Bailments, Sales, Bankruptcy — were more common. *See, e.g., id.* at

Events as well as ideas played a part in creating the climate of intellectual legal opinion that spawned Torts as an independent category of law. But this article focuses on events only as they were used by intellectuals in the legal profession as raw material for the formulation of legal doctrine and theory. My concern is to detail the rule of designated lawyer intellectuals, who can be called glossators, in influencing the development of legal doctrine in America. Glossators — who, after 1870, were primarily academicians — fulfill their professional roles, in important part, through their efforts to derive and articulate theoretical justifications for the working rules of law that have current acceptance. In this "glossing" process, these intellectuals significantly affect the content of legal doctrines and rules and consequently affect the changing state of law in America.[8]

---

458. But both Litchfield and Harvard Law Schools, the primary centers of formal legal education in the early 19th century, listed courses in Contracts and Property. Id. at 454. No courses in Torts were offered, however, and almost no attention was given to individual actions in tort, such as assault, battery, defamation, deceit, or false imprisonment. (Roger Baldwin's lecture notes at Litchfield Law School indicate, however, that brief coverage was given to torts. *See* Stevens, *Two Cheers for 1870: The American Law School,* in LAW IN AMERICAN HISTORY 403, 432 n.31 (D. Fleming & B. Bailyn eds. 1971). Moreover, the great treatise writers of the early 19th century, James Kent and Joseph Story, did not perceive Torts as a discrete legal subject. *See* J. KENT, COMMENTARIES ON AMERICAN LAW (New York 1826-1830); J. STORY, COMMENTARIES ON THE CONFLICT OF LAWS (Boston 1834); J. STORY, COMMENTARIES ON THE CONSTITUTION OF THE UNITED STATES (Boston 1833); J. STORY, COMMENTARIES ON EQUITY JURISPRUDENCE (Boston 1836); J. STORY, COMMENTARIES ON EQUITY PLEADINGS (Boston 1838); J. STORY, COMMENTARIES ON THE LAW OF AGENCY (Boston 1839); J. STORY, COMMENTARIES ON THE LAW OF BAILMENTS (Cambridge, Mass. 1832); J. STORY, COMMENTARIES ON THE LAW OF BILLS OF EXCHANGE (Boston 1843); J. STORY, COMMENTARIES ON THE LAW OF PARTNERSHIP (Boston 1841); J. STORY, COMMENTARIES ON THE LAW OF PROMISSORY NOTES (Boston 1845). For a discussion of Story's *Commentaries,* see G. DUNNE, JUSTICE JOSEPH STORY AND THE RISE OF THE SUPREME COURT 310-15 (1970).

8. Although the American intellectuals discussed in this article are generally members of academic and professional elites, their elite professional status is not intended to be unduly emphasized. But historically certain groups of persons have tended to serve as articulators of values and goals for the legal profession, and those groups have normally possessed elite status. Whether the goals and values of those groups were shared by other Americans of the late 19th century is an inquiry that takes one well beyond the scope of this article. For present purposes a degree of elite intellectual influence in the late-19th-century legal profession is assumed.

I. THE CONCEPTUALIST IMPLUSE IN VICTORIAN AMERICA

Between 1800 and 1850 the attraction of many Americans to the values of individual freedom, equality, and occupational mobility tended to call into question an 18th-century conception of society as an ordered community with designated social roles and relatively limited mobility. In the 19th century, alongside a relatively static, hierarchical vision of man's place in society, there emerged a dynamic, atomistic vision that emphasized the limitless possibilities for individual mobility, creativity, and achievement.[9] For a time these visions were apparently not perceived as contradictory. Leading literary figures could espouse both individual freedom and the ideal of communal life.[10] National politicians could simultaneously portray themselves as guardians of a simpler, more orderly republican society and as apostles of democratic progress.[11] Even theologians, such as the influential Unitarian spokesman William Ellery Channing, could assert that the universe was ordered by God's laws and yet applaud " 'question[ing] [of] the infinite, the unsearchable, with an audacious self reliance.' " [12]

Perhaps the most striking indication that early 19th-century legal scholars were similarly affected by these cultural trends was their possession of both synthetic and atomistic visions of law. Blackstone, in his 18th-century synthetic view, had seen the "Law of England" as a unified entity, capable of being classified into

---

9. This generalization has received widespread support in the historical literature. *See, e.g.,* R. WELTER, THE MIND OF AMERICA, 1820-1860, at 117-22, 141-56 (1975) (citing sources).

10. *See* A. KAUL, THE AMERICAN VISION (1963) (tracing this theme in writings of Cooper, Hawthorne, Melville, and Mark Twain).

11. Andrew Jackson personified these tendencies. *See* M. MEYERS, THE JACKSONIAN PERSUASION (1957); J. WARD, ANDREW JACKSON, SYMBOL FOR AN AGE (1955).

12. J. HIGHAM, FROM BOUNDLESSNESS TO CONSOLIDATION: THE TRANSFORMATION OF AMERICAN CULTURE, 1848-1860, at 6 (William L. Clements Library, 1969).

distinguishable but interdependent parts.[13] By the early 19th century, in Kent's and Story's treatises, law was primarily represented as the sum of its parts (the "law" of bailments, the "law" of agency, etc.), but was still perceived as capable of presentation in the form of a grand synthesis. Nathan Dane's widely used *Abridgment*,[14] which first appeared in 1823, was also an attempt at synthesis, but Dane's organization suggested that American law was a series of diverse interpretations of individual actions that possessed little unity or coherence. And by the 1850s leading treatise writers such as Theophilus Parsons and Emory Washburn stressed encyclopedic coverage more than theoretical synthesis.[15]

Although a sense that American law was dissonant, diverse, and even chaotic developed in early 19th-century legal scholarship, this perception went hand in hand with a belief that American society was still to some extent a communal entity, bound together by shared values. A major source of these shared communal values was religious dogma.[16] Parsons' treatise on contracts, for example, distinguished between "the law of God" and "human law." [17] Parsons argued, building on this distinction, that human laws, with which his treatise was concerned, could not entirely sanction "craft and cunning"; but this fact should not be taken to mean that "whatever human law does not prohibit, [one] has a right to do;

---

13. Blackstone's *Commentaries* had divided "the Laws of England" into "the rights of persons" (*e.g.*, sovereign immunities, master-servant, domestic relations), "the rights of things" (real and personal property), "private wrongs" (*e.g.*, trespass, nuisance, equitable remedies, and civil procedure), and "public wrongs" (criminal law and procedure). This fourfold division constituted the four volumes of his commentaries.

14. N. DANE, A GENERAL ABRIDGMENT AND DIGEST OF AMERICAN LAW (Boston, 1823-1829).

15. *See, e.g.*, T. PARSONS, THE LAW OF CONTRACTS (Boston, 1853-1855); E. WASHBURN, A TREATISE ON THE AMERICAN LAW OF REAL PROPERTY (Boston, 1860-1862). Washburn's treatise was written between 1856 and 1860. *See* THE CENTENNIAL HISTORY OF THE HARVARD LAW SCHOOL 356 (1918).

16. *See* Kennedy, *Form and Substance in Private Law Adjudication*, 89 HARV. L. REV. 1685, 1725-27 (1976).

17. 2 T. PARSONS, *supra* note 15, at 265.

for that only is right which violates no law, and there is another law beside human law." [18]

If the simultaneous possession of synthetic and atomistic visions of society was a defining characteristic of early 19th-century American culture, and if significant manifestations of these two visions were the binding force of religious dogma and a growing awareness of the value of individual autonomy, a significant change in the intellectual history of America took place in the middle of the 19th century. For after 1850 the role of religion as a unifying force among American intellectuals was considerably diminished, and the sense that American civilization offered endless possibilities for individual growth and progress was sharply qualified. With these developments a new phase in the history of ideas in America emerged, best signified by the term "Victorian."

"Victorian" refers to a cultural and intellectual ethos that had originated in England during the middle years of Queen Victoria's reign. [19] The ethos emerged from tensions associated with the realization that material "progress" in an industrializing, urbanizing society had disintegrative capacities. [20] American Victorians discovered that sudden rises in income levels, massive industrial development, and marked urbanization tended to undermine traditional sources of stability, especially religious dogmas, that complemented a homogeneous, village-oriented, preindustrial society. The theological explanations of the universe that were widely shared by early 19th-century intellectuals had assumed an essentially static view of human nature and social organization; such explanations appeared suddenly irrelevant to the rapidly changing cast of American civilization after the Civil War.

Over and over again post-Civil War scholars stressed their interest in deriving secular and scientific theories that would promote order and unity. Henry Adams explained his "instinctive

18. *Id.*
19. *See* W. HOUGHTON, THE VICTORIAN FRAME OF MIND, 1830-1870 (1957).
20. *See* Brown, *Modernization: A Victorian Climax*, 27 AM. Q. 533 (1975); Meyer, *American Intellectuals and the Victorian Crisis of Faith, id.* at 585.

belief" in the theory of evolution as being based on a need for a "substitute for religion," a "working system for the universe," and a means of "enforc[ing] unity and uniformity." [21] The novelist Hamlin Garland, reading Spencer in the 1880s, found that " 'the universe took on order and harmony.' " [22] The architect Louis Sullivan felt that "Spencer's definition implying a progression . . . to a highly organized complex, seemed to fit" Sullivan's own experience.[23] Some scholars, such as the philosopher John Fiske, even believed that secularly based systematic thinking could be reconciled with a religious faith. The authority of religious principles, Fiske wrote in 1875, was no longer derived "from the arbitrary command of a mythologic quasi-human Ruler," but from "the innermost necessities of [the] process of evolution." [24]

In general, post-Civil War intellectuals were interested in restoring the sense of order and unity that had characterized 18th-century thought, but they rejected efforts to derive order and unity from "mythologic" religious principles. A particular interest of intellectuals in the quarter centry after the war was conceptualization — the transformation of data into theories of universal applicability. Their source of unity was to be methodological: the "scientific" ordering of knowledge.[25] As the sociologist Lester Ward put it, "[T]he origination and distribution of knowledge [could] no longer be left to chance and nature," but

---

21. H. ADAMS, THE EDUCATION OF HENRY ADAMS 225-26 (1931). For a collection of essays on the influence of evolution in America, see EVOLUTIONARY THOUGHT IN AMERICA (S. Persons ed. 1950).

22. Cowley, *Naturalism in American Literature,* in EVOLUTIONARY THOUGHT IN AMERICA, *supra* note 21, at 300, 304.

23. L. SULLIVAN, THE AUTOBIOGRAPHY OF AN IDEA 255 (1934).

24. 2 J. FISKE, OUTLINES OF COSMIC PHILOSOPHY 468 (1875).

25. Other recent scholarship has perceived a similar unity in the pattern of reasoning in post-Civil War treatises and judicial decisions. The pattern has principally been characterized by the term formalism. *See, e.g.,* Horwitz, *The Rise of Legal Formalism,* 19 AM. J. LEG. HIST. 251, 255-57, 261-62 (1975); Kennedy, *supra* note 16, at 1728-31 (using the term "Classical individualism"); Nelson, *The Impact of the Antislavery Movement upon Styles of Judicial Reasoning in Nineteenth Century America,* 87 HARV. L. REV. 513, 514-16, 560-66 (1974). *But see* Scheiber, *Instrumentalism and Property Rights: A Reconsideration of American "Styles of*

were "to be systematized and erected unto true arts." [26] The two legal scholars most immediately responsive to this conceptualist impulse were Nicholas St. John Green and Oliver Wendell Holmes, Jr., who, with Fiske, the philosophers William James and Chauncey Wright, and others, were members of the celebrated Metaphysical Club, a meeting ground of Cambridge intellectuals between 1870 and 1874.[27] Green, a practicing lawyer, taught Torts and Criminal Law at Harvard and Boston University Law Schools in the 1870s and wrote several essays in the *American Law Review,* of which Holmes was an editor, between 1869 and 1876. When he died in 1876, Green had a treatise on Torts in preparation.

Green's approach to legal scholarship, which Holmes called philosophical,[28] was characteristically conceptualist. Green refused to accept legal dogmas on faith, being interested in their effectiveness as working analytical guidelines.[29] The classification of legal subjects and the derivation of general principles of law, efforts that Green identified with philosophically oriented scholarship,[30] were in his judgment useless undertakings unless

---

Judicial Reasoning" in the 19th Century, 1975 WIS. L. REV. 1 (criticizing Nelson for oversimplifying changes in styles of judicial reasoning).

26. 2 L. WARD, DYNAMIC SOCIOLOGY 539 (1883). Ward had begun work on *Dynamic Sociology* in 1869. *See* R. HOFSTADTER, SOCIAL DARWINISM IN AMERICAN THOUGHT 69 (1944).

27. For an analysis of the philosophical contributions of another member of the Club, Charles Peirce, see Note, *Holmes, Peirce and Legal Pragmatism,* 84 YALE L.J. 1123 (1975). On the Metaphysical Club, see Wiener, *Peirce's Metaphysical Club and the Genesis of Pragmatism,* 7 J. HIST. IDEAS 218 (1946).

28. *See* [Holmes], Book Review, 5 AM. L. REV. 340, 341 (1871). *See also* Frank, *A Conflict With Oblivion: Some Observations on the Founders of Legal Pragmatism,* 9 RUTGERS L. REV. 425, 434 (1954).

29. In a discussion of proximate causation, Green called the phrase "natural and proximate consequence" a "stereotyped [form] for gliding over a difficulty without explaining it." N. GREEN, *Torts under the French Law,* in ESSAYS AND NOTES ON THE LAW OF TORT AND CRIME 71, 82 (1933) [book hereinafter cited as ESSAYS]. The *Essays* are reprints of notes and unsigned articles and book reviews that Green published in the *American Law Review,* in the eighth edition of Joseph Story's *Commentaries on the Law of Agency,* which Green edited, and in two volumes of criminal law cases entitled *Criminal Law Reports.* All the material in the *Essays* was written between 1869 and 1876, *Id.* at v.

30. N. GREEN, *Slander and Libel,* in ESSAYS, *supra* note 29, at 49, 69-70.

a given classification or principle had a useful purpose. Purposive organization of a legal subject could be achieved, Green maintained, by understanding the subject's history, as with the law of slander and libel,[31] or by understanding the practical considerations on which it was founded, as with the doctrine of vicarious liability.[32]

Thus, while Green expressed an interest in treating the law as a science and analyzing its developments with something akin to mathematical precision,[33] he conceded that absolute lines could not be drawn because change was constant and "[a]ll things in nature . . . shade into each other by imperceptible degrees."[34] Paradoxically, an acceptance of the inevitability of change provided Green with some solace. If one recognized that "[t]he latest decided cases upon [a] subject *make the law,*"[35] Green believed, one could try to "settle more definitely" the analytical rationales for those cases and "to see what, and how many, of such reasons apply, and with what force, to . . . new cases."[36] Through these techniques one derived general principles that had some operative meaning in practice.

Green's conceptualism, like that of other American Victorian intellectuals, was thus an effort to derive certainty in the face of continual change. Certainty was achieved not by appeal to received dogma but by a scientific reorientation of techniques of legal analysis. Green was as interested in "perfect[ing] the law as a science"[37] as his conceptualist contemporaries in sociology, economics, or philosophy were in perfecting their disciplines.[38]

---

31. *Id.* at 53.

32. N. GREEN, *The Liability of a Principal to Third Persons for the Torts of his Agents and Servants,* in ESSAYS, *supra* note 29, at 127, 127.

33. N. GREEN, *Proximate and Remote Cause,* in ESSAYS, *supra* note 29, at 1, 16.

34. N. GREEN, *Insanity in Criminal Law,* in ESSAYS, *supra* note 29, at 161, 166.

35. N. GREEN, *supra* note 30, at 70.

36. N. GREEN, *The Liability of a Master to his Servants,* in ESSAYS, *supra* note 29, at 131, 137.

37. N. GREEN, *supra* note 33, at 9.

38. The interdisciplinary character of conceptualism is discussed in M. WHITE, SOCIAL THOUGHT IN AMERICA: THE REVOLT AGAINST FORMALISM (1949).

Through these techniques new philosophical classifications of law were made possible.

The strong parallels between Green's approach and that of Holmes in the 1870s suggest a degree of mutual influence.[39] Green's interest in the historical origins of legal doctrines, his conviction that rules and principles derived their primary meaning from the circumstances in which they were used, and his fascination with systems of legal classification were mirrored in Holmes's early scholarship.[40] Both men saw themselves as expounders of the law — glossators — whose interest was in treating legal subjects philosophically from the perspective of scientific insight.[41] But despite the increasing acceptance of conceptualist methodologies in American intellectual life after the Civil War, Green, and especially Holmes, might not have been able to apply those methodologies so readily to law had not the principal classification device of 19th-century jurisprudence, the system of writ pleading, collapsed, leaving a void that was ultimately to be filled by the theories of conceptualists.

II. THE COLLAPSE OF THE WRIT SYSTEM

For the first half of the 19th century "'torts' was not an autonomous branch of law at all but merely, as Holmes noted in 1871, a collection of unrelated writs.[42] Lawyers knew how to sue in tort, but they apparently had little interest in a theory of torts. During the early 19th century, however, the writ system became increasingly haphazard as a classification device, in part because of the growing diversity of American law and the tendency of courts to create exceptions to the system's rigorous requirements,

---

39. The impact of Green on Holmes is discussed in Frank, *supra* note 28, at 434-44. Frank argues that "in several notable respects" Green was "Holmes' precursor." *Id.* at 442.

40. *See generally* M. HOWE, JUSTICE OLIVER WENDELL HOLMES: THE PROVING YEARS (1963); M. WHITE, *supra* note 38, at 71-75. For a discussion of Green's interest in history, see Frank, *supra* note 28, at 439-40.

41. *Cf.* L. FRIEDMAN, *supra* note 2, at 531-32 (discussing Langdell's belief that law is a science).

42. [Holmes], *supra* note 28, at 341.

and in part, one suspects, because of the absence of any powerful pressure for conceptual unity in American jurisprudence. By the 1850s, the haphazardness of the writ system was a source of irritation to those working with it in the legal profession, and alternatives to writ classifications came to be considered. The nature of those alternatives was influenced by the conceptualist tendencies of contemporaneous legal thought.

The conventional explanation of the demise of the writ system is that in the early years of the century dissatisfaction arose with the system of pleading, which was founded on enforced conformity to arcane technicalities.[43] Dissatisfaction, according to this explanation, led to the formation of law-revision commissions in states such as New York and Massachusetts. These commissions were charged with making the common law more intelligible to laymen. At the same time a movement for codification of American laws emerged, which in its headiest versions advocated total replacement of the common law with an American civil code. Although the codification movement ultimately failed, its impetus combined with revisionist impulses to produce a reform of civil procedure. The first manifestation of reform came in the New York Code of Procedure, adopted in 1848, which abolished the forms of action on which the writ system was based. Other states quickly followed New York's example, with 11 states abolishing the writ system by 1856 and 23 by the 1870s.[44]

Thus related, the story has a nice historical momentum, with the pent-up demands of the Jacksonians finding voice in the 1840s through the genius of David Dudley Field, author of the 1848 New York Code.[45] Unfortunately not enough scrutiny of the writ system has taken place to justify the conventional explanation. The

---

43. *See, e.g.,* L. FRIEDMAN, *supra* note 2, at 340-46; R. MILLAR, CIVIL PROCEDURE OF THE TRIAL COURT IN HISTORICAL PERSPECTIVE 52-53 (1952); A. SCHLESINGER, THE AGE OF JACKSON 329-33 (1945).

44. *See* R. MILLAR, *supra* note 43, at 54-55.

45. *See* L. FRIEDMAN, *supra* note 2, at 340-43, 351-53; A. SCHLESINGER, *supra* note 43, at 330-33.

scrutiny that has taken place, in fact, reveals a more complex series of developments. A study of Massachusetts pleading in the late 18th and early 19th centuries,[46] for example, has shown that the writ system was not suddenly abandoned in that state, but was gradually and irregularly modified over a 70-year period. Although fraught with technicalities, the Massachusetts system of pleading was not universally rigid: amended pleas were permitted [47] and multiple actions were common.[48] Thus when Massachusetts eventually abolished writ pleading in 1851, that "reform" was not a major modification of existing practice.

Accompanying the overly dramatic account of the writ system's demise has been an overestimation of the amount of dissatisfaction with the system, especially among those who were most significantly affected by it. The writ system served an important jurisprudential function in the early 19th century, that of a surrogate for doctrinal classification. The rigor of the writs, as Green pointed out, tended to make procedural requirements the equivalent of doctrinal categories. "Whatever may be said of [the science of special pleading] as a practical method of meting out justice between private litigants," Green wrote in 1871, "it is certain that the lawyer who was master of it stood upon an eminence which gave him a clearer view of the position of his case, in its relation both to law and the surrounding facts, than there is any other means of obtaining. ... Indeed, a knowledge of criminal pleading is a knowledge of criminal law." [49] One could also master "tort" doctrine by mastering the technicalities of pleading, since, in the writs of trespass and case, the elements of proof that gained one access to a court were often the same elements by which one recovered. Problems of causation were solved by the writ system's requirements, and affirmative defenses such as

---

46. Nelson, *The Reform of Common Law Pleading in Massachusetts 1760-1830: Adjudication as a Prelude to Legislation,* 122 U. PA. L. REV. 97 (1973).

47. *Id.* at 112-15.

48. *Id.* at 119.

49. *N. GREEN, Some Results of Reform in Indictments,* in ESSAYS, *supra* note 29, at 151.

justification or contributory fault were not usually allowed. A plaintiff took pains to show how his injury resulted, either "directly" (trespass) or "indirectly" (case), from a defendant's act. If he were able to establish a chain of direct or indirect causation, and used the proper writ, his chances for recovery were good.[50] Knowing the procedure for suing in trespass or case, then, was the equivalent of knowing the doctrinal elements of those actions.

It is difficult, at least from a 20th-century perspective, to identify the sources of the widespread dissatisfaction conventionally attributed to this system. Few trained lawyers would likely have opposed it, since once mastered it proved a handy digest of the common law.[51] Neophyte lawyers or nonlawyers might fall victim to its technicalities, but if customs prevailing in early 19th-century Massachusetts were followed elsewhere, rigid adherence to the formalities of pleading was not universally required, and leave to amend an ill-considered plea was regularly obtained.[52]

Yet the fact remains that the writ system was widely abolished in the 1850s with remarkably little opposition. In light of the strong lawyer resistance to the codification that took place in the mid-19th century,[53] the abolition of technical pleading might seem a little surprising, since the common law, so vigorously defended by lawyers, derived its substantive doctrines largely from its pleading requirements. But if one conjectures that the change came from within — that the system was discarded by those who had profited most from it — the collapse of the writ system becomes more understandable. If one recalls that the writ system functioned as a device for classifying substantive doctrine, one might hypothesize that writ pleading lost support when it ceased to function successfully in that capacity. Its failure to perform as a means of

53. *See* M. BLOOMFIELD, AMERICAN LAWYERS IN A CHANGING SOCIETY, 1776-1876, at 83-88 (1976); P. MILLER, THE LIFE OF THE MIND IN AMERICA 251-54 (1965).

50. For a description of writ pleading in Massachusetts, see Nelson, *supra* note 46, at 98-116.

51. Dane's *Abridgment* was organized around existing forms of action. N. DANE, *supra* note 14.

52. *See* Nelson, *supra* note 46, at 112-16.

doctrinal organization can be traced to the tendencies toward diversity and dissonance that marked early 19th-century jurisprudence. As the ambit of legal concerns widened and diversified, different localities adopted their own rules of special pleading. In another age the Balkanization of pleading rules might have been intellectually offensive; in the America of the early 19th century, however, jurisprudential order was not universally prized. By the 1850s, however, the haphazardness of the writ system and its structural emphasis — on discrete elements rather than on universals — came to be regarded as analytically unsatisfactory.

With each relaxation of the technicalities of pleading there was a loss of certainty and predictability about substantive legal rules; if the writ system was only indifferently adhered to during the early 19th century, its value as a classification device was undermined. David Dudley Field, for example, called writ pleading " 'clumsily devised,' " and " 'inconvenient in practice.' " [54] In addition, the writ system's emphasis on arcane particulars ran counter to a growing scholarly interest in deriving universal principles. "Like other sciences," a commentator noted in 1851, the law was "supposed to be pervaded by general rules, ... [and] to have first or fundamental principles, never modified." [55] Some years later, Holmes, in discussing a recently enacted state code of procedure, linked this search for scientific universals to a realization of the failings of the writ system:

> If those forms had been based upon a comprehensive survey of the field of rights and duties, so that they embodied in a practical shape a classification of the law, with a form of action to correspond to every substantial duty, the question would be other than it is. But [the writs] are in fact so arbitrary in character, and owe their origin to such purely historical causes, that nothing keeps them but our respect for the sources of our jurisprudence.[56]

---

54. P. MILLER, *supra* note 53, at 259.

55. *Id.* at 161.

56. [Holmes], Book Review, 5 AM. L. REV. 359 (1871) (reviewing THE CODE OF PROCEDURE OF THE STATE OF NEW YORK, AS AMENDED TO 1870 (10th ed. J. Townshend 1870)).

This same dissatisfaction with the particularistic approach of the writs, and a comparable inclination to seek universal guiding principles in the law, motivated Francis Hilliard to write the first generalized treatment of Torts in America. "By a singular process of inversion," Hilliard wrote in commenting on previous treatments of tort actions, "*remedies* [procedural requirements] have been substituted for *wrongs* [substantive elements of an action]." [57] "It is difficult to understand," Hilliard maintained,

> how so obviously unphilosophical a practice became established. . . .
>
> . . . To consider wrongs as merely incidental to remedies; to inquire for what injuries a particular action may be brought, instead of explaining the injuries themselves, and then asking what actions may be brought for their redress, seems to me to reserve the natural order of things. . . .[58]

For Hilliard, emphasis on the writs gave "a false view of the law, as a system of forms rather than principles; [it] elevate[d] the positive and conventional above the absolute and permanent." [59] Hilliard's approach to Torts sought to show that the subject "involve[d] principles of great comprehensiveness, not modified or colored by diverse *forms of action*." [60] In the developing tradition of 19th-century scientific methodology, he proceeded from universals to particulars.

In sum, one can associate the demise of the writ system with the emergence of conceptualism in intellectual thought. By the 1850s the haphazardness of the writ system had become a source of irritation to those working with it in the legal profession, and a search had begun for alternatives to writ classifications.[61] In the

---

57. 1 F. HILLIARD, *supra* note 2, at v (emphasis in original).

58. *Id.* at vi-vii.

59. *Id.* at vii.

60. *Id.* at viii (emphasis in original).

61. Another factor possibly prompting mid-19th-century American lawyers to reassess the worth of the writ system was a growing consciousness of the image of their profession. *See* M. BLOOMFIELD, *supra* note 53, at 136-90.

effort by glossators to replace the writs with generalized substantive legal principles and doctrines, the idea of treating Torts as an independent legal subject came into being. The origins of Torts, then, can be traced to the interaction, in post-Civil War America, of a conceptualist jurisprudence with a deteriorating system of pleading and procedure. Because of this interaction recognition of an independent branch of tort law was, at least, possible. Still wanting was the development of theoretical principles by which Torts could identify itself.

III. A THEORY FOR TORTS: THE EMERGENCE OF NEGLIGENCE

Francis Hilliard conceded in his 1859 preface that although he had "entire confidence in the *idea*" of treating Torts as a separate subject, he had "much diffidence as to the *execution*." [62] His treatise, in fact, was not entirely successful in distinguishing Torts from other legal categories. Included in his discussion of torts were chapters on crimes and property and, in his discussion of slander, treatments of evidence and damages. Hilliard's effort was representative of early attempts to organize the subject matter of Torts. In James Barr Ames's casebook, which appeared in 1874, coverage was limited to intentional torts and trespass.[63] It was classifications like these that caused Holmes, reviewing Charles Addison's treatise on Torts in the *American Law Review* in 1871, to assert that "Torts is not a proper subject for a law book." [64] He found an absence of a "cohesion or legal relationship" between the variously treated topics. Trespass, for example, was far closer to "possession enforced by real actions" than to assault and battery; yet the two were paired as "torts." [65] Holmes "long[ed] for the day when we may see these subjects treated by a writer capable of dealing with them philosophically." [66] By philosophically Holmes meant, as Hilliard and Green had, with sufficient consciousness of scientifically derived universal principles.

---

62. 1 F. HILLIARD, *supra* note 2, at x (emphasis in original).
63. J. AMES, *supra* note 4.
64. [Holmes], *supra* note 28, at 341.
65. *Id.*
66. *Id.*

It was at this point — the 1870s — that an academic search for overriding theoretical principles in Torts seems to have begun in earnest.[67] Two years after Holmes's assertion that Torts was an unfit subject for a treatise, he attempted to formulate a theory of Torts; in passing, he noted that "there is no fault to be found with the contents of text-books on this subject." [68] The study of Torts had become promising for Holmes because he had been able to discover that "an enumeration of the actions which have been successful, and of those which have failed, defines the extent of the primary duties imposed by the law." [69] Examination of the tort writs showed Holmes that in the case of certain civil wrongs, such as allowing dammed water or wild animals to escape, liability was found regardless of the culpability of the actor; that in others, such as assault or fraud, culpability was a prerequisite for liability; and that in still others the culpability of the defendant, although pivotal to recovery, was determined not from "facts" but "from motives

---

67. In 1870, Green, in his preface to Charles G. Addison's *Law of Torts,* wrote that Torts was "the law of those rights which avail against all persons generally, or against all mankind." Green noted that Torts was "usually treated of under the titles of the various forms of action which lie for the infringement of such rights." He felt that such a treatment tended "to confuse these fundamental principles which should be kept distinct in the mind of the student." Green, *Preface* to C. ADDISON, LAW OF TORTS at iii (abr. 1870). Holmes reviewed the book in the *American Law Review. See* note 28 *supra.* Others working on the reorientation of Torts at the same time were Melville Bigelow, Charles Doe, and Thomas Cooley. *See* M. HOWE, *supra* note 40, at 83-84, 139.

Although this article does not focus on the professionalization of the field of law in the late 19th century, there is doubtless some significance to the fact that conceptualism in academic law emerged at the same time that law schools began to hire professors on a full-time basis. *See* Stevens, *supra* note 7, at 424-41. With law designated a "science" and academics urged to develop scientific methodologies, it was perhaps inevitable that an ordering of intellectual fields would take place, if for no other reason than a grand synthesis of Torts or Contracts provided a means of making one's professional mark.

68. [Holmes], *The Theory of Torts,* 7 AM. L. REV. 652, 660 (1873). Mark DeWolfe Howe attributes this essay to Holmes, M. HOWE, *supra* note 40, at 64. ·

69. [Holmes], *supra* note 68, at 659-60.

of policy ... kept purposely indefinite." [70] This last category of cases constituted "modern negligence." [71] Thus Torts could be subdivided into three categories: absolute liability, intentional torts, and negligence.[72]

Holmes's theory was not remarkable in itself; common law writs had, as noted, acquired roughly similar classifications through their procedural requirements. The significant contribution Holmes made was the isolation, in academic literature, of negligence as a substantive tort doctrine. This contribution was significant in two respects. First, it articulated in authoritative terms an expansion in American case law of the concept of negligence from a specific, predetermined duty to a general standard of care. Second, Holmes's isolation of "modern negligence" provided Torts with a philosophical principle [73] (no liability for tortious conduct absent fault; fault to be determined by reference to "the felt necessities of the times" [74]) that, in a short space of time, came to dominate tort law. So infatuated was Holmes with his discovery of "the great mass of cases" in which a negligence standard was applied, and so convinced was he of the soundness of conditioning tort liability on a policy determination that a standard of care had been violated, that only eight years after his first theory of Torts he was prepared to argue that absolute liability had never truly existed in tort law, and that fault, either in the strict (intentional) or looser (negligent) sense, had always been a prerequisite for liability.[75]

---

70. *Id.* at 659.

71. *Id.* at 653.

72. The efforts of Holmes and his contemporaries to develop a general theory of Torts mark one instance in which an American development in 19th-century legal scholarship preceded an analogous development in England. The first English treatise to attempt a generalized treatment of Torts, Frederick Pollock's *The Law of Torts,* did not appear until 1887. It was dedicated to Holmes.

73. *See* [Holmes], *supra* note 68, at 660.

74. The phrase is Holmes's. O. HOLMES, THE COMMON LAW 1 (1881).

75. *Id.* at 89. Holmes acknowledged that fault might not have been a prerequisite "in that period of dry precedent which is so often to be found midway between a creative epoch and a period of solvent philosophical reaction." *Id.*

Holmes's conception of negligence as a general standard of conduct and, parenthetically, as a distinguishing principle for tort law, was one toward which certain American courts had previously been groping. Prior to the 1830s, with the exception of a handful of cases in New York,[76] the term "negligence" generally referred to "neglect" or failure to perform a specific duty imposed by contract, statute, or common law. Examples were the duty of a sheriff to maintain prisoners in custody[77] and the duty of a town to keep bridges in good condition.[78] Suits arising out of the escape of prisoners or damage to bridges or roads alleged that the official responsible had been negligent or neglectful. Commentators used negligence in a similar fashion.[79] There is little indication that prior to the 1830s negligence was generally equated with carelessness or fault. A neglectful person could be found liable simply for nonfeasance.[80]

During the 1830s certain state courts, among them New York, Massachusetts, and Pennsylvania, increasingly came to associate negligence with violations of a general standard of care that was not limited to specific persons, offices, or occupations. *Brown v. Kendall,*[81] A Massachusetts case in which a dog owner inadvertently injured a bystander while attempting to break up a dog fight, is regularly cited as the first American case clearly to employ a "fault" standard in Torts.[82] It was preceded, however, by at least three other cases in New York and Pennsylvania.[83]

---

76. *E.g.,* Percival v. Hickey, 18 Johns. 257 (N.Y. 1820); Foot v. Wiswall, 14 Johns. 304 (N.Y. 1817). *See* M. HORWITZ, *supra* note 5, at 85-97.

77. *E.g.,* Patten v. Halsted, 1 N.J.L. 277 (1795).

78. *E.g.,* Lobdell v. New Bedford, 1 Mass. 153 (1804).

79. *See, e.g.,* 3 N. DANE, *supra* note 14, at 31-33.

80. *See, e.g.,* Patten v. Halsted, 1 N.J.L. 277 (1795). *See also* M. HORWITZ, *supra* note 5, at 86.

81. 60 Mass. (6 Cush.) 292 (1850).

82. *See, e.g.,* M. FRANKLIN, INJURIES AND REMEDIES: CASES AND MATERIALS ON TORT LAW AND ALTERNATIVES 30 (1971); W. PROSSER, J. WADE & V. SCHWARTZ, CASES AND MATERIALS ON TORTS 9 (6th ed. 1976).

83. Livingston v. Adams, 8 Cow. 175 (N.Y. 1828); Panton v. Holland, 17 Johns. 92 (N.Y. 1819); Lehigh Bridge Co. v. Lehigh Coal & Navigation Co., 4 Rawle 8 (Pa. 1833). *Livingston v. Adams* and *Lehigh Bridge* were "bursting dam" cases, and *Panton v. Holland* a case in which a foundation for a house had been dug improperly.

Brown v. Kendall's significance lay in the impressive articulation of a generalized "fault" standard by Chief Justice Lemuel Shaw, a judge who by the 1850s had come to view the common law as a set of broad and comprehensive principles.[84] Shaw did not originate the association of the term "negligence" with violations of a general standard of care in *Brown v. Kendall*,[85] but suggested that the fault principle had wide application. Negligence, Shaw implied, was more than a neglect of specific duties imposed only under certain circumstances; it was the touchstone (and principal limiting factor) of a general theory of civil obligation, under which persons owed a universal, but confined, duty to take care not to injure their neighbors.[86]

Viewed in this fashion, the modern negligence principle in tort law seems to have been an intellectual response to the increased number of accidents involving persons in no preexisting relationships with each other — "stranger" cases.[87] In this limited sense the conventional identification of the rise of Torts with the advent of industrialism is accurate. Advances in transportation and industry — mills, dams, carriages, ships — made injuries involving strangers more common. As judges and legal scholars sought to establish a theory of liability for stranger accidents, older notions of neglect proved inadequate, for increasingly parties involved in accidents owed no previously imposed duties to one another. The special requirements of individual writs may have served to distinguish one tortious injury from another, but they did not address the principal policy question raised by stranger accident cases: As a matter of policy, what general duties were owed to all by all? [88] Once the import of this question became clear, the ground

---

84. Norway Plains Co. v. Boston & M.R.R., 67 Mass. (1 Gray) 263, 267 (1854). *See* G. WHITE, THE AMERICAN JUDICIAL TRADITION 60-61 (1976).

85. *See* M. HORWITZ, *supra* note 5, at 90 (maintaining that "an exaggerated significance" has been assigned to *Brown v. Kendall*).

86. *See* 60 Mass. (6 Cush.) at 296.

87. M. HORWITZ, *supra* note 5, uses similar terminology. Professor Horwitz sees mid-19th-century judges as "develop[ing] the idea of duties owed to noncontracting strangers." *Id.* at 95.

88. *See* [Holmes], *supra* note 68, at 663.

for a new theory of tort liability in stranger cases was broken. Neglect was widened to become a generalized theory of legal carelessness; an objective fault standard emerged as a limiting principle of tort liability; modern negligence was born.

Two stranger cases from the 1870s, one of which made use of Holmes's insights, illustrate the increasing dominance of the newer generalized conception of negligence. Both cases, *Brown v. Collins* [89] and *Losee v. Buchanan*,[90] were reactions against the implications of *Rylands v. Fletcher*,[91] the 1868 House of Lords decision holding a defendant liable regardless of fault for allowing water to seep through his land and damage the mines of a neighbor. Both the *Brown* and *Losee* courts concluded that strict liability for injuries to strangers was not to be retained in modern American tort law. In *Brown* a pair of horses, startled by the engine of a passing train, had shied off the road and damaged a lamppost on an adjoining property owner's lot. The parties stipulated that the driver "was in the use of ordinary care and skill" in managing his horses prior to the time they became frightened. Judge Charles Doe held that, absent a showing of "actual fault" in the driver, no liability would attach.[92] Relying in part on Holmes's observations in *The Theory of Torts*,[93] Doe maintained that to extend the *Rylands v. Fletcher* principle of "absolute liability without evidence of negligence," seemed "contrary to the analogies and the general principles of the common law." [94] Holding a defendant liable without a showing that he had acted negligently was the equivalent of suggesting that "every one is liable for all damage done by superior force overpowering him, and using him or his property as an instrument of violence." [95] Doe argued that liability in tort,

---

89. 53 N.H. 442 (1873).
90. 51 N.Y. 476 (1873).
91. 3 L.R. 1 E. & I. App. 330 (1868).
92. 53 N.H. at 450-51.
93. *Id.* at 445.
94. *Id.* at 450.
95. *Id.* at 451.

where a defendant had acted unintentionally, should be conditioned on a showing of lack of "ordinary care and skill." [96]

One of the precedents Doe relied upon in *Brown v. Collins* was *Losee v. Buchanan,* a New York case also decided in 1873. In the absence of any New Hampshire precedent for applying negligence in the generalized sense employed in *Brown,* Doe had looked to other courts and scholars for support for his critique of *Rylands v. Fletcher.* But in *Losee* Commissioner Robert Earl had the benefit of a prior New York case,[97] which he cited as holding that " '[w]here one builds a mill-dam upon a proper model, and the work is well and substantially done, he is not liable to an action though it break away .... Negligence should be shown in order to make him liable.' " [98] Earl's task was to extend that principle to a case in which a steam boiler had exploded, damaging buildings on a neighboring tract of land. He thought the extension simple enough. "We must have factories, machinery, dams, canals and railroads," he maintained. "If I have any of these upon my lands, and they are not a nuisance and are not so managed as to become such, I am not responsible for any damage they accidentally and unavoidably do may neighbor. He receives his compensation for such damage by the general good, in which he shares ...." [99]

As for *Rylands v. Fletcher,* Judge Earl found it to be "in direct conflict with the law as settled in this country." [100] The "universal" American rule, Earl asserted, was that "no one can be made liable for injuries to the person or property of another without some fault or negligence on his part." [101] Negligence was thus much more than a specific duty. It was a general precondition of liability for unintentional torts — a "universal rule" that helped define the subject of Torts itself. As Holmes wrote eight years later in *The Common Law:* "The general principle of our law is that loss from

---

96. *Id.* at 442.
97. Livingston v. Adams, 8 Cow. 175 (N.Y. 1828).
98. 51 N.Y. at 487.
99. *Id.* at 484-85.
100. *Id.* at 486-87.
101. *Id.* at 491.

accident must lie where it falls .... 'No case or principle can be found ... subjecting an individual to liability for an act done without fault on his part.' " [102]

With the growth of negligence from a specific unperformed duty owed to a particular person to a generalized standard of care owed to all, the emergence of Torts as an independent branch of law was ensured. Impulses to conceptualize law around a series of universal principles had extracted Torts from a diverse series of writs and transformed it into a discernible academic subject; these same impulses were struggling to find some unity in the various civil wrongs that were being cataloged. Negligence provided that unity; it also provided a workable standard — a limiting principle — for the numerous inadvertent injuries involving strangers that had come to be a characteristic late 19th-century tort action. Negligence can thus be identified with all of the trends that combined to produce the emergence of the subject of Torts in America. Negligence was a universal rule, satisfying conceptualist tendencies in legal thought; it was an all-purpose cause of action, supplanting both trespass and case; and it was an evaluative standard for decisionmaking in cases involving unintentional injuries to strangers.

The close identification of Torts with the rise of negligence can be seen in the evolution of Torts casebooks and treatises by legal scholars in the late 19th century. As late as the third edition of Hilliard's treatise in 1866, negligence had only a nine-page treatment, and most of the cases cited used the term in its earlier sense of failure to perform a specific duty.[103] Ames's 1874 casebook, as indicated, contained no negligence cases.[104] By 1880, in Thomas Cooley's treatise,[105] the need for a generalized treatment of negligence had begun to be perceived. Cooley devoted

---

102. O. HOLMES, *supra* note 74, at 94-95 (quoting Chief Justice Nelson of New York). Holmes cited *Brown v. Kendall* with approval at 105-06.

103. *See* 1 F. HILLIARD, THE LAW OF TORTS 115-23 (3d ed. Boston 1866).

104. *See* p. 683 *supra*.

105. T. COOLEY, A TREATISE ON THE LAW OF TORTS (1880).

a chapter to "Wrongs from Non-Performance of Conventional and Statutory Duties," and included negligence among them.[106] But he also recognized that "in every relation of life ... some duty is imposed for the benefit of others," [107] and in a separate chapter discussed "the general principles which must govern when ... one has been injured by the neglect of another to observe due care." [108] His discussion included reference to a great many stranger accident cases.[109] In 1893 Ames's casebook was supplemented by a second volume, authored by Jeremiah Smith, that devoted six chapters to negligence, including discussions of standards of care, the concept of a duty, and contributory negligence.[110] Smith retained a chapter on negligence as a duty imposed by contract; but that chapter was omitted in the 1909 edition.[111] By 1911 John H. Wigmore apparently believed that Torts was sufficiently discrete to merit a fullblown conceptualist treatment. He divided the "Science of Law" into "public" and "private" components,[112] and each component into "groups" and their "topic[s]," [113] and proceeded to analyze the legal relations this categorization created.[144] He found Torts to be concerned with universal, "non-refusable" duties, which created correlative "general rights." [115] He then subdivided "general rights" into three elements — damage, causation, and excuse [116] — and further subdivided these elements [117] in a virtual mania of classification. His technique was made possible, Wigmore felt, because Torts,

---

106. *Id.* at 628-58.
107. *Id.* at 659.
108. *Id.*
109. *Id.* at 661-66 (citing cases).
110. 2 J. AMES & J. SMITH, A SELECTION OF CASES ON THE LAW OF TORTS (J. Smith ed. 1893).
111. *Id.* at iii (J. Smith ed. 1909).
112. 1 J. WIGMORE, SELECT CASES ON THE LAW OF TORTS, app. B, at vii, x (1911).
113. *Id.* at xi.
114. *Id.* at x.
115. *Id.* at x, xi.
116. *Id.* at xi.
117. *Id.* at xi-1.

being a branch of law, had "the quality of being uniform and regular." [118]

Behind Wigmore's nomenclature was the triumph of an insight of Holmes's in the 1870s: Torts was that part of the law concerned with universal private duties "of all to all." [119] It was, in short, virtually synonymous with negligence. Intentional torts were clear violations of duties "of all the world to all the world"; [120] they raised few policy questions and primarily involved only problems of causation and assessment of damages. Inadvertent, nonnegligent torts were not actionable unless a given duty had been imposed on the nonnegligent actor by statute, custom, or practice. Negligence cases most starkly raised the policy issue that Holmes and his followers found most significant: When does society impose a duty not to harm one's neighbor? Thus Torts, by the close of the 19th century, had been transformed from its former status as a handful of civil, noncontractual wrongs, some of which (assault and battery) were retained in the new conceptualization of the late 19th century, others of which (neglect) were cast aside in the treatises and in the courts. Torts had become an entity distinct from the other private-law categories of Contracts or Property: it was that branch of private law which dealt with universally imposed duties.

IV. The 19th-Century Legacy

The climate of opinion in which Torts emerged as an independent branch of the law has had significant effects on its subsequent development. Tracing those effects is beyond the scope of this article, but there is one general legacy of the formative period of Torts worth noting here. The scientific methodologies of Green and Holmes, as well as those of conceptualists in other fields, regularly succeeded in deriving social theories that were "evolutionary" in character, that is, theories that built their intellectual systems on the assumptions that life was constantly changing and man

---

118. *Id.* at vii.
119. The phrase is Holmes's in *The Theory of Torts, supra* note 68, at 662.
120. *Id.* at 660.

continually adapting to change. Looking back on his intellectual experiences in the 1860s and 1870s, Holmes observed that evolutionary theories had affected "our whole way of thinking about the universe." [121] One of the paradoxes of the conceptualism of this period was that although it tended to derive monistic theories, those theories rested on a sense of fluidity: the evolutionary "laws" of the universe were everywhere true but were based on the permanency of change. In both Green's and Holmes's writing in the post-Civil War years one can see a dual concern for achieving order and unity and for recognizing that "all things in nature ... shade into each other by imperceptible degrees." [122] Against a scientifically derived philosophical synthesis was juxtaposed "the felt necessities of the times." [123]

Historians have noted the two-pronged character of these evolutionary theories: they led, in the early 20th century, either to a deterministic view of society, in which the fittest invariably survived, or to a pragmatic view, in which man continually adapted himself to changing conditions.[124] One can see traces of this same duality in early 20th-century scholarly approaches to tort law. Even though a conceptualist methodology persisted among some torts scholars as late as 1920,[125] other torts scholars soon disassociated themselves from conceptualism in its most monistic forms. Shortly after the triumph of negligence as a unifying principle of Torts, scholars suggested that the negligence principle had little meaning outside the changing circumstances in which it was to be applied.[126]

When this critique of conceptualism in Torts, often identified

---

121. 1 HOLMES-POLLOCK LETTERS 57-58 (M. Howe ed. 1941).

122. N. GREEN, *supra* note 34, at 166. *See* Frank, *supra* note 28, at 436-37.

123. O. HOLMES, *supra* note 74, at 660.

124. *See, e.g.,* E. GOLDMAN, RENDEZVOUS WITH DESTINY (1952).

125. *See, e.g.,* Beale, *The Proximate Consequences of an Act,* 33 HARV. L. REV. 633, 636 (1920).

126. *See, e.g.,* L. GREEN, *Analysis of Tort Cases,* in JUDGE AND JURY 21 (1930); L. GREEN, THE JUDICIAL PROCESS IN TORTS CASES iii (1931). (Both of Green's books contain other examples of this critique of the negligence principle.)

with realism in American jurisprudence,[127] is reexamined in light of the intellectual origins of Torts, an additional observation suggests itself. It is conceivable that the evolutionary character of negligence theory may have itself contributed to the dissatisfaction with universal rules in Torts. The dynamic component of evolutionary theories was the component most attractive to early 20th-century intellectuals. Rapid change came to be seen as a permanent feature of American civilization, and legal scholars, as well as other intellectuals, criticized universal rules as mechanical and static.[128] The major late-19th-century rule of Torts, the negligence principle, had an inherent capacity to adapt itself to change, since its operative standard, "ordinary care under the circumstances," presumed that no one set of circumstances was precisely like another. But the negligence principle was also intended to be monistic, in the sense of being capable of universal application in a predictable manner. As suspicion of monistic principles mounted in the early 20th century, the fluid character of negligence was stressed.[129] It was a short step from perceiving the negligence principle as fluid to perceiving it as meaningless outside the circumstances in which it was applied.

CONCLUSION: THE ROLE OF DOMINANT METHODOLOGIES IN AMERICAN LEGAL HISTORY

This article has attempted to stress the importance of the values and thought patterns of 19th-century American intellectuals in fostering the growth of Torts as an independent branch of law. I have resisted a linear explanation for what "caused" the emergence of Torts, suggesting that the growth of

---

127. In his celebrated article, *Some Realism About Realism,* 44 HARV. L. REV. 1222, 1226 n.18 (1931), Karl Llewellyn identified Leon Green as one of the advocates of "realistic" jurisprudence.

128. *See* White, *From Sociological Jurisprudence to Realism: Jurisprudence and Social Change in Early Twentieth-Century America,* 58 VA. L. REV. 999, 1003-05 (1972).

129. *See, e.g.,* B. CARDOZO, THE NATURE OF THE JUDICIAL PROCESS 161 (1921); B. CARDOZO, THE PARADOXES OF LEGAL SCIENCE 85 (1928).

industrialization is only part of the explanation. A fuller understanding of the origins of Torts as a separate branch of law requires, I have maintained, an appreciation of the changes in American intellectual culture that took place after 1850.

By my focus on scholars and academicians within the legal profession, I do not mean to suggest that the role of those groups in shaping the content of law is more significant than that of practitioners, judges, or other persons with legal training. I do mean to suggest, however, that it is more significant than perhaps commonly supposed; that treatise writers and scholars do not merely collect data supplied by courts and practitioners, but organize it in accordance with their existing intellectual inclinations. The raw material for a theory that would distinguish Torts from other areas of law was present in mid-19th-century America. The significance of a classification of Torts as a discrete branch of law was accentuated by the collapse of the writ system, a collapse that was not brought about by scholars. But the methodological apparatus that ultimately derived the modern negligence principle was created by intellectuals. The independence of Torts was ultimately linked to the triumph, in Victorian America, of a conceptualist methodology.

The significance of dominant disciplinary or professional methodologies,[130] and the value choices or assumptions those methodologies tacitly make, seems to me to represent a theme in the history of American law that has received inadequate treatment. Current scholarship in American legal history makes the now-commonplace assumption that law "mirrors" [131] society and that factors "external" [132] to the workings of legal institutions have had an important influence on the course of American law.

---

130. The phrase "dominant methodology" can be analogized to "paradigm" or "disciplinary matrix" as used by Thomas Kuhn. T. KUHN, THE STRUCTURE OF SCIENTIFIC REVOLUTIONS 175, 182 (2d ed. 1970). Kuhn defines "paradigm," in the sense most akin to my focus here, as "the entire constellation of beliefs, values, [and] techniques . . . shared by the members of a given community." *Id.* at 175.

131. L. FRIEDMAN, *supra* note 2, at 10.

132. Gordon, *Introduction: J. Willard Hurst and the Common Law Tradition in American Legal Historiography,* 10 LAW & SOC. REV. 9 (1975).

While this assumption is not unsound, it tends to underemphasize the role of dominant thought patterns within the legal profession that form the intellectual context in which "external" developments take place. We need to know much more about the origins of these patterns of thought, whose primary function seems to be that of shaping and limiting the interpretation of the changing source materials of the legal profession.

My interest here has been in identifying some of the cultural forces that served to focus the theoretical concerns of American intellectuals, including legal scholars, during the period when Torts emerged as an independent branch of law. My analytical model has been one that seeks to identify the features of American culture that, during given periods, shape the intellectual inquiries of scholars in academic disciplines or professions into tacitly approved pursuits, reflecting the acknowledged primacy of certain values, such as order, unity, creativity, or independence, and creating certain methodological orientations, such as conceptualism.

The relationship between ideas and events in American legal history is probably more complex than some current scholarship implies. The fields into which law is classified, the subjects taught in American law schools, the treatise literature, and the doctrinal bases of case law are not merely reflections of current events; to an important extent they are the end products of intellectual trends within the legal profession. These trends themselves develop from complicated interactions of events and ideas which legal historians have not studied in any detail. Examining the dominant methodological assumptions of academicians and other scholars in the legal profession is, in my view, a potentially fruitful way to address the relationship among ideas, events, and the history of American law. This article is intended, therefore, as an initial exploration of a broad and complex subject.

191

CHAPTER 3. THE JUDICIARY

I have written elsewhere* on appellate judges in America and shall not repeat myself here. This chapter merely underscores, through essays on two twentieth-century judges of high stature, my conviction that significant contributions to American legal thought have been made by holders of judgeships, particularly at the appellate levels.

The Rise and Fall of Justice Holmes describes the capacity of well-known American judges to serve as inspirational models for educated persons. Justice Oliver Wendell Holmes' "rise" to folk-heroism and subsequent "fall" from grace among leading professional critics illustrates the extent to which a judge, like a president or other comparably visible public figure, can mirror in his changing reputation a nation's collective value conflicts. The fact that Americans can occasionally endow judges with such emotional significance testifies to the importance we ascribe to the office.

Allocating Power Among Agencies and Courts considers a related dimension of judging in America: the capacity to exert influence across spans of time. Justice Louis Brandeis' image in twentieth-century historiography may have fluctuated in a manner comparable to that of Holmes, but Brandeis' "legacy" remains: the impact his thinking has on current legal doctrine. In administrative law, particularly, Brandeis' conception of the proper allocation of power between administrative agencies and courts continues to influence current practices. Like ancient English forms of procedure, American judges can rule us from their graves.

---

* G. EDWARD WHITE, THE AMERICAN JUDICIAL TRADITION: PROFILES OF LEADING AMERICAN JUDGES (1976).

THE RISE AND FALL OF JUSTICE HOLMES

The University of Chicago Law Review, Vol. 39, No. 1 (1971)

Occasionally the American nation sees itself in the life of one of its citizens. Something about the experiences, background, attitudes, or accomplishments of an individual seems particularly evocative of American culture, or at least a vision thereof. Such a life was that of Justice Oliver Wendell Holmes. In addition to being a man of great popular appeal,[1] Holmes has held considerable interest for the intellectual community. From the publication of Holmes's *The Common Law* in 1881 until the present day, legal scholars, philosophers, political scientists, historians, literary critics, and journalists [2] have attempted to understand and articulate the qualities that have made Holmes, in their eyes, an especially noteworthy representative of American civilization. This article traces the changing image of one man in the eyes of American intellectuals through the years — the "rise and fall" of Justice Holmes.

I. INTRODUCTION

American intellectuals have focused on Holmes in three capacities: as Brahmin, as ideologue, and as stylist. The shifting image of Holmes in the American scholarly community reflects changes in the attitutde of intellectuals toward Holmes in each capacity.

The term Brahmin suggests Holmes's close association with a Boston tradition of social privilege and intellectual enterprise. During the twenty years following Holmes's birth in 1841, Boston and its surrounding countryside produced the first major concentration of intellectual activity in American history. The

---

1. Holmes has been the only Supreme Court Justice in American history whose life has been the subject of a Broadway play, *The Magnificent Yankee,* which appeared in 1951.

2. The enumerated groups compose the "American intellectual community" for the purposes of this essay. Journalists include writers for the *New York Times,* the *New York Herald Tribune,* the *Christian Science Monitor,* and certain periodicals of popular scholarship, such as the *Nation* and the *New Republic.*

individuals who made contributions, which ranged from discoveries in natural science to poetry, were from wealthy or socially respectable families. Many had traveled to Europe in their youth, some for educational purposes; many had attended Harvard College, some also reading law for a time; a distinct minority, such as the Adamses, had served in the government.[3]

Of those names associated with Brahminism — Parkman, Agassiz, James, Lowell, Emerson, Longfellow, Parker, to list some — that of Holmes was among the most celebrated. At his son's birth Dr. Oliver Wendell Holmes, Sr. had already gained notice for an emotional appeal on behalf of the threatened *U.S. Constitution*.[4] During Holmes's youth his father had enhanced his professional status with an influential paper on puerperal fever [5] and ultimately emerged as the leading social historian of his time with the publication of *The Autocrat of the Breakfast Table*.[6] The success of the elder Holmes and the equal success of Holmes, Jr. in a different area of endeavor, coupled with an unmistakable tension between father and son,[7] has served as a starting point for scholarly explorations into the relationship between Holmes and his heritage. The explorations have revealed a relationship rich in ambiguities.

The Brahmins were "gentlemen" at a time when that style of life was still considered a profession. Gentlemanliness stood not only for educated refinement in intellect, taste, and culture, but also for snobbishness and class consciousness. There is abundant evidence that Holmes was as fastidious, clubbish, and condescending as any of his peers.[8] Moreover, he possessed high

---

3. *See generally* V. Brooks, The Flowering of New England (1936).

4. O.W. Holmes, Sr., *Old Ironsides,* Boston Daily Advertiser, Sept. 16, 1830.

5. O.W. Holmes, Sr., *The Contagiousness of Puerperal Fever,* New England J. Medicine and Surgery, Apr., 1843.

6. O.W. Holmes, Sr., The Autocrat of the Breakfast Table (1858); *see* M. Howe, Holmes of the Breakfast Table (1939).

7. *See* C. Bowen, Yankee From Olympus (1943); M. Howe, Justice Oliver Wendell Holmes: The Shaping Years, 1841-1879 (1957).

8. *See* Hamilton, *On Dating Justice Holmes,* 9 U. Chi. L. Rev. 1 (1941); Kurland, *Portrait of the Jurist as a Young Mind,* 25 U. Chi. L. Rev. 206 (1957); Llewellyn, *Holmes,* 35 Colum. L. Rev. 485 (1935); Sergeant, *Oliver Wendell Holmes,* 49 New Republic 59 (1926).

intellectual standards and was generally critical of even those works he considered worth reading.[9] He also held rather elitist political views, confessing late in his life that the only justification he found for a government's undertaking to rectify social ills was "an aristocratic assumption that you know what is good for them better than they (which no doubt you do)." [10]

Alongside these aristocratic characteristics, however, eixsted countertendencies. After a convivial youth as Harvard undergraduate and clubman, Holmes largely withdrew from social contacts with his peers for approximately ten years. He had virtually no intimate friends during his adult life, but his major correspondence friendships were with non-Brahmins. Although he fervently desired to make an intellectual name for himself before his fortieth birthday,[11] he was contemptuous of his father's role as all-purpose man of letters.[12] If Holmes favored government by elites, he believed in sharply curtailing the powers of the elitist judicial branch; [13] if he "loathe[d] the thick-fingered clowns we call the people ... — vulgar, selfish, and base," [14] he praised "that instinct that makes the American unable to meet his fellow man otherwise than simply as a man." [15]

Holmes's ideology was as ambiguous as his identification with his heritage. He emerged from adolescence an agnostic and an opponent both of time-honored moral pieties and of inexorable axioms governing scholarship. Later in his life, his agnosticism merged with a theory of government that stressed the importance of power relationships. Nevertheless, he retained an apparently

---

9. Hamilton, *supra* note 8; Llewellyn, *supra* note 8.

10. Letter from Oliver Wendell Holmes to Harold Laski, July 23, 1925, in 1 HOLMES-LASKI LETTERS 762 (M. Howe ed. 1953).

11. M. HOWE, JUSTICE OLIVER WENDELL HOLMES: THE PROVING YEARS, 1870-1882 (1963).

12. M. HOWE, *supra* note 7, at 19-21.
WENDELL HOLMES JR. 71 (M. HOWE ed. 1947).

13. *E.g.*, Lochner v. New York, 198 U.S. 45, 74 (1905) (dissenting opinion).

14. Quoted in TOUCHED WITH FIRE: CIVIL WAR LETTERS AND DIARY OF OLIVER WENDELL HOLMES JR., 71 (M. HOWE ed. 1947).

15. Quoted in THE OCCASIONAL SPEECHES OF JUSTICE OLIVER WENDELL HOLMES 25 (M. Howe ed. 1962).

passionate devotion to the act of believing in ideals — as distinguished from any particular ideals themselves — and a faith in the redeeming powers of social evolution. The combination of these potentially contradictory precepts has confounded those who have studied Holmes as ideologue. The "nutshell" words for Holmes abound: positivist,[16] Darwinist,[17] skeptic,[18] cynic,[19] idealist,[20] romanticist,[21] mystic,[22] progressive,[23] patriot.[24] Each suggests an aspect of his thought, but no one word can accurately describe the whole.

Holmes has been equally interesting to American intellectuals as a judicial stylist. In a profession in which the mode of expression characteristically has been technical, formal, depersonalized, and restrained, Holmes's opinions are remarkable for their absence of technicalities, their informality, their liveliness, and their poetic flights of language. Holmes's style is better described as a deviation from the judicial norm than as an improvement on it. If clarity, precision, and "reasoned elaboration" [25] can be said to be ideals of judicial opinion writing, Holmes appears to have eschewed these goals in the pursuit of terseness and ambiguity. His opinions have been called as difficult to understand as they are easy to read.[26]

In each of the above capacities, then, Holmes is not only interesting but controversial. As Brahmin, he provokes comment at two levels: his position evokes the tension of social privilege and intellectual superiority in an increasingly socially mobile and

---

16. Howe, *The Positivism of Mr. Justice Holmes,* 64 HARV. L. REV. 529 (1951).

17. Rogat, *Mr. Justice Holmes: A Dissenting Opinion,* 15 STAN. L. REV. 3, 254 (1963).

18. M. LERNER, THE MIND AND FAITH OF JUSTICE HOLMES (1943).

19. Mencken, *The Great Holmes Mystery,* 26 AMERICAN MERCURY 123 (1932).

20. M. HOWE, *supra* note 7.

21. *Id.*

22. Boorstin, *The Elusiveness of Mr. Justice Holmes,* 14 NEW ENGLAND Q. 478 (1941).

23. R. FAULKNER, THE JURISPRUDENCE OF JOHN MARSHALL 227-28 (1968).

24. Villard, *Issues and Men: The Great Judge,* 140 NATION 323 (1935).

25. *Cf.* H. HART & A. SACKS, THE LEGAL PROCESS (tentative ed. 1958).

26. Rogat, *supra* note 17, at 9-10.

mass-educated society; his behavior contains the emotional conflict inherent in a man rejecting his social heritage. As ideologue, his stances raise a series of questions, among them whether power should be the controlling basis of social arrangements and whether social evolution is inevitable. As stylist, his method of judicial communication invites inquiries as to the value of a decision-making process that expresses its conclusions by unelaborated formulae.

The ambiguities and controversy surrounding Holmes have emerged as his image has changed in the eyes of the American intellectual community. Commentators have woven his thoughts and attitudes into their own social, political, or intellectual preoccupations. As those preoccupations have shifted, the image of Holmes has changed accordingly.

II. The Changing Image of Justice Holmes

Holmes's image may be evaluated in six time segments: (1) 1881 (publication of *The Common Law*) to 1902 (appointment to the Supreme Court), (2) 1903 to 1931 (retirement from the bench), (3) 1932 to 1940, (4) 1941 to 1949, (5) 1950 to 1959, and (6) 1960 to the present. Broadly speaking, each time segment is marked by a dominant intellectual attitude; these attitudes I have termed scientism, progressivism, hero worship, demythology, a sense of alienation, and libertarianism-egalitarianism. The time segments are, of course, only approximations for the sake of convenience, since changes in intellectual attitudes do not occur with chronological precision. The segments are intended to convey a general sense of the points in time at which one overriding perception of Holmes began to be replaced by another, rather than to demarcate any abrupt changes in intellectual attitude.

The term "image," as used in this article, is a construct representing the perceptions of a variety of articulate individuals about a public figure. Like any construct employed to derive collective meaning from individual attitudes, it is imperfect. This imperfection flows from the diversity of intellectual viewpoints during any historical period. The primary purposes of this investigation of Holmes's reputation are to emphasize the complexity of the process by which the reputation of a judge is established and to demonstrate the way in which the image of a man is shaped by the attitudes of his critics.

A. 1881-1902: Holmes as Scientist

The late nineteenth century intelligentsia in America were obsessed with what would now be known as model building. Religious and spiritual principles appeared to them to have been made obsolete by more measurable rules of science. The universe, they had discovered, could be explained in terms of recurrent, predictable phenomena such as evolution and competition. Holmes's *The Common Law,* his contemporaties felt, was in the mainstream of the scientific movement in that it systematized jurisprudence on the basis of observable social phenomena rather than through intellectual abstractions. The theories advanced by Holmes, such as the external standard of liability in tort law, were said to rest on "a series of scientific observations" and were thought to indicate "the advance which the common law is now making toward a more scientific structure than it has ever before possessed." [27] By announcing that the felt necessities of the time governed the formulation of policy in the courts, Holmes was setting forth a tangible set of materials on which to erect a jurisprudential system, hence bringing "the . . . office of the courts . . . into unaccustomed clearness." [28] By 1899 a commentator announced that *The Common Law* was "everywhere regarded as a scientific work." [29]

Scientism, in the late nineteenth century, was intellectual radicalism, since it attempted to shift the source of scholarly axioms away from the intuitions and abstractions of an educated elite of religious believers. To believe in science was to challenge established faiths. Insofar as it questioned a set of traditional social values, scientism was associated with political radicalism,

---

27. Book Review, 26 ALBANY L.J. 484, 486 (1882).
28. Book Review, 15 AM. L. REV. 331 (1881).
29. Note, 33 AM. L. REV. 753, 754 (1899).

and there were those who thought that Holmes had tendencies in this direction. In 1899 two law reviews labeled Holmes a radical, pointing particularly to his dissent in *Vegelahn v. Guntner*,[30] in which Holmes had disassociated himself from a majority ruling upholding an injunction prohibiting peaceful picketing by strikers and had announced that "combination [on the part of labor] is a necessary and desirable counterpart [of combination on the part of capital] if the battle is to be carried on in a fair and equal way." [31] Reviewers found such "radical" language "strange . . . from a man of [Holmes's] environments." [32]

Late nineteenth century intellectuals were most interested in Holmes as ideologue. His privileged social position was not regarded as significant to commentators — the only negative remarks made about Holmes's heritage were issued by Wendell Phillips, himself a Brahmin, who complained in 1895 about the unfortunate tendency of Holmes and other of his contemporaries to equate war with heroism.[33] As a stylist, Holmes suffered from too facile an identification with his father. Those who attempted to analyze his opinions or writings invariably prefaced their remarks with a reference to the literary contributions of Dr. Holmes. At his sixtieth birthday, after twenty years on the Massachusetts bench, Holmes had not fully emerged as a unique and original figure. What reputation he had made for himself by 1902 flowed mainly from his efforts to make the study of the law more scientific.

B. *1903-1931: Holmes as Progressive*

The late nineteenth century intellectual community insisted that formal logical arguments rest on a more scientific foundation than intuitive personal insights, but it was by no means prepared to abandon the use of abstract, deductive reasoning as an academic and pedagogic tool. Syllogistic reasoning from assumed intellectual principles represented the primary mode of thought

---

30. 167 Mass. 92, 104 (1896).
31. *Id.* at 108.
32. Note, *Judge Holmes' Opinions*, 60 ALBANY L.J. 118 (1899).
33. Phillips, *Sentimental Jingoism*, 61 NATION 440 (1895).

and expression of the time. After 1900, however, not only the content of particular academic axioms but the formalistic reasoning process itself came increasingly under attack.[34] Antiformalism in the early twentieth century intellectual community was a manifestation of the broader ideological movement known as progressivism. Progressivism emphasized the constantly changing nature of society and the need for testing social propositions and intellectual theories on the basis of contemporary experience. It resisted abstractions that could not be shown to be responsive to modern social conditions and was consequently hostile to intellectual discourse that appeared to rest on untested or untestable assumptions. In particular, progressivism denied the existence of permanent "laws" that governed intellectual disciplines. It preferred dominant academic or ideological trends to emerge through a process of experimentation whereby those ideas or policies that proved useful in achieving "progress" achieved dominant status until they were replaced by still more "progressive" concepts.[35]

In its political form, the progressive movement believed in the management of government by experts responsible to but not deferential toward the public. Progressives sought to expand the public sector of government in order to substitute decision making by an educated, efficient group of impartial administrators for decision making by partisan representatives of special interest groups. Progressive public policy envisaged the expansion of the executive branch of government, primarily in the form of administrative regulatory agencies, at the expense of Congress and the courts. Progressives urged federal or state legislation that attempted to create executive regulatory schemes and demanded a large measure of judicial tolerance for such legislation. They were particularly incensed at the attempts by judges to substitute nineteenth century economic axioms for empirical analyses of contemporary economic conditions.[36]

---

34. *Cf.* M. WHITE, SOCIAL THOUGHT IN AMERICA (1968).
35. *Cf.* D. NOBLE, THE PARADOX OF PROGRESSIVE THOUGHT (1958).
36. *Cf.* White, *The Social Values of the Progressives: Some New Perspectives,* 70 S. ATLANTIC Q. 62 (1971).

The reexamination of American social values stimulated by progressivism led ultimately to a reexamination of the movement itself. In its early years, at the opening of the twentieth century, the movement simultaneously embraced empirical relativism and moral absolutism, advocating social change in accordance with time-honored standards of behavior, such as honesty, industry, and temperance. But as its adherents became more impressed with the impermanence of ideas and institutions, they came to question the inviolability of their once-cherished moral principles. The result was a sweeping attack on the dominant social mores of the late nineteenth century, which were dismissed as "Victorian" and "Puritan."

Holmes's career on the Supreme Court coincided with the dominance of progressivism as an intellectual force in American life. His relationship with movement itself was complex. Insofar as progressivism meant social or political reform, Holmes had little sympathy for the movement. In 1915 he told John Wigmore that "the squashy sentimentalism of a big minority of our people about human life" made him "puke." Among that minority Holmes placed those "who believe in the upward and onward — who talk of uplift, who think that something particular has happened and that the universe is no longer predatory." [37] Holmes continued to believe in nineteenth century concepts of classical economics, which the progressives repudiated, and nineteenth century social theories, such as that proposed by Malthus, which assumed an inherent imperfectibility in the bulk of mankind. He failed to share in any degree the progressives' faith in man's innate goodness or their missionary zeal to inculcate others with their moral beliefs. He remained throughout his life supremely indifferent to social welfare schemes of any sort, with the possible exception of eugenics. [38]

Nevertheless, the progressives found Holmes an especially attractive and sympathetic judicial figure and contributed to the growth of his stature. By an accident of history, Holmes ascended

---

37. Quoted in M. HOWE, *supra* note 7, at 25.
38. *Cf.* Rogat, *supra* note 17, at 282-89.

the Supreme Court bench at a time when a series of constitutional issues were before the Court that progressives considered to be of great importance. The issues involved the constitutionality of state and federal legislative schemes, such as workmen's compensation and wages-and-hours regulation, in which governmental bodies asserted control over private economic relationships. This power the progressives regarded as essential to their campaign to reduce the influence of "special interests." In a series of opinions from 1903 to 1923, Holmes announced his willingness to tolerate legislative experiments and his contempt for judges who used constitutional provisions to further their own social or economic prejudices.[39] The paradigmatic situation Holmes addressed in these years was that posed by *Lochner v. New York,* [40] in which Justice Peckham, for the majority, had found a New York statute establishing maximum work hours for bakers inconsistent with the due process clause of the fourteenth amendment because it interfered with the right of laborers to work as many hours as they wished. Holmes found Peckham's position to be an artificial application of the so-called liberty-of-contract doctrine [41] in the face of conditions in the baking industry that rendered that doctrine meaningless. He stressed the reasonableness of beliefs on the part of New York legislators that the working environment of bakers was deleterious to their health and deferred to these beliefs, without endorsing the soundness of the maximum hours law itself.

Progressives considered Holmes's exposure of the deficiencies of abstract judicial reasoning and his tolerance for the programs of legislative majorities to be manifestations of judicial statesmanship of the highest order. In a series of articles, Felix Frankfurter celebrated Holmes for his ability to separate his personal views from his legal opinions, for his resistance to

---

39. *E.g.,* Adkins v. Children's Hospital, 261 U.S. 525, 567 (1923) (dissenting opinion); Truax v. Corrigan, 257 U.S. 312, 342 (1921) (dissenting opinion); Hammer v. Dagenhart, 247 U.S. 251, 277 (1918) (dissenting opinion); Adair v. United States, 208 U.S. 161, 190 (1908) (dissenting opinion); Lochner v. New York, 198 U.S. 45, 74 (1905) (dissenting opinion); Otis v. Parker, 187 U.S. 606 (1903).
40. 198 U.S. 45 (1905).
41. *Cf.* Pound, *Liberty of Contract,* 18 YALE L.J. 454 (1909).

doctrinaire interpretation, for his understanding of social and economic forces, and for his willingness to allow legislative experimentation.[42] Frankfurter's opinions were echoed by others, including James Tufts,[43] Roscoe Pound,[44] and John Dewey.[45] Praising Holmes's grasp of "economic forces," Charles Carpenter declared in 1929 that "no judge who has sat upon the bench has ever been more progressive in his attitude." [46] Walter Wheeler Cook and Jerome Frank saw in Holmes's interpretation of his office the advent of a new school of jurisprudence. Cook asked rhetorically in 1921: "How many . . . among law teachers, not to mention judges and practicing lawyers, . . . 'consider the ends which [legal] rules seek to accomplish, the reasons why those ends are desired, what is given up to gain them, and whether they are worth the price?' " "[M]uch missionary work remains to be done," Cook maintained, "before the methods of legal thinking exemplified [by Holmes] become characteristic of . . . the leaders of the legal profession." [47] Frank, nine years later, hailed Holmes for "abandon[ing], once and for all, the phantasy of a perfect, consistent, legal uniformity . . . ." "As a consequence," Frank felt, "whatever clear [sense] of legal realities we have attained in this country in the past twenty-five years is in large measure due to him. . . . [Holmes] has developed that remarkable tolerance which

---

42. Frankfurter, *The Constitutional Opinions of Mr. Justice Holmes,* 29 HARV. L. REV. 683, 691, 693, 694 (1916); Frankfurter, *Twenty Years of Mr. Justice Holmes's Constitutional Opinions,* 36 HARV. L. REV. 909, 927, 929 (1923); Frankfurter, *Mr. Justice Holmes and the Constitution,* 41 HARV. L. REV. 121, 132, 134 (1927).

43. "Holmes has . . . firmly set himself against a slack universe of legal conceptions and a rigidly fixed social order" and "has sought to give man room to express his advancing needs in an orderly progressing society." Tufts, *The Legal and Social Philosophy of Mr. Justice Holmes,* 7 A.B.A.J. 359 (1921).

44. Pound discussed Holmes's "conscious facing of the problem of harmonizing or compromising conflicting or overlapping interests . . . ." Pound, *'Judge Holmes's' Contributions to the Science of Law,* 34 HARV. L. REV. 449, 450 (1921).

45. Dewey stressed Holmes's "impatience with the attempt to settle matters of social policy by dialectic reasoning from fixed concepts" and his "faith that . . . our social system is one of experimentation, subject to the ordeal of experienced consequences." Dewey, *Justice Holmes and the Liberal Mind,* 53 NEW REPUBLIC 210, 211 (1928).

46. Carpenter, *Oliver Wendell Holmes, Jurist,* 8 ORE. L. REV. 269, 270 (1929).

47. Cook, Book Review, 30 YALE L.J. 775, 776 (1921).

is the mark of high maturity.... His legal skepticism is clear, sane, vital, progressive...." [48]

One of the social issues to which progressives turned their attention was the place of social privilege in American society. On one level, progressivism was a movement to expand the classes of beneficiaries of governmental reforms and consequently to achieve a more egalitarian society. On another, it represented a reentry of social and intellectual elites into positions of public influence. In specific reforms such as the conservation movement, progressive rhetoric emphasized the importance of diffusing the power of monopolists and of improving the life style of small farmers, while progressive programs envisaged the management of conservation programs by an educated elite of technocrats.[49] In general terms, social privilege was not itself regarded as an evil by progressives, provided that individuals of high status demonstrated a sense of social responsibility and a concern for the less fortunate classes.

With some strain, early twentieth century commentators sought to demonstrate these qualities in Holmes. They attempted this through association of Holmes with two symbols: the socially conscious Puritan and the aristocrat as democrat. The first symbol was an artful redefinition of Puritanism. For early twentieth century American intellectuals, Puritanism symbolized a moral rigidity and parochialism that came increasingly to be considered old-fashioned. But it also suggested an adherence to the dictates of one's conscience. Certain supporters of Holmes tended to stress his social conscience, which they linked to his Puritan heritage. They insisted that Holmes was "a Puritan whom doubt had civilized" so that his "Puritan strength" appeared not as a religious dogma but as a "simple conviction" that the democratic ideals of American civilization should be upheld.[50] Life for Holmes was "a rich but a responsible adventure" in which the "natural Puritan aristocracy" functioned as caretakers of democracy. [51]

---

48. J. FRANK, LAW AND THE MODERN MIND 253, 257, 259 (1930).

49. *Cf.* G. WHITE, THE EASTERN ESTABLISHMENT AND THE WESTERN EXPERIENCE (1968).

50. Littell, *Books and Things*, 3 NEW REPUBLIC 100 (1915).

51. Sergeant, *Oliver Wendell Holmes*, 49 NEW REPUBLIC 59, 60 (1926).

Thus Holmes, especially during his last years on the bench, came to be considered "an aristocrat with a genuine interest in the welfare of the common man." [52] Those attracted to the symbol of Holmes as an aristocratic democrat emphasized the social implications of his free speech opinions. In these cases the defendants whose rights Holmes championed were conspicuously disadvantaged persons, being impoverished immigrants.[53]

Holmes's style was not controversial among members of the early twentieth century intellectual community. Their overriding concern was that judicial opinions not exhibit the abstract reasoning characterized by Roscoe Pound as "mechanical jurisprudence"; [54] on this point Holmes's opinions were eminently satisfying, since they eschewed that process altogether. Holmes's tendency toward formulaic expression was seen by commentators as fresh rather than cryptic. Judge Benjamin Cardozo, himself an aspiring stylist, remarked that "one almost writhes in despair at the futility ... of imitation or approach" upon confronting Holmes's "pointed phrases." [55]

In his metamorphosis from scientist to progressive, Holmes stood on the threshold of deification. He stepped from his father's shadow by transcending his privileged background through tolerance and sympathy for thoughts and life styles foreign to his own. To observers of progressive persuasion his sense of the impermanency of ideas and intellectual axioms became "realism" or "sociological jurisprudence"; his willingness to defer to the wishes of those holding positions of political power became a belief in social experimentation; his tendency to believe that social

52. Pollard, *Justice Holmes, Champion of the Common Man,* N.Y. Times, Dec. 1, 1929, § 4, at 4, col. 1.

53. *E.g.,* United States v. Schwimmer, 279 U.S. 644, 653 (1929) (dissenting opinion); Schenck v. United States, 249 U.S. 47 (1919); Abrams v. United States, 250 U.S. 616, 624 (1919) (dissenting opinion). In the correspondence attendant upon the *Schwimmer* decision, in which WASP militarist Holmes made courteous replies to the tributes of Russian Jewish pacifist Rosika Schwimmer, readers saw another manifestation of the Brahmin's tolerance for ideologies and life styles alien to his own. *See* Sergeant, *supra* note 51, at 60.

54. Pound, *Mechanical Jurisprudence,* 8 COLUM. L. REV. 605 (1908).

55. Cardozo, *Mr. Justice Holmes,* 44 HARV. L. REV. 682, 689 (1931).

upheavals were infrequent and that words alone rarely threatened the fabric of society became a faith in free speech; his general indifference to social problems and political issues became enlightened judicial self-restraint. He lacked only a historical vindication of his attitudes toward judicial decision making and political arrangements — which, after 1931, he received.

C.   1932-1940: Holmes as Myth

Reviewing in 1941 the ten years that had passed since Holmes's retirement, Walton Hamilton found that Holmes had emerged as a "deity . . . an Olympian who in judgment could do no wrong. His opinions were norms by which to measure the departures of his Court from the true path of the law." "The neat phrase, the quotable line," Hamilton observed, "were ultimates; and beauty of form was commuted into wisdom of utterance. For the Court, but especially in dissent, thus spake Holmes and the subject was closed." [56] The years from 1932 to 1940 witnessed the apotheosis of Holmes. His human qualities were enhanced in the eyes of the world: the moving radio address on his ninetieth birthday; [57] the gracious retirement, accompanied by a memorable letter to his fellow justices; [58] the tranquil declining years when, to one observer, his face fairly glowed with an inner radiance.[59] His death, three days short of his ninety-fourth birthday, was cause for inspired reflection — here was a life that could be said to have been fully lived, in terms of both longevity and accomplishment.

Other elements contributed to the deification of Holmes. At a time when economic privilege was in disrepute but gracious life styles retained a romantic attraction,[60] Holmes's role as transcendant Brahmin maintained its fascination. His brand of jurisprudence was labeled "realistic;" it served as an inspiration for legal scholars who desired to publicize the human and

---

56. Hamilton, *supra* note 8.
57. Reprinted in JUSTICE OLIVER WENDELL HOLMES: HIS BOOK NOTICES AND UNCOLLECTED LETTERS AND PAPERS 142 (H. Shriver ed. 1936).
58. *Id.* at 143.
59. C. BOWEN, YANKEE FROM OLYMPUS 413 (1943).
60. *Cf.* D. WECTER, THE GREAT DEPRESSION (1948).

institutional factors operative in judicial decision making and to eradicate once and for all deductive logic from the judging process.[61] His tolerance for experiments in legislation and his relativist approach to ideas contrasted sharply with the stubborn absolutism of the Justices who struck down New Deal legislative programs. As the primary responsibility for reform shifted from the states to the federal government, those who believed that a vast expansion of federal power and activity was needed to save the nation imagined that Holmes would have supported their efforts. He thus became a liberal as well as a realist.

The transcendant Brahmin theme was popularized by the appearance in 1932 of the first full-length biography of Holmes, written by the journalist Silas Bent. Holmes, for Bent, expanded the Puritan view of human nature — that man is inherently selfish — to a "noble conception of a realistic and rationalized science of law." He "perceived that jealousy and envy . . . were in fact when sublimated the basis of human justice." As a consequence, he came to advocate a mode of lawmaking that gave each man fair scope to pursue his own self-interest. Bent saw this as evidence that Holmes had "freed himself from the group loyalties and prejudices and passions which are a heritage of those reared in the security of the genteel tradition." "Never," he maintained, "was aristocrat less class-conscious." [62] Others pursued this tack. "Of the many achievements of Justice Holmes," Adolf Berle wrote in 1935, "none is more glorious than that of transcending the bounds of his apparent emotional security." [63] Augustin Derby, a former clerk to Holmes, found him "the most democratic of men, . . . entirely without pose." [64]

61. *Cf.* W. RUMBLE, AMERICAN LEGAL REALISM (1965).
62. S. BENT, JUSTICE OLIVER WENDELL HOLMES (1932).
63. Berle, *Justice Holmes: Liberal,* 24 SURVEY GRAPHIC 178 (1935).
64. Derby, *Recollections of Mr. Justice Holmes,* 12 N.Y.U.L.Q. REV. 345, 345-46 (1935). Max Lerner called Holmes "the very perfection and flowering of the New England aristocracy." Lerner, Book Review, 46 YALE L.J. 904, 908 (1937). Morris Cohen found him to have "intellectual power and the true liberal attitude that enabled him to rise above his hereditary class prejudices." Cohen, *Justice Holmes,* 82 NEW REPUBLIC 206, 207 (1935).

208

If Bent polished Holmes's image as aristocratic democrat, Karl Llewellyn served a similar function in the emergence of Holmes as realist. Llewellyn had himself been one of the early and major spokesmen for realism — in 1930 and 1931 he had written law review articles that announced the emergence of a realistic jurisprudence which combined a sense of the sterility and artificiality of legal rules with a belief in the importance of manipulation and rationalization in governmental decision making.[65] This point of view was not original, Llewellyn maintained; "Holmes's mind had travelled most of the road two generations back." [66]

By the date of Holmes's death, realism had become a major intellectual force among American legal scholars. Llewellyn took the occasion to pay tribute to the contribution of Holmes to the movement. Because of Holmes's work, Llewellyn maintained, "it is no longer heresy to argue that judges have 'molecular' law-making power .... It is ... no longer heresy to argue that there is no brooding omnipresence in the skies, but that the true measure of law ... is: what, in particular, can or will anybody do about it, here and now? It is no longer heresy to see constitutional law as a field in which economic forces, prejudices and personalities play in an intricate, semi-concealed game, law, politics and statesmanship together ...." [67]

The most compelling image of Holmes in the nine years after 1931, however, was that of liberal. The major representation of him in that role was made by Felix Frankfurter in *Mr. Justice Holmes and the Supreme Court,* published in 1938. Frankfurter had himself made the transition from progressive to New Dealer without strain [68] — he saw the experiments of the Roosevelt administrations as enlightened recognition of the need to adjust

---

65. *E.g.,* Llewellyn, *A Realistic Jurisprudence — The Next Step,* 30 COLUM. L. REV. 431 (1930); Llewellyn, *Some Realism About Realism,* 44 HARV. L. REV. 1222 (1931).

66. Llewellyn, *supra* note 65, at 454.

67. Llewellyn, *Holmes,* 35 COLUM. L. REV. 485, 487-88 (1935).

68. The transition was not so easy for others; many progressives parted company with the New Deal. *See* O. GRAHAM, JR., AN ENCORE FOR REFORM (1967).

social policies pragmatically in order to meet the demands of an increasingly complex civilization. In Frankfurter's view, Holmes "threw the weight of his authority on the side of social readjustments through legislation." Holmes analyzed "with ... clarity the governing elements in the modern economic struggle," Frankfurter maintained, "[and] found nothing in the Constitution to prevent legislation which sought to remove some of the more obvious inequalities in the distribution of economic power." He "[did not] believe that there was anything in the Constitution to bar even a conscious use of the taxing power for readjusting the social equilibrium." He "was loath to find a governmental vacuum ... where there was no intersection of federal and state authority." [69] In short, Holmes was an ancestral New Dealer, as he had been for Llewellyn an ancestral realist.

The intellectual community of the 1930s was quick to support Frankfurter's interpretation. Perhaps the most enthusiastic acclaim came from the *New York Times,* which described Holmes as the "liberal and lovable philosopher" whose "scores of opinions ... testif[ied] to his liberalism" [70] and who was "known through the world for his liberal interpretations of the law in cases involving property rights and personal rights." [71] Upon Holmes's death the *Times* called him the "chief liberal of [the] supreme bench for 29 years." [72]

The 1930s thus saw Holmes elevated to demigod by the intellectual community.[73] If he had been "the idol of the

---

69. F. Frankfurter, Mr. Justice Holmes and the Supreme Court 44, 36-37, 43, 86 (1938).

70. N.Y. Times, Jan. 13, 1932, § 1, at 3, col. 4.

71. *Id.* at col. 6.

72. N.Y. Times, Mar. 6, 1935, § 1, at 1, cols. 2-3.

73. Amidst the shower of praise for Holmes in the 1930s came an occasionally querulous or critical note, foreshadowing a later shift in tone. H.L. Mencken felt that there was "no evidence in Holmes' decisions that he ever gave any really profound thought to the great battle of ideas that raged in his time." Holmes had "no ... genuine belief in democracy," Mencken argued, and his decisions demonstrated "a widespread and beautiful inconsistency." Further, the "peculiar salacity" of Holmes's opinions, which made them "interesting as literature," derived in Mencken's opinion from an "easy-going cynicism." Holmes, Mencken felt, "had a considerable talent for epigrams," and when "once his mood had brought

progressives who believed that America must evolve and change,"[74] he was even more revered by the reformers of the 1930s, who had added to their criteria for statesmanship a commitment to majoritarian relativism and a "realistic" approach to social planning. Although he symbolized the grandeur of a more distant, and for some a more gentlemanly, era, he also appeared — particularly in light of the Court-packing crisis and the "switch in time" — distinctly a man of the times.

D. *1941-1949: Demythologizing*

Holmes's reputation had been too closely linked to an implicit set of social priorities not to be altered with the replacement of that set by another. His unequivocal deference to the whims of majorities was destined to become a subject of controversy as the intellectual community lost faith in the judgment of sheer numbers. As early as 1919 it had been suggested that Holmes believed "that there can be . . . no standard of evaluation except the principle that might makes right."[75] In 1940 Lon Fuller had pursued a similar line of analysis in observing that Holmes's influence as a judge "fell far short of being commensurate with his general intellectual stature." Fuller attributed this condition to Holmes's "notion that the law is something severable from one's

---

him to this or that judgment the announcement of it was sometimes more than a little affected by purely literary impulse. . . . [T]he result was . . . now and then . . . far more literature than law." Mencken, *The Great Holmes Mystery*, 26 AMERICAN MERCURY 123, 124 (1932). Kenneth Reiblich, in a 1939 analysis of Holmes's conflict-of-laws opinions, found that "certain concepts seemed to be accepted [by Holmes] as apriori truths and applied with little indication of the realism which one might have expected to find." Reiblich found puzzling the "conviction that Mr. Justice Holmes, the liberal and realist, becomes in conflict of laws the conservative and conceptualist." Reiblich, *The Conflict of Laws Philosophy of Mr. Justice Holmes*, 28 GEO. L.J. 1, 12, 20-21 (1939). Meanwhile, Walter Nelles and Samuel Mermin had concluded that "in his approach to labor questions Holmes was free from all such sentimentality as is expressed in talk of 'human rights' or 'brotherhood of man.' There was no humanitarian softness in his head." Nelles & Mermin, *Holmes and Labor Law*, 13 N.Y.U.L.Q. REV. 517 (1936).

74. Villard, *Issues and Men: The Great Judge*, 140 NATION 323 (1935).

75. Bode, *Justice Holmes, Natural Law, and the Moral Ideal*, 29 INTERNAT'L J. ETHICS 397 (1919).

notions of what it ought to be." [76] The absence of any overriding set of moral values in Holmes's jurisprudence caused increasing anxiety in the intellectual community after 1941, when ideals of civilization and justice seemed challenged in a variety of ways by the Axis powers.

The most sensational manifestation of this anxiety was a series of articles by Jesuit theologians and law professors which linked Holmes's ideology with that of totalitarian regimes. Between 1941 and 1943, four critiques of this nature appeared. Two of the articles, written by Francis Lucey, attempted to show that Holmes's philosophy was "akin to Hitler's" and that if adopted "would be the death knell of our democracy." [77] For Holmes, Lucey maintained, "there [were] no moral oughts, . . . just plain, unadulterated physical force of the majority imposing itself on all." "If . . . Holmes was correct," Lucey concluded, "Hitler is correct." [78] John Ford published a similar piece in 1942 which summarized Holmes's thought as follows: "The essence of law is physical force. Might makes legal right. The law is to be divorced from all morality. There is no such thing as a moral ought — it is a mere fiction. . . . . There is no absolute truth. . . . . There is too much fuss about the sanctity of human life. To the state man is a means to be sacrificed if necessary in the interest of the state. The ultimate arbiter of all life is physical force." These attitudes scandalized Ford, who saw them as the ultimate rationale for fascist and communist dictatorships.[79] The fourth such critique of Holmes, written by Paul Gregg, equated Holmes's "pragmatism" — a philosophy which for Gregg assumed that "ideas, logic, reason, morals, and all else, are merely tools by which plans of action are forged and made to work" — with "the latest social experiment in Nazi Germany." "Who can say," Gregg asked, "that the United States, at some future time, will not be dominated by

---

76. L. FULLER, THE LAW IN QUEST OF ITSELF 62-63 (1940).

77. Lucey, *Jurisprudence and the Future Social Order,* 16 SOCIAL SCI. 211 (1941).

78. Lucey, *Natural Law and American Legal Realism,* 30 GEO. L.J. 493, 512, 531 (1942).

79. Ford, *The Fundamentals of Holmes' Juristic Philosophy,* 11 FORDHAM L. REV. 255, 275 (1942).

bureaucrats whose social philosophy is kindred to that of Hitler, Goering, Goebbels, and Himmler?" "[T]otalitarianism and dictatorship," Gregg felt, "can live and flourish under pragmatism. ... If totalitarianism ever becomes the form of American government, its leaders, no doubt, will canonize as one of the patron saints Mr. Justice Holmes. For his popularization of the pragmatic philosophy of law has done much to pave the way." [80]

The ideas advanced in these four articles were popularized by Ben Palmer in an essay entitled "Hobbes, Holmes, and Hitler," which appeared in the *American Bar Association Journal* in 1945. In Palmer's view, "the fact that Holmes was a polished gentleman who did not go about like a storm-trooper knocking people down and proclaiming the supremacy of the blonde beast should not blind us to his legal philosophy that might makes right, that law is the command of the dominant social group." Holmes's jurisprudence, for Palmer, sanctioned "the iron fist of absolute power wielded without possibility of external restraint because of any protest of impotent individuals or minorities." "If totalitarianism comes to America," Palmer maintained, " ... it will come through dominance in the judiciary of men who have accepted a philosophy of law that has ... its fruition in implications from the philosophy of Holmes." [81]

The association of Holmes with totalitarianism sparked a debate that was, in its ramifications, to preoccupy legal scholars in America for a further decade. At the core of the debate was the question whether the American legal system embodied any absolute moral principles or whether it merely exemplified contemporary social norms. In the 1940s it seemed especially distressing for American intellectuals, particularly those of a religious persuasion, to deny that lawmaking in the United States flowed from unalterable humanitarian principles. In other parts of the world, denial of such standards seemed to have created patently inhumane governments. America had made a commitment to combat these nations, and philosophies that assumed that

---

80. Gregg, *The Pragmatism of Mr. Justice Holmes,* 31 GEO. L.J. 262, 284, 293, 294 (1943).
81. Palmer, *Hobbes, Holmes, and Hitler,* 31 A.B.A.J. 569, 571-73 (1945).

"whatever works is right" appeared intolerable to those who supported this struggle.

The Jesuit attack on Holmes, then, was an extreme manifestation of a general tendency of intellectuals in the 1940s to reassess Holmes's philosophy in relation to their own thinking. At a time when "pragmatism" and "realism" had evolved, in some circles, from words suggesting progressive social reform to words heralding the coming of totalitarianism, one group of Holmes's critics maintained that such labels were inadequate to describe the breadth and depth of his character. These critics defended Holmes by emphasizing the complexities and contradictions in his thought. Daniel Boorstin suggested in a 1941 article that "the inadequacy of labels like 'liberal' and 'conservative' quickly appears" in describing Holmes. "In his earnestness to encompass all philosophies and yet to commit himself to none," Boorstin maintained, Holmes made "his personal world of ideas" one "of doubt and conflict." He "clearly felt the tug of opposing forces": his "New England conservative tradition" and his "intensely liberal individuality." [82] Max Lerner noted in Holmes "a deep conflict between skepticism and belief, between mind and faith, between a recognition that men act in terms of a cold calculation of interests, and a recognition also that they are moved by symbols." Holmes tried, in Lerner's view, "to construct a philosophy of life for himself which would allow him to take account of both strains." [83] Francis Biddle referred to Holmes's "dualism of skeptic and moralist, of doubter and preacher." "He distrusted affirmations," Biddle felt, "yet . . . made them with an oversimplification that was only partially concealed by the form of witty aphorism which they usually took." [84]

To be sure, the 1940s were marked by some older images of Holmes. Felix Frankfurter persisted in emphasizing Holmes's ability to "transcend his emotional attachments." "New Englander of New Englanders in his feelings all his life," Frankfurter wrote

---

82. Boorstin, *The Elusiveness of Mr. Justice Holmes,* 14 NEW ENGLAND Q. 478, 480-81 (1941).

83. M. LERNER, THE MIND AND FAITH OF JUSTICE HOLMES 373 (1943).

84. F. BIDDLE, MR. JUSTICE HOLMES 95 (1942).

of Holmes in 1944, "[he] disciplined himself against any kind of parochialism in his thinking. . . . He reached the democratic result by . . . his disbelief in ultimate answers to social questions. Thereby he exhibited the judicial function at its purest." [85] Morton White maintained that Holmes was "a serious comrade-in-arms of the liberal, progressive, and professional movement for reform" and felt that his "intellectual outlook was permeated with a good many of the ideas that were stirring the liberals of his time." [86] But the tone of the commentators had altered. If the Jesuit critics and their popularizers were regarded as aberrational, they nonetheless symbolized an unconscious decision by American intellectuals to, as Walton Hamilton put it, "elevate Mr. Justice Holmes from deity to mortality." [87] From that decision emerged a complex image of Holmes as a man whose thought and character contained contradictory forces and whose apparently facile self-assurance masked the considerable strain he must have felt in attempting to reconcile them. If the passions of the war-scarred 1940s stimulated some of the most savage evaluations of Holmes, they also generated some of the most mature.

E.   *1950-1959: Sense of Alienation*

Whatever Holmes had been to American intellectuals from 1880 through the 1940s, he had been relevant. His relationship to his heritage, his approach to constitutional issues, his jurisprudential principles had touched on powerful themes for the intellectual community. But after 1950, critics of Holmes tended increasingly to reveal their sense of the widening gulf between his world and theirs. The man who had been dateless for Hamilton in 1941 suddenly became dated.

The decade commenced with a continuation of the impassioned debate that had begun in the 1940s. Harold McKinnon denounced Holmes's philosophy as "a symbol of our intellectual wretchedness, a conspicuous example of our abandonment of those spiritual,

---

85. Frankfurter, *Oliver Wendell Holmes,* 21 DICTIONARY OF AMERICAN BIOGRAPHY 417, 423 (1944).

86. M. WHITE, *supra* note 34, at 104, 74.

87. Hamilton, *supra* note 8, at 1.

philosophical and moral truths that have been the life of the western tradition." [88] Father Lucey also returned to the attack, again comparing Holmes to Hitler.[89] Supporters of Holmes continued to defend him. Fred Rodell wrote that "Holmes took pains to make clear ... that his skepticism had never bred in him the cynicism of defeat and despair, and that, in the realm of ought-to-be, he held strong moral and ethical views concerning decency and justice among mankind." [90] Mark DeWolfe Howe stated that Holmes "did not deny that a primary source of law is the realm of moral standards in which society has its being, and ... considered the first responsibility of the lawyer and judge to be that of bringing the law into conformity with those moral standards." Howe's essay was colored by a sense that his generation was affected by concerns that had not affected Holmes. The adverse criticism of Holmes's skepticism, Howe felt, was "partly the result of the glimpse which Hitler gave us of cynicism triumphant. We have begun to ask ourselves whether, despite Holmes, there are not some standards of decency so fundamental and so permanent that they may properly be described as absolute." Having experienced a sense of the depths of man's inhumanity to man, Howe and his contemporaries of the 1950s were not, in his judgment, "intellectually willing and emotionally able to accept that total skepticism which led Holmes to question whether man has a cosmic significance 'different in kind from that which belongs to a baboon or a grain of sand.' " [91] They needed to believe that moral principles buttressed the universe; that civilization imposed limits on man's behavior. "Holmes' words are read now," Henry Hart wrote in 1951, "when the foundations of all things are being re-examined. The moral claims of settled law in a constitutional democracy must not today be overlooked." [92]

---

88. McKinnon, *The Secret of Mr. Justice Holmes,* 36 A.B.A.J. 261, 345 (1950).

89. Lucey, *Holmes — Liberal — Humanitarian — Believer in Democracy?,* 39 GEO. L.J. 523, 548, 553 (1951).

90. Rodell, *Justice Holmes and His Hecklers,* 60 YALE L.J. 620, 623 (1951).

91. Howe, *The Positivism of Mr. Justice Holmes,* 64 HARV. L. REV. 529, 544-45 (1951).

92. Hart, *Holmes' Positivism — An Addendum,* 64 HARV. L. REV. 929, 937 (1951).

Holmes himself had not experienced the horrors of a wholly amoral world. Charles Wyzanski emphasized Holmes's faith in the ultimate triumph of reason. Wyzanski attributed this faith to the fact that "Holmes wrote before the world had fully appreciated the wickedness of which civilized man is capable. He knew not the Nazi concentration camps ... nor the Communist disciplined subordination of man's interest in truth to man's interest in material progress." [93]

Intellectuals of the 1950s thus felt that Holmes's conclusions were founded on assumptions about the nature of man that differed from their own. This view led critics to treat him as a figure from another age, an approach that occasionally led to debunking [94] or redefinition [95] of his political views. In the main, however, alienation from Holmes took the form of attempts to

---

93. Wyzanski, *The Democracy of Justice Oliver Wendell Holmes,* 7 VAND. L. REV. 311, 319 (1954).

94. Martin Hickman's "reappraisal" of Holmes revealed "a man arrogant beyond the ordinary, a man of narrow and oligarchical sympathies," whose "indulgence of the legislature ... rested at least as much on contempt as on tolerance." The stereotype of Holmes that he "was a champion of free speech and civil rights, that he was compassionate and solicitous for the defenseless," Hickman argued, was not supported by "an examination of the cases." There "is a hollow ring to the finely turned phrases." Hickman, *Mr. Justice Holmes: A Reappraisal,* 5 W. POL. Q. 66, 83, 73 (1952). Merle Pusey, in his biography of Charles Evans Hughes, wrote that the "Holmes whom the judges knew had little in common with the humanitarian crusader of the same name who has so often been extolled in print. Holmes' brethren knew that he didn't care a straw for the 'social' or 'progressive' legislation that he was said to be heroically defending .... [They] were well aware of his scorn for any deviation from the result he thought the law required because that result might be 'unjust' to the individuals concerned." 1 M. PUSEY, CHARLES EVANS HUGHES 287, 289 (1951).

95. Irving Bernstein announced that the "cherished American myth ... that Oliver Wendell Holmes was a liberal" was "as baseless as the tale of Washington and the cherry tree." Holmes, according to Bernstein, was "as profound, as civilized, and articulate a conservative as the United States has produced." He was "a firm believer in capitalism who looked with distrust upon governmental intervention in economic life. Monopolies won his respect, while he regarded unions and strikes suspiciously .... Movements seeking the reform or reconstruction of economic society won his distrust.... Free speech for Holmes was a Darwinian arena in which ideas would struggle for survival. It was at the same time a prop of a conservative society." Bernstein, *The Conservative Justice Holmes,* 23 NEW ENGLAND Q. 435, 445, 449 (1950).

217

place him at a distant point in time. This was the major thrust of the three principal books written about Holmes in the 1950s: Henry Steel Commager's *The American Mind,* Samuel Konefsky's *The Legacy of Holmes and Brandeis,* and Mark DeWolfe Howe's *Mr. Justice Holmes: The Shaping Years.* Commager identified Holmes with "the progressive movement['s] . . . inability to fulfill itself without imposing far reaching readjustments upon the legal mechanics of economy." [96] Konefsky found Holmes "backward" and "singularly static" in "his conception of the economic universe" and maintained that his thought was "filled with a good many fallacies and superficial preconceptions which he assumed to be basic truths," including his "imperturbable confidence in the capacity of society to defy artificial meddling with its natural evolution." [97] Howe saw Holmes's aesthetic judgment as "responsive to older modes of expression and earlier moods of feeling." His biography of Holmes, Howe observed, was largely "an essay in intellectual history." [98]

The works of the 1950s presented a composite picture of Holmes as a man whose thought failed, despite its breadth, to encompass the problems of mid-twentieth century existence. A series of inevitabilities ruled Holmes's world: iron economic laws, natural selection of ideas and social policies, the continual progress of civilization. These inevitabilities marked the thought of an older age where, in light of a series of consoling faiths, men could afford to be skeptical. Life in the mature twentieth century, in the minds of American intellectuals, encouraged no such faiths.

F. *1960—: Holmes and Libertarianism-Egalitarianism*

In the 1960s, attention turned to the problems caused by the inequalities and diversities among Americans. Integration — racial, psychological, cultural — became a dominant concept as the decade opened. Intellectuals emphasized once more the responsibilities of elites to those less privileged and stressed the fundamental values — liberty, democracy, egalitarianism,

---

96. H.S. COMMAGER, THE AMERICAN MIND 374 (1950).
97. S. KONEFSKY, THE LEGACY OF HOLMES AND BRANDEIS 59, 24, 64, 303 (1956).
98. M. HOWE, *supra* note 7, at 10, vi.

impartial justice — that bound Americans together. Critics of Holmes asked again whether he had understood the social obligations of leadership or the consensual values embedded in the process of lawmaking in America. Their answer, by and large, was negative on both counts. Critics alleged that as both a man and a judge Holmes had been indifferent to the needs of the underprivileged. They pointed to the distance Holmes felt between himself and less socially and intellectually privileged Americans, and to his apparent lack of concern for civil-liberties interests in certain cases.

"It would be easy . . . to create the impression," Edmund Wilson wrote of Holmes in 1962, "that [he] was an egregious social snob of a peculiarly provincial kind." [99] Commentators on Holmes as Brahmin did occasionally attempt to foster that impression,[100] but they were far more concerned with what Wilson called the "carapace of impenetrable indifference to current pressures and public opinion" in Holmes, "due partly to the impregnable security of belonging to the Boston 'Brahmin' caste." [101] Distance, withdrawal, isolation, and detachment became the chief aspects of Holmes's Brahminism that interested critics. Mark DeWolfe Howe emphasized Holmes's prolonged withdrawal from society and his feeling that his destiny lay in areas, such as scholarship, that were isolated from the world at large.[102] Yosal Rogat accentuated Holmes's "preoccupation with the theme of the observer — the spectator." "[His] participation in public, and perhaps even in private, experience had an attenuated quality," Rogat wrote, "and [he] withdrew, perhaps consciously, from important areas of shared human experience." [103] Saul Touster provided a charitable explanation for Holmes's Brahmin detachment. "Holmes," Touster maintained, "was . . . a profoundly injured spirit." "The deadening of sympathetic feelings, the Olympian aloofness, the spectator view, . . . the disbelief in causes" were devices "by which he

---

99. E. WILSON, PATRIOTIC GORE 784 (1962).

100. *E.g.,* Rogat, *The Judge as Spectator,* 31 U. CHI. L. REV. 213, 230 (1964).

101. E. WILSON, *supra* note 99, at 782-83.

102. M. HOWE, *supra* note 11, at 1-8, 256 (1963).

103. Rogat, *supra* note 100, at 230.

somehow [could] gain distance from the world." Touster found that Holmes's "expressions of sympathy and doubt and feelings for the distress of the Negro were suppressed" in his later life; "suppression of feeling," he maintained, "may be the product not of the absence of feeling, but an excess of it." [104]

Others in the 1960s viewed aloofness in Holmes less sympathetically. Francis Biddle, in an otherwise laudatory assessment, described Holmes as "an aristocrat and a conservative" who "had little sympathy with the sufferings and failures of mankind, and no urgent desire to change their lot." [105] Rogat felt that "to a remarkable degree, Holmes simply did not care. . . . Precisely because he thought that 'the crowd' was unwise, he expected them to destroy the way of life that he preferred. But he would have thought it immature to be deeply concerned about that imminent destruction." [106] Robert Faulkner saw Holmes's skepticism and deference to majority views as manifestations of "a certain disdain toward minorities and the weak generally." [107]

For intellectuals of the 1960s, belief in certain fundamental guarantees of equal treatment for minorities and certain permanent individual rights was an important aspect of enlightened social thought. In the context of their own full-blown libertarianism-egalitárianism, representatives of the American intellectual community found Holmes's response to civil liberties shocking. Rogat, the leading critic, set out to disprove the widely held belief that Holmes was a champion of civil liberties. In cases involving "various claims to civil and political rights that arose out of the Civil War Amendments," for example, Rogat maintained that Holmes was "consistent" in "denying the claimed right" and "weighed the substantive claim to equality lightly." In alien cases Holmes "wrote as if anyone seeking entry was merely a suppliant." "Nowhere" did he "help in framing a remedy to secure a

---

104. Touster, *In Search of Holmes From Within,* 18 VAND. L. REV. 437, 470, 450-51 (1965).

105. F. BIDDLE, JUSTICE HOLMES, NATURAL LAW AND THE SUPREME COURT 7 (1961).

106. Rogat, *supra* note 100, at 255.

107. R. FAULKNER, THE JURISPRUDENCE OF JOHN MARSHALL 253 (1968).

constitutional right. He did not develop further any inchoate right or liberty, or broaden the scope of those which were already established." In short, Rogat found that "the accepted image of Holmes as uniquely libertarian owes more to fantasies unloosed by the attractiveness of his personality than to the realities of his career." Holmes's striking insensitivity to civil rights and liberties stemmed, Rogat maintained, from a "fundamentally impoverished account of legal phenomena." He "did not sufficiently distinguish a crude system of social control, resting on naked power, from a distinctively legal method of control." He seemed "never ... to have perceived, and certainly never acknowledged, the extent to which general commitments to fairness, generality and neutrality are built into the idea of legality and constitute part of its meaning. . . . Holmes spoke as if a legal system were simply a mechanism to enforce by whatever means, the desires of the dominant group," ignoring the extent to which law in America was premised on notions of equitable attention to the needs of minorities and guarantees of equal justice.[108]

Faulkner also found that an "orientation by moral and political ends [was] absent from Holmes' jurisprudence." Holmes, for Faulkner, "left vacant [the] essence [of judicial decision making]: a reasonable view of what constitutes justice in America." The "besetting and deepest flaw of Holmes' thought" was a tendency to prefer abstractions to "humane ends." Instead of giving attention to the pressing needs of interests at particular points in time, Faulkner argued, Holmes subscribed to a "fundamentally optimistic fatalism" which allowed history to usurp the role of the judge in doing justice. Holmes believed, according to Faulkner, that "man's interests are automatically ever better served . . . ." "[He] presupposed . . . the justice of history." [109]

Critics of the 1960s expanded the concept of civil liberty in finding Holmes wanting as a civil libertarian. Writers of the 1920s and 1930s who had hailed Holmes as a champion of civil liberties

---

108. Rogat, *supra* note 17, at 254-55, 24, 305, 308; Rogat, *supra* note 100, at 225.
109. R. FAULKNER, *supra* note 107, at 264-65, 263, 247-49.

had made assumptions about the nature of rights in civilized society different from those made by their counterparts in the 1960s. They had assumed that liberties — such as that of contract and that of speech — were not absolutes, but were subsumed in the consensual values of contemporary America. Their view was that expressed by Justice Brandeis in two decisions in 1921: "Rights ... must be remoulded, from time to time, to meet the changing needs of society." [110] "All rights derive from the purposes of the society in which they exist; above all rights rises duty to the community." [111] They considered Holmes a libertarian because in certain decisions he had protected freedom of speech where it did not immediately threaten national interests. For Holmes, the liberty flowed not from any inherent right of the individual but from the interest of society in a free flow of ideas. By the 1960s, however, the standard of libertarianism had altered; a social definition of civil rights seemed inequitable. Racial equality seemed to demand a philosophical definition that provided for the inherent equality of individuals and the absolute nature of human rights. No longer could society have one standard of rights for one set of persons and a second for another — that constituted a deprivation of inalienable guaranties. In this context Holmes's easy approval of majoritarian discriminations against minorities appeared unconscionably nonlibertarian.

The 1960s marked the nadir of Holmes's image. Critics seemed unwilling to undertake charitable interpretations of any of his characteristics: his Brahminism was considered snobbishness, diffidence, and insensitivity; his ideological presuppositions were thought to exhibit both a shocking indifference to humanitarian values and a complacent insularity about the inevitability of progress. The great repute in which Holmes had been held in earlier years seemed to critics of the 1960s to be a glaring example of the distasteful set of values that had dominated American civilization in their immediate past. The ideal they held of a society whose guardians perceived the democratic and egalitarian

---

110. Truax v. Corrigan, 257 U.S. 312, 376 (1921).
111. Duplex Co. v. Deering, 254 U.S. 443, 488 (1921).

222

principles at its core clashed with qualities and beliefs they found in Holmes.

III. HOLMES AND THE CRITICS: A CONCLUDING ASSESSMENT

Despite its diversity, the critical literature on Holmes almost uniformly fails to assess him on his own historical terms. Holmes was, first and foremost, a late nineteenth century intellectual radical. He was concerned with smashing existing fixed systems of the universe and substituting a fluid one. *The Common Law* was his most telling work — it was critical of the quasi-religious formalistic logic of his time and supportive of two fluid organizing concepts, history and community values. At the close of the nineteenth century, Holmes attempted through science to make the concept of community values a tangible, measureable one. In this task he foreshadowed the efforts of social planners in the early twentieth century. But as that century dawned, Holmes gave up his effort and came to rest on the belief that the universe was unknowable, that ultimate values were in the end merely personal prejudices, and that change comes through the fluctuating superiority of such prejudices. Ultimately his ideology presumed an open and ever-changing system of intellectual intercourse — an unregulated market of ideas. This was his famous skepticism.

Because Holmes equated prevailing social values and ideals with prejudices, his ideology was profoundly apolitical. Late nineteenth century commentators made the mistake of identifying his intellectual radicalism with political radicalism. The progressives also erred in thinking that since Holmes believed in fluidity and change, he, like they, ascribed a positive value to change. But in giving up any belief in scientific measurement of social desires, Holmes had also given up a faith in the ability of social planners to achieve progress through an enlightened reordering of social priorities. If beliefs could not be measured, he felt, they could not be ranked. He thus rested on "what the crowd wants." The progressives, in contrast, wanted to educate the "crowd" to desire those things that the progressives believed right-thinking twentieth century Americans should desire.

The hero worshippers of the 1930s made a similar error in their evaluations of Holmes. They ascribed to him the positive as well as the negative components of attitudes, whereas Holmes held only the negative. Because Holmes believed that ideas should have free expression — a belief he often justified by saying that the process of airing those ideas would convince people of their absurdity — and because some of his free speech decisions had involved members of minority groups, Holmes became a protector of minorities and a transcendant Brahmin. His approach to free speech, in fact, assumed the ultimate impotence of all forms of unpopular expression. Because Holmes was critical of nineteenth century judicial formalism and had demonstrated a consciousness of the element of bias in judicial decision making, he was said to support the whole of realism. But Holmes did not believe that psychology was the major component of decision making, and he opposed the kind of empirical internal study of institutions that the realists advocated. Because Holmes had taken a passive stance toward state experimentive schemes in the 1910s and 1920s, critics of the 1930s assumed that he would be not only equally passive toward the federal programs of the New Deal, but sympathetic to what the New Deal represented. But Holmes had never been enthusiastic about paternalistic legislation. He took a fatalistic view of man's nature and muttered about who was going to "pay the bill."

The demythologizers of the 1940s, though more sensitive than their earlier predecessors to the complexities in Holmes, still regarded him as "dateless." His apolitical, laissez faire skepticism was read as the equivalent of those bogeys of the 1940s, pragmatism and totalitarianism. Only in the 1950s did intellectuals begin to see a gap between Holmes's universe and their own. This perception appeared largely in the form of strained efforts to make him "moral" in 1950s terms — to show that had he comprehended the horror of totalitarian regimes he would have demonstrated greater concern for political values.

The critics of the 1960s continued to view Holmes through the lens of contemporary events. Their annoyance at his apparent absence of concern for libertarian principles rested on an expanded definition of liberties. Like the progressives, writers of the 1960s matched all previous eras against their own; Holmes, whose thought was shaped in a world that had far different notions of "liberty" and "equality," was destined to fall short of their standards.

But if Holmes asks, on one level, to be judged by the standards of his age, he invites, on another level, judgment by a more timeless standard: the capacity for being human. Here one finds a disturbing dissonance between Holmes's very conspicuous social and professional success — it is hard to imagine a life less marred by physical, social, or economic deprivations or one marked by a greater length and breadth of achievement — and his gloomy musings that "the crowd has substantially all there is," [112] that "we all are very near despair," [113] that men are like "flies," [114] and that man has no more cosmic significance than a baboon or a grain of sand.[115] The specter of the eminent Holmes uttering such misanthropy smacks of the "old cardinal" prose of Henry Adams that Holmes himself decried.[116]

Holmes's skepticism appears to have been less a striving for a positive goal than a facile means of avoiding commitment, whether to beliefs, institutions, or mankind itself. One is struck by the comments of Holmes that he had remained childless because he could not bear bringing children into the world and because he preferred the less-involved paternalism he felt for his law clerks.[117] These statements suggest a desire to evade the responsibilities and emotional attachments of close involvement with other human beings, or perhaps the adoption of a misanthropic pose to prevent others from probing into areas of his life in which he felt vulnerable.

It is disappointing to find a man who was fortunate enough to

---

112. 1 HOLMES-LASKI LETTERS 207 (M. Howe ed. 1953).

113. O.W. HOLMES, COLLECTED LEGAL PAPERS 248 (1920).

114. 2 HOLMES-LASKI LETTERS 946 (M. Howe ed. 1953).

115. *Cf.* Howe, *supra* note 91.

116. Rogat, *supra* note 100, at 230-31.

117. Letter and Memorandum from Learned Hand to Mark DeWolfe Howe, Apr. 29, 1959, in M. HOWE, *supra* note 102, at 8; Derby, *supra* note 64, at 352.

be made aware in his lifetime of the full measure of his accomplishment (how many men are able to hear themselves called "the greatest of our age in the domain of jurisprudence, and one of the greatest of the ages" [118]? yet who seemed to be so indifferent, at times savagely so, to the lives of his fellow mortals. To be sure, Holmes had his values — civilization, the martial virtues, and, in his own sense, democracy and even liberty. He also had high standards of intellectual performance. But the richness of his mind, the power of his intellect, and even the depth of his feelings tended to degenerate into a cranky negativism that, given his stature, seems peculiarly distasteful. It is Holmes's articulated refusal to take pride in being human that marks him as one of the least "heroic" of America's heroes.

---

118. Cardozo, *Mr. Justice Holmes,* 44 HARV. L. REV. 682, 684 (1931).

ALLOCATING POWER BETWEEN AGENCIES AND COURTS: THE LEGACY OF JUSTICE BRANDEIS

Duke Law Journal, Vol. 1974, No. 2 (1974)

INTRODUCTION

From the turn of the last century, when administrative law was only beginning to acquire an academic and professional identity,[1] through more recent debate concerning the proper function of independent regulatory agencies as agents of government in America,[2] a recurrent theme of conventional wisdom has been that most administrative law issues can be viewed as revolving around the allocation of power between administrative agencies[3] and reviewing courts. Questions involving the scope of judicial review of agency action or the doctrines of primary jurisdiction and exhaustion of administrative remedies, may, under this approach, be viewed essentially as inquiries into whether it is more desirable

---

1. *See generally* T. GOODNOW, COMPARATIVE ADMINISTRATIVE LAW (1893); T. GOODNOW, PRINCIPLES OF ADMINISTRATIVE LAW OF THE UNITED STATES (1905); Schwartz, *The Administrative Agency in Historical Perspective,* 36 IND. L.J. 260 (1961).

HEREAFTER THE FOLLOWING CITATIONS WILL BE USED IN THIS ARTICLE:

J. BLUM, THE REPUBLICAN ROOSEVELT (1954) [hereinafter cited as BLUM];

K. DAVIS, ADMINISTRATIVE LAW TREATISE (1958) [hereinafter cited as DAVIS];

L. JAFFE, JUDICIAL CONTROL OF ADMINISTRATIVE ACTION (1965) [hereinafter cited as JAFFE].

2. *Compare* Davis, *A New Approach to Delegation,* 36 U. CHI. L. REV. 713 (1969), *with* Jaffe, *The Illusion of the Ideal Administration,* 86 HARV. L. REV. 1183 (1973).

3. The term "agency" is used in this Article to designate three different kinds of administrative bodies: independent regulatory agencies such as the Interstate Commerce Commission; executive agencies such as the Post Office or the Department of the Interior; and "hybrid" agencies, which combine the characteristics of the first two types of agency. For a more detailed discussion and explanation of the "hybrid" agencies, see text accompanying notes 159-62 *infra.* The term is also used more generally as a synonym for "administrative body" itself. Whether the term is being used in its general sense or as a means of describing a particular type of administrative body should be apparent from the context in which it appears.

to have a court or an agency exercise supervisory control over some aspect of American life. Even the language employed by the courts in considering such questions, invariably glossed with such terms of art as "expertise," "administrative discretion," and "substantial evidence," suggests a significant preoccupation with power allocation. A court's deference to the "expert" judgments of an agency can be thought of as an implicit concession of supervisory power; a court's refusal to find that an agency determination has been based on "substantial evidence" can be read as implying suspicion of the agency's supervisory competence.

This method of analyzing the interaction between administrative agencies and reviewing courts has been so dominant in administrative law in the last thirty years[4] that any other approach may seem eccentric. Yet the allocative approach reflects concerns that were not the primary interests of the founders of the modern regulatory agency and tends to deemphasize issues which at one time were the major battlefields of administrative law — issues such as the constitutionality of legislative delegations of lawmaking power to agencies and the worth of uniform national regulatory standards.[5] The contributions of one man, Justice Louis D. Brandeis, reoriented the focus of administrative law toward the appropriate allocation of functions and power between courts and agencies. The gradual elevation of Brandeis' approach to such a dominant position and the contemporary ramifications of that development are the subjects of this Article.

I. The Original Conception of Regulatory Agencies: The Hepburn Act Debate

The Early ICC and the Progressives

The first modern federal regulatory agency, the Interstate Commerce Commission, was the logical outgrowth of efforts by

---

4. *See generally* T. Cooper, Administrative Agencies and the Courts (1951); R. Jackson, The Struggle for Judicial Supremacy (1941); Jaffe.

5. See text accompanying notes 34, 35 *infra*. *See generally* Davis, *supra* note 2, at 713; Merrill, *Standards — A Safeguard for the Exercise of Delegated Power,* 47 Neb. L. Rev. 469 (1968).

the states in the early 1880's to deal with abuses generated by the unrestrained growth and power of the great railroads. The device employed by the states in this endeavor was the special study commission.[6] Like those early state commissions, the ICC, as originally structured, was not necessarily intended to be a permanent body: the impetus for its creation arose from inequitable discrepancies in railroad rates, and it was generally believed that as the contours of that problem changed, the Commission's mandate might also vary significantly.[7]

Shortly after its emergence, the ICC became severely hampered in its operations as a result of narrow judicial interpretations of the permissible scope of the Commission's activities. In *ICC v. Cincinnati Railway,*[8] decided in 1897, the Supreme Court held that the Commission had neither the power to prescribe minimum or maximum interstate railway rates nor the power to obtain a court order directing the railroads to follow past rates which the Commission had previously determined to have been "reasonable and just."[9] Additionally, in two other decisions in that same decade, *Chicago, Milwaukee & St. Paul Railway v. Minnesota*[10] and *Smyth v. Ames,*[11] the Court resorted, respectively, to procedural and substantive due process analyses to sharply curtail the ability of state commissions to regulate intrastate railroad rates. The first of these two cases maintained that the reasonableness of railroad rates was ultimately a judicial question under the requirements of procedural due process,[12] while the latter case held that the due

---

6. For a discussion of the essentially ad hoc nature of these early state commissions, see R. CUSHMAN, THE INDEPENDENT REGULATORY COMMISSIONS 22-23 (1941).

7. Id. at 64-65.

8. 167 U.S. 479 (1897).

9. *Id.* at 511.

10. 134 U.S. 418 (1890).

11. 169 U.S. 466 (1898).

12. In *Chicago Railway* the Court held unconstitutional a Minnesota statute regulating railroad rates because it made the state commission's determination conclusive with respect to the reasonableness of those rates. Stressing the procedural infirmities of the statute, the Court stated:

It deprives the company of its right to a judicial investigation, by due

process clause required commission-established rates to yield a "fair return" on a "fair present value." [13] Both decisions reflected the Court's underlying concern for the potential reach of regulatory bodies. As stated by the Court in *Smyth v. Ames,* "[t]he idea that any legislature ... can conclusively determine for the people and for the courts that what it ... authorizes its agents to do ... is consistent with the fundamental law ... is in opposition to the theory of our institutions." [14]

After the turn of the century, however, the concept of regulation by administrative agency was revived as a result of its adoption by a more general and more enduring wave of reform that came to be known as Progressivism. One ingredient of Progressivism was a reexamination of the effectiveness of the traditional institutions of American government and the subsequent formulation of specific proposals for reform. In diverse ways and in varying degrees, the legislative and judicial branches of government were, according to the Progressives, unresponsive to the needs of the time. The Progressives asserted that legislatures, especially at the state level, were corrupt and partisan, furthering "special interests" at the expense of the public; they also contended that the judiciary was hopelessly isolated from social change and therefore unmindful of tne new challenges facing governing institutions in early twentieth-century America.[15] The Progressives resolved to meet these difficulties not only by

---

process of law, under the forms and with the machinery provided by the wisdom of successive ages for the investigation judicially of the truth of a matter in controversy, and substitutes therefor, as an absolute finality, the action of a railroad commission which ... cannot be regarded as clothed with judicial functions or possessing the machinery of a court of justice. 134 U.S. at 457.

13. In *Smyth* the Court held Nebraska's railroad rate regulation statute unconstitutional. Instead of basing its decision upon procedural defects, as was the case in *Chicago Railway* (see note 12 *supra*), the Court found the Nebraska statute defective in that the rates fixed therein did not permit a fair return on the fair market value of property employed for the public use. 169 U.S. at 546-47.

14. *Id.* at 527.

15. *See generally* H. CROLY, THE PROMISE OF AMERICAN LIFE 278 (1909); C. MCCARTHY, THE NEW IDEA 179 *et seq.* (1910).

fighting special interests in the legislatures and by calling for a shift from "mechanical" to "sociological" jurisprudence,[16] but also by expanding the powers of regulatory agencies. Appropriately structured and staffed administrative agencies, they believed, could encompass the blend of technical expertise, enlightenment, and impartiality needed to solve the complex problems besetting an evolving industrial society. Through such nonpartisan agencies, the "best men" of the time could return to public service; in the operations of such institutions, the skills of modern business management could be combined with the old-fashioned virtues of honesty and integrity.[17]

The *Cincinnati Railway* and *Smyth v. Ames* decisions [18] had thus dealt jarring blows to the Progressives' great expectations for the independent regulatory agency in general and the ICC in particular. Robert LaFollette, a leading Progressive, called the *Cincinnati Railway* decision "crushing," asserting that it robbed the ICC of its power to fix rates and left it "worse than helpless." [19] When Theodore Roosevelt became President, he noted that although the ICC technically had power over the railways, its power "was either not exercised at all or exercised with utter inefficiency." [20] The original purpose of the Interstate Commerce Act, Roosevelt maintained, had been subverted.

The Hepburn Act Debate

Accordingly, in 1904 President Roosevelt proposed legislation [21]

---

16. *See* Pound, *Mechanical Jurisprudence,* 8 COLUM. L. REV. 605, 608-10 (1908). A primary attraction of mechanical jurisprudence was its supposedly precise scientific method of administration through deductive logic. Roscoe Pound maintained that to base legal conclusions on preliminary assumptions was neither scientific nor precise. He urged a shift to a "pragmatic jurisprudence based on an empirical examination of human conditions rather than on a priori assumptions." *Id.* at 610.

17. *See generally* White, *The Social Values of the Progressives: Some New Perspectives,* 70 S. ATLANTIC Q. 62, 73-74 (1971) (citing authorities).

18. See text accompanying notes 8-14 *supra.*

19. R. LAFOLLETTE, LAFOLLETTE'S AUTOBIOGRAPHY 172 (1960).

20. T. ROOSEVELT, AN AUTOBIOGRAPHY 473 (1919).

21. Hepburn bill, H.R. 12987, 59th Cong., 1st Sess. (1904).

which was later to become the Hepburn Act of 1906;[22] the provisions of that bill presaged the revitalization of the independent regulatory agency as a unit of government. The Hepburn bill proposed that the ICC be vested with the power to decide what should constitute a reasonable railroad rate in those circumstances wherein an existing rate had been challenged and, after a full hearing, had been found to be unreasonable.[23] This proposal was consistent with President Roosevelt's view that administrative agencies could be utilized to serve as expert watchdogs on large-scale industrial enterprises, penalizing inefficient and criminal practices and rewarding efficient and honest ones. Moreover, it was good politics: the country at large was increasingly disturbed by discriminatory practices in the shipping of goods on railroads and increasingly suspicious of growing industrial combinations.[24] During the summer and fall of 1905, Roosevelt made speeches which suggested that the most effective way of dealing with "the monopoly power" was to curb it through administrative regulation before the industrial combines grew so massive that not even the courts could control them.[25] Augmented power in the Interstate Commerce Commission, he argued, "would put a stop to abuses of big corporations . . . would destroy monopoly, and make the biggest business man in the

---

22. Act of June 29, 1906, ch. 3591, 34 Stat. 584, *as amended* 49 U.S.C. §§ 1-40 (1970). For a full discussion of Roosevelt's role in the passage of the Hepburn Act, see BLUM 87-105.

23. Hepburn bill, H.R. 12987, 59th Cong., 1st Sess. (1904).

24. *See, e.g.,* G. MOWRY, THE ERA OF THEODORE ROOSEVELT 133, 198-99 (1958).

25. T. ROOSEVELT, THE WORKS OF THEODORE ROOSEVELT, PRESIDENTIAL ADDRESSES AND STATE PAPERS 369-71 (address in Chicago, Ill., May 10, 1905), 405-07 (address in Williamstown, Mass., June 22, 1905), 448-55 (address in Chautauqua, N.Y., Aug. 11, 1905), 462-65 (address in Richmond, Va., Oct. 18, 1905), 492-95 (address in Atlanta, Ga., Oct. 20, 1905), 562-67 (address to a joint session of Congress in Washington, D.C., Dec. 5, 1905). *See also* BLUM 87-90. Roosevelt was forced to turn to the regulatory commission as a means of controlling trusts because of the failure of previous antitrust legislation. The Sherman Antitrust Act, July 2, 1890, ch. 647, 26 Stat. 209, *as amended* 15 U.S.C §§ 1-7 (1970), directed at monopolies, had been emasculated by the Supreme Court in such cases as United States v. E.C. Knight Co., 156 U.S. 1 (1895).

country conform squarely to the principles laid down by the American people, while at the same time giving fair play to the little man. . . . " [26] Rhetoric of this kind responded to a widespread public desire for solutions to the alleged abuses of "monopolists," a category in which the nation's large railroads were often placed.[27] The House of Representatives, also attentive to this sentiment, passed the Hepburn bill in February, 1906, by a nearly unanimous vote.[28]

The Hepburn bill then went to the Senate. There it was debated until May, when it was passed after the addition of an amendment introduced by Senator William Allison of Iowa and backed by Roosevelt.[29] The story of the bill's tortuous journey through the Senate is a familiar one, filled with suggestions of intrigue and political tradeoffs.[30] But a central aspect of the Senate debate has often been minimized: the question of judicial review of the ICC's decisions. Although that question dominated the legislators' attention in their deliberations, it has been considered almost inconsequential in contrast to "the large and varied significance of the whole railroad measures." [31] One commentator has described the judicial review question as an issue revealing only "detailed matters of emphasis" rather than differences "of principle and basic political philosophies." [32]

To relegate the controversy over judicial review to a position of peripheral significance, however, is to misconstrue the meaning of the Hepburn Act debate. While other serious issues certainly present themselves in retrospect — such as the role of the Hepburn

---

26. T. ROOSEVELT, *supra* note 20, at 232.

27. *See, e.g.,* BLUM 86; D. BURTON, THEODORE ROOSEVELT 136-38 (1972).

28. 40 CONG. REC. 2303 (1906) (yeas 346, nays 7). See text accompanying notes 22, 23 *supra.*

29. *See* BLUM 92-105. While granting the courts power to "enjoin, set aside, annul, or suspend any order" of the ICC, the Allison Amendment failed to specify the grounds for suspension. *Id.* at 103 (quoting Allison Amendment). This "purposeful obscurity" allowed advocates of both narrow and broad review to claim victory. *Id.* at 102. See text accompanying notes 50-52 *infra.*

30. G. KOLKO, RAILROADS AND REGULATION 1877-1916 at 127-44 (1965).

31. BLUM 96.

32. G. KOLKO, *supra* note 30, at 129.

Act in establishing a trend of governmental regulation of private enterprise or the possibility that the Act may have furthered the interests of those parties it purported to regulate — these matters were not of primary concern to Congress in the context of the actual hearings on the bill. Those hearings reflect less concern with the relative effectiveness of regulation than with the question of which institutional forum — agency or court — should be the primary regulator. This latter question was at the heart of the Hepburn Act debate.[33] It forced consideration of the purposes and functions of regulatory agencies in the American system of government; it tested the commitment of Progressives, particularly those trained in the law, to the agency forum as a viable legal institution.

The controversial nature of the Hepburn bill was immediately emphasized by its opponents in the Senate. On February 28, Ohio Senator Joseph B. Foraker made a lengthy address challenging the constitutionality of the bill on three grounds: first, the bill assumed that Congress had power to make rates, which in Foraker's view it did not;[34] second, the bill combined executive, legislative, and judicial powers in an administrative body, hence violating the separation of powers envisaged by the Constitution;[35] third, the bill constituted an illegal delegation of legislative power, since the provision that rates established by the Commission be "just and reasonable and fairly remunerative" was too vague to serve as a governing standard.[36] Foraker also attacked the bill's provision establishing the scope of judicial review, which was to be confined to the question of whether orders by the Commission had been

---

33. *See, e.g.,* 40 CONG. REC. 4431-46 (1906) (debate on a proposed amendment to the Hepburn Act, limiting judicial review of ICC orders to the question of whether such orders violated constitutional due process by being confiscatory, thus excluding from judicial review any inquiry into whether ICC orders were in fact just and reasonable).

34. *Id.* at 3105.

35. *Id.* at 3108.

36. *Id.* at 3112.

"regularly made." [37] He contended that ratemaking was a legislative act and that, by delegating a ratemaking power to the Commission, Congress had vested the Commission with a legislative discretion for determining what was a reasonable rate. Foraker argued that, absent a contrary statutory provision, such legislative discretion could only be overturned by the courts in those instances where the rate was fixed so high that it was extortionate as to the shipper or so low that it was confiscatory as to the carrier. Hence, he maintained, where the challenged rate fell between these two extremes, the Commission's decisions would be final. The unavailability of judicial review in these "intermediate" rate cases disturbed him; the courts had "been from the beginning of the common law the sure bulwark of the liberties and rights of the Anglo-Saxon race. . . . the conservative, steadying, reassuring factor in American Government." [38] That the Hepburn bill demonstrated an unwillingness to allow the courts unrestricted scope of review was in Foraker's judgment "enough not only to excite distrust [of the bill] . . . but also to condemn it." [39]

Twelve days later Senator Charles A. Culberson of Texas countered Foraker's attacks. After a lengthy discussion of the history of the commerce clause, Culberson concluded that since the congressional power to regulate transportation necessarily implied the power to fix the conditions under which transportation might be conducted, the delegation of that regulatory power to an agency logically implied the attendant power in that agency to fix rates of transportation. [40] Further, he rationalized the combination of legislative and judicial functions in the ICC as necessary to protect the public in some degree against "the selfishness of . . . a body of capitalists who control the great systems." [41] Finally, Culberson asserted that the standard prescribed by the delegation from

---

37. *Id.* at 3117. The concept of limited judicial review of administrative decisions was not unprecedented at this time. It had been previously advanced in American School of Magnetic Healing v. McAnnulty, 187 U.S. 94 (1902).

38. 40 CONG. REC. 3118 (1906).

39. *Id.*

40. *Id.* at 3678.

41. *Id.* at 3682.

Congress to the ICC — that all rates fixed be "just and reasonable" — was "as clear as . . . any other general principle" and was a test that had been so repeatedly declared by judges as to be regarded as a part of American law.[42]

Senator Culberson was also concerned about attempts to insert in the bill a more detailed provision for judicial review. Such an insertion, in his opinion, might extend the jurisdiction of the courts "to matters of business and policy respecting rates with which [they should] not concern themselves, because it is no part of the judicial function . . . ." [43] In Culberson's opinion, the courts could review rates alleged to be extortionate or confiscatory despite the absence of a statutory provision, but they had no authority to interfere with rates established under a "just and reasonable" standard except when the rates in question were so patently unreasonable as to justify the claim that they were equivalent to confiscation.[44]

Of the four points[45] raised by Foraker and disputed by Culberson, the Senate quickly focused on the scope of judicial review of the Commission's decisions. As the debate passed through March to April and May, opponents of the bill conceded the delegation and combination-of-functions points in order to concentrate their energies on attempts to amend the bill to secure broad review. The central issue of the debate was whether rates established by the ICC which were not clearly confiscatory but which were arguably less than "just and reasonable and fairly remunerative" should fall within the permissible scope of judicial review. Advocates of the bill, among them such Progressives as Francis Newlands of Nevada and Alexander Clay of Georgia, wanted to deny the courts any power to inquire into whether the Commission's rates were in fact just and reasonable;[46] they contended that judicial review should be confined to the confiscatory situation,[47] where it was compelled by the

---

42. *Id.* at 3678.
43. *Id.* at 3680.
44. *Id. Cf.* American School of Magnetic Healing v. McAnnulty, 187 U.S. 94 (1902).
45. See text accompanying notes 34-42 *supra.*
46. 40 CONG. REC. 4435 (1906) (remarks of Senators Clay and Newlands).
47. *Id.* at 4434 (remarks of Senator Clay).

Constitution.[48] Articulating the prime rationale of the supporters of narrow review, Senator Newlands noted that most of the amendments proposed by those favoring broad review gave the courts the right to review not only Commission action in determining rates but also ICC orders relating to practices and regulations. "I fear," he proclaimed, "that the result of [the amendments] will be to turn over to the judiciary review of the legislative discretion of the Commission . . . ." [49]

Newlands' remarks dramatizing the conflict between advocates of narrow review and proponents of broad review were made on March 29. Three weeks later the parties appeared to be at an impasse, and the Hepburn bill's chances of passage seemed dubious. Shortly thereafter, however, through a mysterious set of circumstances,[50] a compromise was reached, whereby the Senate adopted the Hepburn bill with an amendment introduced by Senator Allison. The amendment contained language that explicitly granted review of Commission decisions to the federal district courts, struck out the troublesomely vague "fairly remunerative" phrase from the delegation provision of the Hepburn bill,[51] but did not define the scope of review.[52]

Advocates of narrow review claimed victory, and in a sense the absence of a specific authorization for the courts to reexamine Commission orders or practices gave hope to those who believed in agency autonomy. As a practical matter, however, the Allison amendment left the courts with a relatively free hand to define their relationship to regulatory agencies. It also provided judges

---

48. *See, e.g.,* Chicago, M. & St. P. Ry. v. Minnesota, 134 U.S. 418, 458 (1890). For a discussion of the holding in the *Chicago Railway* case, see note 12 *supra.*

49. 40 CONG. REC. 4435 (1906). For further remarks on this issue by Senator Newlands, see *id.* at 4445.

50. Senator Aldrich, the leader of the Senate forces opposing the Hepburn bill, inexplicably retreated from his position. Aldrich may have made the political judgment that further opposition might mobilize support for an event more radical proposal by Senator LaFollette, while the Allison Amendment was at least ambiguous. *See* BLUM 101-03.

51. See text accompanying note 36 *supra.*

52. BLUM 102.

with an opportunity to assess the effectiveness of agencies in solving social problems and to test that effectiveness against the alternative of a judicial solution — to define, in other words, the limits of agency power and, by implication, the correlative extent of judicial power. In one of the ironies of American politics, the legislation which was to revitalize the regulatory agency as an alternative forum for conflict resolution simultaneously set the stage for subsequent judicial limitation of agency autonomy. Those who had welcomed the emergence of regulatory agencies, in part because of their loss of faith in the courts' ability to promote social justice, faced the prospect that further agency growth after 1906 would be subject to the judiciary's willingness to tolerate supervisory power in agencies.

While the outcome of the Hepburn Act debate suggested that future controversies in administrative law would tend to be reduced to exercises in institutional power allocation, such did not prove to be the case. Other questions debated by Senators Foraker and Culberson — notably those concerning the permissibility of combining constitutionally separate powers in one agency and those involving the required specificity of standards governing powers delegated to an agency[53] — were still unanswered. Thus, threshold questions of constitutionality remained; consequently the regulatory agency had not yet achieved legitimacy as an institution of American government. Further, the original conception of regulatory agencies as being independent of both courts and legislatures, uniform in practice and procedures, and zealously opposed to corruption and influence-peddling among regulatees persisted in some quarters,[54] affecting court decisions as well as public opinion. An allocation calculus, weighing the respective powers of courts and agencies, was slow to materialize in the face of these distractions. It gained momentum largely from the accident of Louis Brandeis' appointment to the Supreme Court.

---

53. See text accompanying notes 35, 36 *supra*.

54. *See* H. CROLY, PROGRESSIVE DEMOCRACY 364-67 (1914). *See also* White, *supra* note 17, at 73-74 (citing authorities).

II. Justice Brandeis and the Allocation Calculus

The Rise of the Regulatory Agencies

In the ten years between the passage of the Hepburn Act and Brandies' confirmation as a Supreme Court Justice, regulatory agencies became a more pervasive feature of American government. Woodrow Wilson, with whom Brandeis had developed a close relationship during the 1912 presidential campaign, had taken office determined to insure that large corporate enterprises would not be allowed complete freedom either to grow to gigantic proportions or to dominate their respective markets. After some internal debate, the Wilson administration ultimately settled on the use of federal regulatory agencies as checks upon industrial enterprise.[55] In 1914 Brandeis participated in the drafting of legislation[56] creating the Federal Trade Commission, whose original mandate was to oversee and suppress industrial practices which tended to further unfair competition. Complementing the Federal Trade Commission Act was the Clayton Act,[57] likewise enacted in 1914, which was designed to prohibit practices that tended to substantially lessen competition. By 1916 Progressives were able to maintain that the major industrial and financial centers of power in the country were each subject to agency supervision: the railroads, through the ICC; the trusts, through the FTC, Clayton Act, and revived enforcement of the Sherman Act;[58]

---

55. H. Ford, Woodrow Wilson: the Man and His Work 192-94 (1916); M. Urofsky, A Mind of One Piece: Brandeis and American Reform 90-92 (1971).

56. Federal Trade Commission Act, Sept. 26, 1914, ch. 311, 38 Stat. 717, *as amended* 15 U.S.C. §§ 41-46, 47-58 (1970). For discussion of Brandeis' role in the development of the provision establishing the FTC, see A. Lief, Brandeis, The Personal History of an American Ideal 287-91 (1936); M. Urofsky, *supra* note 55, at 85-92.

57. Act of Oct. 15, 1914, ch. 323, 38 Stat. 730, *as amended* 15 U.S.C. §§ 12-13, 14-21, 22-27 (1970).

58. The Supreme Court, however, showed little sign of cooperating with the government in Sherman Act cases. *See, e.g.,* United States v. United States Steel Corp., 251 U.S. 417 (1920).

and the banks, through the Federal Reserve Board, created in 1913.[59]

Brandeis had been closely identified with these policies[60] and was regarded as favorably disposed toward governmental supervision of free enterprise. But his attitude toward the regulatory agency form of government as such was somewhat ambivalent. His initial critiques of the trusts and the banking industry had focused upon the structural deficiencies of excessive size and overcentralization endemic to those institutions rather than upon the need for federal regulation of their business practices.[61] In accordance with this view, Brandeis had originally favored fragmentation of large industrial combinations and had advocated placing regulatory power in the states rather than in the federal government.[62] He had gone on record before his appointment to the Court as favoring employee participation in industrial management;[63] yet he had simultaneously demonstrated some skepticism about the place of regulatory agencies in furthering that goal. "[N]o commission," Brandeis wrote in 1914, "however able, fearless and diligent its members, can . . . supply the incentive and the eagerness to please the public . . . which [result] from the necessities of competition." [64] Although he played a leading role in drafting legislation establishing the Federal Trade Commission,[65] he had initially

---

59. The Federal Reserve Board was established pursuant to the Federal Reserve Act, Dec. 23, 1913, ch. 6, 38 Stat. 251.

60. In addition to his work on the Federal Trade Commission and Sherman Acts, Brandeis had testified at hearings before the Pujo Committee on banking reform and had written an influential polemic attacking the banks and the trusts. See L. BRANDEIS, OTHER PEOPLE'S MONEY AND HOW THE BANKERS USE IT (1933) (originally published in book form in 1914).

61. See generally L. BRANDEIS, BUSINESS — A PROFESSION (1933); L. BRANDEIS, supra note 60, at 47-62.

62. See L. BRANDEIS, supra note 60, at 310.

63. 8 COMM'N ON INDUS. RELATIONS, FINAL REPORT AND TESTIMONY, S. DOC. 415, 64th Cong., 1st Sess. 7659-60, 7662, 7664 (1916).

64. L. BRANDEIS, BUSINESS — A PROFESSION 295-96 (1933).

65. See note 56 supra.

argued that it be limited to fact-finding and advisory powers.[66] Administrative regulation, he believed, might "prevent positive abuses, like discriminations, or rebating, or excessive rates"; but it could neither "make an inefficient business efficient" nor "supply initiative or energy." [67]

In general, Brandeis supported or criticized the activities of governmental institutions in accordance with their apparent ability to foster social objectives that he believed to be desirable. Among these goals were the preservation of self-reliance and individual initiative; internal efficiency in business management, which flowed, in Brandeis' view, from moderate size and sound accounting; and the preservation of certain moral values, such as temperance, honesty, and industry.[68] To these beliefs Brandeis added a conviction that policy decisions ought to be grounded on carefully analyzed empirical data. These attitudes, over time, would lead him to view the function of regulatory agencies somewhat differently than did the original sponsors of the Hepburn Act.

Defining "Administrative" Functions

A potential consequence of the Progressives' enthusiasm for administrative agencies, as noted, was the emergence of a sphere of governmental influence that could not be invaded by the courts. The creation of permanent regulatory agencies implied a judgment that those bodies were somehow eminently qualified to supervise certain areas of American life. But this judgment had largely been expressed in generalities: by 1916 there had been little definition, by the judiciary or otherwise, of the specific functions that could be called uniquely "administrative" or especially amenable to the

---

66. A. LIEF, *supra* note 56, at 219-20; *cf.* Rublee, *The Original Plan and Early History of the Federal Trade Commission,* 11 PROCEEDINGS OF ACADEMY OF POL. SCI. [666]-[667] (1926).

67. L. BRANDEIS, BUSINESS — A PROFESSION 295 (1933). *But see also* L. BRANDEIS, THE CURSE OF BIGNESS 122-24 (1934) (suggesting that "prohibition of monopoly" coupled with "regulation of competition" would be sufficient to preserve and restore competition).

68. *See, e.g.,* L. BRANDEIS, BUSINESS — A PROFESSION xlvi-lvi (1933).

exercise of agency power. With the proliferation of federal regulatory agencies during the Wilson administration, a need for a more precise articulation of the rationale for agency control emerged. One of Brandeis' major judicial contributions was the formulation of a set of criteria to aid in the process of meeting this need.

Development of the Doctrine of Primary Jurisdiction

The doctrine of primary jurisdiction,[69] by which agencies, as opposed to courts, are deemed the appropriate entities to make initial decisions that are in some sense adjudicative, was one of the early devices utilized for establishing agency autonomy. An initial justification for the doctrine was uniformity. In the 1907 case of *Texas and Pacific Railway v. Abilene Cotton Oil Co.,*[70] for example, Justice White employed the following analysis in deciding that preliminary resort to the ICC was necessary to determine the reasonableness of an interstate carrier rate:

> For if, without previous action by the Commission, power might be exerted by courts and juries generally to determine the reasonableness of an established rate, ... a uniform standard of rates in the future would be impossible, as the standard would fluctuate and vary, dependent upon the divergent conclusions reached ... by the various courts called upon to consider the subject as an original question.[71]

The Interstate Commerce Act of 1887,[72] White maintained, had as its primary purpose the elimination of localized rate discriminations; if courts could revise a uniform ICC rate, that purpose would be defeated.[73] Following *Abilene,* additional

---

69. *See* 3 DAVIS §§ 19.01-.09.

70. 204 U.S. 426 (1907).

71. *Id.* at 440.

72. Act of Feb. 4, 1887, ch. 104, 24 Stat. 379, *as amended* 49 U.S.C §§ 1 *et seq.,* 301 *et seq.,* 901 *et seq.,* 1001 *et seq.,* 1231 *et seq.* (1970).

73. 204 U.S. at 440-41. The result in *Abilene* seemed contrary to the concurrent jurisdiction which the Act of 1887 had seemingly given to the courts:

> [A]ny person or persons claiming to be damaged by any common carrier subject to the provisions of this act may either make complaint to the

Supreme Court cases[74] focused on the uniformity requirement and distinguished between instances wherein, as in *Abilene,* a rate was attacked as unreasonable[75] and instances wherein a carrier was charged with violating an existing common law custom or practice.[76] In the latter class of situations, "where the decision did not involve the determination of matters calling for the exercise of the administrative power and discretion of the Commission," [77] the state courts retained concurrent jurisdiction.

The uniformity rationale for upholding agency decisions became increasingly inadequate, however, as the Progressives formulated more ambitious schemes of regulation through agencies. Enthusiasts for agency government came to be interested in more

---

Commission as hereinafter provided for, or may bring suit in his or their own behalf for the recovery of the damages for which such common carrier may be liable under the provisions of this act, in any District or Circuit Court of the United States of competent jurisdiction . . . . Act of Feb. 4, 1887, ch. 104, § 9, 24 Stat. 379, *as amended* 49 U.S.C. § 9 (1970).

The Supreme Court held, however, that this provisions granted to the courts concurrent jurisdiction only as to the questions which would not necessitate prior action by the Commission. This construction was compelled because,

[i]f the power existed in both courts and the Commission to originally hear complaints on [the reasonableness of rates], there might be a divergence between the action of the Commission and the decision of a court. In other words, the established schedule might be found reasonable by the Commission in the first instance and unreasonable by a court acting originally, and thus a conflict would arise which would render the enforcement of the act impossible. 204 U.S. at 441.

In Professor Davis' opinion "[t]he *Abilene* case is probably one of the outstanding examples in all Supreme Court history of 'interpretation' which leads to a result diametrically opposed to clear and unambiguous statutory language." 3 DAVIS § 19.02, at 7.

74. *E.g.,* Pennsylvania R.R. v. Puritan Coal Mining Co., 237 U.S. 121 (1915); Robinson v. Baltimore & O.R.R., 222 U.S. 506 (1912).

75. *E.g.,* Robinson v. Baltimore & O.R.R., 222 U.S. 506, 509 (1912).

76. *E.g.,* Pennsylvania R.R. v. Puritan Coal Mining Co., 237 U.S. 121 (1915). In *Puritan* there was an alleged breach of the carrier's common law duty to furnish a reasonable number of cars as well as a violation of a state statute prohibiting discrimination between shippers in furnishing cars. *Id.* at 130-31. The Court was of the opinion that the latter factor was irrelevant because the liability would be the same in either event. *Id.* at 132.

77. *Id.* at 130.

than avoiding geographic inequalities in the shipment of interstate goods; they were concerned with nothing less than the revitalization and modernization of the American governmental apparatus.[78] In their minds carving out an area of agency supremacy was equated with the infusion of expertise, efficiency, and integrity into the governing process. The primary jurisdiction doctrine constituted, in their view, a recognition by the courts of the inherent superiority of regulatory agencies in the performance of certain tasks. In the hands of Justice Brandeis, the doctrine began to receive a more elaborate and extended justification: he viewed the exercise of primary jurisdiction as a necessary means of agency self-definition.

In *Northern Pacific Railway Co. v. Solum,*[79] at 1918 decision, Brandeis considered the question of whether a Minnesota state court, in the absence of initial consideration by the ICC, could investigate the reasonableness of the rate-setting practices of railroads operating in interstate commerce passing through Minnesota. At the turn of the twentieth century, the Northern Pacific operated two routes in Minnesota, one intrastate and the other interstate, each of which charged the same rates. Minnesota passed a statute in 1907 fixing intrastate rates at a figure lower than those charged by the Northern Pacific. The Northern Pacific ultimately reduced its intrastate rates to conform with the statute, but it maintained its interstate rates at their previous levels and continued its past practice of routing outbound shipments from some Minnesota cities via the interstate rather than the intrastate line. Several shippers on the Duluth line brought suits in a Minnesota state court to compel the railroad to select the cheaper intrastate route for their future shipments and to recover the rate differential which resulted from past routing on the interstate line. The state court found that under common law the Northern Pacific owed a duty to transport shipments over the line which would give

---

78. H. CROLY, *supra* note 54, at 364-77; H. CROLY, *supra* note 15, at 362. *See also* White, *supra* note 17, at 73-74 (citing authorities).

79. 247 U.S. 477 (1918).

the shipper the benefit of the cheaper rate.[80] On appeal to the United States Supreme Court, the Northern Pacific contended that the duty of the carrier was in part defined by the "general practices" of carriers dealing in interstate commerce and that the reasonableness of those practices was an administrative question which could not be anticipated by the state court. The aggrieved shippers, citing the *Abilene Cotton Oil Co.* case,[81] urged that preliminary resort to the ICC was only compelled in those cases involving the questions of whether a particular rate was unreasonable or whether a particular practice was discriminatory.[82]

Writing for the Court, Brandeis upheld the Northern Pacific's assertion of the primary jurisdiction doctrine, stating that the reasonableness of its practice of shipping over the interstate route was "an administrative question ... of perhaps considerable complexity." [83] He noted that the carrier's obligations required it to consider "its own [interests] and those of the general public" as well as "to deal justly with the shipper," adding that in some circumstances "[r]esort to the more expensive route may be justified." [84] The duty of the carrier, in Brandeis' judgment, was not an absolute one: the standard was the reasonableness of the practice, "all things considered." [85] Brandeis rejected the contention that the primary jurisdiction doctrine was limited in applicability to cases involving the reasonableness of a particular rate or the discriminatory effects of particular practices. Such instances merely represented the minimum reach of the rule.[86]

The rationale for preliminary jurisdiction in *Northern Pacific* was not notable for its clarity. Brandeis did attempt to characterize

---

80. Solum v. Northern Pac. Ry., 133 Minn. 93, 96, 157 N.W. 996, 997 (1916).
81. See notes 70-73 *supra* and accompanying text.
82. 247 U.S. at 480, 482-83.
83. *Id.* at 483.
84. *Id.* at 482.
85. *Id.*
86. *Id.* at 483. In resolving the primary jurisdiction issue, Brandeis also resolved affirmatively the larger question of whether the federal forum was appropriate for regulation in that type of case. *Id.* at 483-84.

situations where the "interest of the general public" was involved as being better suited to agency consideration, and he sought to identify questions involving complicated economic analysis as issues especially suitable for "administrative" determination. But the opinion balked at attempting an actual definition of administrative functions or an indication of the proper scope of agency power — other than to state that "any practice of the carrier which gives rise to the application of a rate" was a matter for initial agency consideration.[87] This latter language, however, was not related to the underlying purposes or functions of agencies; the decision did little more than state one example of an "administrative" question.

In the 1922 case of *Great Northern Railway v. Merchants Elevator Co.,*[88] Brandeis was faced with a similar problem of definition; this time his response was somewhat more specific. Like *Northern Pacific,* this case arose from railroad activities in Minnesota: the plaintiff shipper brought an action in state court claiming that the railroad had overcharged it in violation of the railroad's own tariff schedule. The case appears to have been an attempt to test the power of the ICC to construe tariff provisions, since the sum in dispute was a mere eighty dollars.[89] The Great Northern claimed that primary resort to the ICC was required for a determination of which of two conflicting tariff provisions applied; the shipper claimed that the court could take initial jurisdiction over the entire controversy. Counsel for the Great Northern argued that uniformity in tariff rates was impossible to achieve unless the proper construction of tariffs was determined by the ICC and that the purpose of the Act establishing the ICC was "to secure and preserve uniformity" in the regulation of commerce.[90]

Brandeis conceded that uniformity was the paramount purpose of the Commerce Act, but held that the attainment of uniformity

---

87. *Id.* at 483.
88. 259 U.S. 285 (1922).
89. *Id.* at 288.
90. Id. at 290.

did not require preliminary resort to the Commission in every case where the construction of a tariff was in dispute. In so holding, he attempted to characterize the kinds of questions that gave rise to the doctrine of primary jurisdiction. If the controversy involved "the exercise of administrative discretion" or "issues essentially of fact," preliminary resort to the Commission was necessary.[91] Both of these criteria addressed the relative ability of courts and agencies to deal with the precise question at issue. If answering the litigated point required the exercise of "discretion in technical matters," such as the assessment of large amounts of conflicting factual evidence, the decision should be entrusted to an administrative body of experts. Similarly, if a consideration of extrinsic factual evidence was necessary to establish a usage of trade or to impart special meaning to words, the agency was the appropriate initial forum. Questions of "fact" should be resolved by commissions as a preliminary matter, since their resolution necessitated the gathering and analyzing of empirical data, a task which agencies were better prepared to perform. In *Great Northern,* however, Brandeis felt that there was no occasion for the exercise of administrative discretion and that no "fact" was in controversy. Resolution of the dispute before the court merely called for a construction of the words of the tariff, used in their "ordinary" sense, and the application of that construction to a set of undisputed facts.[92] In such circumstances, the Justice held, preliminary resort to the administrative agency was unnecessary.

The *Northern Pacific* and *Great Northern* decisions, viewed together, employed three criteria to define the circumstances which could trigger the requirement of preliminary agency jurisdiction: whether the questions presented were by their nature "administrative," whether "administrative discretion" was involved, and whether the questions presented involved issues of "fact" or "law." Brandeis tended, especially in *Great Northern*, to equate administrative discretion with technical expertise and thus suggested that he shared in some measure the desire of the

---

91. *Id.* at 295-96.
92. *Id.* at 290-92, 294.

Progressives to infuse government with independent, scientific-minded experts, whose special competence was the justification for their authority. The Justice did not discuss the other criteria in depth. His distinction in *Great Northern* between questions of fact and questions of law, for example, turned on whether words were used in their ordinary sense or as terms of art. But it was difficult to ascertain from that distinction whether the primary jurisdiction doctrine could be invoked upon the mere allegation that words in a statute had specialized import for a particular group of persons.

Nevertheless, Brandeis' decision in *Great Northern* and his brief remarks in *Northern Pacific* moved him towards a fuller articulation of the justifications for the agency form of government. In subsequent cases in which the primary jurisdiction doctrine was not involved, Brandeis maintained his interest in defining administrative functions. In his dissent in *Pennsylvania v. West Virginia,*[93] a 1923 decision, he elaborated on a distinction he had made in *Great Northern* between "legislative or administrative" functions, on the one hand, and judicial functions, on the other.[94] His purpose was to describe the special character of regulatory agencies and to justify entrusting them with authority in particular areas.

The case involved suits by Pennsylvania and Ohio to enjoin West Virginia from enforcing an act of its legislature which was designed to divert or retain, for the benefit of West Virginia consumers, natural gas that otherwise would have gone to consumers in adjacent states through established channels of interstate commerce. The West Virginia statute created a public service commission with power to prevent exportation of gas from the state when, in the commission's judgment, local demand equaled or exceeded the amount of gas produced.[95] At the time the

---

93. 262 U.S. 553 (1923).
94. *Id.* at 605-23 (dissenting opinion of Brandeis, J.).
95. Act of Feb. 10, 1919, ch. 71, [1919] W. Va. Acts.

suits were brought, the commission had taken no action with regard to the distribution of natural gas. A majority of the Court, through Justice Van Devanter, nonetheless held the statute unconstitutional as an impermissible interference with interstate commerce.[96]

Brandeis dissented, maintaining that a determination of what constituted an equitable allocation of natural gas among contiguous states required an investigation of the production and demand, both actual and potential, in each state; an estimate of the undeveloped gas territory; and a review of the business judgment of those managing the gas companies. Such determinations "would be of the character which calls for the informed judgment of a board of experts." [97] A court clearly could not undertake such determinations; equitable distribution was a "task of ... complexity and difficulty" that should be allocated to "an interstate public service commission with broad powers, perfected administrative machinery, ample resources [and] practical experience." [98]

This complexity-expertise rationale was coupled in *Pennsylvania v. West Virginia* with a suggestion that certain problems gave rise to the need for what have come to be called "on-going" solutions. Public service regulation, in Brandeis' judgment, was a field in which the "controlling body" was confronted with "baffling" factors and changing circumstances that required "continuous supervision and control." [99] Courts were simply not equipped to make continual investigations into the variables influencing the growth and change of particular sectors of the economy; they functioned to decide specific controversies presented to them at given times. The investment of resources required to accumulate the kind of information necessary to make an informed decision as to the proper distribution of natural gas among West Virginia and neighboring states was beyond the capability of the courts, whose

---

96. 262 U.S. at 596-600.
97. *Id.* at 621-22 (dissenting opinion of Brandeis, J.).
98. *Id.* at 623.
99. *Id.* at 621.

officers were generalists and advocates rather than experts and fact-finders. Brandeis therefore concluded that the administrative agency — with its presumed abilities to cope with complex economic and social problems, to consider and digest the multiple and diverse interests affected within its area of expertise, and to provide ad hoc and even experimental solutions — was the proper forum in which to address such controversies.

In sum, Brandeis developed four principal criteria to aid in defining administrative functions and in determining whether or not the exercise of primary agency jurisdiction was indicated in a particular context: (1) whether the complexity of the social problem necessitated that it be addressed by a body of experts with specialized training; (2) whether the question presented was one that could be conclusively resolved in one sitting or was one that required the continued involvement over time of the decision-making body; (3) whether the controversy presented questions that were by their very nature "administrative"; and (4) whether particular issues raised were issues of "fact" or "law." The first two criteria served to define the third by providing justifications for why a particular set of issues required for its proper resolution the use of techniques that in themselves served to define the functions and purposes of an administrative agency. The fourth criterion defined "facts" in a special way: evidence that, for reasons suggested in the other criteria, an agency was peculiarly suited to assess.[100]

These criteria became the principal devices for allocating power between courts and regulatory agencies in modern America and, beyond that, a source of post-World War II justifications for the regulatory agency form of government.[101] From them have been

---

100. The last criterion implicitly raised the question of whether there were limits on the power of regulatory agencies to gather facts as opposed to analyzing them. In United States v. Abilene & S. Ry., 265 U.S. 274 (1924), Brandeis considered this question and held, for the Court, that an agency could not rely in making its decisions on evidence that had not been introduced into the record.

101. In its report, the Hoover Commission's Task Force on Regulatory Commissions emphasized the expertise of the commissions and their continuing involvement in the problem being regulated as justifications for Congress'

derived the standard arguments on behalf of agency control: expertise, public-mindedness, flexibility, and the peculiar ability to gather and analyze factual information.[102] In developing these arguments, Brandeis had gone far toward formulating a rationale for the continued presence of regulatory agencies in the American governmental process. As current social problems came to be perceived as "complex," expertise, efficiency, and flexibility came to be viewed as the appropriate institutional virtues required for their solution. Yet Brandeis, as indicated earlier,[103] was not unqualifiedly enthusiastic about the virtues of the agency form of government; he viewed it, rather, as having distinct limitations. Even as his judicial decisions served to augment the powers of agencies, they served to articulate a rationale for judicial limitation of those powers.

The Scope of Judicial Review of Administrative Action

If the doctrine of primary jurisdiction may be said to have invited the formulation of a rationale for agency power, questions involving the scope of judicial review of agency activities stimulated discussion of the limits of that power. Whereas the former doctrine determines whether the court or the agency should make a particular decision in the first instance, the scope of review determines those issues which the court may finally resolve after the agency has initially decided them.[104] The literature on judicial review of administrative action suggests that decisions defining the scope of review can be viewed, ultimately, as indications of the extent of public confidence in an agency's governing abilities.[105]

---

increasing reliance on the agency form of government. *See* COMM. ON INDEPENDENT REGULATORY COMM'NS, TASK FORCE REPORT ON REGULATORY COMMISSIONS PREPARED FOR THE COMMISSION ON ORGANIZATION OF THE EXECUTIVE BRANCH OF THE GOVERNMENT 19, 22-23 (1949) (app. N). *See also* Pritchett, *The Regulatory Commissions Revisited,* 43 AM. POL. SCI. REV. 978, 982 (1949).

102. *See generally* 4 DAVIS §§ 29.01-30.14.
103. See text accompanying notes 60-67 *supra.*
104. *See* 3 DAVIS § 19.01; 4 *id.* § 29.01.
105. *See generally* 4 DAVIS § 30.09; JAFFE 123-24.

Whether an agency or a court is the preferred supervisory unit for a particular area of conflict-generating activity may be determined by the extent to which particular qualities, relevant and desirable in that area, are perceived as characteristic of the one unit or the other. At the time of Brandeis' appointment to the Court, however, the concept of agency government largely remained an unknown quality; and the general perception of agency performance had not yet hardened into fixed opinion. While regulatory agencies had become an approved part of the system of American government, the justifications for their power had been only vaguely formulated, and the limitations upon that power had yet to be fixed.[106] There thus existed a substantial interface between the areas of clearly administrative and clearly judicial activity; the extent to which the agencies would come to preempt that area was to be largely determined by the courts' own definition of the proper scope of judicial review of administrative action. Justice Brandeis was quick to seize the initiative in formulating that definition.

The Uncertain Standards of Union Pacific. Before Brandeis assumed his seat, the Supreme Court formulated some tentative conditions governing the scope of judicial review in *ICC v. Union Pacific Railroad,*[107] decided in 1912. The Court, through Chief Justice White, concluded that orders of the ICC were "final" and nonreviewable in the courts unless they were beyond the power which the agency could constitutionally exercise, beyond its statutory power, or based on a "mistake of law."[108] Such guidelines were vague indeed. They suggested that the courts, on an appeal from agency action, had considerable province to investigate both the statutory scheme creating the agency involved and the particular practice in issue. In a railroad rate case, for example, a court could determine whether the ICC rate was so low as to amount to a confiscation of property without due process of

---

106. See text accompanying notes 53-54 *supra.*

107. 222 U.S. 541 (1912). In American School of Magnetic Healing v. McAnnulty, 187 U.S. 94 (1902), the Court had previously addressed this issue, but the intervention of the Hepburn Act had rendered that holding nugatory.

108. 222 U.S. at 547.

law[109] or decide whether Congress had delegated power to the ICC to interpret provisions in tariffs.[110] The *Union Pacific* decision left a whole range of agency determinations potentially vulnerable to judicial reversal. Brandeis' decisions in subsequent cases involving the scope of judicial review of administrative action attempted to clarify this uncertain agency-court relationship.

Agency Discretion and Judicial Responsibility: Fixing the Focus of Review. In the 1919 case of *Skinner & Eddy Corp. v. United States,*[111] the Supreme Court was asked to determine whether a decision by the ICC to increase rates on iron and steel products shipped from Pittsburgh to Seattle could be reviewed by a district court before the shippers had exhausted their administrative remedies. Prior to *Skinner* a 1910 amendment to the Hepburn Act had declared that railroad carriers who had reduced their rates "in competition with a water route or routes" could not subsequently increase rates in the absence of an ICC finding that the proposed increase rested "upon changed conditions other than the elimination of water competition." [112] In March of 1916, at the request of carriers forming connecting lines between Pittsburgh and Seattle, the ICC had approved a fifteen-cent-per-hundred-pound rate reduction on Pittsburgh-Seattle routes, in accordance with its then existing policy of allowing lower rates for overland routes to coastal terminals than the rates permitted for intermountain routes. At the same time, the Commission's order allowed the carriers to retain the higher rates to intermediate shipping points. The Commission's policy of permitting the carriers to charge these discriminatory rates had been thought justified by the serious competition from coast-to-coast water carriers previously faced by overland shippers to coastal ports.[113] In response to pressures from intermountain merchants and carriers

---

109. *Cf.* ICC v. Cincinnati Ry., 167 U.S. 479 (1897).

110. *Cf.* Great N. Ry. v. Merchants Elevator Co., 259 U.S. 285 (1922), discussed in text accompanying notes 88-92 *supra.*

111. 249 U.S. 557 (1919).

112. Act of June 18, 1910, ch. 309, § 8, 36 Stat. 539 (codified at 49 U.S.C. § 4(2) (1970)).

113. 249 U.S. at 560-61.

who claimed that the setting of lower rates for routes which terminated at coastal ports discriminated against them, the ICC reopened consideration of its March order. Among the grounds for reconsideration cited by the intermountain interests was the decline of water competition to coastal ports. The ICC held a hearing, determined that effective water competition between the coasts had virtually ceased, and in July rescinded the March order.[114] The Commission then ordered the Pittsburgh-Seattle carriers to "reduce the degree of discrimination" in favor of shippers to coastal points and against the intermountain shippers.[115]

Accordingly, the Pittsburgh-Seattle carriers proposed an increase in rates to coastal points from sixty-five cents to ninety-four cents, effective in September, 1916. Skinner & Eddy, an Oregon corporation, protested to the ICC in August and asked for a hearing, claiming that the proposed increase in rates violated the Hepburn Act's provision forbidding an increase in rates unless the increase was justified by changed conditions other than the decline of water competition. The ICC denied Skinner & Eddy's request, but postponed until December the effective date for the ninety-four-cent rate. Subsequently the proposed rate was altered, with the ICC's consent, from ninety-four to seventy-five cents, effective the same date. On the date the revised rates were filed, Skinner & Eddy reiterated its claims and again requested a hearing; the ICC again denied the request.[116] Skinner & Eddy then brought suit in the District Court of Oregon to enjoin the ICC from enforcement of its order granting the increased rates, alleging that in so doing the ICC had exceeded its statutory powers. The suit, heard by a three-judge court, was dismissed for failure to state a cause of action; and a direct appeal was taken to the Supreme Court.[117]

Brandeis, for the Court, held that the district court could immediately review the ICC's order without further proceedings

---

114. *Id.* at 558, 561.
115. *Id.* at 561.
116. *Id.* at 561-62.
117. *See id.* at 558-59.

before the Commission because the plaintiff's claim for relief went directly to the Commission's authority to issue the order rather than to the content of the order.[118] He then proceeded to set forth the considerations which justified the Commission's approval of the proposed increase of shipping rates to coastal points.

Noting that the ICC had no power to prevent directly the setting of unreasonably low rates to eliminate competition, Brandeis explained that the 1910 Hepburn Act amendment,[119] which limited the circumstances under which rates once reduced because of competition with water routes could thereafter be increased, was intended as a substitute deterrent to predatory price-cutting. But the earlier rate reduction made by the Pittsburgh-Seattle carriers, Brandeis pointed out, had not been an instance of such predatory behavior; rather, it had been made with the express approval of the Commission as a justifiable response to previously existing water competition. A reduction so made did not fall within the prohibition against subsequent rate increases embodied in the Act. In any event, as Brandeis noted, to freeze the Pittsburgh-Seattle rates at the lower level when water competition had virtually disappeared would tend to "ensure monopoly [rather] than preserve competition." [120] With railroad rates set so low, the feasibility of renewed water competition would be substantially reduced. Observing that the conditions which had once justified the lower rate level for railroad routes to coastal terminals no longer obtained, Brandeis concluded that the Commission's authority to relieve carriers from orders which had been "improvidently" granted or which had been based upon conditions no longer operative justified approval of the increased rates for the Pittsburgh-Seattle carriers.[121]

The *Skinner* decision demonstrated Brandeis' cognizance of the fact that, although flexibility and autonomy were prerequisites for

---

118. *Id.* at 562-63.
119. Act of June 18, 1910, ch. 309, § 8, 36 Stat. 539 (codified at 49 U.S.C. § 4 (2) (1970)).
120. 249 U.S. at 568.
121. *Id.* at 567-69.

effective agency functioning, the courts could decide for themselves whether particular administrative practices furthered those goals. Agency jurisdiction did not have to be exhausted first in such a case because the appellant was challenging the agency's authority to take a particular course of action rather than the content of the action taken. Hence *Skinner* stood for the proposition that the prospect that certain agency practices exceeded the scope of the agency's authority could justify judicial review, as well as for the proposition that the exercise of power clearly delegated to an agency could be tempered by the agency's sense of justice and fairness.[122] The procedure envisaged by the decision gave freedom to administrative bodies to modify their judgments on the basis of new information, but permitted the courts speedy review of those modifications.

The pattern of *Skinner* was followed in later Brandeis opinions defining the scope of judicial review of administrative action.[123] The Justice was willing to concede substantial deference to administrative expertise and flexibility within what he considered to be the proper confines of agency activity; yet he insisted that the courts vigilantly assure themselves that questions of ultimate judicial cognizance were not left to the discretion of the agencies. When appropriate, Brandeis weighed expertise and flexibility against the threat of administrative usurpations of individual rights. He was inclined to assume, in the regulatory context, that discretion in an administrative official was necessary to accomplish enlightened economic and social planning, but in contexts where individual rights hung in the balance, he was quick to see potential violations of the Constitution in discretionary activity.[124]

Economic Rights and Individual Rights: A Double Standard of Judicial Review. Brandeis' tolerance of adminstrative discretion in

---

122. *Id.* at 562, 567.
123. *E.g.,* Crowell v. Benson, 285 U.S. 22, 65-94 (1932) (dissenting opinion of Brandeis, J.); New England Divisions Case, 261 U.S. 184, 201-04 (1923); Ohio Valley Water Co. v. Ben Avon Borough, 253 U.S. 287, 292-99 (1920) (dissenting opinion of Brandeis, J.).
124. *See, e.g.,* Ng Fung Ho v. White, 259 U.S. 276 (1922); Milwaukee Publishing Co. v. Burleson, 255 U.S. 407, 417-36 (1921) (dissenting opinion of Brandeis, J.).

economic regulation was illustrated by the decision in the *New England Divisions Case,*[125] where, writing for the Court, he sustained the constitutionality of an ICC order substantially increasing the New England railroads' share of the joint rates on freight moving between that section and the rest of the country. This increased allocation had been requested by a group of New England railroads, who argued that their needs required a higher share of the joint rates which were apportioned between the New England carriers and the more prosperous carriers in other locales. The situation was further complicated by the fact that the overall joint rates had themselves been increased just prior to the request of the New England group. Carriers outside the New England area sued to enjoin the Commission's order, claiming that the new apportionment of rates to meet the needs of the New England carriers constituted a taking of their property without due process. Brandeis, in dismissing this argument, noted that the "just share" of a carrier was the amount "properly apportioned" out of a joint rate; and that amount could be fixed by the ICC at a figure which it found to be "just, reasonable and equitable." [126] He added that it might well be "just" to give prosperous carriers a smaller proportion of the increased rate than of the original rate.[127] Furthermore, courts could neither evaluate the weight of the evidence used by the ICC to arrive at its decision nor scrutinize the wisdom of the order entered,[128] even though the evidence on which the ICC had based its judgment was admittedly far from conclusive in this instance.[129] The only recourse the carriers had, if they believed an order of this kind to be unjust, was a petition to the ICC for modification of the order.[130]

In contrast to the broad discretion he was willing to tolerate in the agencies' activities in the economic sphere, Brandeis soon

---

125. 261 U.S. 184 (1923).
126. *Id.* at 195.
127. *Id.*
128. *Id.* at 204.
129. *Id.* at 200.
130. *Id.* at 204. *See also* United States v. Abilene & S. Ry., 265 U.S. 274, 281 (1924).

demonstrated his conviction that close judicial reins were necessary to restrain administrative discretion in those areas where regulatory activity might intrude upon constitutionally protected freedoms. This dualistic approach to the proper scope of judicial review was suggested by Brandeis' dissent in the 1921 case of *Milwaukee Publishing Co. v. Burleson,*[131] which had tested the power of the Postmaster General to deny second-class mail privileges to the *Milwaukee Leader,* a newspaper which had printed allegedly seditious material. That case also forced Brandeis to address the peripheral issue of whether the decisions of executive agencies, as distinguished from independent regulatory agencies, entailed the exercise of such broad discretion as to negate meaningful judicial review.

The Postmaster General maintained that his denial of the privileges rested on "representations and complaints from sundry good and loyal citizens of the United States" and from personal reading and consideration of the *Leader,* which suggested to him, "in the exercise of his judgment and discretion," that the publication systematically and continually violated the Espionage Act of 1917.[132] He further claimed that his order denying the *Leader* access to second-class mail rates was "not subject to [being] reviewed, set aside, or controlled by a court of law" since it involved the exercise of judgment and discretion.[133] The Court majority, while ignoring the Postmaster General's contention that his actions were nonreviewable, conceded that "the conclusion of the head of an executive department . . . on such a question . . . will not be disturbed by the courts unless they are clearly of the opinion that it is wrong." [134] Having determined that the Postmaster General's conclusion that the Espionage Act had been violated was supported by substantial evidence, and having further upheld the constitutionality of the Act, the Court upheld the challenged order.

---

131. 255 U.S. 407 (1921).

132. *Id.* at 420 (quoting return filed by Postmaster General). *See* Espionage Act of 1917, § 3, 18 U.S.C. § 2388(a) (1970).

133. 255 U.S. at 420 (quoting return filed by Postmaster General).

134. *Id.* at 413.

Brandeis, in an impassioned dissent, maintained that the Postmaster General had no power either to exclude the paper from the mails on the grounds given or to deny the publisher the second-class mail rate. The power of exclusion, in Brandeis' view, would make the Postmaster General "the universal censor of publications"; [135] a denial of the use of the mails would be tantamount to a denial of the right of circulation. Rejecting the Government's argument that the maintenance of a second-class mail permit was a "privilege," Brandeis pointed out that the terms and conditions of the permit's existence had been defined by Congress and rested "wholly upon mandatory legislation"; accordingly, in the case of one who met those conditions, the "permit" became a "right," independent of the Postmaster General's discretion. [136] Brandeis further contended that an official's determination of whether the conditions prescribed by law for a certain rate existed was "a strictly judicial one, although exercised in administering an executive office." [137] It was not a function which either involved or permitted the exercise of discretionary power. Delegating discretionary power to an administrative official to police the mails raised a series of constitutional problems: it was arguably violative of the first amendment's guaranty of freedom of the press, of the fifth amendment's prohibition against taking property without due process of law, of the sixth amendment's provision for trial by jury in criminal cases, and of the eighth amendment's protection against cruel and unusual punishment. [138] "If, under the Constitution," Brandeis observed, "administrative officers may, as a mere incident of the . . . administration of their departments, be vested

---

135. *Id.* at 423 (dissenting opinion of Brandeis, J.).

136. *Id.* at 427. In rejecting the "right-privilege" distinction in this context, Brandeis anticipated the later critics of that doctrine by some fifty years. *See generally* Van Alstyne, *The Demise of the Right-Privilege Distinction in Constitutional Law,* 81 HARV. L. REV. 1439 (1968).

137. 255 U.S. at 428 (footnote omitted).

138. *Id.* at 429-30.

with the power to issue such orders as this, there is little of substance in our Bill of Rights . . . ."[139]

The different outcomes reached by Brandeis in cases involving only the proper exercise of administrative expertise and flexibility as distinguished from those cases where individual rights were threatened by administrative usurpations suggest the difficulties he had with undifferentiated application of the model of agency government that had been conceived in the context of economic regulation of large industrial enterprises. For Brandeis, effective government in America depended on governmental institutions' having a clear sense of their purposes and limitations.[140] Regulatory agencies had been created to meet a special need that courts and legislatures were less capable of fulfilling: the resolution of social problems which, because of their recent origin, complexity, and changing shape, necessitated the ongoing attention of a body of experts. The experimental and amorphous character of solutions to these types of problems called for flexibility and discretion in the presiding officials; imposition by the courts of too rigid a set of functional limitations on those officials ran counter to the purposes of regulatory agencies. By and large, in Brandeis' view, the courts should be prepared to defer to administrative discretion in the performance of specialized regulatory tasks.

And yet Brandeis recognized that courts would be remiss in the performance of their own functions if they failed to provide a forum for review of administrative activity. More specifically, in the process of review, the courts had to insure that the discretionary acts of officers or commissions conformed to the specific purposes underlying the administrative regulation, as well as to any constitutional limitations on the reach of the regulatory activity. Agency discretion to regulate prices in the transportation industry was one thing; agency discretion in the area of free speech was quite another. Discretion in the latter class of cases could not

---

139. *Id.* at 436. Justice Holmes filed his own dissent and "agree[d] in substance with [Brandeis'] view." *Id.* (dissenting opinion of Holmes, J.).

140. *See* M. UROFSKY, *supra* note 55, at 57-59.

fairly be related to the purposes of adminstrative bodies as governing institutions; where purported extensions of agency discretion threatened civil liberties, the courts had an obligation to check those extensions.

The Fact/Law Dichotomy in Judicial Review. Brandeis believed, in sum, in a flexible, continuous agency-court partnership in which the "division of labor" would be made on the basis of the peculiar capabilities and ultimate responsibilities of the respective "partners." The "senior partner," the judiciary, would defer to the specialized competence of the agencies whenever its constitutional responsibilities, coupled with considerations of efficiency and expedition, permitted it to do so. But in matters of ultimate judicial responsibility, such as the custodianship of the protection afforded by the Bill of Rights, the courts would retain full supervisory and reviewing power, regardless of more pragmatic considerations.

This approach was illustrated in Brandeis' treatment of the traditional distinction, in cases involving judicial review of administrative action, between questions of law and questions of fact. In his opinion in the *Great Northern Railway* case,[141] Brandeis had cited that distinction as one of the criteria to be employed in determining whether a particular issue was peculiarly amenable to initial agency resolution, so that the application of the doctrine of primary jurisdiction might be invoked. The distinction between questions of law and ones of fact has been employed to describe the paradigmatic functions of courts and agencies (the former deal with matters of "law," the latter "find facts"),[142] but the distinction's value as an analytical device is limited. There are numerous instances, for example, where the finding of a particular fact suggests a particular legal result; this situation is commonly referred to as a question of "mixed law and fact." [143] If agencies are supposed to pass upon "the facts" and courts "the law," which body controls the mixed situation? The answer might appear to be,

---

141. See text accompanying notes 88-92 *supra.*
142. 4 DAVIS § 29.01.
143. *See* JAFFE 546-49.

whichever body a given court on review decides is best suited to supervise a particular area of conduct, because of reasons conceivably extending well beyond the circumstances of an individual case. Brandeis, at least, employed the fact-law doctrine in this fashion.

A celebrated Brandeis decision on the scope of judicial review of fact determinations by executive agencies was *Ng Fung Ho v. White*.[144] Two Chinese immigrants who had been summarily deported by an immigration official challenged the decision on the ground that they were American citizens. Brandeis, writing for the Court, held that their claim of citizenship was entitled to judicial review, since jurisdiction in the immigration agency to pass on deportation cases existed if the person being evaluated was, in fact, an alien. Brandeis viewed the petitioners' claim of citizenship as "a denial of an essential jurisdictional fact"; [145] placed in that context, the agency's determination of the issue could not be conclusive. *Ng Fung Ho* consequently modified an earlier decision, *United States v. Ju Toy*,[146] in which Justice Holmes had suggested that findings of fact by the immigration authorities under the procedures of the Chinese Exclusion Acts were conclusive. Therefore, Holmes asserted, such rulings were not subject to judicial review unless the hearing had been unfair, an erroneous rule of law had been applied, or the evidence had been inadequate. Brandeis, writing for the majority in *Ng Fung Ho*, rejected this suggestion: to deport one who claimed to be a citizen without review of that claim was an obvious denial of due process.[147]

The *Ng Fung Ho* decision implied that Brandeis might have favored judicial review of all constitutionally significant fact determinations even in the absence of a provision for review in the applicable statute. But Brandeis did not consider review of an administrative finding of fact to be automatic in every instance where the result of the fact-finding allegedly would be to deprive

---

144. 259 U.S. 276 (1922).
145. *Id.* at 284.
146. 198 U.S. 253 (1905).
147. 259 U.S. at 284-85.

the party involved of a constitutional right. This relativistic approach to the "fact-law" dichotomy was illustrated by his dissent in the 1920 case of *Ohio Valley Water Co. v. Ben Avon Borough.* [148] The Supreme Court of Pennsylvania had held that courts could not weigh the evidence used by the Pennsylvania Public Service Commission to set water rates, despite the fact that a water company had claimed that the rates were confiscatory.[149] The Supreme Court of the United States, through Justice McReynolds, reversed. Maintaining that the company had not been given a proper hearing on the confiscation issue,[150] the majority further held that the courts, in reviewing commission orders fixing maximum rates, could consider questions of fact as well as questions of law.[151]

Brandeis, in dissent, alluded to the "established principle applied in reviewing the findings of administrative boards, that 'courts will not examine the facts further than to determine whether there was substantial evidence to sustain the order.' " [152] A commission order, he noted, could not of itself create a limitation upon the scope of review, but there was nevertheless a presumption in favor of "the conclusion of an experienced administrative body reached after a full hearing." [153] In Brandeis' view the proper relationship between agencies and courts in matters such as those presented by the *Ben Avon* case was one in which courts accepted the facts found by the agency, even though the findings of fact served to determine whether or not there had been a taking of property. Courts could examine the entire record to determine whether what purported to be a finding of "fact" was "so involved with and dependent upon questions of law as to be in substance and effect a decision of the latter," [154] but they should not pass upon the

---

148. 253 U.S. 287 (1920).

149. Borough of Ben Avon v. Ohio Valley Water Co., 260 Pa. 289, 103 A. 744 (1918).

150. 253 U.S. at 291.

151. *Id.* at 289.

152. *Id.* at 297 (dissenting opinion of Brandeis, J.).

153. *Id.*

154. *Id.* at 298, *quoting* Kansas City S. Ry. v. C.H. Albers Comm'n Co., 223 U.S. 573, 591-93 (1912).

relative weight of conflicting evidence nor substitute their judgment on "pure matters of fact" for that of the agency.[155] Implicit in these concessions was the suggestion that where the constitutional repercussions of an agency's factual determination were *economic* in nature, a court could view those determinations as "pure matters of fact."

The agency-court partnership approach fashioned by Brandeis regarded distinctions drawn between the proper functions of each body not merely as linguistic smokescreens but as viable standards tied to the historical or legislative purposes of the respective institutions. Thus, in matters affecting economic regulation, while agency findings of fact might incidentally affect constitutional rights (such as the right to just compensation), regulatory agencies should be allowed broad discretion to make judgments based on specialized empirical fact-finding, absent an instance of patently confiscatory action.[156] Admittedly, the process of finding facts could function as a limited resolution of questions of law, but this was not particularly troublesome for Brandeis: the purpose of these agencies, after all, was to regulate the excesses of industrial enterprises. In those areas of regulatory activity where civil liberties were involved, however, Brandeis tended to scrutinize executive agency action more carefully and to interpret the fact-law distinction more strictly.[157] Any decision, however closely related to the factual determinations usually delegated to the agencies, was for the courts alone to make if the determination had the ultimate effect of circumscribing the exercise of individual liberties guaranteed by the Constitution. Although he believed that

---

155. 253 U.S. at 298-99 (dissenting opinion of Brandeis, J.).

156. *See, e.g.,* New England Divisions Case, 261 U.S. 184 (1923), discussed in text accompanying notes 125-30 *supra*.

157. *Compare, e.g.,* United States v. One Ford Coupe Auto., 272 U.S. 321 (1926), *and* Lambert v. Yellowley, 272 U.S. 581 (1926) (two decisions where Brandeis interpreted the power of the federal government to enforce the eighteenth amendment very broadly), *with* Whitney v. California, 274 U.S. 357, 372 (1927) (concurring opinion of Brandeis, J.) *and* Gilbert v. Minnesota, 254 U.S. 325, 334 (1920) (dissenting opinion of Brandeis, J.) (opinions in which Brandeis protested against governmental attempts to suppress freedom of speech and association).

government had a duty to maintain moral standards in public life, Brandeis was persistently wary of the potentially stifling effects of large institutions, public or private, on individual freedom.[158]

Refinements on the Allocation Calculus

The proliferation of agencies continued throughout the early twentieth century; and after the election of Franklin Roosevelt in 1932, administrative agencies fairly exploded in number, size, and influence. The diverse character of these burgeoning agencies further accentuated an issue that had already captured Brandeis' attention. The issue, in its starkest form, was whether the partnership model of agency-court interaction could sensibly be applied outside the context of the standard independent regulatory agencies.

The early planners of the New Deal had created a type of administrative agency which was neither a permanent department of the executive branch nor an independent regulatory commission.[159] These agencies were viewed as a temporary, experimental extension of executive prerogative in an economic emergency and thus were somewhat more immune from continued legislative scrutiny than were the standard regulatory commissions. On the other hand, although some of these experimental agencies were equipped to perform fact-finding and adjudicative functions similar to those of independent regulatory commissions, their ability to control the activities of their "regulatees" was not regarded as comparable to that of the existing regulatory commissions.

Because of their eclectic nature, these experimental New Deal agencies may accurately be described as "hybrids." Notable examples of these hybrid agencies were the National Recovery Administration, which proposed codes of conduct for the operations of private enterprise and applied limited sanctions in the event of noncompliance,[160] and the Public Works Administration,

---

158. *See generally* L. BRANDEIS, THE CURSE OF BIGNESS (1934).

159. *See, e.g.,* R. CUSHMAN, *supra* note 6, at 374-89 (discussing the National Bituminous Coal Commission).

160. *See id.* at 354-57.

which centralized the functions of other New Deal agencies, distributed jobs to unemployed persons, and coordinated federal heavy construction projects.[161] Although they exhibited great variety in function and organization, the hybrid agencies of the New Deal could all be fairly described as individualized responses to a national emergency, with loosely defined roles and uncertain futures.

Because of the vast delegation of legislative power involved in the operations of the hybrid agencies, they quickly became objects of political controversy.[162] Since the framers of the New Deal assumed a wide-ranging public commitment to agency government, administrative law doctrine took on more than an academic character when applied in this context. The courts were forced therefore to determine the legal distinctions, if any, between the established independent regulatory commissions and the New Deal hybrids.

The 1932 case of *Crowell v. Benson* [163] had anticipated several of these issues. The case involved an appeal from the decision of a deputy commissioner of the United States Workmen's Compensation Commission. The Longshoremen's and Harbor Workers' Compensation Act of 1927 [164] established this agency and gave it power to adjudicate disputes arising out of injuries suffered by certain employees while working upon the navigable waters of the United States.[165] Empowered with certain fact-finding and adjudicative powers,[166] the Commission was a "hybrid" agency, possessing neither the summary authority of an executive department nor the broad regulatory powers of an independent commission. The principal issue on appeal in *Crowell* was the reviewability of a "finding of fact" by the deputy commissioner that one Knudsen, who had been injured while working on the navigable waters of the United States, was an "employee" within

---

161. *See id.*
162. *See* PEARE, THE LOUIS D. BRANDEIS STORY 266-69 (1970).
163. 285 U.S. 22 (1932).
164. Act of Mar. 4, 1927, ch. 509, 44 Stat. 1424 (codified at 33 U.S.C. §§ 901-50 (1970)).
165. 33 U.S.C. § 919(a) (1970).
166. *Id.* §§ 919(c), 923, 927.

the meaning of the Act.[167] The statute made the employer liable for injuries without fault only if the injured person were such an "employee." [168] The employer, challenging the deputy commissioner's finding as to Knudsen's status as an "employee," sued in federal district court to enjoin enforcement of the Commission's award to Knudsen.[169] The district court granted a de novo hearing upon the facts and the law,[170] reversed the Commissioner's finding that the claimant had been in the employ of the petitioner, and restrained the enforcement of the award.[171]

A majority of the Supreme Court, through Chief Justice Hughes, held that the district court could make an independent determination of the fact of Knudsen's employment.[172] In a remarkable opinion, which blended older conceptions of the inalienable rights of property holders with a recognition of the primacy of modern social welfare legislation limiting those rights, Hughes made it clear that Congress was not at complete liberty to legislate a general prescription of liability without fault in maritime cases. Only the special circumstances of the employment relation, the Chief Justice contended, had allowed no-fault workmen's compensation legislation to withstand due process challenges. Hence, he maintained, the fact of employment was not only a necessary factor in establishing the jurisdiction of the Commission but also an essential element of the statute's constitutional validity.[173] The employer could be required to compensate injured claimants, in the absence of any negligence on his part, only if they were truly his employees. The employer's rights and duties were inextricably bound up in that fact, as was the authority of the Commission to adjudicate such disputes.

---

167. 285 U.S. at 37.

168. 33 U.S.C. § 903(a) (1970).

169. Benson v. Crowell, 33 F.2d 137 (S.D. Ala. 1929), and Benson v. Crowell, 38 F.2d 306 (S.D. Ala. 1930) (supplemental opinion), aff'd, 45 F.2d 66 (5th Cir. 1930), aff'd, 285 U.S. 22 (1932).

170. 33 F.2d at 142.

171. See 285 U.S. at 37.

172. Id. at 65.

173. Id. at 54-56.

Consequently the majority held that the determination of so crucial a fact could not be withdrawn from the purview of the courts.[174]

Brandeis dissented and, in the process, attempted to refute the problems inherent in the application of his agency-court partnership model to cases involving hybrid agencies.[175] He warmed to his task by differing with the majority over the proper construction of the Compensation Act (maintaining that Congress did not contemplate de novo proceedings in a trial court),[176] the correct interpretation of the due process clause (asserting that Congress could prescribe liability without fault outside the employment relation),[177] and the necessity of de novo judicial review when property rights are at stake (claiming that such review was not required under the circumstances).[178]

Brandeis then sought to explain the use of the agency-court partnership concept in different contexts. One category of agencies he described as "fact-finding and fact-gathering tribunals" whose purpose was to "withdraw from the courts, subject to the power of judicial review, a class of controversies which experience has shown can be more effectively and expeditiously handled in the first instance by a special and expert tribunal." [179] Another category, which the majority had lumped with the first, encompassed "in no sense fact-gathering or fact-finding tribunals of first instance," but rather "tribunals of final resort within the scope of their authority." [180] The first category included the compensation commission in *Crowell v. Benson* and similar independent regulatory agencies, such as the Interstate Commerce Commission and the Federal Trade Commission; the "very function" of these agencies was to supplement the courts by making initial determinations of fact.[181] Brandeis asserted that this

---

174. *Id.* at 64.
175. *Id.* at 65-95 (dissenting opinion of Brandeis, J.).
176. *Id.* at 66-72.
177. *Id.* at 77-80.
178. *Id.* at 80-84.
179. *Id.* at 88.
180. *Id.* at 88-89.
181. *Id.* at 93.

supplementary relationship would be subverted by "permitting special reexamination in a trial court of so-called 'jurisdictional facts,'" a practice which the majority was sanctioning in Crowell. [182] Such judicial scrutiny of "jurisdictional facts," he contended, was only appropriate in the case of the second category of agencies — the executive agencies charged with the resolution of matters "ordinarily outside of judicial competence" and "within the power of Congress to commit to conclusive executive determination." [183] Brandeis included in this category such administrative bodies as the Postal Department, the Immigration Service, and the Department of the Interior.[184] Since these agencies possessed "otherwise final jurisdiction over matters properly committed to them," [185] the courts could properly reexamine any factual determinations which were a prerequisite to the exercise of that jurisdiction.

In Brandeis' view the nature of judicial intervention should vary significantly as between these different agency categories. With respect to the "fact-finding tribunals," the function of the courts was to review all questions of law; [186] with respect to executive agencies, it was "essentially [one] of control — the function of keeping [the agencies] within their statutory authority." [187] The latter function might properly entail a reexamination of "jurisdictional facts"; but if those facts existed, the judicial function was complete. The partnership theory of agency-court interaction was therefore best suited to those situations where an agency functioned as a surrogate, though specialized, court, performing "adjudicative" as opposed to "legislative" functions. With respect to the executive agencies, however, which operated in areas beyond the purview of judicial competence, a court was

---

182. *Id.* at 92-93.
183. *Id.* at 89.
184. *Id.* at 90-91 n.26.
185. *Id.* at 93.
186. *Id.* at 88.
187. *Id.* at 89.

more of a censor than a partner.[188] Hybrid agencies such as the commission in *Crowell v. Benson* were at least partially fact-gatherers and adjudicators, and hence the "partnership" approach could be sensibly applied to them.

Brandeis' formulation in the *Crowell* case appeared to be designed to give courts optimum freedom of choice in reviewing the discretionary judgments of agencies.[189] Although the Justice distinguished between fact-gathering and executive agencies as well as between "review" and "control," those distinctions broke down in practice. Executive agencies such as the Immigration Service found facts: *Ng Fung Ho*[190] was a case about the implications of a finding of fact, and Brandeis permitted review. Denominating this type of review as "control" did little to clarify the distinction. The major difference between *Ng Fung Ho* and *Crowell,* for Brandeis' purposes, appeared to be the character of the right infringed by agency discretion. In *Ng Fung Ho* it was citizenship; in *Crowell* it was a property right. The *Crowell* case, for Brandeis, was in that respect like *Ben Avon*:[191] the courts had less obligation to make independent judgments on the validity of an agency decision where property rights were involved.[192] Thus, Brandeis' device of dividing the agencies into categories probably

---

188. *Id.*
189. Professor Jaffe has described the manner in which Justice Brandeis utilized this flexibility of the review-control formulation to achieve the result he desired in particular cases. *See* Jaffe, *The Contributions of Mr. Justice Brandeis to Administrative Law,* 18 IOWA L. REV. 213, 219-24 (1933). In this article, Jaffe maintained that Brandeis'

> devotion is not to doctrine; he is not primarily concerned to presume an artificial consistency with what he may have said in this or that case. Rather he seeks an intuitive judgment of what will be a just, a "social" result, after a very elaborate and careful consideration of the pertinent realities. *Id.* at 226.

190. See text accompanying notes 144-47 *supra.*
191. See text accompanying notes 148-55 *supra.*
192. For a discussion of the Brandeis predilection for protecting intangible personal rights with greater diligence than property rights, as illustrated in his opinions in *Ng Fung Ho, Crowell,* and *Ben Avon,* see Jaffe, *supra* note 189, at 224-27 & n.40.

served a purpose other than that of establishing a general rule as to when judicial review would be appropriate and when not. It would allow the courts to peg the hybrid agencies as "fact-gathering tribunals," thus providing a rationale for their inclusion in Brandeis' formulation of an agency-court partnership.

Shortly after the *Crowell* decision, and during the height of President Roosevelt's New Deal reforms, the political and economic realities of the era seemed to move Justice Brandeis' brethren on the Court closer to his views on the desirability of substantial agency independence in the area of economic regulation. A protracted series of anti-New Deal cases,[193] in which the Court had resurrected such shopworn objections to agency government as the delegation doctrine, had generated such political ill will towards the Court that its very composition had been threatened. In surviving President Roosevelt's Court-packing attempt,[194] the Court found it necessary by the late 1930's to abandon many of the views that served to link it with the jurisprudence of the late nineteenth century. Among the abandoned views, apparently, was that of open resistance to the notion of agency government.[195] Indeed, the language of at least one case from the later years of the New Deal suggested that the Court had accommodated itself to Brandeis' concept of the agency-court partnership.

In *United States v. Morgan*[196] the Court considered the appropriate disposition of a fund of money being held in escrow while a previous controversy over stockyard brokers' rates was being settled. That controversy had itself been before the Court on three prior occasions and had generated three muddled opinions.[197] The apparent outcome of that series of litigation had

---

193. The chronology of this line of cases is exemplified by the following list: Panama Ref. Co. v. Ryan, 293 U.S. 388 (1935); Schechter Poultry Corp. v. United States, 295 U.S. 495 (1935); United States v. Butler, 297 U.S. 1 (1936); Jones v. SEC, 298 U.S. 1 (1936); Carter v. Carter Coal Co., 298 U.S. 238 (1936).

194. *See* R. JACKSON, *supra* note 4, at 187-96.

195. *See id.* at 87-165.

196. 307 U.S. 183 (1939).

197. Morgan v. United States, 304 U.S. 1, *rehearing denied,* 304 U.S. 23 (1938); Morgan v. United States, 298 U.S. 468 (1936).

been a holding that an order of the Secretary of Agriculture fixing brokers' commission rates was defective because of procedural irregularities.[198] Eventually, however, in passing on the disposition of the escrowed fund, the Court held that the Secretary could correct his own procedural missteps without further judicial scrutiny.[199] In the process Justice Stone, for the Court, stated:

> [I]n construing a statute setting up an administrative agency and providing for judicial review of its action, court and agency are not to be regarded as wholly independent and unrelated instrumentalities of justice, each acting in the performance of its prescribed statutory duty without regard to the appropriate function of the other . . . . Court and agency are the means adopted to obtain the prescribed end . . . . [N]either can rightly be regarded by the other as an alien intruder, to be tolerated if must be, but never to be encouraged or aided by the other in the attainment of the common aim.[200]

Thus, at the very end of Brandeis' judicial career, his view of a symbiotic agency-court relationship seemed to have been partially vindicated.

III. THE BRANDEISIAN LEGACY IN MODERN AMERICA

The previous portions of this Article have described the leading role played by Brandeis in formulating a "modern" approach to that aspect of administrative law which is concerned with the allocation of power between courts and agencies. Brandeis' approach may be termed "modern," in this context, because of the nature of the criteria he employed in his allocation calculus. Those criteria, at least on their face, were non-normative: they emphasized "objective" factors such as efficiency and expertise, while deemphasizing the subjective notion that some branches of government were more susceptible to influence and corruption

---

198. *See* 304 U.S. at 25-26.
199. 307 U.S. at 198.
200. *Id.* at 191.

than others. These standards focused on the interdependence of all governing institutions in America and underscored the delicate interactions between governmental institutions and their constituents.[201] The agency-court partnership envisioned by Brandeis entailed no hard and fast lines between court and agency jurisdiction, no competitive assessments of the capacity of institutions to achieve upright or enlightened government, and no rigid barriers between the private and public sectors of the nation.

Brandeis' approach to administrative law, viewed in this fashion, appeared closer to the philosophy of government expressed in the New Deal than to that expressed in the Progressive Era. He was hailed, in 1933, as one of the most contemporary of men; the concerns he had articulated about the proper structure and function of various institutions of government in the early years of the twentieth century had anticipated similar needs felt by many Americans in the depression years.[202] Yet Brandeis' contemporary-mindedness in the Thirties had its paradoxical aspects: his solutions to then current problems demonstrated a suspicion of size in industry and government and a passionate concern for individual freedom that were associated with an earlier era.[203]

The paradox ran deeper on a personal level. Brandeis demonstrated in his private social attitudes an absolutist approach to moral issues and a faith in the capacity of Americans to control their destinies that identified him more closely with Progressives than with New Dealers.[204] It was as though he simultaneously contained within himself two personae: the detached social accountant, whose judgments rested on his cost-benefit analyses, and the moral philosopher/social planner, who passionately wished to see the restructuring of American government in the pattern

---

201. *See* Beard, *Introduction* to THE SOCIAL AND ECONOMIC VIEWS OF MR. JUSTICE BRANDEIS at xix (A. Lief ed. 1930); M. UROFSKY, *supra* note 55, at xii.

202. *See* Hart, Book Review, 82 U. PA. L. REV. 668, 668 (1934).

203. *Id.* at 670.

204. For a description of the differences between the two "reform movements," see R. HOFSTADTER, THE AGE OF REFORM 300-26 (1955); White, *From Sociological Jurisprudence to Realism: Jurisprudence and Social Change in Early Twentieth-Century America,* 58 VA. L. REV. 999 (1972).

of his own high ideals. For Brandeis the two roles were integrated. Detached analysis justified moral commitment, which in turn stimulated further empirical inquiry. For others in the 1930's, however, the roles were separable; hence Brandeis' pragmatic concept of an agency-court partnership could attain great influence while his more visceral opinions on the deficiencies of "Big Government" were being disregarded.

While the experience of the 1930's partially vindicated Brandeis' approach to agency-court allocation problems, subsequent developments suggested that his theories were vulnerable to the pressures of changing events and attitudes. While certain of Brandeis' assumptions about the purposes of agency government — notably the conviction that administrative expertise should be given broad discretion in regulating the economic activity of industrial enterprises — were generally shared by the policymakers of the New Deal, it was clear that an earlier generation of policymakers had rejected those assumptions and that subsequent generations might do so as well.

Thus some two decades after the New Deal had established the administrative agency as an ubiquitous institution of American government, another assumed quality of agency government, that of detached impartiality, was attacked. Agencies came to be criticized as being overly responsive to and protective of the industries which they regulated; some agencies came to be viewed as the "captives" of their regulatees.[205] At the same time, the

---

205. *See generally* M. BERNSTEIN, REGULATING BUSINESS BY INDEPENDENT COMMISSION 154-60, 263-71, 294-95 (1955); 1 DAVIS § 1.03; E. REDFORD, ADMINISTRATION OF NATIONAL ECONOMIC CONTROL 220-71 (1952). For an interesting exchange on the causes of and the cure for the "capture" of the ICC, see Huntington, *The Marasmus of the ICC: The Commission, The Railroads, and the Public Interest,* 61 YALE L.J. 467 (1952); Morgan, *A Critique of* "The Marasmus of the ICC: The Commission, the Railroads, and the Public Interest," 62 YALE L.J. 171 (1953); Huntington, *The ICC Reexamined: A Colloquy,* 63 YALE L.J. 44 (1953). Professor Jaffe argues that the phenomenon should be attributed not to any misfeasance on the part of agency personnel, but rather to Congress' habit of granting to the agencies extremely broad and ill-defined powers which fail to engender a sense of mandate. Jaffe, *The Effective Limits of the Administrative Process: A Reevaluation,* 67 HARV. L. REV. 1105, 1109-10 (1954). *See also* JAFFE

formerly favorable code words associated with administrative regulation took on pejorative meanings: "expertise" came to be viewed as "elitism" and "discretion" as "arbitrariness." [206]

The extent to which the Brandeisian approach retains contemporary viability, then, depends on the degree to which its underlying assumptions are still considered valid. Affecting this variable are the changed circumstances under which administrative agencies currently operate and the jurisprudential theories which those circumstances have helped to foster.

The Ramifications of the Broad Delegation Model

One immediate illustration of the changed character of administrative law since Brandeis' retirement is the "current acceptance of the broad delegation model" [207] governing relations between agencies and the legislatures that create them. Delegation

---

12-13; Jaffe, *supra* note 2, at 1187, 1198-99. *But see* Schwartz, *Legal Restriction of Competition in the Regulated Industries: An Abdication of Judicial Responsibility,* 67 HARV. L. REV. 436, 474 (1954):

> The direction of a mature administrative agency can easily drift into the hands of people, able and devoted indeed, but of the second level of competence or initiative. Often they will be men who find congenial the routine security of office and the reliable deference of the small group of important businessmen and counsel who regularly appear before them. They will naturally be responsive to plans for making business life more orderly and secure through integration and price regulation. Unplanned and ruthless commercial rivalry will be distasteful to them. On the other hand, small victories over those whom they regulate will suffice to maintain their self-esteem, while large issues can be postponed or avoided.

206. *See* JAFFE 576-85; Cragun & deSeife, *A Skeptic Views Twenty-five Years of Administrative Process,* 16 FED. B.J. 556, 559-60 (1956); Schwartz, *supra* note 205, at 471-75. Justice Douglas, dissenting from the Court's affirmance of a rate order the propriety of which he felt the ICC had failed to adequately establish, warned that

> [u]nless we make the requirements for administrative action strict and demanding, *expertise,* the strength of modern government, can become a monster which rules with no practical limits on its discretion. Absolute discretion, like corruption, marks the beginning of the end of liberty. New York v. United States, 342 U.S. 882, 884 (1951) (dissenting opinion of Douglas, J.) (emphasis in original).

207. Jaffe, *supra* note 2, at 1184.

of legislative power to agencies, as noted, was a serious issue in the 1930's: the Supreme Court on one occasion openly stated that Congress could not delegate any part of its legislative power except under the limitation of a prescribed standard.[208] By the advent of the 1970's, however, other trends had surfaced: regulatory agencies customarily asserted and exercised power in the absence of congressional guidelines, and courts had come to tolerate this practice.[209] Noting this development, Professor Kenneth Culp Davis has labeled the nondelegation doctrine a "failure" and has called for open tolerance by the courts of broad delegations from legislatures to agencies.[210]

If broad delegation is assumed to be an important facet of the contemporary American administrative process, the differences between the current environment and that in which Brandeis operated are readily apparent. For the presence of broad delegation implicitly raises a series of problems which Brandeis was not compelled to address. First, agencies have continued to proliferate and diversify since the New Deal: there are more executive and regulatory agencies, in the traditional sense of the terms, and far more "hybrids." [211] Should a broad delegation model be applied across the board, so that differences between types of agencies as well as variations in their statutory underpinnings are minimized?

Brandeis had only begun to examine differences between standard regulatory agencies and "hybrid" agencies in *Crowell v. Benson*, and he viewed questions of delegation of power at a time when the broad delegation model was a mere gleam in the eye of academic apologists for the New Deal.[212] His theory of allocation conceded the importance of having independent, expert regulatory agencies; assumed that Congress would provide them with some

---

208. United States v. Shreveport Grain & Elevator Co., 287 U.S. 77, 85 (1932).

209. *See, e.g.,* Permian Basin Area Rate Cases, 390 U.S. 747 (1968); American Trucking Ass'n v. Atchison, T. & S.F. Ry., 387 U.S. 397 (1967).

210. Davis, *supra* note 2, at 714.

211. See text accompanying notes 159-62 *supra*.

212. *See, e.g.,* J. LANDIS, THE ADMINISTRATIVE PROCESS 68-70 (1938).

guidance, as it had the ICC; assumed further that the agencies would try simultaneously to make use of their expertise and to follow statutory guidelines; and reserved for the courts a power to make judgments about whether the agency's actions usurped important rights or seriously interfered with interests deserving protection. But his theory did not address the question of indiscriminately broad delegations which accompanied the proliferation and diversification of traditional regulatory and executive agencies and of the new hybrids.[213]

A second issue arises from the fact that the broad delegation model encourages informal agency discretion. Broad delegations invite agencies to develop their own informal decision-making criteria, which, from the point of view of administrators, are more flexible and efficient. But as agency jurisdiction expands, the impact of agency decisions broadens correspondingly; and the fairness of informal actions becomes a matter of concern to more persons. Arbitrariness, especially in light of the widening scope of procedural due process safeguards,[214] thus becomes an important

---

213. In three recent cases the Supreme Court has upheld agency assertions of power to deal with problems which were not even contemplated by Congress when the agencies were created. In each of the three decisions, the Court permitted the agency to establish the requisite delegation by relying on general statutory language describing the mission of the administrative body. *See* United States v. Southwestern Cable Co., 392 U.S. 157 (1968) (upholding the Federal Communication Commission's Community Antenna Television (CATV) regulations); Permian Basin Area Rate Cases, 390 U.S. 747 (1968) (upholding the Federal Power Commission's area price-fixing for natural gas); American Trucking Ass'n v. Atchison, T. & S.F. Ry., 387 U.S. 397 (1967) (upholding the Interstate Commerce Commission's "piggyback" regulations). For a discussion of these three cases, see DAVIS, *supra* note 2, at 715-19.

214. For example, the Supreme Court has recently expanded the number of contexts in which a hearing is required by the due process clause. In Goldberg v. Kelly, 397 U.S. 254 (1970), the Court held that public assistance officials must conduct a hearing before terminating a recipient's welfare payments on ineligibility grounds. Sniadach v. Family Fin. Corp., 395 U.S. 337 (1969), invalidated prejudgment garnishment because the system provided for no hearing at the time of garnishment. Similarly, in Fuentes v. Shevin, 407 U.S. 67 (1972), the Court held that prejudgment replevin was impermissible due to failure to assure a hearing before repossession of chattels. *See generally* K. DAVIS, ADMINISTRATIVE LAW TEXT §§ 7.01-.16 (3d ed. 1972).

negative value; informal agency decisions have increasingly been challenged in the courts as arbitrary.[215] Such challenges force consideration of two related questions: can the courts properly function as a check on informal agency discretion by providing ad hoc judicial content to imprecise legislative standards? And, if the first question is answered affirmatively, to what extent are the courts capable of formulating criteria to aid themselves in the performance of this function? The answers to these questions can be expected to determine the continued viability of the pragmatic and flexible agency-court partnership visualized by Justice Brandeis.

Contemporary Challenges to Agency Discretion: Demise of the Agency-Court Partnership?

Both courts and academicians have recently taken positions on these issues. The District of Columbia Circuit has announced a "new era" [216] in agency-court relations, wherein informal agency discretion will receive close judicial scrutiny to insure that the agency has taken a "hard look" at the problems before it and has minimized "unconscious preference and irrelevant prejudice" in its decision.[217] Under the "new era" approach, such traditional standards of judicial review as the "rational basis" test for informal rulemaking [218] may no longer be followed. Thus, at least

---

215. *See, e.g.*, Environmental Defense Fund v. Ruckelshaus, 439 F.2d 584 (D.C. Cir. 1971) (alleging arbitrary refusal to suspend registration of DDT as a pesticide); Holmes v. New York City Housing Authority, 398 F.2d 262 (2d Cir. 1968) (alleging arbitrary exclusion from public housing); Hornsby v. Allen, 326 F.2d 605 (5th Cir. 1964) (alleging arbitrary denial of liquor license); Smith v. Ladner, 288 F. Supp. 66 (S.D. Miss. 1968) (alleging arbitrary refusal to grant charter for nonprofit corporation). *See* Verkuil, *Judicial Review of Informal Rulemaking*, 60 VA. L. REV. 185 (1974).

216. Environmental Defense Fund v. Ruckelshaus, 439 F.2d 584, 597 (D.C. Cir. 1971). *See generally* K. DAVIS, *supra* note 214, §§ 2.09-.10.

217. Greater Boston Television Corp. v. FCC, 444 F.2d 841, 852 (D.C. Cir. 1970).

218. Under the "rational basis" test, "whenever the [reviewing] court believes that substitution of judicial judgment is inappropriate," the court recites "that the administrative determination must be upheld if it has warrant in the record and rational basis in law." 4 DAVIS § 30.05, at 214. *See generally id.* § 30.05.

278

with respect to certain agencies,[219] the District of Columbia Circuit may be expected to examine the discretionary judgments of "expert" agency personnel — not only to assure adequate procedural protections for affected parties [220] but also to assure that such "expert" judgments, even though involving "technical and specialized matters," are based on sound reasons.[221] That court appears to be assuming that it can and should serve as a check on informal agency discretion and that it will be able to develop evaluative criteria that will prove useful in performing this new role. At the moment these criteria seem to focus on assuring "principled decision-making" in an agency through insistence that it give "reasoned opinions" for its informal judgments.[222] So stated, the criteria do not reflect a great deal of analytical crispness. Perhaps they are merely intended to give the District of Columbia Circuit additional time to further develop and refine its position.

Commentators in the field of administrative law have recently addressed themselves to the question of court supervision of agency discretion. Professor Davis, as indicated earlier, has urged the courts to forgo attempts to "prevent delegation of legislative

---

219. A difficulty with making generalizations about the "new era" and the "hard look" doctrine is that the case law has thus far been confined to a few agencies, notably the Federal Communications Commission and the Environmental Protection Agency.

220. See Environmental Defense Fund v. Ruckelshaus, 439 F.2d 584, 594 (D.C. Cir. 1971); Greater Boston Television Corp. v. FCC, 444 F.2d 841, 850 (D.C. Cir. 1970). See also International Harvester Co. v. Ruckelshaus, 478 F.2d 615, 630-33 (D.C. Cir. 1973).

221. See International Harvester Co. v. Ruckelshaus, 478 F.2d 615, 648 (D.C. Cir. 1973); Greater Boston Television Corp. v. FCC, 444 F.2d 841, 850 (D.C. Cir. 1970). But see id. at 651 (concurring opinion), where Chief Judge Bazelon protests court investigation into "the technical intricacies of the agency's decision." See also Mobil Oil Corp. v. FPC, 483 F.2d 1238, 1257-59 (D.C. Cir. 1973).

222. See Mobil Oil Corp. v. FPC, 483 F.2d 1238, 1260, 1262 (D.C. Cir. 1973); International Harvester Co. v. Ruckelshaus, 478 F.2d 615, 647-50 (D.C. Cir. 1973); Greater Boston Television Corp. v. FCC, 444 F.2d 841, 851-53 (D.C. Cir. 1970). See also Phillips Petroleum Co. v. FPC, 475 F.2d 842 (10th Cir. 1973), cert. denied, 42 U.S.L.W. 3401 (U.S. Jan. 14, 1974).

power or to require meaningful statutory standards" and, instead, to focus their inquiries on the ability of administrators to "structure" and "confine" their discretionary power.[223] Realistic reform of administrative procedures should properly be addressed to "the protections the administrators in fact provide, irrespective of what the statutes say or fail to say." [224] In Davis' view broad delegation is helpful because it allows deference to expertise: he has no difficulty with agencies making policy judgments in their area of specialized competence, just as Brandeis was untroubled by the exercise of broad agency discretion in the area of economic regulation. Davis' concerns are that the judgments be reasoned rather than arbitrary and that they be made in a procedural context wich allows affected parties a panoply of safeguards. If the agency can show that it has established, through its own regulations, "procedural safeguards and . . . standards to guide discretion," [225] the courts ought to tolerate its informal decisions.

Professor Louis L. Jaffe has challenged Davis' approach on at least two levels. He questions Davis' reliance on the interplay between agencies and courts rather than on that between agencies and legislatures, and he expresses skepticism concerning universal applicability of the Davis model.[226] Jaffe feels that Davis' approach unduly minimizes "the peculiar political process which provides the milieu and defines the operation of each agency." [227] If openness, as opposed to arbitrariness, is a desirable social goal in the administrative process, Jaffe argues, "the extent to which an agency is open . . . is determined by the definiteness and specificity of the congressional expresssion of the agency's methods and objectives." [228] Consequently Jaffe calls for renewed attention,

---

223. Davis, *supra* note 2, at 713. *See generally* K. DAVIS, DISCRETIONARY JUSTICE (1969). *But see* Wright, Book Review, 81 YALE L.J. 575, 578 (1972), in which Judge J. Skelly Wright of the District of Columbia Circuit expresses skepticism that the agencies will "see the error of their ways."
224. Davis, *supra* note 2, at 713.
225. *Id.* at 732.
226. Jaffe, *supra* note 2, at 1183-84.
227. *Id.* at 1188.
228. *Id. See also* Jaffe, Book Review, 14 VILL. L. REV. 773 (1969).

even in broad delegation contests, to legislative standards and to distinctions between various types of agencies. He prefers that "political choices" be made by the legislature.

By political choices Jaffe means both a balancing of competing social values, such as a need for sources of energy versus a need to protect the environment, and a balancing of competing institutional values, such as expertise and efficiency as opposed to bureaucratic "rigidity and displacement of objectives by ... routine." [229] For Jaffe, a primary purpose of judicial review in broad delegation contexts is to ascertain what sets of choices the legislature has made and whether it has reserved the power to make further ones. Shifting the focus of judicial inquiry to administrative rules and procedures, in Jaffe's view, directs attention away from the crucial question of legislative policy choices. Moreover, it unduly minimizes the possibility that the current diversity in the types of agencies may be a function of legislative judgments.[230]

Statutory standards in broad delegations, then, still have real meaning for Jaffe: they are the means by which a legislature articulates its social and institutional value preferences in a given area. A broad delegation to an agency without precise standards, in this view, may reflect deliberate congressional choice rather than mere oversight—a judgment, in effect, that the agency forum is best designed to assess and solve a social problem. An important question which must be faced on judicial review, then, is whether the courts agree with that judgment or whether, because of the importance of the interests affected or rights invaded by agency decision-making, they would prefer that they themselves make an assessment and offer a solution.

Jaffe, a former Brandeis clerk, appears interested in retaining and refining portions of the Brandeisian model. His blueprint for reviewing courts in the broad delegation context appears designed

---

229. Jaffe, *supra* note 2, at 1188.
230. *See id.* at 1188-89.

to continue the agency-court partnership, with the court, as he has said elsewhere, being the "senior partner." [231] Jaffe is willing to defer to expertise, but only if it is a meaningful prerequisite to the effective governance of an area of American life. His analysis rests heavily on distinctions between types of agencies and statutory contexts. He regards informal policy choices by agencies as appropriate if Congress has opted to allow them broad supervisory powers, but he would retain the option for reviewing courts to scrutinize those choices. In short, Jaffe's approach appears intended to maintain flexibility for both courts and agencies and to insure cooperation among them, as far as possible, rather than to establish the courts as the zealous guardians of the justice and fairness of agency activity.[232] Brandeis' approach to allocation had rather similar goals, albeit in a dramatically different environment.

It is possible to read the "new era" decisions of the District of Columbia Circuit as supporting Jaffe as well as Davis, but on balance this court appears to be moving away from Jaffe's position. Those decisions [233] involved agencies, such as the Environmental Protection Agency, entrusted with broad legislative delegations and therefore especially prone to making informal discretionary judgments. Close scrutiny by the courts of these judgments might be consistent with Jaffe's position if one regards the decisions as sui generis—the products of a peculiar lack of confidence in the judgment of the agency in question.[234] Context, then, might help to explain the decisions. Yet Jaffe's writings point to the conclusion that when such broad delegations have been granted, Congress has provisionally decided to concede an agency substantial discretion in the regulation of a particular area of activity. If this is so,

---

231. JAFFE, 546 (referring to Justice Brandeis' concurring opinion in St. Joseph Stock Yards Co. v. United States, 298 U.S. 38, 84 (1936)).

232. *Id.* 572-73.

233. See cases cited in note 221 *supra*.

234. In some instances, however, such close scrutiny may be the product of particular dissatisfaction with Congress: Jaffee had bemoaned the failure of Congress to provide standards for FCC license renewals. *See* Jaffe, WHDH: *The FCC and Broadcasting License Renewals,* 82 HARV. L. REV. 1693 (1969).

reviewing courts should not lightly assume the function of setting aright the regulatory mechanisms of such an agency.

It is difficult to harmonize the "new era" cases with this last suggestion. The court remanded two of the cases [235] to the agency for a formulation of reasoned criteria to justify its decision; in the third,[236] the court ultimately supported the agency's findings. The approach adopted by the District of Columbia Circuit in those cases reflected little, if any, deference to the notion that broad legislative delegation necessarily entails broad leeway for discretionary administrative procedures. In each of the cases the court seemed preoccupied with insuring that the agency had provided internal procedural safeguards for affected parties and that it had supported its "discretionary decisions by ... reasoned opinions." [237] In language which could just as easily have been uttered by Professor Davis, the court in *Environmental Defense Fund v. Ruckelshaus* maintained that judicial review "must operate to insure that the administrative process itself will confine and control the exercise of discretion." [238] Absent was any talk of an agency-court partnership or of a pragmatic and complementary division of labor between the two institutions.

In sum, the broad delegation model appears to have merged with a greater judicial interest in procedural due process, resulting in a modification of Brandeis' allocation calculus. Brandeis operated in a time when aggressive court intervention on behalf of minority groups or other disadvantaged interests was rare; now the practice has become commonplace. He also formulated his allocation criteria in an age when the case law on judicial review of administrative action was largely concerned with a regulatory context which was far narrower in its scope and impact. No "captive" theory of the administrative process had become

---

235. Mobil Oil Corp. v. FPC, 483 F.2d 1238, 1263-64 (D.C. Cir. 1973); International Harvester Co. v. Ruckelshaus, 478 F.2d 615, 649 (D.C. Cir. 1973).

236. Greater Boston Television Corp. v. FCC, 444 F.2d 841 (D.C. Cir. 1970).

237. Environmental Defense Fund v. Ruckelshaus, 439 F.2d 584, 598 (D.C. Cir. 1971).

238. *Id., citing* K. Davis, Discretionary Justice (1969).

influential;[239] no comparable attention to procedural safeguards existed; agency discretion had not yet been equated with "unconscious preference and irrelevant prejudice."[240] Brandeis had to counter arguments that began with a presumption against administrative regulation of any kind; his successors must contend with a prevalent notion that, while the administrative forum is here to stay, it cannot be presumed to reach just results without continuing judicial supervision of its procedures.

CONCLUSION

Despite these trends, the legacy of Justice Brandeis to contemporary administrative law is still considerable although as the differences widen between the social and jurisprudential climate of his time and ours, tenets of his philosophy may have to be modified to reflect current conditions. Two examples will suffice. As noted, Brandeis played an important part in the refinement of the doctrine of primary jurisdiction, which, in his decisions, came to serve as a technique for allocating the initial supervision of a social or economic controversy between courts and agencies. One of his decisions previously discussed, *Great Northern Railway v. Merchants Elevator Co.*,[241] reserved considerable power to the court to construe the language of regulatory agency tariffs. That decision has been narrowed by later cases,[242] which suggest that agency jurisdiction can extend to matters of tariff interpretation and that judicial review should only be exercised after a regulating agency has construed a tariff and has clarified its underlying purposes. This development is viewed by some as a response to growing faith in agency expertise,[243] but it can also be characterized simply as a tactic designed by the courts to relieve increasingly crowded dockets by

---

239. *Cf.* Jaffe, *supra* note 2, at 1187. See note 205 *supra* and accompanying text.

240. See note 217 *supra* and accompanying text.

241. 259 U.S. 285 (1922). See notes 88-92 *supra* and accompanying text.

242. *See* United States v. Chesapeake & O. Ry., 352 U.S. 77 (1956); United States v. Western Pac. R.R., 352 U.S. 59 (1956).

243. *See* Jaffe, *Primary Jurisdiction,* 77 HARV. L. REV. 1037, 1045 (1964).

consigning more disputes to agencies as a preliminary matter. The expanded role and impact of courts on society since the 1950's has had a reciprocal effect: the more "justice" is to be dispensed on a broadening scale, the greater the number of controversies requiring supervision, and, as a necessary corollary, the greater the need to enlarge the scope of agency primary jurisdiction.

A second modification of a Brandeis contribution can be seen in the law of standing. Standing issues have not previously been discussed because they raise questions of allocating power between courts and agencies only peripherally; their essential impact is on the initial scope of agency decision-making. But insofar as a standing issue requires the courts to determine the potential reach of an agency decision—since it is the reviewing court, ultimately, which decides how many sets of interests an agency rule or regulation may fairly affect—the issue may be viewed as raising allocation questions.[244] In two important pre-New Deal decisions,[245] Brandeis formulated a test for standing based on the aggrieved party's membership in a class protected by the statute creating the agency. Under this test a party did not have standing merely if he was injured, economically or otherwise, by the agency's action; he needed to be within that class which the statute specifically sought to protect.

Recent cases have substantially altered that test.[246] Plaintiffs have been conceded standing to sue if they can show that they are *arguably* within the zone of interest to be protected [247] and have

---

244. *See* Scott, *Standing in the Supreme Court—A Functional Analysis,* 86 HARV. L. REV. 645, 683-90 (1973).

245. Alexander Sprunt & Son, Inc. v. United States, 281 U.S. 249 (1930); Chicago Injunction Case, 264 U.S. 258 (1924).

246. *See* Investment Co. Institute v. Camp, 401 U.S. 617 (1971); Arnold Tours, Inc. v. Camp, 400 U.S. 45 (1970); Association of Data Processing Serv. Organizations v. Camp, 397 U.S. 150 (1970); Barlow v. Collins, 397 U.S. 159 (1970); Hardin v. Kentucky Util. Co., 390 U.S. 1 (1968) (all granting standing). *See generally* Davis, *The Liberalized Law of Standing,* 37 U. CHI. L. REV. 450 (1970); Jaffe, *Standing Again,* 84 HARV. L. REV. 633 (1971).

247. Association of Data Processing Serv. Organizations v. Camp, 397 U.S. 150, 156 (1970).

suffered some injury.[248] Direct statutory support for a plaintiff's interest no longer seems to be a *sine qua non,* nor need the injury be economic in nature.[249] The broadening of the standing test since Brandeis' tenure may likewise be attributed to changed social conditions and jurisprudential perceptions. As agencies have become more pervasive in their impact, more persons have been affected, directly and indirectly, by their decisions; as this phenomenon of "polycentrism" [250] is perceived, it summons up a new spate of due process questions in a society increasingly conscious of the values of procedural fairness and justice. The fact of increased agency presence generates a perception of growing agency power; a fear of the effect of unchecked power on disadvantaged persons has been one of the sources of the "due process revolution" [251] of the fifties and sixties. Changes in the law of standing have reflected these developments.

The Brandeisian approach, then, will not have the impact in the future that it once had; one could not expect otherwise if history has a meaning. Brandeis was peculiarly suited, intellectually and temperamentally, to make a major contribution to administrative law in its formative years. So wide-ranging and influential was that contribution that it has survived well beyond Brandeis' own career; and it may, with refinements and modifications, continue to make its mark on administrative law. But just as Brandeis helped shift the original focus of administrative law during his career, so a

248. Sierra Club v. Morton, 405 U.S. 727 (1972). The plaintiffs in *Sierra Club* were denied standing because they had failed to allege that any club members had suffered any direct environmental injury. It would appear, however, that this pleading defect can be rectified in future cases if public interest organizations merely allege direct harm to their members. *See* Note, *The New Law of Threshold Standing: The Effect of* Sierra Club *on Jus Tertii and on Government Contracts,* 1973 DUKE L.J. 218.

249. Although the cases cited in note 246 *supra* all involved economic interests, *Sierra Club* (see note 248 *supra*) did not. *Sierra Club* can be read to obviate any economic-interest component in standing, assuming that direct noneconomic injury has been properly pleaded. *See generally* Scott, *supra* note 244, at 667.

250. *Cf.* Fuller, *The Forms and Limits of Adjudication,* in H. Hart & A. Sacks, The Legal Process 421 (tent. ed. 1958).

251. *See, e.g.,* Holmes v. New York City Housing Authority, 398 F.2d 262 (2d Cir. 1968). *See generally* F. GRAHAM, THE DUE PROCESS REVOLUTION (1972).

combination of changed circumstances and ideas may already have shifted that focus once more. One need not lament this situation: Brandeis' views reflected his special concerns and in one sense had a certain narrowness and rigidity, for all their usefulness. From a contemporary perspective, one can admire Brandeis' achievement without longing for his reincarnation.

CHAPTER 4. CONSTITUTIONAL LAW

Every law professor likes to think of himself as something of an expert on the Constitution, but some of us are more expert than others. In my case constitutional law has not been a major area of my scholarship or teaching, although I like to view some of my work as making interstitial contributions to the field. In this chapter of essays my concern is not so much with analyses of specific constitutional law doctrines or cases as it is with the significance of the Constitution for American legal thought.

Two consequences of the presence of a Constitution are addressed in the succeeding essays. *The Supreme Court's Public and the Public's Supreme Court* takes for granted the entrenchment of constitutional law as "supreme law" and the place of the Supreme Court as the final interpreter of that body of law, and proceeds to ponder some of the consequent problems for a society in which public opinion is taken seriously. The essay suggests that communication between the elite professional Court and the non-elite lay public is not as simple, or as one-sided, a process as may commonly be thought.

The essay on *Constitutional Protection for Personal Lifestyles,* written with J. Harvie Wilkinson, III, explores the ability of the Constitution to serve as a source of protection against newly perceived social grievances. How can a document be both a repository of timeless legal principles and a proving ground for "new" legal rights? The paradox has fascinated constitutional scholars over the years, and continues to fascinate one who does not regularly write orthodox constitutional analysis. Professor Wilkinson and I argue in the essay that "lifestyle choices" of domestic companionship, sexual conduct, and personal appearance deserve, within limits, the status of constitutional rights, even though their importance in American society has only recently been perceived.

289

THE SUPREME COURT'S PUBLIC
AND THE PUBLIC'S SUPREME
COURT

The Virginia Quarterly Review, Vol. 52, No. 3 (1976)

This essay has two related themes, which will be considered in inverse order from their appearance in its title. The first is the problem of making the Supreme Court of the United States and its justices accessible and understandable to the public at large. The second is the problem of ascertaining the proper audience to which Supreme Court decisions should be directed. Both themes are suggested by the recent publication of Richard Kluger's important book, *Simple Justice* (Knopf, $15.95), a history of the Court's decision in *Brown v. Board of Education,* outlawing racial segregation in the public schools.

Brown's impact, Kluger rightly senses, was not confined to schools, nor even to race; it reaffirmed and gave concrete meaning to "the inherent equality of mankind." After the unanimous dictates of the Court in *Brown* were pronounced, one could argue, it did not matter what Americans *thought* about race relations and racial superiority and inferiority; they had, in their public lives at any rate, to *act* as if human beings really were created equal. Over time, so runs the argument, thinking one way and acting another becomes a strain, and finally one shapes thoughts to actions. All people become equal because the law, personified by the Supreme Court, says they must be so regarded. Conformity to law finally becomes conformity to a different way of thinking.

But the Supreme Court, Kluger shows, was acutely aware of the controversial nature of racial segregation, anxious to avoid offending large segments of the public with its decision, and as concerned with the immediate practical consequences of a holding invalidating segregated public schools as it was with the juristic rationale for the holding itself. The external politics of the *Brown* decision illustrate that judge-made law in America commands respect but does not necessarily compel obedience. If sufficient numbers of the public profoundly disagree with a judgment of the

Court — the *Dred Scott* case, for example — the judgment will not stand. *Brown* changed the character of American public education not simply because the Supreme Court said that racial segregation in the public schools was "against the law" but because the Court correctly understood that most Americans, on reflection, would find the public practice of racial segregation antithetical to fundamental ideals of the nation.

If the Supreme Court's relation to the American populace, then, is more reciprocal than might sometimes be thought — if the Supreme Court needs the public as much as the public needs the Supreme Court — how can the two entities better understand one another? Surveys and polls continually reveal that although the office of Justice of the Supreme Court perhaps commands more public respect than any other, very few Americans know who sits on the Court at any given time, what functions the justices perform, or what the Court's decisions mean. Conversely, service on the Court tends to protect the confidentiality of a justice, sharply limit public access to him, and discourage him from seeking public contacts. Roughly speaking, it seems as if the public at large cannot fully understand the Court, nor can the Court fully understand the thoughts and feelings of the public. How, then, can the two entities effectively interact?

II

Simple Justice dramatizes the interaction of law with the movement for black equality in modern America. Three literary analogies to *Simple Justice* come to mind. *Simple Justice* is like a Homeric epic in its slow progression of stories within stories, intermingling finally with one another in a grand and heroic climax. It is like a 17th-century morality play in its recurrent insistence that the values of decency and humaneness can and should triumph. And it is like a Victorian novel in its skillful interplay of personal and social themes, its threads of plot and subplot that are finally bound together.

Seldom, in my view, is so value-oriented a piece of scholarship so successful as an historical contribution. There are quarrels lawyers or historians could pick with Kluger's perspective: he characterizes 19th-century judges as "liberals" or "conservatives," using these terms in their 20th-century sense; he occasionally reads cases loosely and thereby evaluates decisions as speaking more broadly and decisively than they were likely intended. One senses Kluger is not really too concerned with the technicalities and qualifications of legal and historical scholarship: his purpose is to dramatize, and he is willing to oversimplify a little to maintain the emotional intensity of his narrative.

Brown was an unusual case in that it affected many more persons than an ordinary Court decision, was written — deliberately, as Kluger points out — in a much less "legalistic" tone, and received widespread publication outside the normal channels through which judgments of the Court are communicated. It was also, unlike many other controversial Warren Court cases, a decision touching the nerve fibers of American society and exposing that society's basic contradictions. The juxtaposition of race and equality has been a central issue of American civilization since its origins; it remains such; *Brown* purported, at one level ("law") and in one context (public elementary schools), to assert that equality transcended race consciousness. Consequently the public had a strong need to understand *Brown* and to relate to it. One could argue, in fact, that the primary roadblock to the *Brown* decision was a sense on the part of several justices that the public would not comprehend a decision that racial segregation in public schools was impermissible and would therefore not accept it.

Brown, then, because it was a case to which so many Americans needed to relate, is an especially good subject for a narrative that seeks a wider audience than the usual Court-watchers and commentators. But the question goes beyond *Brown*: in seeking to relate to a particular Supreme Court decision can the public relate to the Court at large?

Three public impressions of the Court suggest themselves, each with its own germ of an insight. One is that the Supreme Court is "nine people"; a second that the Court is "a branch of government"; a third that the Court is "the supreme law of the land." *Simple Justice* deals most fully with the first and the third, only sparingly and not altogether successfully with the second.

Each impression, taken alone, is an inadequate description of the Court. In combination, and with some added reflection, the three may capture its essence.

Much of Kluger's narrative could be said to stand for the proposition that although the Supreme Court is composed of nine people, it is "really" made up of far more. The scenario of *Simple Justice* contains the activities of hundreds of persons over vast amounts of time. It includes not only blacks, such as Reverend Joseph A. Delaine, who turned to the courts to challenge segregated practices, but lawyers for their cause, such as Spottswood Robinson and Thurgood Marshall; social scientists, such as Kenneth Clark, who helped in the litigation; lower court judges, such as John Parker, Waties Waring, and Collins Seitz, who passed on the constitutional validity of segregated public schools; and advocates on the other side, such as Lindsay Almond and John W. Davis. It takes in judges — Lemuel Shaw, Samuel Miller, Henry Billings Brown, John Harlan the Elder — who considered questions of racial segregation throughout American history. It includes law clerks to the justices who sat for the three years of arguments surrounding *Brown* and its companion cases.

The sweep of Kluger's narrative seems designed not merely to set standards for exhaustive research, but to make a broader point: the process of a Supreme Court decision involves many more individuals than those who are publicly identified with the result. The additional individuals not only take part in the decision-making process; they help shape the outcome. Aggrieved blacks in the 1940's had the fortitude to seek remedies in the courts. Lawyers agreed to represent them and shaped arguments that they intended to persuade judges. Judges searched for pronouncements of other judges on similar matters as authorities to follow, disagree with, or disregard. Judges talked to their law clerks and digested the latter's research. Judges read the newspapers and tried to ascertain the tolerance of public opinion for change in the area of race relations. The nine Justices who finally decided *Brown* were not deciding alone. The Supreme Court may be isolated from partisan politics, and its members may even on occasion be out of touch with contemporary attitudes, but its decisions cannot fairly be reduced to the idiosyncratic judgments of nine men.

Yet the personnel of the Court at a given time surely makes a difference in the outcome of decisions. Regardless of the swirl of outside pressures surrounding a justice as he enters the conference room to discuss and vote on a case, his presence there, as opposed to the presence of some other individual, is important. Therein lies the germ of truth in the public impression that the Court is "nine people." Kluger argues in *Simple Justice* that the death of Chief Justice Vinson in the summer of 1953, and the subsequent appointment of Earl Warren to succeed to the Chief Justiceship, was decisive in the outcome of *Brown.* Vinson had been wedded, though not exclusively, to the principle of segregation; he had influenced the views of others, such as Justice Clark. Warren was not similarly wedded and had the advantage of being regarded as a former public official and politician with his "finger on the nation's pulse." Warren's presence, for Kluger, not only tipped the scales in favor of the eventual result in *Brown* but ultimately secured unanimity for the decision.

I shall have more to say in the latter portion of this essay about the difficulties of determining the precise interplay of personalities in the Supreme Court's decisions. At this point it suffices to note that while the Court cannot fairly be equated solely with "nine people," the interaction of its nine members strongly affects its decisions.

"Interaction" on the Court is nonetheless not simply the agreements and disagreements of individuals. It is also discussions between persons who hold the highest office of one of the principal branches of American government. Here one confronts the "branch of government" perception of the Court, which suggests that the Court's decisions are not so much the judgments of persons as they are the pronouncements of a permanent and continuous American governmental institution. There is something to be said for this perception, to which Kluger gives only slight attention. Justices on the Court are continually seeking to square their decisions with the extant judgments of their predecessor Courts. In the discussions of *Brown,* for example, a most serious argument for maintaining the existence of racially segregated facilities was that a prior Court had sustained their constitutionality and nearly 60 years had passed without that Court's judgment being invalidated.

On the surface, institutional continuity may look simply like blind adherence to the past. A Court that slavishly follows precedent, one might assume, imprisons the law in time. But institutional continuity is not so much an appeal to history as it is an appeal to the mystique of American governmental bodies, who are designed, in theory, to serve the public rather than to promote the interests and values of those who are associated with them. The Supreme Court is peculiarly vulnerable to the charge that it does not serve the public because of the undemocratic character of its appointments process and the life tenure of its members. If the Court is not somehow distinguishable from its current occupants — if the institution itself has no identity over time — then law becomes equated with idiosyncratic judgments by people on whose actions there is no effective political check.

Thus Justices take seriously matters of institutional continuity and feel strongly the constraints on their actions that come from a sense of association with the Supreme Court of the United States. Some Justices, such as Felix Frankfurter, try to make a sharp distinction between their personal sympathies or antipathies and their judicial obligations; others, such as Earl Warren, find such a distinction artificial. No Justice functions, however, without a sense of holding an office in the American system of government and being bound, to some extent, by the traditions of that office and by public expectations about its performance. *Brown* was a difficult case not because arguments for maintaining segregation were humane or fair or just, but because they represented the majoritarian legal and social thinking of six decades, and they had been regularly, albeit sometimes grudgingly, accepted by the United States Supreme Court. A rationale for overruling the legal and social principle of *Plessy v. Ferguson,* an 1896 decision sustaining the constitutionality of "separate but equal" racially segregated public facilities, was hard to find, not simply because of indecisiveness among some of the Warren Court's members about the value of integrated public schools, but because of the strong weight afforded institutional continuity in Supreme Court decisions.

Among those justices who had difficulty finding a rationale to overrule *Plessy* was Robert Jackson, who worried, Kluger maintains, that an overruling would undermine respect for "a supposedly stable organic law." Jackson's fear, while partially directed at the theme of institutional continuity, was also directed at a third public image of the Court, that it is "the supreme law of the land." Earl Warren was also cognizant of this perception, Kluger believes, and may have shared it. "You did not 'work out something' with the decrees of the Supreme Court," Kluger characterizes Warren as thinking, "you obeyed them. That is what a government of laws meant."

On reflection, this public perception of the Court, like the prior two discussed, needs refinement. "Law" in America is, of course, much more than the pronouncements of nine justices or one institution. Other institutions make law, and some — Congress most notably — can legislate Supreme Court decisions out of existence. The Supreme Court may be, since *Marbury v. Madison,* the ultimate interpreter of the Constitution, but state legislatures, through the amendment process, can change the Constitution's text. A corpus of officials is charged with enforcing the Court's decisions and may, according to some evidence, retain an unchecked discretion to deviate from them if they choose. A Court decision outlawing prayers in public schools has not fully had that effect; another insisting that criminal suspects be fully apprised of their rights while under police custody has apparently been only indifferently implemented. Irate Presidents, from Jefferson through Nixon, have considered refusing to comply with Court decrees or have allegedly refused outright. Andrew Jackson has for years been associated with the ultimatum, "John Marshall has made his decision (one favorable to the interests of the Cherokee Indians and hostile to those of Jackson), now let him enforce it." Jackson apparently never made such a categorical statement, but the possibility of noncompliance with a Court decision always exists.

The Court is an institution charged with a responsibility to make authoritative pronouncements about what the state of a current branch of the law is. Its pronouncements carry great weight, and, as indicated, speak well beyond the time in which they are made, but they are not "the law" unless the American public, in the main, accepts them as such. Overwhelmingly insensitive or unpopular Court decisions never achieve the legitimacy necessary for public acquiescence. *Plessy v. Ferguson* did, for a time, but less than 40 years after its enactment its fullest meaning — a racially segregated society at all levels — began to be undermined.

Thus the Court is the "supreme law of the land" only in a limited sense. Yet the authority of the Court in matters of social controversy remains immense. Habitually Americans have tried to resolve divisive social issues by appeal to legal institutions; historically the judiciary, personified by the Court, has been perceived as the ultimate arbiter of "legal" questions. When competing social attitudes, such as equality and racial prejudice, become issues of constitutional law, as in *Plessy* and *Brown,* and when the Supreme Court purports to resolve those issues, its participation has immense social significance. The Court lends all its majesty and dignity to one outcome or another. It says either "segregate with our blessings" or "integrate whether you like it or not." One may not like what the Court says or even vow to disobey its edicts. But in so doing one opposes a force of great power and stature in American life. Kluger shows in *Simple Justice* the great importance of the participation of the Court in the civil rights movement. The Court did not initiate the movement, nor was it primarily responsible for the transformation in racial attitudes that has taken place in America between World War II and the present. But the momentum that civil rights received from *Brown v. Board of Education* was incalculable.

The impact of *Brown* swept away one vestige of racial segregation after another, but recently countervailing forces have collided with the integrationist impulse, producing serious dilemmas that the current Court can no more "solve" than the nation can apparently reach agreement upon. Benign racial quotas in education and forced busing to achieve racial balance are issues on which Americans seem deeply divided at present. In none of these areas has the Court taken a ringing, unanimous stand comparable to its posture in *Brown*. Perhaps this is because the nine people currently on the Court cannot agree on a stand, perhaps because the judicial branch of government is limited in its ability to make decisions in certain contexts, perhaps because "the law of the land" is not perceived as clear on such issues. What needs to happen for these issues to be satisfactorily resolved is a continuing dialogue between the Court and the nation, so that individual Justices can be exposed to the same swirl of attitudes and arguments that they encountered in considering *Brown*.

III

To be thus exposed, one might assume, the Supreme Court needs an understanding of the public, just as the public needs one of the Supreme Court. But what is the Supreme Court's "public"? To whom should Supreme Court decisions be directed? Here the issues seem not so much in need of refinement as in need of initial examination. Who are the classes of persons to which Supreme Court decisions are addressed? Although we may surmise that some decisions, like *Brown*, affect countless numbers of people, being affected by a decision and understanding it may be two different things.

Simple Justice raises the question of the impact of various kinds of publicists in communicating the decisions of the Court beyond their usual circles. In addressing that question I will be distinguishing between three segments of the public, "professional," "informed," and "lay," and between two kinds of publicists, "insider" and "outsider."

The average Supreme Court decision is written for and communicated to a "professional" audience. This audience is primarily made up of persons with legal training and a specialized interest in the Court's proceedings. The Court speaks to some members of this audience in a precise fashion by resolving a particular controversy in which they were involved. Such persons include the litigants before the court, their counsel, and lower court judges that have passed on the specific legal questions decided. Beyond this group are additional "professionals": similarly situated litigants or potential litigants for whom the decision gives guidance; practitioners whose future advice to clients is affected by the decision; law professors who address the decision in the course of their scholarship or teaching. Most cases decided by the Supreme Court communicate almost exclusively to this group.

Other decisions of the Court, especially those in the area of constitutional law, may be perceived as having wider applicability. The Court's decision finding the practice of compulsory prayers in public schools unconstitutional, for example, affected not only the individual litigant in the case, his counsel, lower courts, and the specialized bar, but also numerous school children, their parents, and educators. But did those classes of persons understand the decision? In such cases the question of multi-leveled communication is squarely raised: can the Court write for more than one audience?

In one sense the answer to that question is no. The reasoning of a Supreme Court decision is necessarily technical, involving an analysis of legal source materials communicated in legal language. Persons not trained in the law cannot easily fathom intricacies in legal reasoning. Indeed, a widely shared perception of legal reasoning is that it is "lawyer's gobbledegook," and there is some truth in the perception. Like other professions and guilds in American society, lawyers and judges have a distinctive vocabulary and a distinctive mode of reasoning. The patterns of that reasoning are not always intelligible to laymen.

Yet surely another audience exists for Supreme Court decisions: those persons without legal training who attempt to keep informed on contemporary issues and who take an interest in the social or political implications of Supreme Court decisions. Being "a branch of government" and "the supreme law of the land," the Supreme Court is associated with politics and social life in a broad sense. Its decisions are widely characterized as "liberal" or "conservative," as "progressive" or "reactionary," and even as "right" or "wrong." These characterizations are frequently made by "informed" nonlawyers: representatives of the media, writers, politicians, government officials, academicians. Such characterizations may be noted and appraised by the constituents of these various groups — the archetypal "laymen" who buy books, read newspapers, listen to influential people, and help create "public opinion."

Brown v. Board was a decision deliberately intended to reach beyond the professional audience of the Court. Chief Justice Warren's opinion in *Brown* was written in simple, almost colloquial language. It was short enough to have its complete text published in newspapers. Kluger maintains that Warren intended the opinion to be "readable by the lay public, non-rhetorical, unemotional, and above all, non-accusatory." The opinion had, Kluger feels, a "bleached-out quality" to its language, and a "thinness of legal materials." James Reston said the opinion read "more like an expert paper on sociology than a Supreme Court opinion."

Although *Brown* represents the exceptional Supreme Court decision rather than the ordinary one, it starkly presents communication dilemmas faced by the Court. How does the Court reach beyond a professional audience and yet retain its stature as a learned professional institution? How does it speak to the public in a comprehensive way without appearing to give over-simplified solutions to complex issues? How can its reasoning be both emotionally directed — through appeal to unifying values like "good citizenship" or universal bogeys like "inferiority" — and intellectually rigorous?

The short answer to these questions is that the Court cannot simultaneously communicate to the "professional," "informed," and "lay" segments of the public with perfect success. Its pithy aphorisms and catch-phrases ("three generations of imbeciles is enough"), ("one-man, one-vote") conceal complexities and suffer under intense academic analysis. Its technical masterpieces — some of the opinions of Justice John Harlan II come to mind — are sometimes incomprehensible even to "informed" nonlawyers. But the appropriate communication standard, it seems, can be something short of perfection. Indeed, it may be more important for the Court to take cognizance of its "informed" and "lay" audiences than for it to actually reach them. For the principle behind communication efforts is not to make everyone a lawyer (surely ample numbers exist) but to justify the Court's power. The Court seeks public understanding because it seeks public legitimation of its decisions; otherwise its authority is eroded. Having limited enforcement powers, no political base, and few purse strings — little save its authority — the Court must justify its stature through its reasoning. If its communication is unpersuasive or unintelligible, its stature may be threatened.

Given the technical nature of Court decisions and the imperatives of communication, the Court is forced to rely in part on publicists. Some of these publicists are hired by the Court: its press staff, its Clerk's and Marshal's offices. The latter two offices "publicize" by serving as liaisons, respectively, between the bar and the tourist public. Among the functions of the Clerk's office is to apprise counsel and other interested parties of the state of the Court's docket; among the duties of the Marshal's office is to provide public tours of the Supreme Court building and to allow the public limited access to oral arguments while the Court is in session.

The above "insider" publicists are privy, in varying degrees, to confidential information about Court personnel and procedures. They are not expected, by and large, to communicate this information to the public; they are expected, rather, to communicate only that information which is deemed appropriate for public consumption. Like other high-level governmental officials, the Justices of the Supreme Court are screened from the public by their staffs, and information released about their activities by "insider" publicists is selected information. Here one notices a trade-off common to public life in high circles: a public "right to know" about the activities of notable figures is recognized and catered to, but balanced off against the needs of such persons for privacy in their working and private lives. In the case of Supreme Court Justices a need for privacy is thought to be particularly acute since the Court is expected to be aloof from partisan strife and justices are expected to make "independent" decisions.

Another set of "insider" publicists is the law clerks who serve as research aides to individual Justices. Calling such persons "publicists" may seem anomalous, since the task of a law clerk, ostensibly, is to aid a Justice in the preparation, not the dissemination, of an opinion. But the law clerks have traditionally been regarded as serving a broader function. They not only give a Justice access to the services of a person with supposed intellectual ability; they allegedly give the Justice access to contemporary ideas. Law clerks normally serve for only a year and are comparatively recent law school graduates: they arguably reflect contemporary waves of educated legal thought. According to this hypothesis, clerks may have a fuller sense than a Justice for the contemporary impact of a decision, or they may be, by virtue of their age, able to view delicate political judgments from a different perspective. Kluger surmises that Barrett Prettyman, Justice Robert Jackson's clerk for the 1953 Term, was highly influential in persuading Jackson to suppress a concurring opinion in *Brown*.

Whether law clerks actually help the Court expand the range and impact of its opinions or merely reinforce the views of the Justices they serve is a question whose answer undoubtedly varies from case to case and which is not, on balance, very significant. Of greater interest, for present purposes, is the fact that law clerks have the same limitations of confidentiality placed upon them as do other "insiders." These limitations are made quite explicit: a clerk is not to reveal privileged information to which he has access during his tenure. The confidentiality limitation informally extends beyond the duration of a clerkship; former clerks are normally cautious about discussing the details of their past service with a Justice. The tradition of confidentiality sometimes puts former clerks and other "insiders" in the awkward position of believing they may know "the truth" about a particular episode in the Court's history but being enjoined from contradicting erroneous accounts of that episode.

Beyond the "insider" publicists previously described are "selected" insiders: journalists or academicians granted access to otherwise privileged information for the express purpose of revealing that information to the public. Sometimes the information is in the form of a "leak," designed to have contemporary impact; sometimes it serves to provide a biographer or historian fuller background to the career of a Justice or to the work of a particular Court. Justices have taken radically different views on the use of selected insiders. Chief Justice Marshall himself wrote a defense of *McCulloch v. Maryland* under a pseudonym; Justice Story used the Court's Reporter, Henry Wheaton, to disseminate copies of Story's opinions to private persons; Chief Justice Stone granted Alpheus Mason access to intraCourt memoranda to aid in the preparation of a biography. Chief Justices Hughes and Warren, on the other hand, attempted to maintain confidentiality about the Court's internal business and refrained, in autobiographies, from giving particularized accounts of their tenures.

Countless "outsider" publicists of the Court exist: commentators in the popular press; academicians writing on a selected aspect of the Court's performance or on the contributions of individual justices; educators seeking to describe the Court in any of its perceived roles. A distinction between "insider" and "outsider" publicists may be thought of, at first blush, as serving no purpose. If the Court needs to communicate its work to the public, and yet is limited, by the nature of its work, to communication to a very narrow audience, should it not welcome other publicists who can expand that audience? Should the precise access of the publicist to information emanating from the Court matter? After all, the purpose of a Court decision is to resolve a point of law and to advance reasons why the resolution has taken a particular form. If the reasons are circulated for public appraisal, why does it matter who circulates them?

The difficulty, of course, is that American society has fostered the development of hierarchies of persons with "expertise" or lack thereof on contemporary issues, and has regularly attributed expertise to those with "inside" information. Thus in writing *Simple Justice* Kluger has not only set out to humanize the *Brown* decision but also to establish his credentials as an "insider" publicist. He has sought to do this by not only reading a great deal of the available popular and contemporary literature on *Brown* and the issues it raised but also by interviewing as many participants in the *Brown* decision as he could. Kluger attempts to create, along with a strong impression of what the *Brown* decision *means* to contemporary American life, an equally strong impression of the *way Brown was*: the "inside" story of the decision.

This writer, while applauding Kluger's high professional standards as a historian and a journalist, and while admiring his zeal and persistence, finds the "insider" stance of *Simple Justice* troublesome in places. Its difficulty stems from the apparently skewed focus it sometimes creates for readers. Instead of savoring the symbolic meaning of *Brown* — something no legalistic commentary on the decision can adequately capture — a reader is invited to ask what "really" happened "inside the Court" in the *Brown* case. And that inquiry, in this writer's view, is nearly irrelevant. Can one ever "know" the connection of circumstances that produces a unanimous Court decision? Can one ever be sure which Justices took what positions in conference, or changed their votes, or suppressed dissents or concurrences, or made private deals? And does it matter?

Kluger gives an account of the internal deliberations of *Brown* which is well reasoned and documented. He identifies some Justices as supporting and others as originally opposing the eventual outcome of *Brown*. He characterizes the various positions of the opponents and sketches a narrative of their eventual capitulation to the majority view, as expressed in Warren's opinion. On two separate occasions this writer, while a law clerk at the Court many years after *Brown*, heard accounts of the deliberations that differed from Kluger's. Other scholars have advanced hypotheses about the deliberations that are different still.

But whether one chooses to accept Kluger's account or those of others seems beside the point. *Brown* was a decision that confronted the Court with the possibility of profound change; it was a case laden with moral overtones; it was not easily "settled" one way or another by constitutional language. Such decisions inevitably produce uncertainties among some Justices and strong feelings among others. In the expression of these uncertainties and feelings complexities of personal relations come into play. Many years later "what happened" becomes elusive; it was never clear to start with. Each Justice brought his individual perspective to *Brown;* for each the meaning of the decision was not quite what it was for the others. The "way it was" inside the Court's conference room in the *Brown* discussions consisted of a composite of thoughts and feelings that can never completely be recaptured, nor can the subsequent actions and thoughts of the participating Justices. Major historical events all have this quality; their "reality" is not completely reproducible.

In suggesting that Kluger's effort to describe "what happened" in *Brown* is not, and cannot be, completely authoritative, I do not mean to indict Kluger. He has succeeded, within his own limitations of access, in producing a plausible "inside" history of the case; contemporary Americans are fascinated with "inside" accounts of famous events; Kluger's focus thus gives his book a wider appeal and thereby supports what I take to be his major task, that of universalizing the process of a Supreme Court decision by stressing its human elements.

In this capacity Kluger is a superb "publicist" for the Court, for he shows that Supreme Court Justices, like the rest of us, make decisions as human beings, regardless of the constraining factors of their office and the technical requirements of their profession. The civil rights movement affected the nine Justices in *Brown,* at one level, in the same manner that it affected most other Americans: that is, it forced people to ask themselves why the accident of race should be a criterion for keeping some human beings forcibly separated from others. The answer the *Brown* justices gave to this question made more impact than the answers of numerous other people because of the multiple roles of the Supreme Court in American life. But the fundamental importance of *Brown* is that the question was asked. The symbolic meaning of *Brown* is thus primarily its human dimension, what it says about living in America. In stressing this dimension Kluger has done justice to the decision and to the Court.

IV

The Court's "public" is therefore ultimately Americans as humans; the public's "Court" is ultimately an institution composed of nine people who claim the power to affect our current definitions of humanity. Communication between the Court and the public, although fraught with complexities and difficulties, is essential because human beings are united in their humanity yet differentiated by their social and institutional roles. If the humans composing the Court are to wield greater power than most others in America, and are nonetheless incapable of surrendering their humanity, it would seem that they ought to advance some reasons why this power rests in them and not in others. Every time the Court makes a decision, then, it implicitly justifies its power. Thinking of the Court as "the law of the land" or "a branch of government" may help some Americans tolerate that power, but the Court is "nine people," too, and nine singularly powerful people.

Legitimacy is thus the recurrent quest of the Court. Legitimacy follows from the involvement of the public in Court decisions so that the decisions are largely accepted and followed, not so much because of the authority of the Court, but because of a general belief in the principles for which the decisions stand. The Court therefore needs to tell the public, as fully and carefully and clearly as it can, what its decisions stand for. Many times, because of its professional status, the Court cannot easily make such communications. But if no one does, the public is forced to rely on the Court simply because of its authority. In a period in which the accountability of authoritative institutions seems necessary for their successful functioning, blind public faith in the Court seems highly unlikely.

If legitimacy is tied to communication, and if the technicalities of Court communications narrow their impact, it seems that the Court must communicate in other respects. The humanness of the Court, in particular, ought to be communicated. Yet there are difficulties, as noted: the need in the justices for some measure of privacy and confidentiality; the importance of the Court as an institution transcending personalities; the majesty of the judicial branch of government, which stems in large part from its identification with the values of impersonality and detachment. The triumph of *Simple Justice* is that it humanizes the Court without

306

entirely losing sight of its transcendent institutional qualities. We see the nine Justices struggling with the personal difficulties *Brown* raises for each of them, and coping with the presence of each other; but we see also, if we look hard enough, their sense of being judges and being members of the Supreme Court of the United States, and, finally, their sense of the symbolic meaning of *Brown*. *Brown,* it seems, is a legitimated decision: its general principle of racial equality before the law seems largely accepted in America. A striking indication of *Brown's* legitimacy is that the Court's basic message was communicated to Richard Kluger, who has done his best to justify it in further communication. That seems to be what the process of legitimating Court decisions is all about: unraveling the complexities of Court-public communication to reveal the basic principles of concordance. Legitimacy comes when enough of the public understands, and believes, what the Court has said; it cannot come, in cases of massive potential impact like *Brown,* until the Court has truly spoken to the public. The "public" and the "Court" may not be entirely comprehensible to one another, but they are nonetheless mutually interdependent.

CONSTITUTIONAL PROTECTION FOR PERSONAL LIFESTYLES

Cornell Law Review, Volume 62, No. 3 (1977)

INTRODUCTION

Personal tastes, preferences, impulses, and expressions appear to be candidates for a new constitutional protection. No recent constitutional trend, in fact, seems more significant. One is hard pressed to account fully for this development, much less for the recurrence of personal lifestyle issues in what is supposedly a more conservative and more traditionalist Supreme Court. Perhaps the new trend portends a fundamental shift in values: the emergence of a national ethic that, in matters of style and morality, personal choice is paramount. Perhaps the momentum of racial and sexual egalitarianism has brought with it a demand for acceptance of a panoply of personal lifestyles. Or perhaps it is simply that as we perceive ourselves less capable of influencing our national and communal fates, we demand greater freedom to direct our lives as individuals.

Although its causes are complex, the phenomenon itself is clear. The Supreme Court is increasingly being invited to extend constitutional protection to personal lifestyle choices.[1] By "lifestyle choice" we mean an individual's decision to exercise control over the most personal aspects of his or her life. The term lifestyle is used in its original sense, stripped of popular connotations: it refers to the capacity to craft one's intimate, personal existence in the manner that one sees fit.

Such is the pace of constitutional litigation in this area that *Griswold v. Connecticut*[2] already seems something of a

---

1. The invitation is not always accepted. *See* Kelly v. Johnson, 425 U.S. 238 (1976); Doe v. Commonwealth's Attorney, 403 F. Supp. 1199 (E.D. Va. 1975), *aff'd mem.,* 425 U.S. 901 (1976).

2. 381 U.S. 479 (1965).

grandfather case. Part of *Griswold's* mystique is its utter imprecision: Justice Douglas' opinion has generated more emanations than those on which it purported to draw.[3] It is no accident that Justice Douglas was the most ardent and explicit champion of lifestyle freedom yet to sit on the Court.[4] He left much in the way of stirring words and phrases, precious little in the way of analytic definition. The void seems unfortunate, because no constitutional issue has been more prone to loose platitude and sweeping assertion than the relationship of law to personal lifestyle choice.

Our discussion of lifestyle freedom attempts to refine some existing constitutional categories and to present a unified framework for analysis of lifestyle issues reaching the Court today. We do not focus exclusively on a right of privacy, although privacy may at times be a propitious and even a necessary condition for personal lifestyle choices to operate. But many of the personal choices deemed eligible for protection — personal appearance, for example — are at least in part visible to the public and do not involve governmental intrusion or surveillance. Nor are we discussing only a right of autonomy, if that term is confined to personal activities that involve no demonstrable harm to others.[5] Exercise of lifestyle freedom may adversely affect others, whether they be the children of a broken marriage or even, in the Supreme Court's words, those having merely "the potentiality of human life."[6]

Our treatment of the lifestyle cases concentrates initially upon three basic categories, which can be represented in terms of "freedoms." The first is a freedom of personal companionship, where the individual claims the right to select his most intimate

---

3. See the extensive Comments on the *Griswold* case by Professors Dixon, Emerson, Kauper, McKay, and Sutherland in 64 MICH. L. REV. 197-288 (1965).

4. *See, e.g.,* Department of Agriculture v. Moreno, 413 U.S. 528, 538 (1973) (concurring opinion, Douglas, J.); Doe v. Bolton, 410 U.S. 179, 209 (1973) (concurring opinion, Douglas, J.); Ham v. South Carolina, 409 U.S. 524, 529 (1973) (concurring in part and dissenting in part, Douglas, J.); Papachristou v. Jacksonville, 405 U.S. 156 (1972). *But see* Village of Belle Terre v. Boraas, 416 U.S. 1 (1974).

5. *See* G. GUNTHER, CASES AND MATERIALS ON CONSTITUTIONAL LAW 654-55 (9th ed. 1975); Henkin, *Privacy and Autonomy,* 74 COLUM. L. REV. 1410 (1974).

6. Roe v. Wade, 410 U.S. 113, 162 (1973).

domestic associates. The second is a freedom of personal sexual conduct. The third is a freedom of personal dress and appearance.

The scope of each of these freedoms will be analyzed in detail in succeeding sections. Our analysis implicitly asks three related questions: First, what kinds of lifestyle issues is the Court currently confronting? Second, what lifestyle freedoms is it protecting and what competing state interests is it taking into account? Third, what standards for judicial review currently dominate the personal lifestyle area?

Finally, in a concluding section we consider lifestyle issues from a more general perspective. We set forth justifications for judicial intervention to protect lifestyle freedoms; we discuss the scope of a general constitutional lifestyle right; and we survey and assess the state interests in restricting lifestyle choices. We conclude that within certain limits judicial protection of personal lifestyle choices is constitutionally warranted and socially desirable, that the Court reaffirms its historic function by protecting lifestyle choices, but that indiscriminate and unreasoned vindication of lifestyle freedoms is no more desirable than insensitivity to them.

I. Domestic Companionship

The peculiar intimacy of the home environment and the relationships within it have in the past decade caused the Court to guarantee a significant measure of personal control over domestic companionship. This section will demonstrate that the right of domestic association is broader than is commonly supposed, that it is, within certain limits, a legitimate candidate for constitutional protection, but that unless the Court gives serious thought to those limits, the right may soon take on "strange boundaries as yet undiscernible." [7]

The Court's struggle with the new right of domestic companionship has been inextricably related to recent pervasive changes in American family life. Those changes have been the

---

7. Stanley v. Illinois, 405 U.S. 645, 668 (1972) (dissenting opinion, Burger, C.J.).

subject of such intense discussion elsewhere [8] that a brief summary suffices here. The trend has been from uniformity to diversity and individuality in domestic lifestyles. Larger numbers of Americans are rejecting the idea that marriage is a lifelong union and that the formal family is the exclusive unit for bearing and raising children.[9] Marriage itself is changing as men and women alter such traditional roles as providers and housewives. Divorce is becoming more commonplace and less stigmatized.[10] Children are more likely to be born out of wedlock and raised by a single parent.[11] Indeed, more Americans are finding it advantageous to bypass formal marriage altogether and cohabit in what one writer terms the "shadow institution [of] informal de facto marriage." [12]

The primary legal battleground for such changes is, of course, state domestic relations law and not constitutional law. The state, through its police power, has traditionally regulated popular

---

8. *E.g.*, L. CASLER, IS MARRIAGE NECESSARY? (1974); N. O'NEILL & G. O'NEILL, OPEN MARRIAGE (1972); A. SKOLNICK & J. SKOLNICK, FAMILY IN TRANSITION (1971); B. YORBURG, THE CHANGING FAMILY (1973); Glick, *A Demographer Looks at American Families*, 37 J. MARR. & FAM. 15 (1975); Novak, *The Family Out of Favor*, HARPER'S MAGAZINE, Apr. 1976, at 37.

9. *See* R. LIBBY & R. WHITEHURST, RENOVATING MARRIAGE: TOWARD NEW SEXUAL LIFESTYLES (1973); C. ROGERS, BECOMING PARTNERS: MARRIAGE AND ITS ALTERNATIVES (1972); Ramey, *Intimate Networks: Will They Replace the Monogamous Family?*, 9 FUTURIST 175 (1975).

10. *See* H. CARTER & P. GLICK, MARRIAGE AND DIVORCE: A SOCIAL AND ECONOMIC STUDY (1970); J. EPSTEIN, DIVORCED IN AMERICA (1974); Bernard, *Note on Changing Life Styles, 1970-1974*, 37 J. MARR. & FAM. 582, 583-84 (1974); *More and More Broken Marriages*, U.S. NEWS & WORLD REPORT, Aug. 14, 1972, at 30.

11. As one reporter describes this trend:

Despite the array of alternatives for today's woman — contraception, abortion, adoption — the number of unmarried women giving birth and then raising their children has risen dramatically. Though still just under 1 percent of all families, their numbers have increased five-fold in the past fifteen years, with the fastest rise taking place since 1970. . . . Associated primarily with poor people, or occasionally with the Bohemian chic of the upper classes, the phenomenon of the unmarried mother, though still rare, is becoming more visible among women with middle class backgrounds. Sawyer, *For Unmarried Mothers, There are Feelings of Fulfillment Mixed With Resentment*, Washington Post, Apr. 15, 1976, § D.C. (district weekly), at 1, col. 3.

12. Glendon, *Marriage and the State: The Withering Away of Marriage*, 62 VA. L. REV. 663, 665 (1976).

mortality, and the Supreme Court still formally acknowledges that domestic relations "ha[ve] long been regarded as a virtually exclusive province of the States." [13] State law has not invariably been resistant to changes in domestic lifestyles. Divorce laws have become more lenient and now include no-fault grounds alongside or in lieu of fault grounds. [14] New alimony and support statutes require state courts to rely less on gender and more on the circumstances of a particular marriage. [15] Criminal laws prohibiting extramarital sexual behavior have been either relaxed or indifferently enforced. [16] State barriers to marriage, always minimal, have become even less stringent. [17] Indeed, state law will inevitably be encouraged to keep pace with shifting lifestyle trends, or else risk evasion or irrelevance. If, for example, the barriers to marriage become too strict, couples may be encouraged to ignore them and cohabit. If divorce becomes too difficult, spouses might be inclined to remarry surreptitiously before an existing marriage has been formally dissolved, or simply to terminate their marriage informally. If prospects of alimony or child support appear unfair or burdensome, spouses might be tempted to flee the jurisdiction and so escape the obligations of formal marriage separation.

Thus state law, however sluggishly and reluctantly, is forced to accommodate domestic lifestyle changes. But the question of how

---

13. Sosna v. Iowa, 419 U.S. 393, 404 (1975).

14. *See* Foster & Freed, *Divorce Reform: Breaks on Breakdown?,* 13 J. FAM. L. 443 (1973-74). As of June 1, 1974, only five states — Illinois, Massachusetts, Mississippi, Pennsylvania, and South Dakota — retained marital misconduct as the sole ground for divorce. Freed, *Grounds for Divorce in the American Jurisdictions,* 8 FAM. L.Q. 401, 401 (1974).

15. *See, e.g.,* the 1975 amendment to VA. CODE § 20-61 (1975), requiring reciprocal support between the spouses during marriage, and the 1975 amendment to VA. CODE § 20-107 (1975), insuring that alimony could be awarded to either spouse upon dissolution of marriage.

16. *See, e.g.,* Project, *The Consenting Adult Homosexual and the Law: An Empirical Study of Enforcement and Administration in Los Angeles County,* 13 U.C.L.A. L. REV. 643, 688-89 (1966).

17. *See, e.g.,* R. BARROW & H. FABING, EPILEPSY AND THE LAW 30 (2d ed. 1966) (noting removal of marriage prohibitions on epileptics); M. PAULSEN, W. WADLINGTON & J. GOEBEL, CASES AND OTHER MATERIALS ON DOMESTIC RELATIONS 131 (2d 3d. 1974) (noting similar removal in favor of persons with tuberculosis).

constitutional law ought to respond to this evolving domestic lifestyle pattern is more subtle and difficult. Constitutional law, unlike state law, has the unique potential to bestow a national benediction upon unconventional domestic lifestyles. The Supreme Court, more than any other instrument of American government, is institutionally receptive to pleas for national tolerance of those whose domestic arrangements have heretofore received little popular support. As we shall see, the effect of constitutional law in the domestic lifestyle area is potentially fourfold: to guarantee greater freedom of entry into and exit from formal family relationships, to encourage and validate role changes within the family or marriage partnership,[18] to make available formal family status to unorthodox groups, and to confer legitimacy and recognition upon extrafamilial relationships.[19]

In each of these instances, the force of constitutional law confronts the traditional order. The Court must often decide whether to use the Constitution to deprive the family — long regarded as the cornerstone of American society — of its favored status under law. It is true that the law has always been limited in its capacity to maintain conventional family arrangements; witness the widespread use of perjury and collusion to evade statutes limiting divorce to fault grounds alone.[20] Yet in areas involving traditional morality, society values law as much for its instructional as for its coercive effect. Law is a vehicle by which democratic majorities reaffirm shared moral aspirations and summon society's allegiance to a common set of behavioral goals. Deploying the Constitution to undermine conventional precepts of domestic morality is a step not lightly taken.

It is, however, a step the Court will sometimes take. There will always be some Americans who resist traditional conceptions of

---

18. This has been the effect of the Court's recent attack on sex discrimination, discussed in Ginsburg, *Gender in the Supreme Court: The 1973 and 1974 Terms,* 1975 SUP. CT. REV. 1.

19. *E.g.,* Stanley v. Illinois, 405 U.S. 645 (1972).

20. *See* Wadlington, *Divorce Without Fault Without Perjury,* 52 VA. L. REV. 32, 33 (1966).

family life and regard the favored legal status of the nuclear family as economically oppressive and a source of indignity and affront. Most obvious are those Americans who live outside the traditional family unit for reasons at least partly beyond their control. Such a category would include illegitimate children, homosexuals whose preferences preclude marriage, fundamentalist Mormons for whom polygamy is religiously mandated, and members of minority groups for whom economic, social, and cultural pressures cause disproportionate rates of family breakdown. To date the Court has dealt erratically with these "outsiders," vindicating on occasion the rights of illegitimates,[21] while upholding enactments against homosexuals [22] and polygamists.[23]

Other Americans deliberately choose to live outside the traditional family unit, preferring for a variety of reasons to live together without the legal ties of marriage. With regard to such persons the Court faces a formidable dilemma. The family is indubitably a cornerstone of American society and should be favored by the law; yet choice of domestic companionship constitutes the kind of intimate personal decision that also deserves constitutional respect. With such tensions in mind, three sets of lifestyle choices are discussed herein: marriage and divorce, procreation, and extrafamilial association.

---

21. *E.g.,* New Jersey Welfare Rights Org. v. Cahill, 411 U.S. 619 (1973) (invalidating statute denying welfare benefits to households with illegitimate children); Gomez v. Perez, 409 U.S. 535 (1973) (invalidating statute denying right of parental support to illegitimate children); Weber v. Aetna Cas. & Sur. Co., 406 U.S. 164 (1972) (invalidating statute denying right of illegitimate child to recover workmen's compensation benefits); Levy v. Louisiana, 391 U.S. 68 (1968) (invalidating statute denying right of illegitimate child to recover for wrongful death). *But cf.* Mathews v. Lucas, 96 S. Ct. 2755 (1976) (upholding statute requiring that, in order to qualify for Social Security benefits, illegitimate child must prove that deceased wage earner was parent and was living with or contributing to child's support at time of death); Labine v. Vincent, 401 U.S. 532 (1971) (upholding intestate succession statute excluding illegitimate child in favor of collateral heirs).

22. Doe v. Commonwealth's Attorney, 403 F. Supp. 119, *aff'd mem.* 425 U.S. 901 (1976).

23. Reynolds v. United States, 98 U.S. 145 (1978).

A. *The Choices of Marriage and Divorce*

The first modern case to significantly protect domestic companionship was *Loving v. Virginia*,[24] where the Court held unconstitutional a Virginia statute prohibiting interracial marriage. It is true, of course, that marriage and the sharing of a household need not always coincide. Persons may marry without living together, and they may live together without marrying, but the general meaning of marriage remains that of a shared life within a common abode. Had its result rested solely upon equal protection grounds, *Loving* would have been a case addressed more to the evils of racial discrimination than to the blessings of marriage. But the Court held that the Virginia statute violated the due process clause as well, explaining that "[t]he freedom to marry has long been recognized as one of the vital personal rights essential to the orderly pursuit of happiness by free men." [25]

The due process rationale of *Loving* calls into question other state restrictions on the right of consenting persons to marry. It appears, on reflection, that the Court could extend *Loving* beyond the confines of race without granting an unrestricted marriage right, but that such a course would not be without its complexities and difficulties.

Minimum age requirements are, for example, one restriction upon marriage that ought to survive post-*Loving* scrutiny, provided that the minimum age is the same for male and female [26] and, arguably, that disabilities on youthful marriage are removed by the age of eighteen.[27] Minimum age restrictions are constitutionally justified because the age disability is temporary, because it applies equally to all members of society, and because it is obvious that with respect to age some arbitrary line must be drawn. The Court, in fact, has consistently noted that the

---

24. 388 U.S. 1 (1967).

25. *Id.* at 12.

26. Stanton v. Stanton, 421 U.S. 7 (1975), appears to require as much.

27. Although the twenty-sixth amendment of the Constitution secures the vote for 18-year olds in state and federal elections, it is doubtful that the Court would decree a substantive due process right to marry at the same age.

fundamental right to vote can be denied to those under a state-prescribed minimum age.[28] Finally, in light of the frequent failure of early marriages, age restrictions serve as a logical means of controlling the ill effects of youthful marriage on the parties, their offspring, and the public generally.[29]

More troublesome are prohibitions based upon consanguinity and affinity which *permanently* prevent, as did the *Loving* prohibition, desirous parties from marrying. Civil laws against consanguineous marriages, often paralleled by criminal prohibitions of incest, are said to prevent the genetic deformities of inbreeding and to promote family harmony by preventing intrafamily sexual jealousy and rivalry.[30] Both of these ends are clearly legitimate, and the maintenance of family tranquility alone should permit the state to prevent parent-child and brother-sister unions, even if no genetic evidence supports such a bar. It is questionable, however, whether either of the above interests are served by prohibiting, for example, marriages between first cousins. The enammorment of first cousins seems not nearly so traumatic to the family structure as are sexual attractions within the nuclear unit itself. *Loving* would suggest that the state at least ought to bear the burden of establishing a greater than normal likelihood of birth defects arising from marriages of first cousins before being allowed to prohibit such unions.[31]

The Court has not had frequent occasion to test other possible parameters of *Loving*. One recent case,[32] which the Court declined

---

28. *E.g.,* Kramer v. Union Free School Dist., 395 U.S. 621, 626 (1969).

29. *See* Monahan, *Does Age at Marriage Matter in Divorce?,* 32 Soc. Forces 81 (1953); Schoen, *California Divorce Rates by Age at First Marriage and Duration of First Marriage,* 37 J. Marr. & Fam. 548 (1975); Weed, *Age at Marriage as a Factor in State Divorce Rate Differentials,* 11 Demography 361 (1974).

30. *See* I. Herskowitz, Genetics 207-08 (2d ed. 1965).

31. *See* Moore, *A Defense of First-Cousin Marriage,* 10 Clev.-Mar. L. Rev. 136 (1961). Prohibition on marriage by affinity, or among in-laws not related by blood, differs from consanguineous marriages only in that the state interest in preventing deficient offspring is not present. As with consanguineous marriages, however, *Loving* ought to require that any prohibition be shown by the state to have more than a speculative bearing on the goal of easing intrafamilial tension.

32. *In re* Goalen, 30 Utah 2d 27, 512 P.2d 1028 (1973), *cert. denied,* 414 U.S. 1148 (1974).

to hear, involved the request of an inmate in the Utah prison system and one Ann Goalen to marry. The Utah Supreme Court, in an intemperate opinion, held that "the refusal of the warden to permit the marriage ... does not violate petitioner's [Goalen's] constitutional rights or those of her convicted friend." [33] Justice Stewart, joined by Justices Douglas and Brennan, dissented briefly from the denial of certiorari, noting that "[t]he extent to which this right [of marriage] may be diluted for one in prison is something the Court has never decided." [34]

Reversal of the Utah Supreme Court in this instance would not have involved an undue extension of the *Loving* rationale. The claim that marriage would create disciplinary problems in prison ignores the fact that inmates married at the time of incarceration often remain so while in prison. Contact between the inmate and his wife could still be carefully regulated. Indeed, the state's only justification for its denial rested on the premise that an inmate denied the right to marry might behave better in prison so as to obtain early release; thus, the state claimed that the denial "act[ed] as an incentive for the convict to aid in his own rehabilitation." [35] Yet there are sufficient rehabilitative incentives in the form of good-time credits, prison privileges, and the possibility of joining one's spouse full time upon release that would serve the same end without denying the inmate a basic civil right.

A first look thus suggests that the inmate's claim should have been upheld. On a second level, however, the claim raised a volatile issue at the outer perimeters of *Loving* — the very nature of the marriage contract itself. The inmate was capable of deriving psychological pleasure and comfort from the thought of being married; he could, in addition, meet many legal obligations of marriage despite his incarceration.[36] He was incapable, however, of experiencing many conventional aspects of marriage: a shared

---

33. *Id.* at 31, 512 P.2d at 1030-31.
34. 414 U.S. at 1150.
35. *Id.* at 1149.
36. It would make little difference in the administration of tax and inheritance statutes, for example, whether a partner to marriage were an inmate or not.

home, regular and unsupervised sexual access to his partner, and the paternal care of offspring. In this light, the question is whether the state can deny the right to marry to persons who cannot, at least for a while, engage in many of its conventional incidents. With respect to many such persons, the state makes no effort to deny the right: soldiers going off to war and women beyond menopause remain free to marry. The prospect of the soldier's prolonged separation from the common abode or of the woman's childlessness are not thought sufficient to deny such persons the other gratifications of a married state.

The question raised by inmate marriage thus has wider implications. The Court may one day face the question of why a homosexual couple, professing deep mutual affection and willing to assume the requisite legal obligations, should be denied the pleasure, the legitimacy, or even the tax benefits of being married.[37] The fact that homosexuals cannot fulfill our conventional idealizations of marriage — and bear children — may not appear to the Court a permissible reason to proscribe such a union, any more than a state could deny marriage to sterile heterosexuals or to those who chose to remain childless. Likewise wanting is any state interest in banning promiscuous sexual habits, since marriage is presumed to stabilize rather than to diversify sexual activity.

More persuasive, however, would be the state's assertion that granting homosexual affection the regard long accorded heterosexual matrimony would undermine the stability of traditional family life. It is fair to argue that the stability of the nuclear family in America has been fortified by a conception of marriage as an exclusively heterosexual union. There is, moreover, a difference between decriminalizing private, consensual conduct between homosexuals and affirmatively blessing such relationships through marriage. The former step signifies a removal of hostility and an expression of social tolerance that stops

---

37. *See* Comment, *Constitutional Aspects of the Homosexual's Right to a Marriage License,* 12 J. FAM. L. 607 (1973); Note, *The Legality of Homosexual Marriage,* 82 YALE L.J. 573 (1973).

short of approval. The latter requires the state to give elevated and hallowed status to an alternative sexual lifestyle fundamentally at odds with the moral precepts of most Americans. Thus, even if private homosexual conduct were decriminalized as a matter of constitutional right, a freedom to marry would not follow.

The outer limits of *Loving* press still further. One can argue, simplistically, that *Loving* ought to guarantee all consenting adults the right to be bound in civil marriage, whether the combination be one male and two females (polygyny), two males and one female (polyandry), or, for that matter, three males and two females, as long as each additional partner joins a consensual union. Bigamous unions have faced a long history of prohibition, with which the Supreme Court has been closely involved. The Court in *Reynolds v. United States*[38] upheld a federal criminal statute prohibiting bigamous marriages, even against Mormon claims that such marriages were religiously mandated. What was denied then against assertions of free religious exercise is not likely to be sanctioned, close to a century later, as a lifestyle right. Indeed, despite the plea of one recent Justice for reversal of *Reynolds,*[39] the Court has flatly stated that "[s]tatutes making bigamy a crime surely cut into an individual's freedom to associate, but few today seriously claim such statutes violate the First Amendment...."[40]

The case against constitutional protection of bigamy is rather more complicated than the Court suggested. The state interests opposing recognition of bigamous marriages are several. Public administration of tax laws, welfare benefits, estate distribution, and alimony and support payments would become more complex if bigamous marriages were recognized, although such "administrative inconvenience," as the Court is wont to term it, is not normally given great deference when a constitutional right is

---

38. 98 U.S. 145 (1878). *See also* Cleveland v. United States, 329 U.S. 14 (1946); Davis v. Beason, 133 U.S. 333 (1890); Cannon v. United States, 116 U.S. 55 (1885); Murphy v. Ramsey, 114 U.S. 15 (1885).

39. Wisconsin v. Yoder, 406 U.S. 205, 247 (1972) (dissenting in part, Douglas, J.).

40. Paris Adult Theatre I v. Slaton, 413 U.S. 49, 68 n.15 (1973).

involved.[41] The claim that bigamous marriages threaten our traditional monogamous family arrangements might be met with some skepticism, given the strength of the monogamous tradition, the practical difficulty of supporting two or more families simultaneously, and the fact that divorce and successive remarriages are becoming more readily available to one who falls in love with someone other than his or her present spouse. Finally, one may question whether children of bigamous marriages would suffer greater deprivation than those presently living in single-parent homes. And if *Stanley v. Illinois* [42] prohibits a conclusive presumption that a single parent is unfit to raise children, can a ban of bigamous marriages be justified on the conclusive presumption that all bigamous parents are unfit?

The disinclination of the Court to extend *Loving*-type protection beyond the heterosexual and monogamous context suggests that the Court fears extension of constitutional protection to bizarre lifestyle choices would threaten traditional American conceptions of family life. So great, in fact, is our emotional investment in orthodox family life that the rationality of these fears and the reality of the threat may never be fully tested. The final irony of *Loving* is thus laid bare. Too tightly constricted, that decision becomes the repository for our most provincial mores; too freely expanded, it might make traditional marriage a meaningless concept. Unlike universal voting, for example, a universal right for consenting persons of whatever sex and in whatever number to marry could well undermine the very sanctity that led the Court to regard the right to marry as fundamental in the first place.

Loving protected the right to join together in marriage. The constitutional right to be rid of an unwanted spouse was first addressed in *Boddie v. Connecticut.*[43] There the Court held that

---

41. *See, e.g.,* Cleveland Bd. of Educ. v. LaFleur, 414 U.S. 632, 646 (1974); Frontiero v. Richardson, 411 U.S. 677, 690-91 (1973); Reed v. Reed, 404 U.S. 71, 76 (1971). *But cf.* Mathews v. Lucas, 96 S. Ct. 2755 (1976) (upheld validity of administrative convenience as state concern in cases of less than strict scrutiny). *See* note 21 *supra.*

42. 405 U.S. 645 (1972).

43. 401 U.S. 371 (1971).

Connecticut's sixty dollar filing fee in divorce actions was, as applied to indigents, a violation of due process.

It is not readily apparent which current of fourteenth amendment analysis *Boddie* best represents. Justice Harlan's opinion for the Court spoke in terms of procedural due process, claiming that "the State's refusal to admit these appellants to its courts, the sole means in Connecticut for obtaining a divorce, must be regarded as the equivalent of denying them an opportunity to be heard upon their claimed right to a dissolution of their marriages ...." [44] Yet the fit with pre-*Boddie* procedural due process decisions was less than perfect. Those decisions had, as Justice Harlan recognized, "typically involved rights of defendants — not, as here, persons seeking access to the judicial process in the first instance." [45]

The *Boddie* Court also sidestepped an equal protection rationale for the decision that would have required either extending the fundamental right of court access to civil actions,[46] or labeling de facto discriminations against indigents suspect.[47] Instead, Justice Harlan laid the foundation for a substantive due process right to divorce, against which he found the state interests of recouping court costs and of discouraging frivolous actions insufficiently compelling, and the means of promoting those interests through a fee requirement too drastic.[48] Such heightened scrutiny of the burdens placed upon the right to divorce comports with Harlan's willingness elsewhere to discern substantive content in due process.[49] The rhetoric of *Boddie* suggests that the right to divorce

---

44. *Id.* at 380.

45. *Id.* at 375.

46. The right was first thought to have been established for criminal actions in Griffin v. Illinois, 351 U.S. 12 (1956).

47. Every public fee, whether a sales tax, municipal water rate, or tuition charge at a public university, operates as a de facto discrimination on those least able to pay. *See* Douglas v. California, 372 U.S. 353, 361-62 (1963) (dissenting opinion, Harlan, J.).

48. 401 U.S. at 381-82.

49. *E.g.,* Griswold v. Connecticut, 381 U.S. 479, 500-02 (1965) (concurring opinion). For intriguing speculation on how Justice Harlan might have voted in the abortion decisions, see Redlich, *A Black-Harlan Dialogue on Due Process and Equal Protection: Overheard in Heaven and Dedicated to Robert B. McKay,* 50 N.Y.U. L. REV. 20, 33-34 (1975).

has become a necessary, if less than glorious, feature of our "living tradition" of due process; divorce is identified as "the adjustment of a fundamental human relationship" [50] and the method by which "two consenting adults may ... mutually liberate themselves from the constraints of legal obligations that go with marriage, and more fundamentally the prohibition against remarriage ...." [51] A subsequent case, which upheld filing fee requirements, distinguished *Boddie* as turning "on the marital relationship and on the associational interests that surround the establishment and dissolution of that relationship." "On many occasions," the Court noted, "we have recognized the fundamental importance of these interests under our Constitution." [52]

The emergence of divorce as a lifestyle right was sidetracked by *Sosna v. Iowa*,[53] where the Court upheld Iowa's requirement that a person reside one year in the state before bringing an action for divorce against a nonresident. Harmonizing *Sosna* and *Boddie* is difficult. The *Sosna* majority disregarded the heightened standard of scrutiny applied by the *Boddie* Court to a law burdening the right to divorce and reverted to a rational basis test. The Court deferred to Iowa's interests in not becoming a "divorce mill" and in protecting its divorce decrees against collateral attack,[54] even though less drastic means of promoting those interests were available.[55] More important was the *Sosna* Court's purported distinction of *Boddie*. The Connecticut statute, noted the Court, worked a "total deprivation" of divorce opportunities; the Iowa law resulted only in a delay.[56]

One clear implication of the delay-deprivation distinction is that state laws requiring lengthy periods of separation before couples

---

50. 401 U.S. at 383.

51. *Id.* at 376.

52. United States v. Kras, 409 U.S. 434, 444 (1973). *Accord,* Ortwein v. Schwab, 410 U.S. 656 (1973).

53. 419 U.S. 393 (1975).

54. *Id.* at 407.

55. A less drastic alternative would have required that the party seeking divorce prove himself to be a domiciliary of Iowa. *See id.* at 424-27 (dissenting opinion, Marshall, J.).

56. *Id.* at 410. The distinction was critized in Justice Marshall's dissent. *Id.* at 422 n.2.

become eligible for divorce are clearly constitutional. Before *Sosna,* such laws might have been attacked as impermissible burdens upon the right of divorce. What public interest, one might argue, is threatened by the essentially private matter of whether *X* and *Y* remain married? A state interest in the welfare of the children appears insufficient, since unhappy parents can separate anyway, and a life of constant parental friction may harm the child more than divorce. Another state interest in separation periods, that marital relationships not be lightly broken off, can be adequately protected by the obstacles of property settlement, alimony, child support and custody decrees, the embarrassment of public declaration of marital failure, and the emotional cost of terminating so intimate a relationship. At least, one might argue that a six-month waiting period, as opposed to two years, for example, adequately serves any state interest in providing a reasonable period for a couple to reflect upon the prospects of reconciliation.[57]

After *Sosna*, however, such arguments are fanciful. The right of divorce now seems constitutionally inert and much less fundamental than the right of marriage. The present Court would presumably tolerate a two-year separation requirement prior to divorce, while it is hard to imagine any court upholding a two-year waiting or acquaintanceship period prior to marriage. The logical consistency of granting a right freely to enter a relationship that one has no right freely to dissolve is questionable. Confinement in a destructive relationship is arguably as damaging as being prevented from forming a desired union. The destructive impact of the former may indeed be lessened by physical, if not legal, separation, but so may unmarried persons maintain physical, if not legal, togetherness. In fact, state burdens upon divorce might be challenged under *Loving* itself as impermissible infringements upon the right to marry, or to remarry, as the case may be.

Despite such arguments, the Court is well advised to accord the right of marriage a more elevated status than that of divorce. The

---

57. A shortened time period in the context of durational residency requirements for voters was required by the Court in Dunn v. Blumstein, 405 U.S. 330, 348 (1972).

Court's position comports with a persistent assumption in American life that marriages are more easily made than broken. The very conception of marriage as a contract implies that marital unions, once made, may not be trivially or inconsequentially undone. The Court has some obligation to further this conception. If marriage is to exist primarily for the self-gratification of the individual partners, then perhaps it should be permitted to dissolve at the first diminution of affection. If, on the other hand, the state intends it to signify an enduring relationship of reciprocal duty and commitment,[58] as well as of mutual emotional involvement, then a required pause before dissolution should not be unconstitutional. Constitutional law must confront the paradox that making divorce fundamental, and thus readily obtainable, might in the end make marriage seem much less so.

All this is not to say that the right of divorce ought to be stripped of all constitutional protection. The law should not force a person to endure indefinitely a close relationship he or she has come to despise. Divorce is a lifestyle choice of sufficient intimacy to override laws that, at least in comparison with those of sister states, make divorce unduly difficult to obtain.[59] Such a comparative standard may contradict the maxim that "a single courageous State may, if its citizens choose, serve as a laboratory; and try novel social and economic experiments without risk to the rest of the country." [60] Yet the Court has often noted that states may not experiment at will with important human rights.[61]

---

58. The duty seems stronger in the case of families with children, where the state has a heightened interest in the prospects of marital reconciliation. Thus, more stringent divorce laws for married parents than for childless couples might be constitutionally permissible.

59. For example, before being amended in 1966, 1962 N.Y. Laws, c. 313, § 170, permitted divorce only on grounds of adultry. And presently, some states still adhere solely to fault grounds for divorce. E.G., S.D. COMPILED LAWS ANN. § 25-4-2 (1967).

60. New State Ice Co. v. Liebmann, 285 U.S. 262, 311 (1932) (dissenting opinion, Brandeis, J.).

61. The fourteenth amendment incorporation of the federal Bill of Rights proceeds on such an assumption.

B. *The Choices of Procreation and Nonprocreation*

The Supreme Court has afforded further constitutional protection to lifestyle choices customarily associated with, although not limited to, the formation and character of the nuclear family. As one has at least a limited right under *Loving* to marry whom one pleases, so one enjoys constitutional protection in the fundamental decision "whether to bear or beget a child." [62] The leading procreational case, *Skinner v. Oklahoma,*[63] struck down as violative of the equal protection clause an Oklahoma statute that inflicted compulsory sterilization on habitual larcenists but not on habitual embezzlers. Procreational rights have also been protected short of state-imposed incapacitation. In *Cleveland Board of Education v. LaFleur,*[64] the Court found that mandatory maternity leaves for public school teachers after the fourth and fifth months of pregnancy unduly burdened a teacher's decision to bear a child. *LaFleur* may in fact vindicate more than the right to procreate, for it upholds the right of a woman to combine a career with motherhood without unnecessary state restriction of either element.

The right to procreate also suggests a right not to procreate. The latter may have emerged sub silentio in *Griswold,* where the right to use contraceptives seemed secondary to the Court's focus on the "intimate relation of husband and wife." [65] Seven years later, in *Eisenstadt v. Baird,*[66] the Court announced that "whatever the rights of the individual to access to contraceptives may be, the rights must be the same for the unmarried and the married alike." [67] Only in *Roe v. Wade,*[68] however, did the right not to procreate gain firm recognition as a lifestyle decision. In upholding

---

62. Eisenstadt v. Baird, 405 U.S. 438, 453 (1972).
63. 316 U.S. 535 (1942).
64. 414 U.S. 632 (1974).
65. 381 U.S. at 482.
66. 405 U.S. 438 (1972).
67. *Id.* at 453.
68. 410 U.S. 113 (1973).

the right to abortion, the Court recognized that an unwanted child might create a "distressful life and future," with psychological, physical, and financial burdens for the woman concerned.[69] Although *Roe* has been severely criticized,[70] the decision is not an illogical extension of the Court's earlier decisions in matters of intimate association. Indeed, if procreation is to be labeled a constitutional right, it may imply a full freedom of negative choice, in the same sense that marriage implies a full choice not to marry, voting not to vote, and travel to remain at home. For the constitutional right of procreation can hardly be fundamental if one is compelled to exercise it.

The Court has extended the right of procreation rather freely. Procreational choice has been protected for males as well as females,[71] and for unmarried as well as married persons.[72] Moreover, the right may extend beyond the acts of intercourse and childbirth to the parent's right, as yet poorly defined, to make certain lifestyle choices of a practical and spiritual nature for his offspring.[73] Yet clearly this lifestyle choice is not absolute, and labeling procreation "fundamental" creates more difficulties than it resolves. The Court itself has hinted that the right need not be underwritten by the public fisc: it has upheld maximum family-grant ceilings under the AFDC program,[74] as well as a state's exclusion of pregnancy and childbirth expenses from

---

69. *Id.* at 153.

70. *E.g.*, Ely, *The Wages of Crying Wolf: A Comment on Roe v. Wade*, 82 YALE L.J. 920 (1973); Epstein, *Substantive Due Process By Any Other Name: The Abortion Cases*, 1973 SUP. CT. REV. 159. The latter concludes that *Roe* is "symptomatic of the analytical poverty possible in constitutional litigation." *Id.* at 184. *But cf.* Perry, *Abortion, the Public Morals, and the Police Power: The Ethical Function of Substantive Due Process*, 23 U.C.L.A. L. REV. 689 (1976) (*Roe* represents ethical function of following cultural transformations in society).

71. *Compare* Skinner v. Oklahoma, 316 U.S. 535 (1942) (males), *with* Cleveland Bd. of Educ. v. LaFleur, 414 U.S. 632 (1974) (females).

72. *Compare* Griswold v. Connecticut, 381 U.S. 479 (1965) (married), *with* Eisenstadt v. Baird, 405 U.S. 438 (1972) (unmarried).

73. Wisconsin v. Yoder, 406 U.S. 205 (1972); Pierce v. Society of Sisters, 268 U.S. 510 (1925); Meyer v. Nebraska, 262 U.S. 390 (1923).

74. Jefferson v. Hackney, 406 U.S. 535 (1972); Dandridge v. Williams, 397 U.S. 471 (1970).

disability insurance coverage.[75] And Congress undoubtedly could "constitutionally seek to discourage excessive population growth by limiting tax deductions for dependents." [76]

Other purposeful and common burdens are placed on procreation, as there must logically be on any act with consequences so formidable as the creation and introduction into society of a new being. For example, there is yet no legal right to procreate with impunity, for parents in every state may be made liable for child support. Nor is there a right to have sexual relations, much less to procreate, with any willing partner, for criminal and civil sanctions still attach to incest and adultery. Thus procreational choices are, despite their constitutionally protected status, limited by laws that identify marriage with possessive and exclusive sexual relations and that favor the family as the best environment for raising offspring.

The focus of the right to procreate is often less on the sexual act itself than on the gratifications and burdens of raising children. In a society where sexual and procreational choices seem ever more distinct, this emphasis is appropriate. Thus, in *Stanley v. Illinois* [77] the Court spoke of "the interest of a parent in the companionship, care, custody, and management of his or her children," [78] and of the "warm, enduring" bonds between parent and child.[79] This emphasis on the rewards of child-rearing may in time lead to recognition of a fundamental right of adoption or of child custody, insofar as courts may insist that public agency procedures affecting placement of children be both open and fair.[80]

For example, characteristics of prospective adoptive parents such as age, physical resemblance to the child, length of residence in the community, or length of marriage might not be allowed to

---

75. Geduldig v. Aiello, 417 U.S. 484 (1974).

76. Cleveland Bd. of Educ. v. LaFleur, 414 U.S. 632, 651 (1974) (concurring opinion, Powell, J.).

77. 405 U.S. 645 (1972).

78. *Id.* at 651.

79. *Id.* at 652.

80. For an overview of the procedures of adoptive agencies, see CHILD WELFARE LEAGUE OF AMERICA, STANDARDS FOR ADOPTION SERVICE (rev. ed. 1973).

operate as conclusive presumptions of parental unfitness,[81] although an adoptive agency might still be allowed to consider carefully such factors in making a placement. Although the doctrine of conclusive presumption has been repeatedly criticized,[82] it has gained its greatest acceptance in the area of child-bearing and custody rights.[83] Certainly the use of *rebuttable* presumptions would have the advantage of not replacing agency expertise with constitutional command. Thus, the Court might not overturn the use of certain factors as presumptions, but instead might require adoptive agencies to give prospective parents a brief hearing on their application, a statement of reasons for an adverse decision, and, perhaps a limited opportunity to review an initial rejection. Such a course would not be without substantial costs,[84] but the Court may find it more awkward to differentiate the rights of natural parents, whose custody right it has already protected,[85] from the rights of persons seeking the grafications of parenthood through adoption.[86]

As with other lifestyle choices, the right to procreate has been imperfectly analyzed by the Court; only a few of its many implications have been examined.[87] Before the post-World War II

---

81. Professor Clark has argued similarly with respect to religious belief: "Many, if not most, adoptions affect children too young to have formed religious beliefs. With the contemporary trend toward earlier adoption, some children go direct from the hospital to their adoptive parents. It makes little sense to talk of their religion." H. CLARK, LAW OF DOMESTIC RELATIONS 647 (1968).

82. *See* Bezanson, *Some Thoughts on the Emerging Irrebuttable Presumption Doctrine,* 7 IND. L. REV. 644 (1974); Note, *The Irrebuttable Presumption Doctrine in the Supreme Court,* 87 HARV. L. REV. 1534 (1974); Note, *Conclusive Presumption Doctrine: Equal Process or Due Protection?,* 72 MICH. L. REV. 800 (1974).

83. *E.g.,* Stanley v. Illinois, 405 U.S. 645 (1972); Cleveland Bd. of Educ. v. LaFleur, 414 U.S. 632 (1974).

84. For an analysis of the costs of procedural due process, see Wilkinson, *Goss v. Lopez: The Supreme Court As School Superintendent,* 1975 SUP. CT. REV. 25, 52-62.

85. Stanley v. Illinois, 405 U.S. 645 (1972).

86. Parents seeking to adopt a child would, however, be requesting a hearing on an *application* for child custody. The Court to date has only required hearings on a *threatened deprivation* of a liberty or property interest.

87. The whole question of compulsory sterilization, for example, raises complex constitutional problems. *See* Gray, *Compulsory Sterilization in a Free Society:*

baby boom, *Skinner* declared that the right to procreate was "fundamental to the very existence and survival of the race." [88] Certainly, this rationale is not persuasive in an overpopulated world. Although all lifestyle rights are linked to an unusual degree to the moral perceptions of the times, the right to procreate seems peculiarly vulnerable to shifting social and political perceptions. The stature of the right may diminish in a period more concerned with the legitimate dangers of overpopulation, or with the related and volatile question of public support for dependent children. How a future Court might react to such state motivations for burdening the right is unforeseeable.

C. *Extrafamilial Lifestyle Choices*

Each of the constitutional rights discussed above is associated with the creation or dissolution of the nuclear family or, in the case of procreation, with a lifestyle choice that is most often exercised within the formal family unit. A crucial question, however, is whether extrafamilial lifestyle choices of domestic companionship and association likewise merit constitutional protection. The first cases where the Court extended such protection to biological relationships outside the formal family involved discrimination against illegitimate children. The Court forbade states from disadvantaging illegitimates in the recovery of wrongful death [89] and workmen's compensation benefits,[90] and in their right to support from their natural fathers.[91] The primary state interest in burdening illegitimacy — that of expressing disapproval of extrafamilial sexual activity — was held insufficient to support such discrimination.

Choices and Dilemmas, 41 U. CINN. L. REV. 529 (1972); MURDOCK, *Sterilization of the Retarded: A Problem or a Solution?*, 62 CALIF. L. REV. 917 (1974); Note, *Legal Analysis and Population Control: The Problem of Coercion*, 84 HARV. L. REV. 1856 (1971).

88. 316 U.S. at 541.
89. Levy v. Louisiana, 391 U.S. 68 (1968).
90. Weber v. Aetna Cas. & Sur. Co., 406 U.S. 164 (1972).
91. Gomez v. Perez, 409 U.S. 535 (1973). The protection for illegitimates has not, of course, been complete. *See* Mathews v. Lucas, 96 S. Ct. 2755 (1976); Labine v. Vincent, 401 U.S. 532 (1971).

The illegitimacy cases make clear, however, that the Court was more concerned with the penalties suffered by innocent offspring than with the extramarital lifestyle choices of parents.[92] The Court did not intend to disparage support of the formal family unit as a legitimate state end; it was concerned with the means — the stigmatizing of innocent offspring — by which the end was furthered.[93] Yet it is significant that the Court was willing to undertake even this scrutiny of means, given that the state's interest in preserving family stability was at stake.

More dramatic than the illegitimacy cases is *Stanley v. Illinois.* [94] There the petitioner was not the innocent victim of an extramarital liaison, but rather was one who had shunned formal wedlock during eighteen years of friendship with a woman by whom he had fathered three children. Indeed, Chief Justice Burger in dissent suggested that the petitioner's chief interest was "with the loss of the welfare payments he would suffer as a result of the designation of others as guardians of the children." [95] In any event, the petitioner challenged an Illinois procedure under which children of an unwed father automatically became wards of the state upon the death of the mother. In holding that the petitioner was entitled to a hearing on his fitness as a parent before his children were taken from him, the Court rejected the dissent's argument that Illinois was justified in recognizing only "those father-child relationships that arise in the context of family units bound together by legal obligations arising from marriage or from adoption proceedings." [96] The law should not refuse, the Court stated, "to recognize those family relationships unlegitimized by a marriage ceremony . . . . [F]amilial bonds in such cases [are] often

---

92. *But cf.* Glona v. American Guar. & Liab. Ins. Co., 391 U.S. 73 (1968) (construction of statute as barring wrongful death recovery by mother of illegitimate child held violative of equal protection).

93. *See* Weber v. Aetna Cas. & Sur. Co., 406 U.S. 164, 175-76 (1972).

94. 405 U.S. 645 (1972).

95. *Id.* at 667 (dissenting opinion, Burger, C.J.).

96. *Id.* at 663 (dissenting opinion, Burger, C.J.). *See also* New Jersey Welfare Rights Org. v. Cahill, 411 U.S. 619 (1973) (statute limiting benefits to "ceremonially" married parents with children held violative of equal protection).

as warm, enduring, and important as those arising within a more formally organized family unit." [97]

On its face *Stanley* stands for the proposition that a father's personal interest in the raising and companionship of his children is not defeated by his decision to remain unwed. Thus *Stanley* may be seen to protect two lifestyle freedoms: a person may choose both to remain unwed and to raise children, and the law may not force a choice between the two. Read in such a manner, *Stanley* may suggest, in an adoption setting, that an agency may not declare a man or woman ineligible as an adoptive parent solely because he or she is single. Read even more expansively, *Stanley* may suggest that the raising of children in a commune may not be declared impermissible by the state solely on the ground that the three, four, or ten adults most directly responsible for a child's upbringing are not united by formal ties of marriage. It is true, of course, that prospective adoptive parents and adults in a commune are not all, as was Peter Stanley, the natural parents of the child. Yet it may be questioned whether the lack of a blood relationship should override *Stanley's* basic premise that the absence of a legal marriage may not alone disqualify otherwise capable adults from child-raising and custody.

Such thoughts seem to be journeys in fantasy. The context of the *Stanley* decision suggests that its implications for extrafamilial lifestyle choices must be cautiously interpreted. To begin with, the Court may have been persuaded to the petitioner's claim of parental fitness by his personal circumstances. He had "lived with the two children whose custody [was] challenged all their lives, and ... [had] supported them." [98] In addition, the Court was seemingly moved by the fact that Illinois forced unwed fathers to forfeit their offspring, yet permitted "married fathers — whether divorced, widowed, or separated — and mothers — even if unwed — the benefit of the presumption that they [were] fit to raise their children." [99] Finally, Stanley's victory was a partial one, for he won

---

97. 405 U.S. at 651-52.
98. *Id.* at 650 n.4.
99. *Id.* at 647.

only the right to a hearing on his parental fitness under ground rules as yet unclear. A state may not, after *Stanley,* use unwed fatherhood as conclusive evidence of unfitness, but, conceivably, it may still establish a rebuttable presumption that such a father is unfit.[100] And if an unwed father is not as easily identified and located as was the petitioner in *Stanley,* the state may yet be able to terminate the right of parenthood without any hearing at all.[101]

In *Stanley,* a biological relationship buttressed the claim of domestic companionship. The Court has also heard cases where unrelated persons asserted a right to share a home. Such claims confront the Court with a dilemma: should the right of domestic companionship be extended to protect those whose living arrangements are not "domestic" in the conventional sense of the word?

The home occupies a special place in constitutional law. It has been protected against the groundless intrusion of the state; it is a sanctuary where our most intimate feelings may flower. Sharing home life with others has helped serve humanity's most elemental needs: to fulfill sexual desires, to provide a place to raise a family, and to ward off spiritual desolation through close companionship with others. For some, sharing a home may mean a "doubling up against the adversities of poverty" [102] or the taking in and ministering to a stranger, or a simple coming together of "persons bound by profession, love, friendship, religious or political affiliation." [103] But while the home may serve as the locus of rewarding and enduring human relationships, it may also be the site of the most corrosive and destructive ones. In the latter instances the question, as we have seen, is whether a household has a constitutional right to dissolve as well as to form.

---

100. *See id.* at 657 n.9; Bezanson, *supra* note 82, at 651-52.

101 *See* 405 U.S. at 657 n.9.

102. Department of Agriculture v. Moreno, 413 U.S. 528, 542 (1973) (concurring opinion, Douglas, J.).

103. Village of Belle Terre v. Boraas, 416 U.S. 1, 16 (1974) (dissenting opinion, Marshall, J.).

The earliest case involving the right of household association for unrelated individuals was *Department of Agriculture v. Moreno.*[104] At issue in *Moreno* was a 1971 amendment to the Food Stamp Act that excluded from the food stamp program any household whose members were not all related. The *Moreno* claimants included a fifty-six-year-old diabetic woman who lived with a female friend and the latter's three children, and two women sharing living expenses together in an apartment so that the daughter of one might attend a nearby school for the deaf. Wishing to assist such people, yet concerned to avoid creating a broad constitutional right to live with whom one pleases, the Court merely declared the "unrelated person" amendment to be "wholly without any rational basis." [105]

The Court's evasion did not go unnoticed. Justice Rehnquist, in dissent, found it rational for Congress to conclude that funding only family units "provides a guarantee which is not provided by households containing unrelated individuals that the household exists for some purpose other than to collect federal food stamps." [106] Given such a rational basis for the family unit preference, it is difficult to resist the conclusion that *Moreno* represents the "unacknowledged application" of a more stringent standard of scrutiny.[107] The elevated scrutiny most likely was triggered by the Court's awareness, as Justice Douglas put it, of an associational right of "[p]eople who are desperately poor but unrelated [to] come together and join hands with the aim better to combat the crises of poverty." [108] The Court's opinion itself may subtly support such a lifestyle right, for it condemns the amendment as an exclusion of *"only* those persons who are so desperately in need of aid that they cannot even afford to alter their living arrangements so as to retain their eligibility." [109]

---

104. 413 U.S. 528 (1973).
105. *Id.* at 538.
106. *Id.* at 546 (dissenting opinion, Rehnquist, J.).
107. *The Supreme Court, 1972 Term,* 87 HARV. L. REV. 1, 133 (1973).
108. 413 U.S. at 543 (concurring opinion, Douglas, J.).
109. *Id.* at 538.

The issue of associational choice for unrelated persons was more directly confronted one term after *Moreno* in *Village of Belle Terre v. Boraas.*[110] Unsuccessfully challenged in *Belle Terre* was a village zoning ordinance restricting land use to one-family dwellings and to household units containing not more than two unrelated persons. Justice Marshall, in a vigorous dissent, characterized the ordinance as permitting "any number of persons related by blood or marriage, be it two or twenty, to live in a single household, but [limiting] to two the number of unrelated persons ... who can occupy a single home."[111] The village, Marshall argued, had "in effect ... acted to fence out those individuals whose choice of lifestyle differs from that of its current residents."[112] Nevertheless, in upholding the ordinance the Court appeared to condone, at least tacitly, the preservation of social and class homogeneity as a valid zoning goal:

> A quiet place where yards are wide, people few, and motor vehicles restricted are legitimate guidelines in a land-use project addressed to family needs.... It is ample to lay out zones where family values, youth values, and the blessing of quiet seclusion and clear air make the area a sanctuary for people.[113]

Moreno and *Belle Terre* are not easily reconciled. Both cases concerned laws that burdened the right of domestic association of unrelated persons. Although rational basis scrutiny was ostensibly employed in both cases, the scrutiny in *Belle Terre* was of the traditional toothless kind, while that in *Moreno* was of the modern, more interventionist variety.[114] In upholding the zoning ordinance in *Belle Terre,* the Court observed that it was dealing with "economic and social legislation,"[115] where legislative judgment routinely merits deference. Yet the statute overturned in *Moreno*

---

110. 416 U.S. 1 (1974).
111. *Id.* at 16 (dissenting opinion, Marshall, J.).
112. *Id.* at 16-17 (dissenting opinion, Marshall, J.).
113. *Id.* at 9.
114. *See generally* Gunther, *The Supreme Court, 1971 Term — Foreword: In Search of Evolving Doctrine on a Changing Court: A Model for a Newer Equal Protection,* 86 HARV. L. REV. 1 (1972).
115. 416 U.S. at 8.

was likewise "economic and social" and involved the area of public appropriations, where the Court has tolerated burdens even upon well-established lifestyle rights.[116] So ambivalent an approach to the associational rights of unrelated persons defies easy explanation. Perhaps the Court in *Belle Terre* simply recoiled from a full investigation of exclusionary zoning practices, which fairly bristle not only with burdens upon lifestyle rights but with difficult questions of wealth discrimination.[117] Or perhaps the difference in the two cases reflects nothing more than the fact that in *Moreno* the plaintiffs were representatives of the handicapped poor, while in *Belle Terre* they were six college students.

The Court's performance in *Moreno* and *Belle Terre* is disappointing not only in its inconsistency but in its failure even to address the central issue pervading both cases: the extent to which unrelated persons have a constitutional right to one another's personal, domestic companionship. A starting point for such an inquiry is *Stanley v. Georgia,*[118] which upheld the right of an adult to possess and view obscene materials in the privacy of his home. Courts may extend *Stanley* to the right to share the home with whom one pleases, for the home furthers the pleasures of intimate companionship as much as it permits the solitary viewing of obscene materials.[119] Yet it is likewise clear that *Stanley*'s

---

116. *See e.g.,* Geduldig v. Aiello, 417 U.S. 484 (1974); Jefferson v. Hackney, 406 U.S. 535 (1972); Dandridge v. Williams, 397 U.S. 471 (1970). *See generally* Wilkinson, *The Supreme Court, The Equal Protection Clause, and The Three Faces of Constitutional Equality,* 61 VA. L. REV. 945, 1005-17 (1975).

117. *See* Sager, *Tight Little Islands: Exclusionary Zoning, Equal Protection, and the Indigent,* 21 STAN. L. REV. 767, 780-98 (1969).

Voiding the ordinance in Belle Terre need not have involved the Court in the zoning thicket. That ordinance imposed a direct prohibition on unorthodox lifestyles. All zoning laws are not so blunt. Minimum lot and minimum house size ordinances, for example, may make it more difficult for persons of certain lifestyles to associate, but they do not constitute outright prohibitions on unconventional associations.

118. 394 U.S. 557 (1969).

119. One reading of *Stanley* might suggest that the petitioner was protected only because he exercised a consitutional right, *i.e.,* the first amendment "right to receive information and ideas." *Id.* at 564. The Court's emphasis on the special nature of the home suggests, however, that it was at least as much the setting as the nature of the activity that prompted protection. This interpretation prevailed in Paris Adult Theater I v. Slaton, 413 U.S. 49, 65-66 (1973).

protection of the home as a haven is not unlimited, for the Court would not uphold a constitutional right to murder in the home, to emit raucous noise, or to possess narcotics, illegal firearms, stolen goods, or even such quantities of obscene materials as are inconsistent with personal possession and use.[120]

Courts may ultimately hold *Stanley* to represent the proposition that one enjoys a constitutional right to do anything in one's home that does not harm others. In other words, the state would have no right to prohibit persons from sharing a home, absent some showing of community harm.

A standard of community harm is, however, more easily stated than applied. Assuming that a state or township wishes to regulate population density — and surely such regulation would serve a legitimate interest by reducing the imposition on the community of more guests and friends, more noise and arguments, more comings and goings, and more cars, motorcycles, household trash, and the like — the state could do so by flatly prohibiting more than two, or three, or whatever number of adults from sharing the same dwelling unit. Thus, the state could satisfy its legitimate interest in regulating population density — itself reflective of lifestyle values — without using means that so broadly discriminate against the lifestyle choices of unrelated persons.[121]

The real issue in *Moreno* and *Belle Terre* leads to other problems. Legal discrimination against households of unrelated persons often has as its chief object the regulation of sexual activity outside marriage.[122] Yet a major failing of the "unrelated persons" provision in *Moreno* lay in the burden it placed on even the elderly poor of the same sex who shared joint living arrangements.[123] Thus, the lesson of *Moreno* may be that extramarital sexual

---

120. *See* 394 U.S. at 468 n.11.

121. *See* Village of Belle Terre v. Boraas, 416 U.S. 1, 19 (1974) (dissenting opinion, Marshall, J.).

122. The Court in *Moreno* noted that a central purpose of the food stamp amendment may have been to exclude "hippie communes" from participation in the program. It then declared that purpose impermissible. 413 U.S. at 534.

123. In this respect, the ordinance in *Belle Terre* may have seemed less punitive to the Court; it at least permitted two unrelated persons to share a home. *See* 416 U.S. at 8.

activity cannot be reached by such overbroad means as a blanket discrimination against unrelated households. Direct prohibition of extramarital sexual activity, however, is another subject.

II. PERSONAL SEXUAL CONDUCT

Sex in American society has traditionally been identified with heterosexuality, with monogamous marriage and the nuclear family. Outside these contexts, personal sexual conduct has been regularly tabooed, through the use of law as well as of other social sanctions. The emerging constitutional dilemmas in the area of sexual conduct involve challenges to those taboos. The challenges, taken together, raise the question whether intimate sexual relations in forms not traditionally sanctioned are constitutionally protected. Should certain values associated with sexual conduct — love, pleasure, intimacy, mutual interdependence — be given the protection of the Constitution, or is that protection reserved for other values — childrearing, monogamous marriage, heterosexuality, adulthood — with which intimate sex has customarily been linked?

The current lifestyle choices spawning controversy in the area of sexual conduct, then, are choices to engage in unconventional sexual relations. Such modern lifestyle choices result in what many legislatures have termed "unnatural" sexual practices. Because of the intimate nature of sexual conduct, "unnatural" sexual practices have not been regularly analyzed or even legislatively particularized; hence an implicit legislative association has been made. A form of intimate sex (homosexuality) has been thought "unnatural" and therefore outlawed; practices (fellatio or cunnilingus) identified with that form have similarly been prohibited, even in their heterosexual variations.[124]

---

124. A typical example is Virginia's statute, VA. CODE § 18.1-212 (Cum. Supp. 1974): Crimes against nature. — If any person shall carnally know in any manner any brute animal, or carnally know any male or female person by the anus or by or with the mouth, or voluntarily submit to such carnal knowledge, he or she shall be guilty of a felony and shall be confined in the penitentiary not less than one year nor more than three years.

Current sexual conduct cases typically involve violations of sodomy statutes. The following discussion seeks to show that recent decisions on sodomitic conduct are not merely delineating the scope of the constitutional right of privacy, but are confronting a more basic issue. That issue is whether the state has an interest in confining intimate sexual conduct to "acceptable" contexts, or whether sexual conduct is to be constitutionally protected regardless of the unpopular, offensive, or "unnatural" form it may take.

A. *The Doctrinal Framework: The Evolving Meanings of Constitutional Privacy*

The courts have regularly analyzed sodomy in terms of constitutional privacy, a concept that in the course of its evolution has embraced three distinct ideas. One is protection from intrusion, summed up in the maxim that a man's home is his castle. This concept of privacy derives from the fourth amendment, which forbids the state's invasion of one's home, office, automobile, person, or effects absent the issuance of a warrant or, in carefully specified situations, a law enforcement officer's determination of probable cause.

A second concept of privacy might best be labeled seclusion. In *Griswold* and in *Stanley v. Georgia,* the Court attempted to link privacy to intimate places, such as the marital bedroom or, more generally, the home. *Stanley* left open the question of the limits of this zone of privacy, and later decisions, notably *Paris Adult Theater I v. Slaton,*[125] have confined the protected zone to the home. This has resulted in some anomalies, such as a distinction between obscene books read in the home (protected) and obscene books in transit from one home to another or read on a wilderness vacation (apparently unprotected).[126] The boundaries of constitutional privacy as seclusion are thus indeterminate, but it is clear that some peculiarly intimate places associated with an

---

125. 413 U.S. 49 (1973).
126. *See id.* at 66.

individual's private life are protected simply because the individual has a right "to be let alone." [127]

Moreover, the concept of seclusion implies protected acts as well as protected places. The concept suggests that one can, in seclusion, engage in activities that would be offensive and even illegal outside a protected, private zone. But the locus of the activity is not dispositive: protection for activity within the home is, as previously noted, far from absolute.[128] Equally important in the *Griswold* and *Stanley* results was the Court's conviction that the acts in question — sexual intercourse and reading obscene literature — had a relatively low potential for working harm beyond the secluded zone.

Meanwhile still another *Griswold* source of privacy — the marital relationship — was undergoing refinement, and a third meaning of constitutional privacy, as personal autonomy, began to emerge. *Griswold* had tied privacy, or at least sexual privacy, to approved relationships. Unmarried persons might not be able to assert privacy claims since they could not identify themselves with the "sacred" institution of marriage.[129] *Eisenstadt v. Baird*[130] undercut any such reasoning by requiring that access to contraceptives, however defined, "be the same for the unmarried and married alike." "[T]he marital couple," noted the *Eisenstadt* Court, "is not an independent entity with a mind and heart of its own, but an association of two individuals each with a separate intellectual and emotional makeup."[131] Hence *Eisenstadt* freed the right of privacy from the marital context and seemed to liberate the right from any preoccupation with place. Privacy, the Court hinted, might mean not only freedom from intrusion or a right to seclusion, but freedom to make decisions about certain personal matters. "If the right of privacy means anything, it is the right of

---

127. Olmstead v. United States, 277 U.S. 438, 478 (1928) (dissenting opinion, Brandeis, J.).
128. *See* text accompanying notes 118-21 *supra*.
129. *See* 381 U.S. at 485-86.
130. 405 U.S. 438, 453 (1972).
131. *Id.* (emphasis added).

the *individual* ... to be free from unwarranted governmental intrusion into matters so fundamentally affecting a person as the decision whether to bear or beget a child." [132]

Roe v. Wade,[133] the Court's principal abortion decision, expanded the *Eisenstadt* meaning of privacy as autonomy to uphold a limited constitutional right to decide to have an abortion. Again, privacy was not confined to freedom from intrusion or to the *Stanley v. Georgia* meaning of seclusion: abortions take place in public hospitals, and participants are not subjected to searches and seizures. What is private about a decision to have an abortion, the Court argued in *Roe,* is the element of personal choice. The decision to have an abortion is intimate because it reflects the special concerns of one individual, not because it occurs in a private place. Hence privacy in the *Eisenstadt-Roe* sense primarily means freedom to make personal choices about one's intimate affairs. Yet the *Roe* Court stopped short of completely equating privacy with autonomy. "[I]t is not clear to us," the Court stated, "that the claim ... that one has an unlimited right to do with one's body as one pleases bears a close relationship to the right of privacy previously articulated in the Court's decisions." [134]

The evolving meanings of constitutional privacy reflect the growing confidence of the Court in the privacy concept. Intrusion, the earliest meaning, derived from rights explicitly protected by the fourth amendment. Seclusion, a broader meaning, then increasingly overshadowed intrusion as privacy rights became more entrenched. Finally, protection for a right of autonomy developed out of the Court's recognition that the right to privacy was a doctrine which had taken hold of the public's imagination: it did not make its appearance until seven years after *Griswold.*

Clashes between the divergent meanings of privacy seem inevitable, especially in the area of sexual conduct. On some occasions a personal choice to engage in intimate sex simultaneously affirms the values of seclusion and autonomy,

---

132. *Id.* (emphasis in original.)
133. 410 U.S. 113 (1973).
134. *Id.* at 154.

thereby creating a privacy right of considerable strength; but at other times that choice invades the seclusion and restricts the autonomy of others. Forcible rape in public involves neither seclusion nor autonomy values and is obviously not protected. Seclusion without autonomy is likewise insufficient. Rape in a private residence may be sufficiently secluded, but of course forfeits protection in its invasion of the victim's autonomy. Autonomy without seclusion may also be unprotected: a consensual sexual act in public invades the seclusion rights of onlookers. Only private, consensual sexual behavior taps both strains of the Court's recent privacy cases and, in so doing, creates a substantial lifestyle right against which various state interests must be carefully weighed.

B. *Judicial Confrontation of Taboos: Some Recent Sodomy Cases*

Recent challenges to state sodomy statutes on privacy grounds illustrate the need to unravel the various meanings of constitutional privacy. Most such statutes flatly outlaw "unnatural" or "deviant" sex; they fail to create exemptions for classes of persons or specific conditions. Fellatio, cunnilingus, and other forms of sodomy are banned whether engaged in openly or in seclusion, and whether engaged in by consenting married adults or by other persons. In light of the evolving meanings of privacy, such statutes seem vulnerable to constitutional challenge. They restrict personal decisions about intimate matters, and their prohibitions reach into areas, such as the home, associated with seclusion. In short, they intrude into the very core of constitutional privacy.

Essential to a blanket prohibition of "unnatural" sexual conduct on moral grounds is a firm and generally shared belief that the prohibited conduct is in fact immoral. When such a general understanding exists, reasons justifying suppression of certain conduct leap to mind. Murder is prohibited because it takes another life, and to take another life without privilege is considered immoral. Arguably, a comparable understanding does not exist to justify the prohibition of "unnatural" sexual conduct. Indeed, one consequence of the more extended and open discussion of sexuality characterizing American life in the 1960's and 1970's has been a greater collective doubt as to which sexual practices are "unnatural" and why. The reflex leap of faith that allows American legislators to punish murder under their police power does not exist for private consensual sexual conduct. Consequently, the state interest in prohibiting "unnatural" sexual practices simply as a regulation of public morality needs particularization.[135]

A significant "unnatural" sexual practice case is *Doe v. Commonwealth's Attorney.*[136] There a group of male homosexuals sued in federal district court for declaratory and injunctive relief, arguing that Virginia's sodomy statute[137] was unconstitutional as applied to consensual homosexual acts performed in private by adult males. The case was first heard by a three-judge panel that voted two to one to sustain the statute, both on its face and as applied to the petitioners.

The majority opinion asserted that state legislation regulating personal sexual conduct is constitutionally suspect only when it "trespasses upon the privacy of the incidents of marriage, upon the sanctity of the home, or upon the nurture of family life."[138] To support this assertion the majority announced that *Griswold* was controlling,[139] yet it failed even to mention the possible extensions of *Griswold* in *Stanley v. Georgia, Eisenstadt,* and *Roe.* The majority then quoted at length[140] from dicta in a dissent by Justice Harlan in *Poe v. Ullman,*[141] where Harlan had argued that homosexuality could be criminally prosecuted even if privately practiced, and closed by recapitulating the long ancestry of sodomy legislation. In short, the majority confined permissible sexual conduct to contexts — marriage, home, family — where it had

---

135. *See* W. BARNETT, SEXUAL FREEDOM AND THE CONSTITUTION 103-08 (1973).
136. 403 F. Supp. 1199 (E.D. Va. 1975), *aff'd mem.,* 425 U.S. 901 (1976).
137. *See* note 124 *supra.*
138. 403 F. Supp. at 1200.
139. *Id.* at 1200-01.
140. *Id.* at 1201-02.
141. 367 U.S. 497, 546, 552-53 (1961).

traditionally been accepted, and demonstrated no awareness whatsoever of the evolving meanings of constitutional privacy.

An emerging constitutional quandary — whether after *Stanley*, *Eisenstadt*, and *Roe*, a right existed to engage in private sexual practices outside the traditional marital context — was thus assumed away by the *Doe* majority. Judge Merhige, however, argued in dissent that *Roe* and *Eisenstadt* demonstrated that "intimate personal decisions or private matters of substantial importance to the well-being of the individuals involved are protected by the Due Process Clause," and that "[t]he right to select consenting adult sexual partners must be considered within this category." [142] Merhige maintained that "fundamental rights of such an intimate facet of an individual's life as sex, absent circumstances warranting intrusion by the state, are to be respected." [143] This was especially true where the activity took place within "the private dwelling of a citizen." [144]

The Supreme Court, on direct appeal, summarily affirmed. Justices Brennan, Marshall, and Stevens voted in favor of noting probable jurisdiction and setting the case for oral argument. In some respects, however, the procedural posture of the case made it an unattractive one for a full-blown decision. At most a threat of prosecution had taken place; no circuit court had considered the case; and the complexity of the issues involved had been aired only preliminarily in Merhige's dissent. Given these circumstances, we suggest that the decision of the Court to summarily affirm, although an adjudication on the merits, should not be taken as an indication that the Court is prepared to sustain sodomy statutes in all situations. Rarely does the Supreme Court understand a prior summary affirmance to preclude subsequent plenary consideration of an important issue. Nor can significant issues of constitutional law be definitively resolved in so peremptory a fashion.

Nonetheless, *Doe v. Commonwealth's Attorney* does establish the proposition that state efforts to prohibit private, consensual

---

142. 403 F. Supp. at 1204.
143. *Id.* at 1205.
144. *Id.*

homosexual conduct are constitutionally permissible, despite *Stanley v. Georgia, Eisenstadt,* and *Roe.* Pending more thorough Supreme Court review, lower courts are bound to that proposition. Unfortunately, the Court announced its decision without any accompanying rationale. If a lifestyle right for consenting adults to engage in intimate sex free from governmental interference is taken seriously, a rationale for the *Doe* result will not be easy to formulate. Consent assumes that neither partner has imposed his sexual inclination on the other; adulthood assumes that any special interest the state might have in the sexual protection of minors is absent; seclusion assumes that others are not exposed to the practices. Thus, an autonomy right to freely engage in sex combines with a seclusion right not to be disturbed in the private practice of intimate sex to produce a constitutional lifestyle claim of some power.

Despite these considerations, state interests of significant strength support a prohibition of homosexuality. First, a state may be interested in discouraging public behavior that gives widespread offense. This legitimate interest cannot be dismissed by simply announcing, as did Judge Merhige, that constitutionally permissible homosexual conduct is limited to private settings.[145] Sexual liaisons necessarily involve some public contact, especially at their inception. Heterosexuals meet in public places, share each other's company, flirt, and indulge in various displays of affection; homosexuals do as much. To equate sexual conduct wholly with private, intimate acts is to compartmentalize sexual encounters in an unrealistic fashion.

Thus, constitutional protection for secluded homosexual acts might well produce a greater public exposure to homosexuality in general. Criminalizing homosexual acts has certainly not succeeded in suppressing all public display of homosexual affection; conversely, decriminalization would not eliminate the social disapprobation that causes many homosexuals to conceal their sexual preference. But it is safe to assume that removal of criminal sanctions from private acts would lead to more open

---

145. *See id.* at 1204-05.

homosexuality, both because homosexuality would no longer expose one to criminal penalties, and because of the greater degree of tolerance that the removal would imply.

Stanley v. Georgia and *United States v. Reidel* [146] suggest one answer to the state interest in avoiding increased public exposure. Taken together, these cases hold that although possession of obscenity in the home is protected, the preconditions to such possession, such as distribution of obscenity, are not. By analogy, the state's interest in saving its citizens public offense could be protected by obliging the state to respect secluded activity, while permitting arrest even for mild public displays of homosexual affection. Such a suggestion, however, is fraught with difficulty. Law enforcement officials might well be unable to differentiate milder forms of homosexual affection from normal expressions of friendship and camaraderie. The *Stanley* "solution" would thus perpetuate the sporadic and volatile street enforcement that exists under present law. [147]

Moreover, it is debatable whether the state interest in protecting the public from offense is alone sufficient to support the *Doe* result. Surely the state may continue to prohibit the assault on sensibilities that would be caused by public performance of the most intimate homosexual acts, just as it now possesses that unquestioned power with respect to heterosexual acts. And, it will be argued by some that public sensibilities would adjust to the milder sight of homosexuals holding hands or walking arm-in-arm just as easily as those sensibilities have adjusted to the presence of long hair, "suggestive" dancing, and other contemporary sights that once were considered shocking.

The very fact of such adjustment, however, brings us to consideration of a final state concern. The most threatening aspect of homosexuality is its potential to become a viable alternative to heterosexual intimacy. This argument is premised upon the belief that the practice of an alternative mode of sexual relations will

---

146. 402 U.S. 351 (1971).

147. *See* H. PACKER, THE LIMITS OF THE CRIMINAL SANCTION 286-95 (1968).

inimically affect the predominant mode. Thus, any recognition of a constitutional right to practice homosexuality would undermine the value of heterosexuality and the institutions and practices — conventional marriage and childrearing — associated with it.

This state concern, in our view, should not be minimized. The nuclear, heterosexual family is charged with several of society's most essential functions. It has served as an important means of educating the young; it has often provided economic support and psychological comfort to family members; and it has operated as the unit upon which basic governmental policies in such matters as taxation, conscription, and inheritance have been based. Family life has been a central unifying experience throughout American society. Preserving the strength of this basic, organic unit is a central and legitimate end of the police power. The state ought to be concerned that if allegiance to traditional family arrangements declines, society as a whole may well suffer.

Disapproving sexual conduct that might threaten traditional family life is arguably a means related to this end. Criminal law provides perhaps the strongest vehicle for expressing such disapproval. On the other hand, it is not the only vehicle for enforcing conventional mores; community disapproval of errant behavior is arguably a more potent enforcement mechanism than the law. Moreover, the criminal law's effectiveness will be reduced if social practices and attitudes run counter to its underlying assumptions. Yet criminalization, whatever its lack of perfection as a deterrent, is a dramatic symbol of social disapprobation.[148] Decriminalization means, quite literally, the removal of disapproval, the recasting of the state's posture as one of neutrality.

In seeking to regulate homosexuality, the state takes as a basic premise that social and legal attitudes play an important and interdependent role in the individual's formation of his or her sexual destiny. A shift on the part of the law from opposition to neutrality arguably makes homosexuality appear a more

---

148. *See id.* at 42-43.

acceptable sexual lifestyle, particularly to younger persons whose sexual preferences are as yet unformed. Young people form their sexual identity partly on the basis of models they see in society.[149] If homosexual behavior is legalized, and thus partly legitimized, an adolescent may question whether he or she should "choose" heterosexuality. At the time their sexual feelings begin to develop, many young people have more interests in common with members of their own sex; sexual attraction rather than genuine interest often first draws adolescents to members of the opposite sex. If society accorded more legitimacy to expressions of homosexual attraction, attachment to the opposite sex might be postponed or diverted for some time, perhaps until after the establishment of sexual patterns that would hamper development of traditional heterosexual family relationships. For those persons who eventually choose the heterosexual model, the existence of conflicting models might provide further sexual tension destructive to the traditional marital unit.

Thus, *Doe v. Commonwealth's Attorney* ultimately presents a significant lifestyle claim balanced against at least one important countervailing state interest. The question raised by *Doe* is a difficult one: Should the state be constitutionally required to abandon an ancient sanction, when abandonment might in time lead to increasing, although statistically unpredictable, defections from heterosexual behavior and traditional family life?[150] On the answer to this last question the authors have been unable to agree. Mr. Wilkinson would uphold the state's interest in the preservation of the traditional family; Mr. White would desire stronger empirical proof that the state interest is truly put in jeopardy by homosexual practices amoung consenting adults. Both authors acknowledge the intuitive elements in their judgments.

The balancing analysis we suggest for *Doe*-type cases is appropriate in other instances where the concept of seclusion is

---

149. *See* Acosta, *Etiology and Treatment of Homosexuality: A Review,* 4 ARCHIVES SEXUAL BEHAVIOR 9, 16-18 (1975).

150. *See* G. HUGHES, THE CONSCIENCE OF THE COURTS 23 (1975) for a view that the defections would not prove substantial.

involved. Such a case was *Lovisi v. Slayton*,[151] a recent Fourth Circuit decision. The question in *Lovisi* was whether a married couple could be constitutionally prosecuted for consensual sodomy in the presence of a third party.

Aldo and Margaret Lovisi, a married couple, were convicted of sodomy under the same Virginia statute at issue in *Doe*. Prosecution of the Lovisis came when one of their daughters brought an erotic photograph to elementary school and claimed that her home was filled with similar pictures. A properly executed search revealed many such photographs, including one depicting Margaret Lovisi performing fellatio on her husband. A third party, one Earl Romeo Dunn, was present when the photographs were taken and had engaged in sexual activity with the Lovisis.[152]

In a habeas corpus proceeding, the Lovisis challenged the constitutionality of Virginia's statute as applied to their sodomitic conduct with each other. The district court found that *Griswold, Eisenstadt,* and *Roe* secured protection of individual sexuality, but held that the Lovisis had waived that protection by allowing their activity to become public through careless exposure of the photographs.[153] The Fourth Circuit, splitting five to three, affirmed, but used a different rationale. Although the court recognized a right of privacy that embraced "marital intimacies," protection dissolved when "a married couple admit[ted] strangers as onlookers" to their sexual activities.[154] The test for protection was apparently secrecy-in-fact: the presence of "observed 'peeping Toms'" or "chance acquaintances" would be considered "accept[ed]," and constitutional protection would thereby be lost.[155] In addition, the Fourth Circuit majority read *Doe v. Commonwealth's Attorney* as "necessarily confin[ing] the constitutionally protected right of privacy to heterosexual conduct, probably even that only within the marital relationship." [156]

---

151. 539 F.2d 349 (4th Cir. 1976), *aff'g* 363 F. Supp. 620 (E.D. Va. 1973).

152. There was sharp controversy throughout the case over whether the pictures were taken by the daughters or by a self-timing camera. *See* 363 F. Supp. at 622.

153. *Id.* at 627.

154. 539 F.2d at 351.

155. *Id.*

156. *Id.* at 352 addendum.

In two dissenting opinions, three judges in *Lovisi* found constitutional immunity for consensual sodomy practiced by a married couple, "whether practiced in secret or in the presence of a third party or a camera."[157] "Privacy," one of the dissenters maintained, was a freedom "not limited to the conduct of persons in private." It was better described as "personal autonomy" or "the right to be let alone."[158]

Lovisi thus illustrates how sexual conduct cases reveal the multiple meanings — sometimes reinforcing and sometimes opposing — of the concept of constitutional privacy. An autonomous lifestyle choice to engage in sodomy sometimes combines with a choice to be left alone. A consensual sodomitic act by a married couple in their bedroom presents a paradigm instance where the two privacies reinforce one another. On other occasions, a choice to practice sodomy is deliberately not secluded in the conventional sense. It involves more than two persons; it takes place outside the home; it may even take place in the presence of strangers. In such instances, the autonomy of the actors may conflict with the seclusion rights of others. The two currently dominant meanings of privacy collide.

In *Doe*, of course, the strength of the lifestyle right derived from the convergence of the autonomy and seclusion aspects of privacy. In *Lovisi,* the constitutional claim is not self-evident: the autonomy dimension of privacy is present, but seclusion is more doubtful. The leading cases are of limited help in determining the meaning of seclusion. Both *Griswold* and *Stanley v. Georgia* involved unquestioned instances of secluded activity. The Court depicted Stanley as "sitting alone in his own house," [159] and the Court in *Griswold,* in discussing the privacy of the marital bedroom, surely did not contemplate the presence of a third party.

The scope of the seclusion aspect of sexual privacy remains uncertain. It obviously does not extend to sexual activity on a

---

157. *Id.* (dissenting opinion, Winter, J.)
158. *Id.* at 356 (dissenting opinion, Craven, J.).
159. 394 U.S. at 565.

streetcorner, or sexual activity before an unwilling viewer dragged into the marital bedroom. Nor do seclusion rights hinge solely on the willingness of the observer; a couple clearly could not, after *Paris Adult Theatre I v. Slaton*,[160] offer admittance to every member of the public who wished to see them perform sexual intercourse. The really difficult questions of seclusion come in cases of selective viewing in intimate places. Should a *Stanley*-type petitioner, for example, be able to claim seclusion rights for a dinner party at which guests are invited to view obscene slides? Should protection for sexual seclusion rights turn on the presence of two, and only two, consenting persons?

Before *Eisenstadt,* courts might have seized upon the presence of a third-party observer as evidence that the marital sexual intimacy of *Griswold* had been converted into something more akin to sport, and thus have denied constitutional protection. After *Eisenstadt*, however, it is uncertain whether the Court regards protected sexual intimacy as a function of marriage or as a function of a prescribed number of persons.[161] It is debatable whether the Lovisis lost the seclusion half of their right to privacy the moment third-party observers were admitted to their bedroom solely because such observers were likely to spread word of the Lovisis' sexual peccadilloes.[162] But we believe that the Lovisis did forfeit their seclusion right when they took and carelessly stored photographs of their activity. Photographs are, of course, a way of preserving and reliving pleasant experiences, of which marital sex is surely one. Yet any couple that fails to take precautions against so vivid and durable a record of their intimate relations

---

160. 413 U.S. 49 (1973).

161. Presumably large numbers of persons engaging in sexual activity within a home could be regulated under a properly drawn breach of the peace and public nuisance statute.

162. The Fourth Circuit believed that the Lovisis could "converse with friends or write books about their sexual relations, recounting in explicit detail their own intimacies and techniques, [and still] remain protected in their expectation of privacy within their own bedroom." 539 F.2d at 351. This concession seems inconsistent with the Fourth Circuit's conclusion that the presence of a third party onlooker alone destroyed the Lovisis' seclusion rights.

reaching the hands of others risks losing the seclusion right important to any lifestyle claim of sexual privacy. Thus, the district court more correctly pinpointed the rationale for the decision: "that snapshots taken by the Lovisis were not kept at home in such a way that the children would be denied access to them." [163]

Notwithstanding the difficulties of determining the limits of seclusion, we believe it to be a necessary and indispensable part of a lifestyle claim of sexual privacy. Not only may nonparticipants be offended by the debasement of intimacy suggested by public sexual acts, but they may also take offense at the acts themselves. And if public offense is certain, seclusion becomes a necessary condition for the legitimate practice of "unnatural" sex. Even if one takes seriously the right of an individual freely to choose his sexual practices, that right must end where it infringes upon the right of others to reject as offensive the mere observation of those practices. If the autonomous choices of some are not to invade the autonomous choices of others, seclusion appears necessary.[164]

Finally, it must be reemphasized that even though a constitutional right to private sexual activity may exist, it still must be weighed, as in *Doe v. Commonwealth's Attorney,* against countervailing state interests. Adultery is one type of sexual activity in which seclusion and autonomy rights may combine, but which the state may still regulate to further its interest in the preservation of the traditional family. Clarification of the values at stake in the area of sexual conduct can only come, we suggest, when taboos are examined with a view toward understanding the social assumptions on which they rest, and when those assumptions are scrutinized in practice, so that corrosiveness is distinguished from unconventionality, and harms are differentiated from fears. The balancing process we have proposed

---

163. 363 F. Supp. at 627. The district court noted testimony by an investigative officer that " 'thousands'of photographs were to be found all over the house" and "were freely available throughout the house to whomever lived there." In such circumstances the court concluded that the Lovisis had "relinquished their right to privacy in the performance of these acts." *Id.*

164. *See* Knowles & Poorkaj, *Attitudes and Behavior on Viewing Sexual Activities in Public Places,* 58 J. Soc. & Soc. Research 130 (1973-74).

seeks, above all, a forthright discussion of matters heretofore treated euphemistically.

III. PERSONAL APPEARANCE: HAIR STYLE AND DRESS

Kelley v. Johnson [165] tested and upheld the validity of a police department regulation limiting the length of policemen's hair. In dissent, Justice Marshall argued that the "liberty" protected by the fourteenth amendment encompassed "matters of personal appearance." [166] Such a reading, Marshall suggested, was consistent with "the values of privacy, self-identity, autonomy, and personal integrity that ... the Constitution was designed to protect." [167] After *Roe, Stanley v. Georgia,* and *Griswold,* Marshall maintained, the right of a citizen "to choose his own personal appearance" was unquestionable; historically it had "simply been taken for granted.[168]

In contrast, Justice Rehnquist's opinion for the majority seemed less certain about the existence of a right to choose one's personal appearance. Rehnquist found the asserted appearance liberty to be distinguishable from the liberties protected by the *Griswold-Stanley v. Illinois-Eisenstadt-Roe* line of cases: those cases involved choices "with respect to certain basic matters of procreation, marriage, and family life." [169] Whether a choice of appearance was comparable, Rehnquist maintained, was a question on which previous cases offered "little, if any, guidance." [170] Indeed, he characterized appearance claims as involving "only the more general contours of the [fourteenth amendment's] substantive liberty interest," [171] and ultimately held, for the Court, that a member of a uniformed civilian service had no fourteenth amendment right to wear his hair as he chose.

---

165. 425 U.S. 238 (1976).
166. *Id.* at 250 (quoting majority opinion at 244).
167. *Id.* at 251.
168. *Id.*
169. *Id.* at 244.
170. *Id.*
171. *Id.* at 245.

Kelley highlights the threshold difficulties in subjecting personal appearance choices to constitutional analysis. The contours of an "appearance right" remain uncertain; the context for protection of that right, if it exists, has not been delineated; the entire area lacks evaluative criteria. In the courts, impressionistic judgments have predominated, ranging from Justice Black's belief that long-hair cases were "purely local affairs," [172] to Justice Marshall's association of appearance "with the historically recognized right of 'every individual to the possession and control of his own person,' ... and ... with 'the right to be let alone ...' ".[173] The following discussion examines the sources of constitutional protection for the appearance right and the diverse context in which claims have recently surfaced. We end by proposing a framework for substantive due process analysis of appearance issues.

A. *The Doctrinal Background*

One intriguing aspect of the history of the United States Constitution has been the emergence of constitutional protection for various liberties at times when, for complex cultural reasons, political suppression of those liberties was considered desirable. For many years after the repeal of the Alien and Sedition Acts,[174] free speech issues were seldom raised in the courts; only in the early twentieth century, when fears of radical European ideologies and anxieties associated with World War I produced anti-subversive legislation, did the first amendment begin to take on its modern protective significance.[175] If one believes, with Justice Marshall, that the assumption that "a man should have a right to wear his hat if he pleased" [176] was so widely shared at the

---

172. Karr v. Schmidt, 401 U.S. 1201, 1203 (1971).

173. 425 U.S. at 253 (citations omitted).

174. Act of June 25, 1798, ch. 58.1 Stat. 570; Act of July 6, 1798, ch. 66, 1 Stat. 577; Act of July 14, 1798, ch. 74, 1 Stat. 596.

175. *See generally* Z. CHAFEE, FREE SEECH IN THE UNITED STATES (1941).

176. 425 U.S. at 252 (quoting I. BRANT, THE BILL OF RIGHTS 54 (1965), in turn quoting Rep. Sedgwick, August 13, 1787) (emphasis deleted).

time the Constitution was drafted that statement of an appearance right would have belabored the obvious,[177] an analogy to the history of free speech is suggested. Pressures to define a freedom to choose one's personal appearance have surfaced only when that freedom was threatened. Such threats have occurred when certain appearances were thought subversive. This perceived subversion has been a consequence of the association of unconventional hair and dress styles with political protest. If modern protection for free speech is a child of World War I, potential protection for appearance choices is largely the offspring of the Vietnam years.

Two Warren Court doctrinal innovations are among the sources of constitutional protection for appearance choices. First is the Warren Court's retreat, late in its history, from the dichotomy between first amendment "speech" and "conduct." In cases such as *Cohen v. California*[178] and *Tinker v. Des Moines School District*,[179] the Court protected expressions — the wearing of a sweatshirt and the wearing of an arm band — which were meant to communicate political ideas, but which were not "pure" speech. Although the Court's rationale in *Cohen* and *Tinker* stressed the content of the messages conveyed, the cases could be read to extend first amendment protection to symbolic speech as manifested in dress.

Second, in *Griswold* the Warren Court developed a "penumbral rights" theory that allowed the Court to derive constitutional rights from emanations from textually designated rights. *Griswold* furthered the potential emergence of an appearance right in two respects. Substantively, the decision created protection for privacy, which in the Burger Court has taken on a meaning of personal autonomy, a value that arguably should encompass appearance choices. And methodologically, Justice Douglas' *Griswold* opinion appeared to free constitutional protection from the limitation of explicit textual designation. If judges could protect marital sexual

---

177. *Id.* at 251-52.
178. 403 U.S. 15 (1971).
179. 393 U.S. 503 (1969).

privacy even though the Constitution did not single it out for protection, why could they not protect other privacies as well?

In its effort to secure certain privacy-derived protections, the Burger Court created another, and perhaps more powerful, potential source of constitutional protection for appearance choices. One textual means of protecting privacy lay in labeling the right a "liberty" interest protected by the fourteenth amendment. The *Griswold* Court had been unwilling to exercise that option: judicial glosses on "liberty," it said, revived the discredited technique of substantive due process.[180] But by *Roe v. Wade* the Burger Court was prepared to concede, for the purposes of candor or clarity, that a limited right to have an abortion was a fourteenth amendment "liberty." [181]

The revival of substantive due process in the privacy cases of the seventies reminds us that although substantive readings of the due process clause have gone in and out of fashion, a desire for some judicial freedom from the restraints of constitutional literalism has always existed. Substantive due process, ordered liberty,[182] fundamental fairness,[183] and other phrases associated with judicial glosses on the Constitution have sought to respond to a problem inherent in an enumerated Bill of Rights: How shall rights too obvious to be enumerated receive constitutional protection if their obviousness evaporates? Personal appearance choices pose a recent concrete example.[184]

B. *A "Liberty" of Hair Style: Due Process Analysis*

There is, of course, no designation of personal appearance as a "liberty" encompassed in the due process clause. The Court in *Kelley* assumed arguendo that such a liberty exists, but held that

---

180. 381 U.S. at 481-82.

181. 410 U.S. at 153.

182. Palko v. Connecticut, 302 U.S. 319, 325 (1937).

183. Duncan v. Louisiana, 391 U.S. 145, 172 (1968) (dissenting opinion, Harlan, J.).

184. *See generally* Grey, *Do We have An Unwritten Constitution?*, 27 STAN. L. REV. 703 (1975).

it could be infringed. The Court's rationale was, as we shall argue, flawed in giving such short shrift to the constitutional significance of appearance choices. To introduce our argument it is helpful to consider initially a more fully reasoned appearance case: the Fifth Circuit's en banc decision in *Karr v. Schmidt,*[185] which held that a Texas school board's regulation restricting the length of male students' hair violated no constitutionally protected right.

Although student "long-hair" cases are now diminishing in number, they remain an important benchmark in the debate over lifestyle rights. The majority in *Karr* seemed concerned about two aspects of such cases: the burden they placed on the federal courts and the relatively trivial nature of the claims they raised. "[N]either the Constitution nor the federal judiciary," the majority announced, "were conceived to be keepers of the national conscience in every matter great and small." [186] Concerned that different federal judges might interpret the reasonableness of hair-length regulations differently, anxious to avoid court congestion, and unable to conceive appearance claims as rising to the dignity of a great constitutional right, the Fifth Circuit laid down a per se rule that school board hair-length regulations were constitutionally valid. In the process the court considered and rejected each of the potential sources of constitutional protection for appearance choices.

Of the various sources reviewed by the Fifth Circuit, only substantive liberty under the due process clause received extended treatment. The majority dismissed the relevance of the first amendment to appearance cases by asserting that the wearing of long hair did not have "sufficient communicative content" to invoke first amendment protection.[187] Karr, a student affected by the regulation, had protested its enforcement because he "like[d] [his] hair long." [188] Nor was a penumbral analysis persuasive.[189]

---

185. 460 F.2d 609 (5th Cir.), *cert. denied,* 409 U.S. 989 (1972).
186. *Id.* at 618.
187. *Id.* at 613.
188. *Id.* at 614.
189. *Id.* at 613.

Karr antedated *Eisenstadt* and *Roe,* and the Fifth Circuit read *Griswold* as being confined to intrusions into the home.[190] Substantive due process arguments, however, raised more substantial issues for the court. But fourteenth amendment liberties, it felt, could be "ranked in a spectrum of importance," at one end of which were "the great liberties" of speech, religion, association, and marital privacy, and at the other "lesser liberties." [191]

The right of a male student to choose his hair length was a "lesser" liberty. It was such because, first, cropped hair eventually grows back and thus "the interference with liberty [was] a temporary and relatively inconsequential one"; [192] second, school boards enact numerous other regulations equally restricting the conduct of students, from parking rules to lunch privileges; and third, the federal courts ought not interfere with the management of local school affairs except where truly "fundamental liberties" were involved.[193]

The Fifth Circuit's triviality point is more easily stated than explained. If the triviality argument reflects a subconscious judicial downgrading of the rights of mere high school students, by far the most frequent long-hair plaintiffs,[194] that downgrading is unsupportable. If, however, it is the choice that is trivial, as opposed to those who exercise it, one wonders why school officials need bother to regulate the matter at all. Finally, in any ordering of appearance rights, a choice of hairstyle may rank among the most important, for unlike uniforms and other prescribed modes of dress, hair length follows a student from school into private life. Student hair-length regulations, then, may illustrate the presumptuousness of officials who interpret their power to regulate part of a person's daily regimen as a mandate to regulate the whole.

---

190. *Id.* at 614.
191. *Id.*
192. *Id.* at 615 (footnote omitted).
193. *Id.* at 616.
194. *See* Note, *On Privacy: Constitutional Protection for Personal Liberty,* 48 N.Y.U.L. REV. 670, 764 (1973).

Moreover, if labeling the hairstyle right trivial is a shorthand way of declaring that the appearance right as a whole lacks importance, the court's position is unacceptable. The values furthered by protection of personal appearance choices are quite similar to the values protected by the right of privacy — individual dignity, freedom of choice, and personal autonomy and integrity. Appearance, like speech, is a chief medium of self-expression that involves important choices about how we wish to project ourselves and be perceived by others. To link appearance with privacy and speech values is not, of course, to require similar constitutional treatment. It does imply, however, that we deal with a substantive constitutional liberty that "may reflect, sustain, and nourish ... personality," [195] and the repression of which may, in the words of Judge Wisdom, "smac[k] of the exaltation of organization over member, unit over component, and state over individual," forcing an "unwilling complier ... to submerge his individuality in the 'undistracting' mass." [196]

Therefore freedom to choose one's manner of appearance, like the freedoms discussed earlier, is a lifestyle right of some significance. And it is clear that at least one member of the *Kelley* majority proceeded on that assumption. Justice Powell, in his concurrence, found "no negative implication in the [majority] opinion with respect to a liberty interest within the Fourteenth Amendment as to matters of personal appearance." [197] Yet acknowledging a lifestyle right of appearance is no more than a first step in constitutional analysis under the due process clause. The second is to ascertain the context in which the choice has been made: What class of persons seeks to exercise the right, and what reasons has government advanced to regulate it? We focus, then, on the different contexts of *Karr* and *Kelley:* Should a choice of hairstyle be protected for students but not for policemen?

In *Karr* the school board argued that regulation of hair-length would serve the goals of inhibiting "classroom distraction,"

---

195. Kelley v. Johnson, 425 U.S. 238, 250 (1976) (dissenting opinion, Marshall, J.).
196. Karr v. Schmidt, 460 F.2d 609, 621 (5th Cir. 1972) (dissenting opinion).
197. 425 U.S. at 249.

avoiding fights between long- and short-haired students, and eliminating potential health and safety hazards.[198] The Fifth Circuit called these "legitimate objectives," [199] clearly within the state's police power. But proper due process analysis hardly stops with the abstract finding of a legitimate state interest. Where regulation impinges on a constitutional right — here, that of appearance — the means chosen by the state ought significantly to further the announced state objectives.[200]

Forcing only male students to cut their hair is an impermissible means of achieving the state interests at stake. Long hair on males is intrinsically no less healthy and no more distracting and disruptive of classroom work than long hair on females. Any difference is the result of custom alone; men, and not women, are traditionally short-haired. If conformity to custom is the unarticulated rationale for hair-length regulations in schools, it seems insufficient to justify the limitation on individual choice. The rationale suggests the untenable: that mere unconventionality of appearance is enough to bring the state's regulatory apparatus into play.

Finally, it must not be forgotten that the context of the student hair-length cases is the public school system. Certainly order and discipline are values that public education in America seeks to foster, and conventionality and uniformity may be fairly thought prerequisites to the furtherance of those values. But American education prizes other values as well: diversity, individuality, and self-expression.[201] If public education aims to teach children how to adjust to a changing and pluralistic society, then schools ought to foster independence as well as instill respect for authority. Thus schools are distinguishable from professions, such as the military, where conformity to an authoritarian ethos may be the overriding goal.

---

198. 460 F.2d at 617.

199. *Id.*

200. Although serious scrutiny of means has thus far been utilized by the Court primarily in equal protection decisions, it seems equally necessary in cases which involve a significant due process right. *See* Gunther, *supra* note 114, at 42.

201. *See* Tinker v. Des Moines School Dist., 393 U.S. 503, 511 (1969).

The student long-hair cases thus pit values fostered by protection of appearance choices against articulated state interests not served by the chosen means of regulation and unarticulated premises about the function of education in America that seem half-truths at best. There are, of course, stages of dress or undress that would quickly activate the state interest in orderly classroom instruction, and degrees of personal uncleanliness that would raise legitimate health concerns. But absent a showing of some definite relationship between hair-length regulations and legitimate educational goals, the regulations should not be permitted to stand.

Assuming one adopts the above analysis for student cases, should hair-length cases involving policemen and firemen, like *Kelley* and *Quinn v. Muscare*,[202] be analogized to the student decisions? The first step in the due process analysis is necessarily the same: appearance choices are liberties against the government, presumptively immune from regulation. But the second step reveals a different context for the appearance claim. Policemen and firemen, unlike students, are professionals who, because of their hazardous working conditions, must number group discipline and order among their paramount goals. The ambiguities of freedom versus order and self-assertion versus socialization that were identified with education are not found in professions that must necessarily be more authoritarian.

Conventionality of dress and appearance can therefore be more easily linked to the need for discipline, order, and efficiency. Uniformity of appearance may convey to the public and instill in the profession itself a more alert and rigorous approach to the job. But although such factors may make the state's case stronger, they do not end the constitutional inquiry. One may concede that some restrictions on the appearance of policemen and firemen are justifiable, without necessarily conceding that meticulous hair regulations, on and off the job, are constitutionally valid.

For example, suppose a policeman accepted uniform standards for hair length, but demanded a short-haired wig while on duty.

---

202. 425 U.S. 560 (1976).

Arguably, a wig would not sufficiently implement the profession's goals. Those goals go beyond mere functional convenience; they involve the promotion of a sense of professional homogeneity and togetherness, as symbolized by uniformity of appearance. The state might argue that wigs would convey the impression that uniformity of appearance was no more than sham and pretense, thereby undermining professional homogeneity and morale.

The *Kelley* and *Quinn* results may rest on a further, unexpressed premise. The Court perhaps assumed that when an adult chooses a profession, he accepts, within certain limits, restrictions on his behavior that flow from his professional status. Appearance restrictions, in varying degrees, are part of almost every profession. Where without undue strain they can be tied to a profession's basic functional imperatives, as in the case of police and firemen, they become part of the costs and benefits one weighs in choosing an occupation. It is possible, of course, that many persons do not "choose" to become firemen or policemen, but rather act from economic necessity, that they do not have perfect information about restrictions on their lifestyle when they make that choice, and that they therefore stand in roughly the same position as students, who up to a certain age do not choose to attend school. These arguments may have some validity in individual cases, but we think that a consciousness of reasonable lifestyle restriction inheres in most occupational choices.

Kelley and *Quinn* are thus defensible results: the hairstyle choices of policemen and firemen raise different issues from those of students. Yet the *Kelley* opinion provided only the most cryptic rationale for evaluating lifestyle choices of appearances. The majority found the policeman's occupational status "highly significant," [203] and referred to Suffolk County's "recognition" that "similarity in appearance of police officers is desirable." [204] From these offhand statements the majority moved swiftly to conclude: "Certainly . . . the claim of a member of a uniformed

---

203. 425 U.S. at 245.
204. *Id.* at 248.

civilian service based on the 'liberty' interest protected by the Fourteenth Amendment [need not] necessarily be treated for constitutional purposes the same as a similar claim by a member of the general public." [205] And thus Suffolk County's long-hair regulation for policemen "did not violate any right guaranteed . . . by the Fourteenth Amendment." [206]

We wish the *Kelley* majority had developed its reasoning, especially since lower courts, notwithstanding Justice Powell's caveat, may treat the case as foreclosing constitutional protection for appearance claims. The Court in *Kelley* ultimately applied a "no-scrutiny" rational basis test to the police hair-length regulations,[207] partly on the ground that they involved the exercise of authority "unquestionably at the core of the State's police power." [208] But why and to what extent this supine rational basis standard will be used to test other burdens upon appearance choices [209] are questions the Court must soon clarify.

C. *The Appearance Overtones of "Unfettered Discretion" Cases*

Although the Court has only reluctantly involved itself in hair-length cases, it has extended constitutional protection to persons whose dress and demeanor may trigger discretionary character judgments by state officials charged with arrest or detention duties. The Court has thus far cast these "unfettered discretion" [210] decisions primarily in terms of the vagueness and overbreadth doctrines, which fail to reflect the analytical heart of the cases. The principal operational difficulty with vague or

---

205. *Id.* at 248-49.

206. *Id.* at 249.

207. The Court cited earlier opinions applying a rational basis standard to state economic regulation, especially Day-Brite Lighting, Inc. v. Missouri, 342 U.S. 421 (1952) and Williamson v. Lee Optical Co., 348 U.S. 483 (1955). 425 U.S. at 247-48.

208. 425 U.S. at 247.

209. There is some fragmentary evidence that the Court will extend this standard. In Ham v. South Carolina, 409 U.S. 524, 527-28 (1973), the Court readily approved a state voir dire procedure that precluded questions to prospective jurors about bias against bearded defendants.

210. The phrase is from Justice Douglas' opinion for the Court in Papachristou v. City of Jacksonville, 405 U.S. 156, 168 (1972).

overbroad ordinances is not the lack of notice to detained parties — few people read state or municipal ordinances — but rather is the opportunity such ordinances create for arbitrary judgments by the police. In particular, ordinances with terms such as "common night walker,"[211] "annoying,"[212] or "suspicious"[213] invite the police to make subjective associations of conduct, including appearance, with criminality. Given the brevity of most police contacts with citizens who stand or walk on city streets, a citizen's appearance may play a substantial part in forming an officer's judgment about the citizen's "suspiciousness" or "annoying" qualities. Speaking for the Court in *Papachristou v. City of Jacksonville,*[214] Justice Douglas suggested that imprecise municipal ordinances may require "nonconformists ... to comport themselves according to the lifestyle deemed appropriate by the ... police."[215]

The appearance aspect of "unfettered discretion" cases underscores one of the basic rationales for protection of appearance choices. Americans purport to believe that a healthy society tolerates a multiplicity of viewpoints and lifestyles. The values of diversity and nonconformity have been identified as buttressing the first amendment. Hence, unconventional appearance choices test our commitment to the preservation of those values outside the area of speech. In a case overturning on grounds of statutory vagueness the conviction of a Massachusetts resident for "treat[ing] contemptuously" the American flag by wearing it sewn to the seat of his trousers,[216] the Court observed that "casual treatment of the flag in many contexts has become a widespread contemporary phenomenon," and that "[f]lag wearing in a day of relaxed clothing styles may be simply for adornment .... "[217] The Court refused to reflexively equate

---

211. *See id.* at 156 n.1.
212. Coates v. City of Cincinnati, 402 U.S. 611, 611 (1971).
213. Palmer v. City of Euclid, 402 U.S. 544, 544 (1971).
214. 405 U.S. 156 (1972).
215. *Id.* at 170.
216. Smith v. Goguen, 415 U.S. 566, 568 (1974).
217. *Id.* at 574.

unorthodox dress with contemptuous treatment of an important national symbol.

In sum, recent "unfettered discretion" cases suggest that appearance choices may no longer be restricted without precise articulation of the reasons for so doing. Although the decisions rest on the vagueness doctrine and mention appearance rights only in passing, they demonstrate at least an embryonic concern for the protection of appearance choices themselves. Significant testing of the appearance dimension of these cases awaits challenge to a more specific ordinance, not open to a vagueness attack. Such a challenge would present a situation analogous to the hair-length cases, and should, in our view, invoke the substantive due process analysis advanced therein.

D. The Current Stature of Appearance "Liberties"

Constitutional protection for appearance choices remains in an undeveloped state. First, there are doctrinal difficulties. Appearance choices are more conduct than pure speech and communicate with insufficient precision and consistency to invoke fruitful first amendment analysis. Substantive due process, in our view the most satisfactory doctrinal setting for appearance cases, has not been in fashion for much of the twentieth century and places special pressures on a judiciary that aspires to impartiality and neutrality. Thus, a credible, textual rationale for protection — a crucial element in effective constitutional adjudication — is not readily available.

Second, appearance choices have been burdened with the implicit judgment, made by judges from Justice Black [218] to the majority in *Karr,* that their stature as liberties is simply not very high; that if they are rights, they are de minimis. Our discussion has emphasized that this offhand treatment needs revision, despite the generally accepted feeling that personal modes of dress and styles of hair are of less than cosmic importance. Like the other lifestyle choices analyzed in this Article, appearance choices reflect a

---

218. *See* Karr v. Schmidt, 401 U.S. 1201 (1971).

dimension of our individuality. If respect for the uniqueness of each person is a core value of American civilization, some degree of constitutional protection for personal appearance choices should follow.

IV. CONSTITUTIONAL PROTECTION FOR PERSONAL LIFESTYLES: AN OVERVIEW

A. *The Case for Creation of a Constitutional Lifestyle Right*

A basic question throughout this Article is why the Constitution should protect lifestyle choices at all. In *Griswold* and *Roe* the Court sensed that lifestyle values deserved constitutional protection but failed to articulate persuasively an analytical basis for conferring it. Providing the necessary articulation, however, is no easy task; lifestyle choices, as such, receive no explicit protection in the Constitution. As a result the Court has invoked the vaguest and most nebulous of constitutional doctrines and provisions — substantive due process,[219] the Bill of Rights' penumbras,[220] and the ninth amendment [221] — to safeguard them.

Although lifestyle freedoms are not expressly safeguarded, we believe that the spirit of the Constitution operates to protect them. We are aware of the historic dangers that attend judicial departure from specific constitutional mandates. Judging by inference from constitutional provisions, or from the Constitution as a whole, has plunged the Court into difficulties in the past.[222] Notwithstanding textual and institutional difficulties, judicial recognition of lifestyle freedoms as due process liberties better serves the basic purposes of the Constitution than dismissal of them.

---

219. Roe v. Wade, 410 U.S. 113, 152-56 (1973).

220. Griswold v. Connecticut, 381 U.S. 479, 483 (1965) (Douglas, J.).

221. *Id.* at 488 (concurring opinion, Goldberg, J.). The three-judge district court in Roe v. Wade, 314 F. Supp. 1217 (N.D. Tex. 1970), also rested its decision upon a ninth amendment rationale. *See id.* at 1219.

222. *E.g.,* Lochner v. New York, 198 U.S. 45 (1905). For an interesting attempt to vindicate rights of "personhood" without reviving the drawbacks of the *Lochner* approach, see Craven, *Personhood: The Right to be Let Alone,* 1976 DUKE L.J. 699.

A compelling mission of the Constitution has been to protect sanctuaries of individual behavior from the hand of the state. The choice of religion and the advocacy of ideas have been deemed matters outside the state's concern; [223] the privacy of the home [224] and the inner sanctity of the mind [225] have been guarded against governmental intrusion; the individual is protected from cruel and unusual punishment,[226] and indeed from any criminal punishment at all unless guarantees such as the right to counsel,[227] to jury trial,[228] and to confrontation [229] are observed. In this context, the Bill of Rights teaches that human dignity is meaningless without a proper measure of personal freedom from governmental interference.

That dignity is seriously diminished unless it includes those choices that most express our uniqueness and individuality. By our style of dress and appearance, our personal associations, our manner of speech, and our sexual behavior we seek to express our uniqueness as humans and to realize our destinies as individual beings. This does not mean that these expressions must be free from all governmental regulation, any more than is our freedom of speech under the first amendment. It does mean that as a starting point of analysis, courts should acknowledge their constitutionally protected status. For nothing is more central to self realization and fulfillment than these very personal decisions. If the concept of individuality is to have meaning, these choices must be protected.

There is another important reason for constitutional shelter of lifestyle choices. The Constitution, as interpreted by the Supreme

---

223. "If there is any fixed star in our constitutional constellation, it is that no official, high or petty, can prescribe what shall be orthodox in politics, nationalism, religion, or other matters of opinion or force citizens to confess by word or act their faith therein." West Virginia Bd. of Educ. v. Barnette, 319 U.S. 624, 642 (1943).
224. Mapp v. Ohio, 367 U.S. 643 (1961).
225. Malloy v. Hogan, 378 U.S. 1 (1964).
226. Weems v. United States, 217 U.S. 349 (1910).
227. Gideon v. Wainwright, 372 U.S. 335 (1963).
228. Duncan v. Louisiana, 391 U.S. 145 (1968).
229. Pointer v. Texas, 380 U.S. 400 (1965).

Court, has increasingly served to protect powerless minorities — casualties of a majoritarian political process. There are, to be sure, distinct and important limits to the Court's role as protector of the powerless. But from the initial *Carolene Products*[230] formulation of "discrete and insular minorities,"[231] to the Warren and Burger Courts' protection of blacks,[232] indigents,[233] illegitimates,[234] resident aliens,[235] criminal suspects,[236] and disenfranchised[237] and underenfranchised voters,[238] solicitude for the disadvantaged has been a central theme in Supreme Court jurisprudence. Similarly, the subjects of lifestyle protection are likely to be persons unable to gain redress through the political process. A person of conventional tastes, having reputable friends, a courteous vocabulary, and unobtrusive appearance, is for those very reasons not often considered offensive to the state in his lifestyle choices. Obloquy is reserved for those whose tastes are unconventional, whose tongues are thought sharp or vile, and whose dress or behavior seems irregular or shocking. Yet it is just such persons who give a constitution its mettle, and without whom human freedom would be limited to choices of which prevailing majorities approve.

It would, in fact, be incongruous for an American Supreme Court to be insensitive to diversity in lifestyle choices. From its origins America has contained a variety of races and peoples, with a multiplicity of thoughts and habits. Different ethnic and racial origins have invariably bred different ways of living. Protection for diverse lifestyles thus conforms to the character of a heterogeneous nation. Moreover, conventional roles are increasingly being discarded. Current lifestyles, for example, seem

---

230. United States v. Carolene Prods. Co., 304 U.S. 144, 152-54 (1938).
231. *Id.* at 152 n. 4.
232. *E.g.,* Brown v. Board of Educ., 347 U.S. 483 (1954).
233. *E.g.,* Boddie v. Connecticut, 401 U.S. 371 (1971).
234. *E.g.,* Levy v. Louisiana, 391 U.S. 68 (1968).
235. *E.g.,* Graham v. Richardson, 403 U.S. 365 (1971).
236. *E.g.,* Miranda v. Arizona, 384 U.S. 436 (1966).
237. *E.g.,* Harper v. Virginia Bd. of Elections, 383 U.S. 663 (1966).
238. *E.g.,* Reynolds v. Sims, 377 U.S. 533 (1964).

less the product of one's sex or race or social background and more the result of personal preference. The Court has been an important part of this process. The higher standard of equal protection applied to suspect classes has the stated purpose of freeing persons from the bondage of racial and other stereotyping and of encouraging them to seek their destinies as individual human beings.[239] For the Court to deny protection to unorthodox lifestyles would appear at odds with much of its modern history.

The purposes served by protection of lifestyle choices are also strikingly similar to those served by the first amendment. In personal behavior as well as in ideas, protection of individual choices preserves dissent from the tastes of the majority. Like protection of first amendment values, lifestyle protection attests to society's faith that a free market in lifestyles, as well as in ideas, best aids the individual in developing his own identity. And, as with the first amendment, lifestyle protection may require defense of the most idiosyncratic among us in order to discourage, at the outer perimeter, the state's natural inclination to compel its citizens to think and behave in orthodox patterns.

Thus, there appear to us general considerations, touching the very heart of the constitutional process, that argue for judicial recognition of a lifestyle right. It is imperative, however, that so amorphous a concept as "lifestyle choice" be defined more precisely, a task to which we now turn.

B. *The Limits of the Lifestyle Concept*

The existence of persuasive reasons for the creation of a constitutional lifestyle right suggests a further elusive question. Which of our personal choices are to qualify for constitutional protection? These choices are literally endless: we decide where to live, what career to pursue, whether to seek a college degree, whether to indulge in tobacco, alcohol, or drugs, whether to buy

---

239. This was especially evident in Frontiero v. Richardson, 411 U.S. 677 (1973), where four members of the Court argued in favor of making sex a suspect class. See also such "middle-level" scrutiny cases as Reed v. Reed, 404 U.S. 71 (1971), and Stanton v. Stanton, 421 U.S. 7 (1975).

or ride a motorcycle, or, to take even more common examples, whether to jaywalk, go to the movies, or buy chocolate or vanilla ice cream. All decisions at least potentially involve an assertion of personal freedom at the expense of the state's power to regulate. It is necessary, therefore, to consider why our discussion of lifestyle freedom should be limited to choices of domestic companionship, sexual conduct, and personal appearance, in the face of so many other individual decisions of comparable or greater magnitude.

We begin by noting that the individual lifestyle choices surveyed in the preceding sections need not constitute an exhaustive list. For example, an additional lifestyle freedom, which the Court appears to have recognized, is that of "personally flavored" speech. Thus, we may express our ideas and may do so in whatever manner and idiom we choose. In the leading decision, *Cohen v. California*,[240] the Court decided that to protect emotive vernacular such as "Fuck the Draft" was to safeguard the verbal lifestyles of America's countercultures.[241] "Indeed," the Court in classic lifestyle terms observed, "we think it is largely because governmental officials cannot make principled distinctions in this area that the Constitution leaves matters of taste and style so largely to the individual."[242] Under *Cohen* and its progeny,[243] freedom of idiomatic expression has prevailed over the state's interest in protecting the sensibilities of bystanders[244] and over everything, in fact, save a narrow public power to prevent the imminent outbreak of street violence.[245]

---

240. 403 U.S. 15 (1971).

241. Note the view of Professor Haiman that *Cohen* involved a verbal lifestyle that rose in popularity as "establishment figures revealed the fear and abhorrence produced in them by such words." Haiman, *How Much of Our Speech Is Free?*, 2 Civ. LIB. REV. 111, 125 (1975).

242. 403 U.S. at 25. This lifestyle freedom may be constitutionally unique in that it is protected as a first amendment rather than as a due process or equal protection right.

243. Lewis v. City of New Orleans. 415 U.S. 130 (1974); Brown v. Oklahoma, 408 U.S. 914 (1972); Rosenfeld v. New Jersey, 408 U.S. 901 (1972); Gooding v. Wilson, 405 U.S. 518 (1972).

244. 403 U.S. at 21-22.

245. Indeed, *Cohen* and its progeny may have narrowed "fighting words"

To note that our discussion of lifestyle freedoms is not exhaustive, however, is not to imply that such freedoms are numberless. The lifestyle freedoms discussed in this Article combine several prevalent characteristics. First, the choices themselves are intimate, whether that intimacy derives from a place, such as the home, or from personal use of one's body, as in the sexual conduct and personal appearance cases. And, although it cannot be said with assurance that even the most intimate choice of one person will not somehow affect those about him, lifestyle choices for the most part involve little prospect of direct or intentional harm to others.[246] Where they do involve personal harm to other parties, as to the children of a divorced couple or to parents upset about an adult child's choice of a spouse, society would very likely conclude that the lifestyle interests of the principals in being able to legally separate or marry override the potential side-effects on those nearby.

A further characteristic of lifestyle choices is their perceived importance, indeed their indispensability, in fulfilling individuality. Every personal choice is, of course, in part an expression and fulfillment of individuality, whether it be the choice of a home or car, a career, a college education, or whatever. Yet these latter choices, lying outside our lifestyle category, depend greatly upon economic means or personal ability; in a competitive world of limited resources, everyone will not obtain the career or home or college he prefers. Conversely, there is a greater universality to lifestyle choices. Marriage, child-raising, and intimate sexual expression are arguably more inalienable rights of living; they exist or should exist for all human beings, however circumstanced.

Thus it is ultimately irrelevant to our analysis that the right to choose a career seems easily more important than the right to wear long hair. Career choices simply lack, in our view, the degree of personal intimacy necessary to characterize them as lifestyle

---

(Chaplinsky v. New Hampshire, 315 U.S. 568, 572 (1942)) to direct facial insults to someone other than a police officer. *See* Lewis v. City of New Orleans, 408 U.S. 913 (1972) (concurring opinion, Powell, J.).

246. Roe v. Wade, 410 U.S. 113 (1973), is an exception, if one takes the view that a fetus is a person.

choices. Expanding the concept of lifestyle freedom to include all important marketplace decisions having some personal element would eventually weaken the force of a lifestyle right and dilute the protection our most intimate choices ought to receive.[247]

Finally, the term lifestyle choice means a choice in the trust sense: the voluntary exercise of free will. Although courts ought to be reluctant to infer that one's choice is not one's own,[248] it would be anomalous and self-defeating to extend a theory of lifestyle freedom to forbid state regulation of, for instance, the injection of heroin, which for physiological reasons may not long remain a matter of choice at all. On the other hand, that physical or psychological gratification is the aim of a lifestyle choice is obviously no reason for failing to protect it.[249]

Drawing the line, however, is an exceedingly complicated and treacherous task. In order to avoid the difficulties of assessing the addictive qualities of different drugs and the compulsiveness of various personal habits, we would recommend that regulation of drugs and alcohol be left to the political process. Unlike marriage, divorce, and personal appearance, for example, drugs and alcohol have traditionally been associated with potential harm to others of a magnitude justifying criminal sanctions. As a result, courts, and certainly the Supreme Court, have largely stayed the hand of the Constitution in this area.[250] We wish we could predict with certainty that such judicial self-restraint will continue.

---

247. This does not imply that career choices ought not to receive constitutional protection under some other method of analysis. *See* Wilkinson, *supra* note 116, at 984-98.

248. The question of voluntariness will pose difficulty in the area of lifestyle rights for minors, especially for those who are very young. In voiding a blanket requirement of parental consent as a condition to abortion in the case of an unmarried minor during the first 12 weeks of pregnancy, the Court noted that "our holding ... does not suggest that every minor, regardless of age or maturity, may give effective consent for termination of her pregnancy." Planned Parenthood v. Danforth, 96 S. Ct. 2831, 2844 (1976).

249. It is difficult, in fact, to imagine a lifestyle choice not motivated, at least in part, by such considerations.

250. Robinson v. California, 370 U.S. 660 (1962), in holding that the status of narcotics addiction may not be criminally punished, did not affect the state's power to regulate drug possession or use. *But see* Ravin v. State, 537 P.2d 494 (Alaska

In sum, we are considering a domain of personal choice whose outer boundaries are not sharp, but which encompasses the most intimate and the most personally distinctive of life's decisions. We turn next to a review of the state interests that are most often advanced as justifications for restricting lifestyle freedoms. Throughout this Article we have stressed that constitutional analysis of lifestyle claims is a balancing process, necessitating judicial evaluation of both the asserted substantive due process lifestyle right and the various state interests supporting its restriction. We now turn to a more detailed examination of those state interests.

C. *An Assessment of Competing State Interests*

Regulation of lifestyle freedoms falls within the classic formulation of the state's police power, for "society ... has traditionally concerned itself with the moral soundness of its people." [251] The lifestyle choices previously discussed each contain a significant moral component. The efficacy of legal enforcement of moral behavior has been the subject of inevitable controversy, but the interest of the state in the manners and morals of its citizens is well established. What seems to us required in constitutional analysis is a discerning look at the state interests advanced to restrict lifestyle choices, so as to ascertain, first, whether those interests are legitimate, and second, whether they are actually threatened by the particular lifestyle choice in question. In discussing the state interests in this area we avoid terms such as "rational" or "compelling," both because those terms carry unwanted freight from their use in other constitutional contexts and because the relationship of legislated morality to personal choice involves sensitive judgments having numerous subtle gradations. What follows is a brief and generalized treatment of several state interests in roughly an ascending order of importance.

1975) (adult possession of marijuana for personal home use protected under Alaska Constitution).

251. Poe v. Ullman, 367 U.S. 497, 545-46 (1961) (dissenting opinion, Harlan, J.).

Least persuasive of the state's justifications for restricting lifestyle freedoms is the general promotion of morality. Such an interest requires a court to accept on faith, in the name of the police power, the state's moral judgment. Unfortunately, the Supreme Court has reacted to this interest most ambivalently. Chief Justice Warren once suggested in dissent that there is a "right of the Nation and of the States to maintain a decent society." [252] The Court in *Paris Adult Theatre I v. Slaton* [253] carried forward this theme and spoke approvingly of the state's power to regulate "the tone of society, . . . the style and quality of life, now and in the future." [254] It noted that "[f]rom the beginning of civilized societies, legislators and judges have acted on various unprovable assumptions," [255] and stated: "In deciding *Roth* [*v. United States*], this Court implicitly accepted that a legislature could legitimately act on such a conclusion to protect 'the social interest in order and morality.' " [256]

Other recent Court opinions, however, indicate that such general state assertions of moral righteousness will not suffice. The *Moreno* Court strongly hinted that attempts to regulate lifestyle choices on the bare assertion that the regulation serves morality would be impermissible.[257] Indeed, it seems impossible that the Court could have reached the results it did in *Griswold, Stanley v. Georgia, Eisenstadt,* and *Roe* without proceeding on just that premise. Somewhat ironically,[258] Chief Justice Burger's opinion in *Wisconsin v. Yoder* [259] provides the most explicit evidence that conclusory invocations of morality on the part of public authority will be found wanting: "There can be no assumption that today's

---

252. Jacobellis v. Ohio, 378 U.S. 184, 199 (1964).

253. 413 U.S. 49 (1973).

254. *Id.* at 59 (Quoting Bickel, *On Pornography: II, Dissenting and Concurring Opinions,* 22 PUB. INTEREST 25, 25-26 (1971)).

255. 413 U.S. at 61.

256. *Id.* (quoting Roth v. United States, 354 U.S. 476, 485 (1957), in turn quoting Chaplinsky v. New Hampshire, 315 U.S. 568, 572 (1942).

257. Department of Agriculture v. Moreno, 413 U.S. 528, 535 n. 7 (1973).

258. It is ironic because Chief Justice Burger was also the author of the opinion for the Court in Paris Adult Theatre I v. Slaton, 413 U.S. 49 (1973).

259. 406 U.S. 205 (1972).

majority is 'right' and the Amish and others like them are 'wrong.' A way of life that is odd or even erratic but interferes with no rights or interests of others is not to be condemned because it is different." [260]

Absent refinement and particularization, state interests in preserving morality lack the weight necessary to support restriction of the free exercise of lifestyle choices. Certainly it would seriously abuse the legal process to condemn private and remote acts simply because the acts strike the majority as repulsive.

The privilege of living in a free and open society entails, we believe, some obligation to tolerate ideas and moral choices with which one disagrees. To think one's own moral predilections should invariably be embodied in law is unrealistic in a society committed, as ours is, to the freedom and dignity of the individual. Moreover, to uphold legal proscriptions on grounds of abstract morality would permit the state to ferret out and ultimately to try and punish offenders upon the assertion, not that the given behavior was socially harmful, but that it was revolting and unnatural. Such a rule of law would invite the majority to act upon its least noble and most prejudiced impulses.[261] Courts have the initial obligation to ensure that invasions of lifestyle choices rest upon firmer and more particularized grounds.

---

260. *Id.* at 223-24.

261. The question of the state's capacity to regulate unorthodox lifestyle choice in the name of morality is illuminated by the debate over Lord Devlin's position that society, for its protection, may criminalize deviant behavior on the basis of a strong community feeling of moral disapproval. P. DEVLIN, THE ENFORCEMENT OF MORALS (1965).

Although it is beyond the scope of this Article to recapitulate the debate in its full subtlety, the response of Lord Devlin's opponents pinpoints our own reservations about the dangers of state regulation of lifestyle choice under so vague a guise as "morality." One commentator chides Devlin for inviting "intolerance, indignation and disgust" as the prerequisites for legal action. Anastaplo, *Law and Morality: On Lord Devlin, Plato's Meno, and Jacob Klein,* 1967 WIS. L. REV. 231, 238. Professor Dworkin criticizes Lord Devlin for permitting legal judgments on morality to be based on nothing more than "prejudice . . . and personal aversion." Dworkin, *Lord Devlin and the Enforcement of Morals,* 75 YALE L.J. 986, 1000-01 (1966). *See also* Hart, *Immorality and Treason,* 62 THE LISTENER 162 (London 1959); Hughes, *Morals and the Criminal Law,* 71 YALE L.J. 662 (1962).

A second justification, aligned with the foregoing but deserving of more serious consideration, is that state regulation of lifestyle choices protects the individual from self-inflicted harm or self-degrading experiences. Here the state professes not to be regulating morality, but rather to be paternalistically saving the individual from himself.[262] Since society often wishes to save the individual from conduct society abhors, however, the moralistic and paternalistic rationales are frequently identical.

Paternalism underlies a great variety of state legislation, including that regulating gambling, drugs, and alcohol, that prohibiting suicide and "immoral" sex, and that requiring the payment of social security taxes and even the wearing of motorcycle helmets.[263] Such legislation, however, often protects against public as well as private harm. Drug legislation seeks to protect society against the crimes of an addict supporting his habit; motorcycle helmet laws allegedly prevent accidents and certainly minimize the costs to society of supporting injured riders and their dependents. In general, protection of the individual from readily demonstrable physical harm, whether from addictive drugs or motorcycle accidents, may be more supportable than protection of persons from acts alleged by the state to be "unnatural" or "immoral." Saving bodies, to be blunt, may be a more justifiable governmental purpose than saving souls.

Difficult questions yet remain. Almost every lifestyle choice involves some possibility of physical harm, especially with intemperate indulgence. A substance such as tobacco presents the hard case: the danger to heart and lungs is cumulative and eventual, and not as dramatic as heroin addiction or a motorcycle crash. Perhaps, as one commentator suggests, society's paternalistic interest should be limited to confronting

---

262. The seminal discussion of this interest is in J.S. MILL, ON LIBERTY, Ch. IV, *Of the Limits to the Authority of Society Over the Individual* (London 1859).

263. The helmet requirement has created considerable controversy. *See e.g.*, State v. Cotton, 55 Haw. 138, 516 P.2d 709 (1973); People v. Fries, 42 Ill. 2d 446, 250 N.E.2d 149 (1969); American Motorcycle Ass'n v. Department of State Police, 11 Mich. App. 351, 158 N.W.2d 72 (1968). *See generally* Howard, *State Courts and Constitutional Rights in the Day of the Burger Court,* 62 VA. L. REV. 873, 929-30 (1976).

smokers with the ugly medical facts so that there is no escaping the knowledge of what the medical risks to health exactly are. Constant reminders of the hazards should be at every hand and with no softening of the gory details. The state might even be justified in using its taxing, regulatory, and persuasive powers to make smoking ... more difficult or less attractive ....[264]

But to proscribe smoking outright, and thus to substitute the medical judgment of the state for the personal lifestyle choice "is paternalism of the strong kind ... and creates serious risks of governmental tyranny." [265]

The notion that the state may inform, warn, tax, and regulate, but not flatly proscribe allegedly self-destructive lifestyle choices, provides a useful touchstone. But it still does not resolve many difficulties. We would surely, even after *Griswold,* allow Connecticut to advise and inform potential users of the medical risks and dangers inherent in contraception. But to what extent might Connecticut publicly advertise the "immorality" of contraceptives, if a majority of its citizens regarded them as immoral? To what extent could it tax contraceptives? Could a state or locality that considered interracial marriages self-degrading and morally depraved post notices to that effect in public buildings? At some point such notices would raise a strong inference that the state intended to discriminate against those who pursued the disfavored activity. In short, professedly beneficent, paternalistic motives should not be an automatic justification even for regulation that stops short of proscription.

Curtailing activities that offend the public is a third rationale for state regulation of lifestyle choices. Certainly a citizen can assert some right not to be assailed in public by deeply revolting behavior. On the other hand, the very act of stepping out in public inevitably entails a risk that one's personal sensibilities will be offended. The public is by definition a diverse, variegated collection of individuals, with a multitude of idiosyncratic habits. Some of these habits —

---

264. J. Feinberg, *Legal Paternalism,* in TODAY'S MORAL PROBLEMS 33, 43 (1975).
265. *Id.*

of dress, personal association, and mode of expression — constitute the exercise of lifestyle choices. And striking the balance between public and personal rights in this area is often difficult.

Certain guidelines are helpful, however, in evaluating this third state interest. In assessing the degree to which certain behavior offends the public, courts ought to employ an objective rather than a subjective standard and ask whether the behavior in question would offend a reasonable person, not whether it distresses the most sensitive member of the community. Any lesser standard fails to give proper effect to the constitutional stature of lifestyle choices. Courts should also consider whether the offending behavior is a localized incident from which one can avert the eyes or walk away, whether it is temporary or permanent, whether it is unobtrusive or insistent in character, and whether either the state interest or the lifestyle choice could be exercised in a less intrusive manner.

A simple illustration may help. Compare, for example, the appellant in *Cohen v. California,*[266] who wore a "Fuck the Draft" message on his jacket in the Los Angeles County Courthouse, with a couple engaging in sexual intercourse in a visible area of a public park. In both situations a passerby could retreat from the incident by averting his gaze or step. And both Cohen's act and the couple's activity are presumably one-time incidents of limited duration. But the similarity ends there. A reasonable person would be substantially more offended by the sight of sexual intercourse in public than by a message reading "Fuck the Draft," a sentiment regularly encountered on the walls of public restrooms. Furthermore, Cohen's message might be less effective if conveyed in a less dramatic or personalized manner, and totally ineffective if confined to the privacy of his quarters. And although the shock value of whatever the copulating couple might be attempting to communicate would also be eliminated by privacy, the feelings of intimacy and pleasure associated with sexual intercourse would

---

266. 403 U.S. 15 (1971).

not. Thus the state interest in avoiding public offense more readily suffices to limit the lifestyle freedom of the couple than of Cohen.[267]

A fourth state interest in restricting lifestyle choices is the prevention of physical violence and disorder. Public display of unorthodox habit often meets with onlooker disapproval. Thus authorities will inevitably be heard to argue that shocking manners of dress and speech, for example, pose serious threats to the maintenance of public peace.

Preservation of order is certainly a legitimate state concern. But the mere recitation of this interest would not justify state restriction of the lifestyle right. In analyzing tensions between lifestyle choices and the preservation of order, the "street speech" cases of the 1950's and 1960's seem particularly apt. Like verbal dissent, unorthodox lifestyle choices may "strike at prejudices and preconceptions" and "invite dispute." [268] Yet official condemnation of such choices should be based upon more than an "undifferentiated fear or apprehension of disturbance." [269] Authorities, in fact, may rightly be charged with some duty of protecting rather than restraining their exercise,[270] especially where such exercise is "peaceful" in character.[271]

An important variation on this fourth state interest lies in state protestations that restriction of the lifestyle right prevents public harm of a nonviolent nature. Examples would be a school's assertion that long hair poses not so much a risk of disruption, as a problem of hygiene, or the claim of the Village of Belle Terre that cohabitation by more than two unrelated persons threatens not a riot, but the community's general repose. In such situations, involving important constitutional claims and legitimate state concerns, scrutiny of means becomes especially important. The

---

267. For a demurrer to *Cohen,* see Rehnquist, *Civility and Freedom of Speech,* 49 IND. L.J. 1 (1973).

268. Terminiello v. Chicago, 337 U.S. 1, 4 (1949).

269. Tinker v. Des Moines School Dist., 393 U.S. 503, 508 (1969). The state may, of course, act to prevent the outbreak of violence. *See* Feiner v. New York, 340 U.S. 315 (1951).

270. *See id.* at 326 (dissenting opinion, Black, J.).

271. Edwards v. South Carolina, 372 U.S. 229, 237 (1963).

means employed by government ought to significantly advance the asserted legitimate state interest, not some punitive alternative one. Thus, in *Belle Terre* the limitation only upon *unrelated* persons living together may not fully implement the village's asserted interest in tranquility, and in the long-hair cases, the means often sweep too broadly by eliminating all unusual hairstyles without regard to cleanliness. Such dramatically under- and over-inclusive selection of means, in relation to the asserted state purposes, creates suspicion that the true aim of the state is more the elimination of variant lifestyle behavior than the promotion of its legitimate goals.

A fifth and final state interest is that removal of legal constraints on lifestyle freedoms may jeopardize the most hallowed and basic institutions of society. Thus state regulation of matters such as divorce and sexual conduct becomes a means of fortifying institutions, such as marriage and the family, that impart meaning and elevation to human life.

The state interest in preserving the family unit needs to be carefully understood. Arguably, the state has no legitimate interest in restricting living arrangements to a narrow ideal of domestication: to, for example, the middle-class family of four safely cottaged in the suburbs. That model has been with us too briefly [272] and is changing too quickly [273] to be the real basis of the state's interest in this area. Rather, the state's proper concern derives from the basic functions performed by "family" units in society: from sexual fulfillment and reproduction, to education and rearing of the young, to economic support and emotional security.[274] It is true, of course, that sexual and reproductive acts

---

272. The common view is that urbanization and industrialization have encouraged shifts in American family structure from an extended kinship pattern to the present nuclear unit. Sociologists disagree on the degree to which American family life resembles the isolated nuclear or the extended kinship model. *See* Winch, *Some Observations On Extended Familism in the United States,* in SELECTED STUDIES IN MARRIAGE AND THE FAMILY 127 (R. Winch & L. Goodman eds. 1968).

273. *See* notes 8-12 and accompanying text *supra.*

274. *See* Murdock, *The Universality of the Nuclear Family,* in A MODERN INTRODUCTION TO THE FAMILY 37, 43 (N. Bell & E. Vogel eds., rev. ed. 1968).

take place outside the family unit, and that education of the young and economic support often come from the state.[275] Still, the vital purposes of the family — child rearing and emotional fulfillment of its members — appear to require some fidelity and constancy of relationship. Margaret Mead recently put it best:

> There needs to be a place where children will know that they belong, where they have an unquestioned right to be, where there will always be responsible adults to welcome them and care for them. For teenagers there needs to be a place from which they can run away without going too far, and come home again, as they try out what it is like to be on their own. For adult men and women, there needs to be a place where someone will always know and care if they fail to return when they said they would, however far they have traveled.[276]

This necessary stability of home and family life is often fostered by legal recognition of marriage, legal regulation of marital dissolution, and legal condemnation of promiscuous sexual behavior. Law adds to such stability both by defining acceptable standards of behavior and by discouraging deviation from them. Where vindication of lifestyle diversity can be shown to damage so basic an institution as the family, courts should not order it.

The difficulty comes in the showing. The withdrawal of law from certain areas of moral choice does not inevitably portend a collapse of the social order. In this regard, a historical analogy may be

---

275. For the view that the family has now lost many of its central and traditional functions, see Ogburn, *The Changing Functions of the Family,* in SELECTED STUDIES IN MARRIAGE AND THE FAMILY, *supra* note 272, at 58.

276. *The Once and Future Home,* Washington Post, July 4, 1976, B1, B5. Dr. Mead continues:

> Over and over again, throughout history, there have been attempts to destroy this family unit and to invoke mythological past happenings to justify contemporary social experiments, such as the assertion that in earlier times there was no family and human beings practised "group marriage," for example. So far in human history, however, societies have not found a way to rear children without the ties of parents to children and children to parents.

Id.

appropriate. Perhaps no moral and social force has been as powerful and pervasive in America as organized religion. Yet the framers of the Constitution deliberately removed religious choice and allegiance from the domain of law and placed them within the realm of personal decision. Nonetheless, organized religion and religiosity have survived the first amendment and have remained important ingredients in American life over the generations. And atheism and agnosticism, despite being protected by the Constitution, have never really taken root.

Understanding why organized religion and religiosity have remained important forces in American life provides an instructive lesson. They have flourished, in large part, because there exist, independent of law, powerful ways for society to check unorthodox and dissident behavior. Even if the law may not be used to enforce conventional lifestyle choices, the private forces of society will retain other means of maintaining conformity: for example, social exclusion from private gatherings and organizations, denial of employment and career advancement, and use of derogatory epithets, all of which largely lie beyond the reach of the Constitution. A reality of American life is that community acceptance, respect, and influence are bestowed upon those whose behavior is generally conventional.

Our plea, finally, is for a balanced and sensitive approach to the central dilemma examined in this Article. Every great society, as a predicate of existence, has rallied the allegiance of its members to some common responsibilities and patterns of living, an allegiance backed to a significant extent by the power and majesty of the law. Definite accommodation must be reached with the rights of dissident members, but not so complete an accommodation as to leave the conventional social fabric without legal support. We must be wary of creating, in the high name of constitutional right, nothing more than a regime of self gratification and indulgence. Equally distressing, however, would be an orthodoxy so pervasive that personal creativity, expression, and realization would be stifled and denied. The Constitution must remain a charter of tolerance without becoming an instrument of social dissolution. There will be no more difficult task.

CONCLUSION

American legal history has developed in the 1970's into an exciting and promising field of study. But areas of intellectual inquiry can not always sustain excitement and promise, and temporal enthusiasms are no substitute for a solid base of scholarship. Impressive beginnings have been made since the late 1960's toward the widening and deepening of that base, which already included a sample of notable contributions.* For American legal history to mature, however, continued scholarly production in a number of diverse areas is necessary.

The intellectual history of American professions and academic disciplines gives one pause in this connection. In many previous instances the growth to maturity of a profession or discipline has been accompanied by a narrowing of the range of "approved" research topics and inquiries.** While this narrowing tendency can be associated with the development of higher critical standards, it can also have a stifling effect. In particular, a choice of research topics can sometimes represent more than a neutral judgment about scholarship; the choice can also be seen as a philosophical or political statement. In my judgment a lack of philosophical diversity in a discipline can retard its possibilities for creativity and thereby adversely affect its stature. One hopes that as American legal history matures it will not narrow its interests.

In one respect my decision to issue this volume of essays follows from the above concerns and hopes. A good portion of the monographic and synthetic energies of American legal historians has recently been directed toward themes not stressed in this book: private as distinguished from public law; nonconstitutional as distinguished from constitutional areas; lower courts and

---

* Compare White, *Some Observations on a Course in Legal History,* 23 J. LEGAL ED. 440 (1971), with Holt, *Now and Then: The Uncertain State of Nineteenth-Century American Legal History,* 7 IND. L. REV. 615 (1974).

** Two stimulating treatments of professionalization in academic disciplines are THOMAS L. HASKELL, THE EMERGENCE OF PROFESSIONAL SOCIAL SCIENCE (1977) and BRUCE KUKLICK, THE RISE OF AMERICAN PHILOSOPHY (1977).

legislatures as distinguished from the Supreme Court and other appellate courts; the marketplace of events, "interests," and "forces" as distinguished from the world of educated thought. I have found this tacit set of decisions about the proper direction of research to have generated some genuine intellectual excitement and to have helped American legal history declare its independence as a discipline. I also find it is time now to broaden, rather than to narrow, the "approved" set of challenges for future scholarship in the history of American law.

This set of essays, then, can be taken as one person's continued interest in exploring, from fresh perspectives, what might be considered orthodox themes. The book can also be taken as a plea for breadth and diversity in American legal history and a hope that inevitable differences in philosophical and political persuasions will not lead to scholastic narrowness and rigidity. The patterns of American legal thought discussed here are by no means the only ones, although I believe them to be central ones. Whether others agree with that last conviction is much less important than the continuation of openness, tolerance, and diversity in professional scholarship.

INDEX

A

Administrative law: early history, 228-238; judicial review of administrative agency decisions, 228-284

American jurisprudence: origins, 18-31

American legal history: evolution, 3-6; characteristics, 16-17; ideas of leading legal historians, 61-71

Appellate opinions: as source material for historians, 74-95

B

Bickel, Alexander, 151-152

Bingham, Joseph, 107-111

Boddie v. Connecticut, 320-322

Brandeis, Louis: and administrative law, 228, 239-287

Brown v. Board of Education, 290-300, 303-305, 307

Brown v. Collins, 183-184

Brown v. Kendall, 181-182

C

Cardozo, Benjamin, 87-95

Common law: function in pre-Revolutionary America, 19-24; interaction with constitutional law, 48-56

Conceptualism: defined, 164, 167-172; relationship to intellectual origins of Torts in America, 167-172

Constitutional law: interaction with nonconstitutional law, 48-61

Crowell v. Benson, 266-271

D

Davis, Kenneth Culp, 279-284

Delegation, doctrine of, 275-284

Department of Agriculture v. Moreno, 333-336

Disciplinary matrixes, defined, 71-73, 189-191

Doe, Charles, 179, 183-184

Doe v. Commonwealth's Attorney, 342-347